CROSSINGS

ALSO BY WALT HARRINGTON

American Profiles:
Somebodies and Nobodies Who Matter

At the Heart of It:
Ordinary People, Extraordinary Lives

Intimate Journalism:
The Art and Craft of Reporting Everyday Life

CROSSINGS

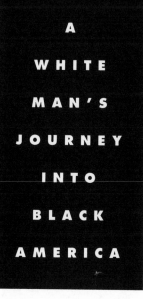

A
WHITE
MAN'S
JOURNEY
INTO
BLACK
AMERICA

WALT HARRINGTON

University of Missouri Press
Columbia and London

Library of Congress Cataloging-in-Publication Data

Harrington, Walt, 1950–
    Crossings : a white man's journey into Black America / Walt Harrington
        p.   cm.
    Originally published: New York : HarperCollins, c1922
    Includes Index.
    ISBN 0-8262-1259-X (alk. paper)
    1. Afro-Americans—Social conditions—1975– 2. United States—Race relations.
    3. Harrington, Walt, 1950- —Journeys.
I. Title.
E185.86.H34   1999
305.396'073—dc21   99-15519
                                                                                    CIP

∞™ This paper meets the requirements of the American
National Standard for Permanence of Paper for Printed
Library Materials, Z39.48, 1984.

To Keran, my wife

Why, the dumbest black bastard in the cotton patch knows that the only way to please a white man is to tell him a lie!

FROM *INVISIBLE MAN*,
BY RALPH ELLISON

It must be hard for a foreigner to know anything about us.

MABEL LINCOLN,
FROM *DRYLONGSO*,
BY JOHN LANGSTON GWALTNEY

And there's one thing I learnt about white people: if they don't understand what you saying, they just ain't gonna hear it.

FROM "PROBLEMS OF ART,"
COLLECTED IN *ELBOW ROOM*,
BY JAMES ALAN MCPHERSON

CONTENTS

Photographs follow page 180.

WASH.

MONT.

N. DAK.

ORE.

IDAHO

S. DAK.

Lacomb

WYO.

NEB.

Sacramento

Oakland

NEV.

UTAH

CALIF.

COLO.

Nicodemus

Allensworth

KANS.

Bakersfield

Beverly Hills

Hollywood

South Central

View Park

Irvine

ARIZ.

N. MEX.

Bc
OK

La Cruces

TEXAS

Pacific
Ocean

MEXICO

-------► Journey One: Into the South

——► Journey Two: Up North

-----► Journey Three: Going West

CROSSINGS

PROLOGUE

My journey begins in the dentist's chair.

The nurse is pressing dental dough into my lower incisors, and she and the doctor are playing dueling banjos with funny stories about their kids. They've paused for me to nod or grunt as if I, too, were part of their conversation when in walks a man, another dentist, dropping by to say hello. "I've got a good one," he says cheerfully, and goes on to tell a racist joke. I can't recall the joke, only that it ends with a black man who is stupid. Dead silence. It's just us white folks here in the room, but my dentist and his nurse know my wife, who is black, and they know my son and my daughter, who are, as they describe themselves, tan and bright tan.

How many racist jokes have I heard in my life? Five thousand, maybe ten thousand, at least. But today, for the first time—who knows exactly why?—I am struck with a deep, sharp pain. I look at this man, with his pasty face, pale hair, and weak lips, and I think: This idiot's talking about my children!

I want to shake him, shove him against the wall. But I say nothing. Hastily, my dentist grabs a tool, the nurse extracts the dough, and the idiot leaves. But I remain in suspended animation. It isn't just the joke. It isn't the tension in the air. It isn't even the idiot. It's my recognition that I've crossed a line, and that for an instant I've traveled to a place where white Americans rarely go. I feel revulsion and anger at this man. I feel fear and anguish for my children. I feel helpless. Am I, I wonder, feeling like a black man?

I have a memory of a long time ago, when I was eight, maybe nine, when I sat with my grandmother on the steps of her house in the country, thirty miles outside Chicago, snapping fresh beans. My grandmother was a large, stern woman with a baritone voice, round wire-rimmed glasses, and ashen hair swept up from her forehead, temples, and neck in that old Gibson Girl fashion. I called her Big Grandma with fear and respect. That day she told me she'd been to "the city"—Chicago Heights, which in the 1950s was an industrial town of about thirty-five thousand people. Big Grandma said she'd seen "coloreds" everywhere. She said that while standing in line at the Walgreen's she'd heard one colored lady tell another colored lady, "I *always* carries a razor in *my* purse." Big Grandma said this with dramatic inflection, a shiver, and a kind of rage, but I missed her complex meanings. Coloreds, I thought. What in the world are coloreds? I had no idea. But from her tone, I knew enough not to ask. I decided that coloreds were people whose skin, for mysterious reasons, resembled a concoction of melted crayons stirred into a weird, beautiful swirl. When I eventually went to Chicago Heights with Big Grandma and she pointed out a colored, I was amazed. I was disappointed. They weren't colored after all.

Three decades later, sitting in the dentist's chair, I'm struck by how much I am still like that little boy who believed he understood what he absolutely did not. I have been married to a black woman for ten years, and we have two children. I've had years of visiting my wife's family in rural Kentucky, years of births and deaths and holiday meals, of hunting with my father-in-law and his friends, of shared shots of Old Forester, shared jokes, lies, and hunting knives— years of what I believed was a life lived across the color line. Yet only today, at age thirty-nine, have I really felt the intimate intrigues and confusions of race in America.

Only today, for the first time, have I crossed the line.

When does a journey begin? Is it the day or the hour or the minute you finally stash your bags, wave good-bye, and set out?

Or does a journey begin way back before you ever knew you'd set out, when the idea was still locked in some undiscovered place in your mind or your heart, surfacing in only fleeting, misunderstood images and half-noted thoughts for years or even decades? So that when the idea occurs to you—say, in the dentist's chair—it seems you've always had it? That's how it was for me, anyway. From the moment I realized that I needed to do this—go out and travel America's parallel black world—it seemed as if I had always needed to do it. Thank the idiot in the dentist's office. His callousness had pierced my lifetime of distant intellectualizing about race and struck at the place where my hopes for my children reside, struck at my heart and not my head. In that instant, I was touched and humbled, converted. In that instant, I knew in my heart that I didn't know anything about race, that I never had. That I had to start again.

For as long as I can remember, the coloreds, then Negroes, then blacks, and now African Americans, have been somewhere on my mind. I suspect this is true for most white people. In our heads, race is always back there somewhere, on a back burner, bewildering us, making us shake our heads and wonder at "those people," alternately blaming ourselves and them for the conundrum that is race in America. But that's where most of us white folks stop. We've got lives to lead, mortgages to pay, birthdays to celebrate. But for me, from that moment in the dentist's chair, the matters of black and white in America were no longer curiosities. I no longer had the luxury of keeping "those people" on my mind's back burner.

Those people were my kids!

The more I thought about this and listened to my white friends, family, and neighbors, the more I realized how little any of us knew. How few of us had even one close black friend, how few of us had ever had an honest conversation with a black person, how many of us were still hiding behind the same frightened rage I'd seen in Big Grandma on the porch thirty years ago. Looking back, I know now that race has baffled and fascinated me all my life, that I've always yearned to understand "those people," to feel something of what it is they feel. I suspect that this is true for most white people. Because in some way, blacks are our other half. In some way, we can't understand ourselves if we don't understand them. It is racism's oldest dynamic.

So with a lifetime of curiosity to satisfy, and a father's need to protect and guide his children, I am heading out into black America to learn something—not from the statistics and politics of race, but

from the lives and voices of real people, black people from every
imaginable age, income, occupation, and locale. I've tacked a map of
the United States to my wall, and I begin a list of places and people,
one filtered through the suggestions of friends and colleagues, black
and white, and my own curiosities. I have these goals: When I'm done
with my travels, I want to have experienced the breadth of black
America. I want to be the blind man who touches the whole elephant. I
want the story of my journey to be less like a social scientist's analysis
and more like an artist's collage. I want my children, when they are old
enough, to be able to pick up this single volume and see, hear, feel,
taste, and understand the sweeping arch of people, places, and opinions that make up half of their heritage. Some of my destinations are
obvious: Montgomery, Alabama, where Rosa Parks refused to move to
the back of the bus in 1955. Some are deeply personal: I hope to find
the first black man I ever knew in my life, someone I met when we
were both teenagers. In between are dozens of other people I plan to
visit: a city police chief, a jazz trumpeter, a convicted murderer, a
farmer, an architect, a welfare mother, a corporate mogul, a rap star,
moviemakers, Hollywood stars, novelists, poets. All across the country, black people have agreed to show me around, introduce me to
their families and friends, tell me the stories of their lives.

That's the plan, anyway. But as I pack clothes, books, notebooks,
pens, tapes, and tape recorders, I think of Mark Twain's words, "Circumstances do the planning for us all," and I decide to go where the
circumstances take me.

My kids say their quick good-byes and run off to play, not really
comprehending that I will be gone more than a little while. My wife
walks with me out to my tan Isuzu Trooper with too many miles on it
already, kisses me good-bye, and stands with her hands on her
cheeks, crying. I think about how much I love her. And I think how
strange it is that I'm about to leave this black woman behind so that I
might learn more about black America. But this much I take for
granted: no one person is black America, not even if she is my wife.

As I wave good-bye and coast down the gentle hill of my driveway, I suddenly think, I'm crazy! Why am I doing this? But I keep
going, because I do know why. I'm doing this for myself, my children, and the dentist with his racist jokes. What do I hope to discover? Who knows? As John Steinbeck wrote, "You don't take the
trip. The trip takes you."

JOURNEY ONE

INTO THE SOUTH

1

BACK TO BEGINNINGS

GLASGOW, KENTUCKY

My wife's father, Alex, slips the rubber band off the large, tightly rolled parchment, uncurls it, smooths it out on the coffee table, and then begins tracing the antecedents of his life. He starts in the upper left-hand corner, touching each name with the fingertips of his left hand: Tyler, Otha, Beulah, Shed, who was his father. Alex's finger follows the branches of the handwritten family tree to his mother, his four brothers, himself, his two sons, his only daughter, who is my wife, and beyond to myself and my two children, Matthew and Kyle. For this genealogical tour, for the first step in my tour of another world, I've come to my wife's family farm in Glasgow, Kentucky, where Alex grew up.

I think of my father-in-law as a friend. He's a soft-spoken man who cannot, to my mother-in-law's constant consternation, be hurried no matter what the occasion. At fifty-eight, Alex is still handsome, lean, and youthful. His sideburns and sparse mustache are sprinkled with gray. My children describe his complexion as brown-tan. He wears low-hanging Rustler jeans and a red-plaid flannel shirt over a crew-neck T-shirt, and he gently pads around the house in gray-speckled hunting socks. He's—how shall I say it?—something of an eccentric. He fries bull gonads for breakfast (served with well-seasoned brown gravy, they taste like tender chicken gizzards). He maintains an antique Model A Ford, an antique Coke machine, and an antique Seeburg jukebox. He will drive a hundred miles for a bottle of moonshine. Alex is a country boy who left the country at fifteen, lying to the air force about his age. A few years ago—after serving in Germany, England, France, California, Washington, and Illinois—Alex and his wife, Celeste, retired to Glasgow. "I gotta die somewhere," he says.

Today is the first morning of my journey into the South from my home near Washington, D.C. I begin in the South because it's where America's black and white disease began and where half of America's blacks live today. I begin in Kentucky because it's where black and white began for me when I married and because, after ten years of visiting my wife's family and their friends in Glasgow, I still know very little about how race has mattered in their lives.

So at 5:30 A.M., Alex and I are up and on the road, driving to Alex's beginnings on Route 90. It is the only road that runs the fifty miles from Glasgow, a town of 12,351 people in southwestern Kentucky, to Lawson Bottom, a deep country hollow southeast of Glasgow and nearly to the Tennessee border in the lush, remote farmland and forest along the Cumberland River. Alex has told me that I cannot understand blacks anywhere in America if I don't understand Lawson Bottom, or at least the thousands of places like Lawson Bottom, because somewhere back in nearly every black person's past is a little Southern farm. "A lot of people try to forget that," Alex says. "I try to never forget."

It's chilly this morning, thirty-five degrees, but the Kentucky sky just after dawn is so blue that it seems to disappear into itself, and the air is as clean as freshly washed glass. We pass ancient tobacco barns. We enter and leave towns with names like Eighty Eight, Marrowbone, and Summer Shade. We curve slowly around roads that hug the sides of mountains, surprise five deer feeding in a pasture, and, finally, enter Lawson Bottom. A hundred years ago, isolated Lawson Bottom was home to Alex's mother's family. It was even named after her family, quite an accomplishment and quite an anomaly in the South of those days.

Alex didn't grow up in Lawson Bottom. His mother had migrated to Glasgow as a young woman, and Alex visited the farm only sporadically as a boy. Yet he has always seemed to have Lawson Bottom in him. He carries its memory proudly, in a way that my wife, who is thirty-seven, and her younger brothers do not. As we make the final turn onto Lawson Bottom Road, Alex—for at least the hundredth time since I've known him—tells me the story of taking his future wife to visit the farm in 1951. When they arrived there, folks were so happy to see them that one of Alex's aunts called for a feast. She yelled to her son (as Alex recalls with an exaggerated Cain-tucky accent), "*Paee*-tehr! Go out and kill a *chai*-kin." Peter did, shooting its head off with a single rifle shot. The car swerves to the left as Alex laughs deeply and wipes tears of laughter from his eyes. Alex loves that story. Yet it makes city folks—black and white—cringe, and it reminds Alex of how far he and his family have come. These days, the Lawsons are gone from Lawson Bottom—except for Alex's cousin Reid, a sixty-six-year-old man who has lived away from the "holler" only six months of his life. Since his brother died in 1979, Reid has been alone on the farm. He likes the quiet.

When Alex and I pull into the muddy drive, Reid is outside in the early morning light hefting the wooden top off the well. He's a tall, lean man, only slightly stooped with the years. He wears jeans, leather boots, and a tan work shirt. On his head rests an orange hunting cap: "Burkesville Fertilizer." The hat sits back, angled to the right atop a full shock of chalk-white hair. Reid's well pump has stopped, but he's unconcerned. Lawson Branch, a tiny mountain-fed stream, runs only twenty feet away, and it is an "everlasting" stream, as they call it, meaning that it never runs dry. If Reid must, he'll simply dip water from the branch for washing clothes or even for drinking. But that won't be necessary. Alex was a master sergeant and an airplane mechanic in the air force—at least he was once they stopped dumping blacks into kitchen, janitorial, and paper-shuffler jobs in the fifties—and for the cost of a $4.50 electrical switch, he'll have Reid's pump whirring in a couple of hours.

While Alex works, Reid leads me to his house, the only one I can see among the trees that climb up the nearby mountainside, the overgrown brush thick with rabbits, and the large, unkempt garden. Once inside, I sit in a creaking chair, one of only three, and survey the single room in which Reid lives. It's as if I'm inside an old, sepia-toned photograph: the "Warm Morning" wood-burning stove in the center of the room, the bare light bulb overhead, the brown crucifix painted on the unpainted drywall, the dog-eared Bible, the strong and—to my own city-dweller nostrils—nauseating smell of dead mice in the walls, a winter condition that can't be avoided on the farm. Reid is like a movie frame halted in time, the living embodiment of where my wife's family began a century ago.

Through the clouded window next to his bed, Reid points to a tuft of young trees, mostly gnarled elm, just across the drive on this side of Lawson Branch. There stood the family home place, the house of patriarch Berry Lawson—born 1865, died 1915. The legend of Berry Lawson has been handed down in my wife's family for generations, and I've heard it not only from Reid but from my wife's grandmother before she died and, just yesterday, from my wife's great-aunt Minnie, a short, eighty-one-year-old wisp of a woman with light, soft skin and wavy gray hair (she's known to everyone as Aunt G, after her middle name, Glatha).

There are no pictures of my wife's great-great-grandfather Berry, only the memories of his children, who say Berry was small and strong—and nearly white, with muted African features and straight, jet-black hair. "Good hair," Aunt G called it. Berry's parentage, like that of so many in the Jim Crow yet miscegenational Old South, is fuzzy. He was raised by a white bachelor farmer and his spinster sister. Everyone assumed Berry was the farmer's son by a neighbor black woman, a Lawson, who had died when Berry was five. Anyway, when the farmer and his sister died, they left Berry the 250-acre farm. But a black man—even a half-black man—owning so much land didn't sit well with everybody, particularly one white farmer who complained that no colored man should be allowed to own such fertile land.

"But *we* did!" says Reid gleefully.

With the land, Berry Lawson and his wife, Ada, set about raising a family. The log cabin they built was magnificent against the shacks and shanties of other blacks in the bottom. The house sat snugly between Lawson Bottom Road to the front and a nine-hundred-foot forest ridge to the rear. Its rough-hewn logs were sealed with wattle and daub and its roof was covered with foot-long split hickory shakes. Inside, the house was dominated by its massive gray stone fireplace—five feet high with a hearth big enough for a six-foot backlog and guarded by heavy dog irons Berry had tempered in his own blacksmith shop.

The Lawsons had plenty. Little cash, but plenty. For the winter, Berry stored mountains of bagged flour made from wheat grown in his fields. He grew corn, hay, and tobacco. He raised cows, hogs, horses, mules, chickens, and ducks. What the farm didn't produce, the steamboats on the Cumberland delivered for barter—candy, coffee, and Red Rolling Fork whiskey. Such black affluence didn't go unnoticed, because even in the nineteenth century in Lawson Bottom race was mingled and confused with the ageless struggles of the haves versus the have-nots. "Of all the Negroes over there," Aunt G told me, muting a joyful little cackle with a hand put discreetly to her mouth, "we was the only ones with land and horses and wagons. All the others would be walkin' and we'd be ridin'. They said we thought we was better, rich, because we were Berry Lawson's kids." Truth is, Aunt G *did* think she was better than other Lawson Bottom blacks. "I thought it was their fault they were poor," she told me with uncertain contrition. "I don't guess it was, lookin' back."

Aunt G's grandmother—my wife's great-great-grandmother— was the light-skinned child of a union between a slave and a slave master. She married a dark man. Sadly, Aunt G said, "All her kids had nappy hair. They had bad hair. She'd say, 'I don't know nothin' about combin' those nappy-headed niggers.' She made Grandpa tend their hair." It was a sentiment Aunt G would carry into her generation: "I just had a horror of little black children, just thought I couldn't tend to 'em," she said, without guilt or self-reflection. "I don't know why. It's something within me."

Reid and I sit in front of the hot stove and talk about these things until it is time for him to go to work. Outside, the sun has warmed the morning and I unzip my coat as we walk to the tobacco barn several hundred feet toward the ridge—past overturned and rusted trucks and automobiles, ancient and abandoned farm equipment, oil tanks, and feeding troughs. In the barn, made of vertical, unpainted splinter wood, sweet-smelling tobacco stalks hang, curing, from three layers of cross beams. Reid says, "Be sure to duck," but I still hit my head hard on the lowest beam. He lights a kerosene heater—a whiff of fuel rises into the air—and then he begins stripping the "trash" and the "lugs" from the three-foot-long tobacco stalks, leaving the lowest-quality leaves—the "tips"—for me to strip and bale for the burley market, where tobacco is bringing $1.67 a pound.

"Ain't been much changed up here," Reid says, his breath hovering like a cloud in the windless barn. "Except whites and blacks go to school together and eat together." He laughs and hands me another stalk. "We'll make a farmer out of you yet," he says, smiling. Reid and I strip and bale, strip and bale silently for a long time, until Alex has the well pump running again. Then Alex and I say good-bye and drive off, back into the late twentieth century, leaving the last Lawson in Lawson Bottom in the cold barn, still stripping tobacco.

The signs on the gas pumps at the Gulf station in downtown Burkesville, Kentucky, read: "You may have won a BMW." Driving past the Gulf into town the next day, it seems that nothing could be more out of sync with Burkesville, a town of 1,815 people located eleven miles southwest of Lawson Bottom. It's a town of pickup trucks, a town of old men with leather faces and weathered jackets standing outside the county courthouse across from the Dollar Store. When I stop a delivery man to ask directions, I see a holstered pistol on the dash of his truck. Nope, this is not BMW country. But Alex has suggested I visit Burkesville to talk with his cousin Nell, because at fifty-five she's the last Lawson Bottom native of his generation still living in the country. I'd met Nell years before at Alex's home, and I'm embarrassed to admit the urban prejudices I revealed that day. Nell wore modest clothes and her hair was parted in the middle and turned up with simplicity. She said, "Hello, nice to meet you." Or at least I suppose she did, because I couldn't understand a word. She was, it seemed to me, strictly back-woods. I imagined her as a character out of Alex's story about Lawson Bottom: "*Paee*-tehr, go out and kill a *chai*-kin."

Only after Nell left did Alex tell me she was a schoolteacher with a master's degree. I felt stupid, though I'll say in my defense that it was also the beginning of my realization that what I had assumed was poor, uneducated, black Kentucky dialect was simply Kentucky country dialect. Nell had reminded me that things are not always what they seem. Tonight, when I sit down with Nell and her twenty-five-year-old daughter, she will remind me of this again.

For some reason, Nell is late. So I sit on the front steps of her brick house high on a hill that overlooks little Burkesville, and I wave to everyone who drives past because everyone waves to me, blacks and whites. I think of the old wisdom: in the North blacks could go as high as they wanted but couldn't get close to whites. In the South, blacks could get close to whites, but couldn't go too high. In the South, it was always a rare white person who didn't count at least some blacks as friends.

As for me, I can't recall ever talking to a black person until I was a teenager playing with an all-black baseball team from Ford Heights, Illinois. I remember my working-class parents always preached "right-thinking" attitudes about race: people are people and everyone should be treated the same. It was easy to think right on race in my suburban Chicago hometown—with no blacks, no Hispanics, maybe an Italian or two. As far as I knew, the platitude that people were people was correct—black people were people just like us, like me. I vaguely remember fat Southern cops and vicious dogs on TV. I remember the Reverend Martin Luther King, Jr., being pelted in Cicero, which was only an hour's drive away. I remember thinking that "those Polacks" were really ignorant.

But despite learning such properly open-minded notions, I also discovered that I could make my parents vaguely uncomfortable if I spouted off too liberally about race. My sister even recalls a time in high school when I asked my mother, "So what would you do if I married a Negro girl?" I don't recall the taunt, but it sounds like me. I remember also that when Moses Turner, the coach of the all-black Ford Heights baseball team, asked me to play for him the summer I turned sixteen, I quickly agreed. Big Grandma thought I'd gone mad. But I relished the renegade image. I loved it when an umpire from my suburban league pulled me aside and asked angrily, "Why are you wasting your time with these niggers?" My little step across the color line seemed to make everybody uncomfortable, which I enjoyed immensely.

But that summer, I also learned something else. I became friends with the team's six-foot-three pitcher, Pee Wee Hampton—a tall, strong kid with a fastball that wouldn't quit. I often drove Pee Wee back and forth to games, and I can still see his street: wide and tree-lined and gray, with mangy dogs and broken bicycles, with grassless yards, tar-paper roofs, unpainted picket fences, and missing screen doors. Kids were everywhere. The summer was 1967 and all around Chicago, racial violence was breaking out.

It was an angry time, and one day, as I turned onto Pee Wee's street, he said, in a voice husky and slow, "Whatever you do, don't hit one of these kids. If you do, there won't be nothin' even I can do for you." This wasn't a threat, but good advice, and you've never seen a person drive more carefully. After Pee Wee got out, I cruised around the block and back to the highway so slowly that people were staring at me. I smiled and nodded. But after that, I wasn't so eager to give Pee Wee a ride home. Twenty-five years later, I still think of Pee Wee sometimes, and in my travels I'm going to find out what became of him, his withering fastball and his desperate hometown of Ford Heights, Illinois.

Until I went away to college in 1968, Pee Wee and his teammates were the only more-than-causal acquaintances I had ever had with black people. In college, I thought that I didn't have a racist bone in my body. Then, at the height of the Black Power movement, black students circulated a petition to turn a little-used building on my rural Illinois campus into a club for black students, which meant they'd be the only group on campus with their own building. I didn't speak against the idea. I didn't campaign against it. But I did decline to sign the petition when it came my way. I thought the idea was unfair to everyone else. I did not think this was a big deal. I was wrong.

Overnight, the several black members of my dormitory basketball team—including the campus black radical leaders Jim Green and Davill Armstrong—announced they wouldn't play as long as I was on the team. Shocked and embarrassed, I offered to quit. But one team leader, a big white guy with definite racist tendencies, declared that I would not resign. *We* would not be bullied! *We* would play without *them!* And that's what we did.

To keep the peace, the college broke its own rule and allowed the black guys from all the dorms to form a team and play in the dorm league. It was something of an event when my dorm played them, with me as point guard. We won that game, although it was little consolation. I'd been tarred as a racist, a reputation I was stuck with for my four years of college. Today, Jim Green is a sergeant in the army in Portsmouth, Virginia, and Davill Armstrong is a doctor in Houston, Texas. I wonder how the last twenty years have changed them, and what they'll say when I knock on their doors.

Nell and her daughter finally arrive well after dark. Nell makes her apologies, hustles around turning on lights, and then sits down with me in the living room while her daughter works in the kitchen. I don't know where to begin and so I casually ask, "So who was your father?" Nell is not one to mince words. After a deep breath, she says,

"I'll be honest with you. My father was white and he never did pay me any attention. He would come to my mother's father's house and sit out, and I'd jump flips but he paid me no attention. His attitude was, 'Yes, I did this to your daughter and there's nothin' you can do about it!'"

Nell's white daddy, it turns out, was the same white man who complained that no colored should be allowed to own land as fertile as Berry Lawson's. "When my father died, I didn't even go see him. I thought: 'If you don't care, I don't care either.' But I did care. I still do." She pauses but I do not speak. "I guess I didn't realize I really cared about my father just until you asked. I guess he's still controlling me from the grave. He never even spoke to me. I think he could at least have done that. I was called 'half-white' and 'bastard' by my own people. I don't know which was more painful. Just not being accepted by anyone, really. I've got a white half-brother right here in this town, and he does not acknowledge me."

Nell's eyes are filled with tears. What am I to say? I think of good-hearted whites I know, even young affluent blacks, who would like this ever-present "race thing" to disappear, go away, because life is different now, changed, better. Isn't it? Then I look at Nell, who is only fifty-five but who, like any abused or beaten or abandoned child, will carry this "race thing" forever. And beyond. "I tell my daughters to stay away from white men," Nell says. "I'd be afraid they'd be using them the way we were done."

"But what about me?" I ask. "I'm white."

"I knew you were different," Nell says, and at first I think she's talking about my wife and me. But as she speaks, I realize she's talking about someone else, too. "I knew that you wouldn't be ashamed to be seen walking down the street with me, that you'd do more than take me behind closed doors. You married her." I look at Nell's twenty-five-year-old daughter Donna, who has joined us in the living room. She says, "White men usually want one thing." What am I to say? Normally, this attitude would strike me as quaint, a throwback to another time, another place. But not tonight, not in this town, this room, not in Nell's house.

Back in Glasgow the next day my father-in-law wants to give me a tour of Lewis Street in the "Kingdom," the nickname for the original few square blocks of black neighborhood in Glasgow. The Kingdom is still a black neighborhood, but today the black-owned businesses are gone—King's restaurant and the Royal Cafe, Mr. Troop's barber shop, the pool and dance halls, Kurd's cab stand, and, of course, the little gypsy restaurant Alex's father ran in a tiny wooden trailer on rubber-and-spoke wheels near Lewis and Brown Streets. In dry Glasgow in dry Barren County, Alex's father sold hooch from that trailer, as he also did from his kitchen half a block away at 506 Lewis, as his teenaged sons Alex and Bobby later did on the streets. The house has fallen to a modern brick funeral home today, and vacant lots and a B-Kwick Food Mart have replaced the rest. But the old Kingdom was the world as my children's grandfather's family knew it after they migrated from Lawson Bottom to Glasgow in the twenties.

Alex's father, my children's great-grandfather, was king of the Kingdom's bootleggers. He was a short, dark man with a confident look in his eyes. He wore a skimmer hat and string ties. He was proud and told his sons he was a blacksmith, but Alex recalls seeing him with a horse only once. At the Spotswood Hotel on Glasgow's Square he worked as a janitor, bus boy, carpenter, bellhop, and, for a long time, a dishwasher. But he was always a bootlegger—until the day Alex, eight years old, watched as the police lugged jug after jug from beneath the house. Alex's father went to prison and died soon after his release.

For a time, Alex's mother—radiant, kind, gentle, and religious—took over the family enterprise. "I got these five boys," she told Aunt G. But she, too, was busted. Finally, Alex's mother retired from the hooch business to do what respectable blacks did in her day: she worked as a nanny and as a maid in Glasgow's hospital. Before her death, she described her predicament by telling me this story: A friend of hers once applied for a factory job. The white boss called her in and told her he knew she could do the work, but he also knew she was the cook of his friend Mrs. Richardson. With a friendly laugh, the boss said he couldn't have Mrs. Richardson mad at him for stealing her favorite cook, now could he?

The men I hunt rabbits with each Thanksgiving holiday in Glasgow—Alex and his younger brother Bobby, who is fifty-six, and their friend Carl, who is fifty-five—were all bootleggers in the Kingdom in the forties. In those days, Lewis Street was much like the corner drug markets that proliferate in American cities today. "It's just a difference in product," Bobby once told me. On weekends, a horde of young black males would mill about waiting for mostly white customers to drive through, roll down their windows, and buy whiskey. Today Alex, Bobby, and Carl aren't embarrassed that they were bootleggers. They're proud of it. "A black man couldn't get a good job in those days," says Bobby, a short, round man who absently lifts his blue cap and smooths his hand over a bald head. In Toughskins bib overalls and a gray hooded sweatshirt, Bobby is working at his barn today, creating a small corral of electric wire to enclose two black steers he plans to fatten for slaughter. "Nope," Bobby says, "the best job a black could get was being a janitor, and there weren't many of them."

Bobby had a respectable job for a while after high school. He was a janitor at Glasgow's hospital, where his mother worked. He earned $100 a month and bolstered his income with light bootlegging. Then one day, Bobby saw the paycheck of a white kid, whose job was to scrape gum off the hospital floors. "It was more than mine!" he says, still incredulous. Bobby went to the hospital chief, a white man who was one of his best bootlegging customers, and asked for a raise. "Bobby," the chief said, "they won't let me pay coloreds what I pay whites." So Bobby quit and took up bootlegging full-time. At his peak, between the ages of sixteen and nineteen, Bobby made more than $800 a month. "Let me tell you," he says, "you won't find a black in Glasgow who's got anything that somewhere along the line bootlegging didn't touch their lives. Because the people workin' weren't paid anything. It was work and be dirt poor, or be a bootlegger."

In those days, race was everywhere and nowhere. The movies, restaurants, and public bathrooms were segregated, of course, as were the downtown Glasgow water fountains. As boys, Alex and Bobby gleefully rubbed their spit onto the spout of the whites-only fountain. Yet, Kentucky wasn't Mississippi and neither Alex nor Bobby can recall a single time anyone in Glasgow treated them rudely because they were black. Race was like a colorless, tasteless, odorless gas in the air. Alex remembers that he was once sent to a white school to pick up his black teacher's paycheck, and he noticed something amazing: on the tables in the white cafeteria sat entire bowls of fresh apples. Alex didn't think this was unfair, only that it was strange and mysterious.

Bobby tells this story: As he would walk to school, the white kids would ride by in their bus and make faces at him, but he would think nothing of it. "It's like the old joke about the Indian riding a horse with his squaw walking next to him," he explains. "A guy asks the Indian, 'Why are you ridin' and your squaw's walkin'?' The Indian looks up at the man, thinks, and then says, 'She no have 'em horse.'" We both laugh at the punch line. "Well, it was like that. We didn't have a horse."

Yet it's eerie how the memory of things no one seemed to notice can live so long, as in the mind of Carl, who is Alex and Bobby's friend and my hunting companion. Carl grew up outside Glasgow in a barn-wood shack. These days, he is never without at least the stub of a cigar working in the corner of his mouth. He's big as a bear, thick everywhere—stomach, chest, neck, legs, arms, even his fingers. Not fat, but thick. This morning, he's out checking on his cows, breaking the ice in their water trough with a shovel. He wears insulated camouflage overalls and green rubber boots. He has a deep, bass voice and a head that seems to sit directly atop his massive shoulders.

When Carl was a boy, there were no black schools near his house, so he didn't start until he was nine. "I'm still awful proud I graduated high school," he says, "considering where I began." Unlike Alex and Bobby, who joined the military and got out of Glasgow for decades, Carl stayed here. He worked at a gas station in town for twelve years—as a "wash boy," scrubbing cars, cleaning the grease pit. He earned $60 a week, far less than his white co-workers. One day, Carl noticed that a white mechanic had worked on a car all morning and gone to lunch without getting it started. Carl got it started. The boss was so happy, he bought Carl a Coke. In 1965, Carl got one of the first area factory jobs that went to a black man, and at age thirty-one he was finally paid a white man's wage.

Carl now drives a forklift at a factory and makes good money. Some of his good friends are white. Thirty years ago, Carl would have said that was impossible. He marvels when he hears young blacks and whites at work bantering back and forth with racial digs. Even today, Carl couldn't do that without getting mad.

Just the other day, he was listening to a couple of young white men bragging about the University of Kentucky basketball team, and Carl felt as if they were pulling an invisible thread in his brain. He thought about when, three decades ago, he happened to sit down next to Kentucky's venerated and racist coach, Adolph Rupp, while fishing. That year, a local black basketball star was trying to get into Kentucky, which had never had a black player, and Carl asked Rupp if he was going to take him. "He can't pass the academic tests," Rupp said smugly. The men had "words," as Carl says, and Rupp packed up his fishing gear and left.

Then Carl thought about all those years at the Texaco station, how he acted like "a nice colored man" when he sometimes wanted to slug the white men who made more money but didn't work any harder. And about the day he got that car started and the boss bought him a Coke. A *Coke!* He thought about how they wouldn't let him go to school until he was nine, how far behind he was, how foolish he felt. He thought about the days when banks wouldn't loan a black $500 without a white cosigner, how as a boy he had to stand in the store and wait until all the whites were served, how even his daddy, his *daddy*, had to wait patiently, like a nice colored man.

"I had to catch myself not to say anything," Carl says. "These are good guys. They're thirty years old. They didn't know Adolph Rupp. But all that brings back through your head everything else that came before. It can eat at you. And you start lookin' for each and every thing. It eats you up. The next thing you know, you're angry and you don't know what you're angry about."

I didn't know exactly what race my wife was when we first met. She's got high cheekbones, electrified hair and a nose that isn't European, but she has no accent except middle-American and her skin is the color of honey. "Maybe," I told a friend, "she's part Filipino." He said, "No, she's black." I didn't think much about it and when I first met her parents a month later and realized she was black, I didn't think much about it then either. Keran was the only black woman I'd ever dated, and I simply told myself that I would not let race matter, that I was beyond it. Besides, marriage wasn't on my screen in those days. My mother, it turned out, was more farsighted, and I once got an anguished late-night call from her, asking me, please, to think about what I was doing, please, think about the children. I told her not to worry, that I hardly knew the woman, that I wasn't marrying anybody for a long time. She said, "But this is how these things start." My mother, the prophet.

Five years later, Keran and I were married. In the years we had dated, strange as it seems, we never had a problem with race that I knew of. I never heard a slur. I didn't notice stares. Nobody seemed to care, at least not in the urban Northeast. I was amazed at this, and always figured it had to do with Keran, who didn't wear race as a badge, who talked middle-class talk, and who was light-skinned enough that whites weren't knee-jerk threatened by her.

But I never forgot my mother's phone call and, about a year before we married, I broke off with Keran. I told myself it was because I wasn't ready to get married, but I knew even then it was also because I feared my parents' reaction. If I were going to marry Keran, I reasoned, I'd better be awfully sure about it. After a few months apart, I was sure.

My parents, who'd always taught me to think right about race, freaked out. I'd been a rebellious kid, and my folks saw my marriage as one more act of rebellion against them. Keran knew me better. She joked, "You have to marry a black woman to prove you're not hopelessly middle class." Indeed, it was my hopelessly middle-class sensibility that attracted her. "I can't marry a jive man," she said. My parents understood none of this. They were dirt poor as children. They struggled all their lives to keep me and my sisters in a decent home, decent schools. They struggled to move us up and out. My father, who was a milkman, worked seven days a week to accomplish this. He was a good man, my father, and I knew it then. But he also was a stranger who seemed to enter my life from an outside world to dispense punishment, make decisions, and pass judgment. I came to deeply resent this, and it was the true seed of my later rebellion. But my parents believed my marriage mocked them and their values and squandered their sacrifices.

"I'm sure Keran is a nice girl from a nice family," my mother said. "This has nothing to do with her." In her mind, as in the minds of so many—including Aunt G—skin color, status, social class, and getting ahead in life were hopelessly confused and intertwined. To my parents, race was a stand-in for a whole constellation of class-laden fears. Who'd hire me? Who'd have me to dinner? What nice neighborhood would take me? After my marriage, my folks and I didn't really talk for several years. Then one day, as my mother looked through photos I'd sent—photos of my nice home, my nice yard, my nice kids—she made this telling remark to my sister: "It looks like your brother has made a life for himself." After I heard this, I visited my parents unexpectedly. For two days no one mentioned my wife or my children, and during a Sunday snowstorm I left as depressed as I've ever been. But a few days later, I got a letter from my father, the only letter he has ever sent me. It was fitting that his letter of reconciliation didn't mention race, because it had never really been the issue.

"I know that if I had it to do over again," he wrote, "I would somehow find more time to spend with you. It seems we never realize this until it's too late." Soon, we were a family again.

Keran's parents had a different reaction to our marriage, and they said not a word about race. They remained true to their lifetime belief that race shouldn't matter, that it should never be an excuse or an explanation. Their philosophy was simple: blacks must act as if they can control their lives, whether or not they can, because otherwise their ambition is sapped and their life consumed by self-pity. It is the way they lived their lives, the way they raised their children, although as kids my wife and her two younger brothers saw their father's beloved Kingdom through a different lens. They were military brats who'd spent half their childhoods in Germany, France, England, on the West Coast, always in military housing, always attending integrated military schools. Alex can tell some grim tales about his early days in the air force. The only day blacks could use the swimming pool, for instance, was Wednesday—after which the water was changed for the week. But by the fifties, Alex believed no place in American society gave blacks a better shake. By then, the military was integrated—housing, clubs, jobs, schools.

Into this brave new world came my wife and her brothers. Their playmates were mostly white, and out of, say, twenty kids in a military classroom, only one, two, maybe three, would be black. In Europe, there were no "Whites Only" signs and no one was turned away at a restaurant door. My wife and her brother, Alex Jr., can't recall a time overseas when race seemed to make a difference in their lives. Keran was wild about the Beatles and thought she'd die if she couldn't marry Paul. Alex Jr. was always the most popular kid in his class. Howard, the youngest, does remember that at the Oktoberfest in Munich, people stared awfully hard. He remembers kids with Southern accents who wouldn't play with him. But Howard must wrack his brain for these small indignities.

So when the kids came home to Glasgow, it was culture shock. Blacks and whites didn't mingle, and that was odd enough. But the rural poverty was shocking. Two generations out of Lawson Bottom, a generation out of the Kingdom, the kids would sit on the porch of the house their grandmother shared with Aunt G since their husbands had died, and they'd look across Back Street at mind-boggling destitution. "It wasn't race," says Howard, who after flying jets in the air force is now a pilot for UPS. "It was poverty. It was poverty like in Africa." He remembers the nights they'd sit on the front porch of their grandmother's house and listen to the people across Back Street chasing the rats from their bedrooms.

"We used to make fun of those people," says Alex Jr., now a casino executive in Las Vegas. "I just couldn't comprehend them." Of his father's Kingdom, he says, "The whole area around Aunt G's was a craphole. And all the black kids had these strange accents. It was hillbilly to me. I had the sense of not wanting to be associated with them. Growing up like I did, I missed an understanding of the anger so many blacks feel toward whites and toward everything to do with whites, including success. I just never felt that. I'm glad I didn't."

My wife and her brothers all graduated from college. Today, they all have good jobs. They are newly affluent, post–civil rights blacks. And they all say that, as far as they know, being black has only helped them. Howard says UPS didn't even answer his job application letter until he sent a picture. "Maybe I'm going through life with blinders," he says, shaking his head, "but when I hear people crying, 'Racism, racism,' I say, 'What are you talking about?' I just haven't seen it." Yes, there were slurs at the mostly white high school they attended in southern Illinois when the family finally moved off base. Yes, they remember family vacations in the fifties when motels turned them away. Yes, they remember some mean redneck stares. And yes, they also remember stares from black kids, who seemed angry and resentful of their white friends.

"I noticed it, but I didn't let it bother me," Howard says. "I've been stared at all my life—at the Oktoberfest, in Illinois, and years later when I'd take planes into Iceland. People stare for a minute and then they come up and talk to you. It hit home very early that through hard work you can make it too. That wasn't true in my dad's day, and that's different."

A FINAL VISIT IN GLASGOW

Aunt G's sitting room is a shrine of photographs—her sister, brothers, daughter, grandchildren, great-grandchildren, nephews, a great nephew. People of all shapes and shades. From her recliner, Aunt G holds court.

As a young woman, Aunt G moved to Glasgow from Lawson Bottom and married the whitest and richest black man she met. She and Mr. Troop, a barber and businessman, had one of the biggest houses in the Kingdom. They also had a daughter—beautiful Mackiva, with soft, pearly skin and flowing, wavy hair. Aunt G, who feared she simply couldn't care for a dark-skinned child, was elated. Her daughter felt differently. "The kids called me a half-white, stringy-hair bitch," says Mackiva, who is fifty-six. Little Mackiva would scream, "I hate this hair! I hate it!"

"You're the biggest fool," Aunt G would tell her. "I'd rather look like you than Auntie Mame." But Mackiva did a 180-degree turn on her mother's outlook. "I decided I'd never marry a bright-skinned man," she says. "My kids would never go through what I went through." And that's what Mackiva did: her husband, Evans, is a handsome dark-skinned man, as are their three grown sons and as are their grandkids, who are Aunt G's great-grandkids.

"Your children are white," Aunt G says to me rather abruptly, using her own either-or standard of skin color to describe my tan-skinned children. "So many whites have a horror of black babies. You didn't know what you'd have. How could you have coped if you'd had a black child?" I can't help but smile, because right now Aunt G is babysitting her great-grandchildren—Brittany, age two, and Michael, six months old. They are, in Aunt G's vocabulary, "black" children.

"Aunt G," I say, "you were terrified to have black babies. You married a bright man. Then your daughter went off and married a dark man and had dark children, who went off and had these dark grandchildren. So let me ask you, how do you cope?" Aunt G looks startled for a moment, but then she lets out a joyful little cackle that she mutes with a hand again put discreetly to her mouth.

"I got one as black as July jam and another with hair nappy as a sheep's back," she says, cackling freely now. "And I just love 'em better than anything! I just love 'em!"

"Aunt G," I say, "I feel the same way about my kids."

2

A SLAVE'S LIFE TODAY

COLONIAL WILLIAMSBURG, VIRGINIA

I'm ready to hit the road through the South for the next few months, and the weather has fallen into one of the hottest summers in years. I keep thinking how miserable the Mississippi Delta will be come August. Today, in the eighty-nine-degree sunlight, I'm headed for Williamsburg, Virginia, on the state's eastern coast at the James River, to visit a woman who plays the part of a slave in Colonial Williamsburg's reconstructed vision of colonial American life. What is it like, I wonder, to act out a slave's behavior and a slave's thoughts each day in the modern world?

I arrive in Williamsburg at an orange dusk. With nothing to do until tomorrow, I drive over to Colonial Williamsburg to see *The Runaway*, a short play about an escaped slave. The play is set in eighteenth-century Williamsburg, which was, for most of that century, the political, social, and cultural center of the largest and most influential American colony. The Virginia colony also saw the first cargo of twenty African indentured servants dropped off at Point Comfort on the James River in 1619. I've never been to Colonial Williamsburg before, and I find the place stunning—all pillars and clapboard, gingerbread and cobblestone, a kind of archaeological dig cum Disneyland. I walk up Waller Street toward Duke of Gloucester, the main drag. The streets are nearly deserted and in the cool evening air the setting is idyllic. Trees line Waller, where the birds are uncorking and the lightning bugs are just beginning their luminous feats. I can smell the clover bursting at my feet. A huge magnolia tree reigns nearby in pale green plumage. Ah, this was the life—at least for white people.

Until only a decade ago, this meticulously reconstructed town, founded in 1926 with the bucks of old John D. Rockefeller, Jr., played a dirty trick on its visitors: it air-brushed African Americans out of the picture, even though in 1790 they made up 702 of the town's 1,422 residents. The policy—and policy it was—of sanitizing Colonial Williamsburg's past seems more than ludicrous as I walk up Duke of Gloucester. The reconstructed Colonial capitol building, with its double turrets, has its red bricks laid alternately the long way and then the short in the Flemish bond style of the era. For exact historical accuracy, the narrow sides of the bricks have even been cured close to the kiln's fire to create a black, glasslike finish, which gives the whole building a checkerboard-squares look. Halfway up Gloucester, I stop at Wetherburn's Tavern, where tomorrow I'm to meet Sylvia Tabb-Lee, the woman whose job it is to play the part of a slave. Wetherburn's, in Williamsburg's tradition of authenticity, is painted in the colonial "Spanish brown" style—a thick, reddish paint covered with a colonial stew of whitewash made from boiled oyster shells that have been crushed and mixed with water. It gives the Wetherburn's walls the same mottled, translucent finish seen on Williamsburg's walls two hundred years ago. Details! Details!

For fifty years, Colonial Williamsburg employed an army of experts to unearth such details, to pore over old books, court documents, and arcane records so it could correctly portray the so-called facts of its colonial life—the facts of dress, manners, furniture, silverware, basketry, food, humor, education, and religion—all the while ignoring half the town's population. By the late seventies, it was getting ridiculous, with tourists increasingly asking where the slaves were. So in 1979, Williamsburg's actors began slowly to blend African American history into their telling, and the African American interpreters' troupe began. Today, out of 120 historical interpreters, twenty are black. Recently, Colonial Williamsburg also opened a reconstructed slave quarters at its Carter's Grove plantation outside of town.

The play I've come to see, *The Runaway*, is about a slave named Simon. A field hand at the nearby Carter's Grove Plantation, he lost his temper and shot and wounded his black slave foreman. Simon flees to Williamsburg because here, among the town's hundreds of slaves, a runaway has the best chance of hiding until he can be smuggled upriver. Yet *The Runaway* ends with Simon being caught by the town constable. "See, nigger!" he bellows. "We live by rules—and the first rule is: you be the slaves, we be the masters."

The epilogue has Bridgette Jackson, a black performer in the play, standing beneath the magnolia tree in the dimness of the street lamp. Bridgette explains to the audience that because this was Simon's first runaway attempt and because he shot a black man, not a white man, he would have gotten off easy: ten to thirty-nine lashes. Another runaway attempt, she says, would have brought dismemberment, usually an ear. A third would have demanded execution. Slave owners hated to lose valuable property that way, Bridgette explains, but the government did reimburse them for their loss, because a slave execution was a kind of tax-deductible expense. At this, Bridgette smiles wryly, magnifying the horror of it all.

I get to Wetherburn's Tavern in the morning before Sylvia arrives. Nobody's around so I wander into the backyard and into the tavern's unlocked slave residence, which consists of two twenty-foot-square rooms with an attic upstairs. By colonial standards, this was a luxury for slaves, who sometimes lived twenty-five to a tiny mud-and-stick hut as field hands at a poor plantation. Only about a dozen slaves lived in Wetherburn's back house, which is brick and painted white. A large, brick fireplace takes up one wall in the room that is the kitchen, living room, and sleeping room. On the only table is a head of lettuce, browning at its edges, a bowl of onions, a loaf of unsliced bread, and a colander filled with black-eyed peas that have been neatly shaped into the form of a star.

In a few minutes Sylvia, recently turned thirty-three, arrives in her slave's costume—a colorless skirt and pullover blouse made of coarse English osnaburg linen, a cheap but resilient eighteenth-century fabric. On her head is a straw hat and beneath it is a blue handkerchief that pulls her shoulder-length hair back from her face in the fashion of Aunt Jemima. She hates the handkerchief, not because it's stereotypical, but because she doesn't believe she looks good with her hair pulled back and her face so prominently displayed. I think she's wrong, that her thin face, moist skin, and arching brows and cheekbones are perfect for the look. She shows me her red-polished fingernails, which she didn't have time to strip bare this morning, and says she'll have to hide her hands when the tourists come. "That's the part about the job I hate," she says. "No polish, no makeup, no eyeliner. Look, I'm a twentieth-century woman."

The tours begin, and Sylvia and her partner (by coincidence, it's Bridgette Jackson, the woman who gave the wry epilogue to the play last night) take up their posts in wooden chairs behind the table. For an hour, I stand in the corner, watching and listening. The women alternate between being first-person characters—acting as if they are slaves, using slave dialect, gossiping about the everyday trivialities of colonial life—and being third-person characters—when they stop playing slaves and become tour guides describing the past. This is called going "in" and "out" of character. Most Williamsburg interpreters are forbidden ever to go "out" of character, but this dual approach was created because slavery is still considered too sensitive to leave to first-person play-acting alone. Slave dialect might sound demeaning to modern sensibilities, like an "Amos 'n' Andy" skit.

"Is you people heard about the runaway?" Sylvia asks an all-white tour group, using a thick, Southern country drawl.

"He's a runaway from Maryland," Bridgette says in a dark whisper, "and he's burnin' down white people's houses. He's upset! Massa sold off his whole family, and he been with 'im ten tobacco season—wife and three chil'ren. And he sold 'em off! I doesn't understand what gives 'em the right to own us no how. I mean the chickens and pigs, I can see that, but not me!"

"Right!" an elderly woman in the crowd suddenly blurts out, as the twentieth century unexpectedly intervenes.

"A Christian woman!" hollers Bridgette. "Is you a Quaker?"

"Yes, I am," answers the woman, quite seriously, reminding me that some things haven't changed: it was the Pennsylvania Quakers who first called for the end of slavery in 1688, a century before the abolitionist movement took off in America.

"You people got slaves backs home?" Sylvia asks.

"No, we do not!" says the woman proudly.

Here, Bridgette and Sylvia go "out" of character, explaining that slaves composed the entire foundation of Colonial Williamsburg society, working in nearly every job and craft except in the apothecary and gunsmith shops, because whites feared slaves might poison or shoot them. Slaves were the Atlases who held up the world—working as cooks, maids, menservants, and waiters, as well as barbers, blacksmiths, butchers, cabinetmakers, carpenters, harness makers, shoemakers, tanners, tailors, nurses, seamstresses, gardeners, and coachmen. Some were even trusted to serve as doctors to the rich, using ancient African herbal remedies in an era when medicine was nonexistent. Four slaves were even bought to help build the capitol, where their complete enslavement and dehumanization would later be codified into the earliest slave laws.

After the group leaves, Sylvia says, "It bothers me that black people are embarrassed to talk about slavery."

"More like ashamed," says Bridgette.

"And angry," says Sylvia. "Really angry, still."

Because this is not the eighteenth century, Sylvia gets a morning break from her job, and we walk up Duke of Gloucester through the horde of tourists and past the traffic jam of horse-drawn carriages toward the formal gardens behind the colonial governor's mansion. The gardens are Sylvia's favorite place. She has gone there since she was a high school girl living in the real Williamsburg, which surrounds Colonial Williamsburg and has a population of 11,530 people. Her father was a Baptist preacher who owned a small trash company, so small that he often picked up the trash himself. Sylvia was among the handful of black children who integrated Williamsburg's elementary schools, and she was often the only black child in her classroom. Today she's married with two children, a four-year-old girl and a six-year-old boy. She has worked at Colonial Williamsburg for three years. Before that, she studied acting and voice in New York and worked as a waitress and hostess in fine restaurants.

"It's funny how working here, playing a slave, has released my own anger about race," she says as we walk, adding that a lot of the controversy about doing slave interpretations at Colonial Williamsburg didn't come from whites, but from blacks. Sylvia says black friends have asked, "How can you lower yourself to play a slave?" "It's hard to find blacks to do what we do," Sylvia says. "It's because of their anger. They think, 'Why do we need to talk about slavery? That will only make me angry, and I already hate whites anyway.' That is their attitude. But working here has made me prouder to be black. When I look at the strength of the people who came before me, I can't believe it. The whole substructure of society was African Americans." They accomplished so much—in addition to getting married, raising families, keeping their faith and music and humor, and holding on to their dignity. They just happened to be slaves, Sylvia says, which makes it all the more remarkable.

We arrive at the gardens, which are magnificent, with rows of purple ageratum and orange day lilies surrounded by boxwood and huge holly bushes trimmed in perfect geometric shapes. I ask Sylvia if she has any close white friends. Yes, she says, but only one, a woman. "There's almost always a distance," she says. For instance, she'll sometimes be at lunch with a group of whites, having a good time, when suddenly she'll find herself thinking, "Gee, I wish some

other black people were here right now." She can't say why. Does it
have something to do with white humor, she wonders? Or style? She
can't put a finger on it, but she feels more comfortable if she isn't the
only black in a white crowd. "I don't believe I'm prejudiced against
white people. It's just tough in Williamsburg. It's still a little Southern
town. We're cordial, but we don't socialize much outside of work."
Sylvia once had a white man who was a friend. They talked all the
time, and she once suggested they do some things together. He said
he couldn't do that. He was a professional and other people wouldn't
like it. It wasn't him, you understand. Says Sylvia, "I have not spoken
to him since."

Then she says this: When she is out with black women friends for
the evening, the only white men who come up to their table to talk
are men from out of town. Sylvia wonders if this is because Williamsburg's white men are racist, or because white men everywhere only
approach black women when they are out of town. It seems this is a
question put to me as a white man, and I say that I don't know the
answer, that perhaps both are true.

Sylvia must go back to work, but later she'll give me a tour of the
Carter's Grove slave quarters. Then she'd like to show me Kingsmill,
an exclusive retirement community on the James River, where she
used to work as a restaurant hostess. Laughing, she says, "I'll wear
street clothes."

The country road to Carter's Grove is named, creatively enough,
Country Road. It begins in Colonial Williamsburg and zig-zags east-
erly as a single gravel lane through a wood of oak and loblolly pine,
past four lonely graves inscribed only with the names Robb and Taylor. Just before Tutter's Neck Creek, the road curves sharply to the
east through marshlands filled with mud turtles and muskrats, raccoons and great blue herons, one of which high-steps regally in the
distance. On the seven-mile Country Road's final stretch—through
marsh grass, cattails, and sedges—we get a glimpse of the James
River, the highway to Europe's tobacco markets and to the old Virginia colony's slave-driven prosperity.

"I worked out here for a year," Sylvia says, "and I never drove
out this way, always took Route 60. Ten minutes. It took a slave two
hours to walk from Carter's Grove to Williamsburg. And that was
nothing. To see their families, slaves sometimes walked the seventy-

five miles to Richmond." Sylvia, as she promised, has changed into
street clothes—black gym shorts, white socks and tennis shoes, and a
black T-shirt that reads: "The Liberation of Nelson Mandela. Freedom." Being a twentieth-century woman, she's also wearing lipstick,
makeup, two orange bracelets, a gold watch, and earrings.

"A man named Carter Burwell, a wealthy plantation owner, built
Carter's Grove in the 1750s," she says, "and it's been here ever since,
almost 250 years." At the plantation, we walk through a woods and
into a clearing where the slave quarters sit on parched gray dirt. The
quarters consist of four small wooden cabins, two of which are
mortared with chinking and daub—mud, straw, small sticks, and
lime mixed with water. Even the chimneys were made with the brew,
which meant the places burned often. The quarters are impressive.
Colonial Williamsburg's obsession with detail is everywhere, especially in the quarter's round wooden corrals, which are distinctively
West African. During the year since the quarters opened, Sylvia has
watched to see how visitors react. "Some whites walk right past and
go up to the mansion, not wanting even to look," she says. "Others
quietly go through, asking no questions and then they cry and hug
me and say, 'Thank you.'" Sylvia wipes tears from her eyes as she
says this. "That's when I think about the blacks who say I'm demeaning myself working here."

"How do blacks respond?" I ask.

Sylvia sighs. "How can I put this?" she says. "A lot of them are
glad to see it and they say so. But a lot come in with an attitude.
They're just waiting to see how we're going to polish slavery so its
palatable to whites. 'What are these Uncle Toms gonna do to cover up
for whitey?' they're thinking. They don't know enough about slavery
to be proud. That makes me sad."

Kingsmill is so amazing to Sylvia that she says I must see it while I'm
in town, so we drive out for dinner. It's like any of the many country-
club communities around the United States, but the view of the
James River is spectacular. We go to the restaurant where Sylvia once
worked and take a table outside on the balcony. The golf course, the
pool, and a children's playground are in front of us. Beyond is the
James, rolling gently in the sunset, a few sailboats decorating the
scene. Kingsmill is integrated, of course, and several black men in the
bright outfits of the golf-playing class sip drinks on the grass beneath

us. "Kingsmill isn't segregated," Sylvia says. "The cost of the homes will segregate it just fine."

We watch the sunset and the boats for a while, and then Sylvia says that when she worked in the restaurant she often found herself feeling resentful. "And I'm not that kind of person," she explains. Out here, where people treat all this comfort so naturally, as if they had been born to deserve it, "I started to wonder why I couldn't have a shot at this luxury," she says. "Why have I been excluded? What if you can't afford to go to college for six years? I kept feeling like I wanted to be served once in a while, rather than always doing the serving." Sylvia didn't like that feeling and so she quit. "At Williamsburg, I play a slave," she says. "But I feel less like a slave than I did at Kingsmill."

3

THROUGH A CHILD'S EYES

FARMVILLE, VIRGINIA

The heat wave continues, but when I pass through the concrete corridor from Williamsburg to Petersburg and head west on old U.S. Route 460, it's as if both the temperature and the decade have dropped back. Route 460 is an aging four-lane highway separated by a small forest, which gives the road the feel of a mountain trail. After a while, I pass a decrepit farmhouse with two black women and three children sitting on the porch. It's two o'clock in the afternoon, the heat of the day, but I suppose it's cooler on the porch than inside the house, even with its screenless windows thrown open like wide eyes.

The image of these people lingers, reminding me of the Great Depression—at least of the image I have of the depression from the photos my modern eyes have seen. History is like that. It doesn't only exist as a collection of details to be uncovered and compiled, as in the detailed monuments of Colonial Williamsburg. History's old images are seen through the eyeglasses of our own time. Who can understand today how decent men of the Old South could speak of slavery and honor in the same breath? Or how, only a century before them, almost no one in the world found slavery a bothersome moral issue? Today whites and blacks can finally see and accept the painful truths of Colonial Williamsburg's history because we have changed, which is good. But even better is that this truth-telling has changed Sylvia Tabb-Lee, made her prouder, more confident, less angry. The harsh truth has set her free.

This morning just before I left Williamsburg, I met a white man named Don R. Hill, a tourist at Colonial Williamsburg and an anthropologist by profession. I told him about my trip, and he told me that in 1958, as a college student, he and a friend had traveled to Clarksdale, Mississippi, in the heart of Jim Crow country, to collect tape recordings of black blues singers. With a young black man they met in Clarksdale, they went to Mississippi's notorious Parchman Farm state prison and asked if they could record inmates' songs. Don Hill and his friend were run out of Mississippi by the police.

"If you get to Clarksdale," he said, "look up Wade Walton. He took us to Parchman. He's a barber who's played harmonica with a lot of great bluesmen. Tell him I said hello." I have put Clarksdale and Wade Walton on my list.

Quite unexpectedly, I drive into the little town of Crewe, Virginia, which I hadn't realized was on my route. I know the town because my wife was born here, at the home of her maternal grandmother while her father was stationed in Germany in 1952. She stayed only a year, and driving through I realize what a good thing that was for me. Imagine if she had never left, never moved off to Europe or the North or the West Coast, just stayed here in rural Virginia, where the strategy of "massive resistance" to integration was born and carried out by U.S. Senator Harry Byrd's racist political machine. She would have known Jim Crow, attended segregated and inferior schools, used coloreds-only bathrooms and fountains. She could never have washed herself clean of those hateful experiences. She'd be different, no doubt.

As I pick up speed after exiting the other side of Crewe, I think that that is what's so insane about racism—my wife doesn't hate whites, nor is she embarrassed to share their values or goals, nor is she more mistrustful of them than she is of blacks. I'm sure most white people wish all blacks were as easy to get along with as my wife. But she's that way because she wasn't a victim. She escaped

Crewe—escaped America during much of her childhood—and lived among whites as an equal. This is what we whites rarely comprehend: it is we who create the anger, resentment, and mistrust in blacks. We create the very qualities we despise and fear. If we stop one madness we stop the other.

Speaking of madness, today I'm headed to a small town in south-central Virginia named Farmville, the seat of Prince Edward County, where from 1959 to 1964 the white county board of supervisors closed the public schools rather than integrate them. The case went to the U.S. Supreme Court, where the white mossbacks lost in a historic decision that ensured public school integration. Through the eye-glasses of today, the battle seems positively antebellum, positively South African. But it happened, and white people who believed they were acting as inspirations to their children took to the barricades without blinking, like good Afrikaners.

Near Farmville's eastern boundary runs the bucolically named Persimmon Tree Road, but I soon see that Farmville is no quaint, picture-postcard town with church steeples round the old town square. It's dingy and gray, a dumpy little town. Even in the hot, bright, ninety-degree sunlight it seems to reek of decay. About a mile off Broad Street on South Main, I find the house of Rudolf Doswell, one of Farmville's two black town councilmen. Mr. Doswell is a tall and dignified man who remained on the fringes of Prince Edward's great school integration battle, because he feared for his job as a government extension agent. He helped out in the struggle by teaching children in the evenings. Prince Edward's black children from those days have been called the "lost generation." There are no figures on how many youngsters didn't finish high school as a result of the half-decade school closing, but Mr. Doswell estimates it was at least several hundred, which is a lot in a county of only 17,320 people. A Michigan State University study once estimated that 1,100 of the county's 1,700 black kids got little education during the closings.

But what's lost in pondering the horror of what white Prince Edward County did to its black children is the memory of the amazingly creative ways that many, if not most, black residents tackled the school closing. There were classes held in local churches all over the county, although the curriculums were catch-as-catch-can. Hundreds of black families went to far greater lengths: they rented houses in nearby counties and moved there during the week. Or before dawn, they drove their children to the homes of friends or relatives in those counties and had these children get on the bus as if they lived there. Or they sent their children—boys and girls as young as first-graders—to live in the homes of sympathetic strangers in Richmond or Washington, D.C., where they went to school. For five years these wrenching dislocations took place, and I've come to learn how the children, now grown up, feel about it today.

With Mr. Doswell's help, I spend the next two days talking to men and women who were once locked out of their own schools. In Farmville, I notice black faces behind the counters of small shops and clothing stores, something that was taboo a few decades ago. There are black bank tellers, black policemen, and black professors at Long-wood College, which is part of Virginia's state university system. Mr. Doswell even sits on the county planning and zoning board, whose members decide what land will be developed for homes or busi-nesses, thus helping to determine the fortunes of the lawyers, bankers, real estate brokers, and large landowners, who are nine-hundred-pound gorillas in little places like Prince Edward County.

I find thirty-eight-year-old Chuck Reid working at the Longwood College recreation center, handing out bowling shoes and billiard equipment. He's the assistant rec center director and the second of Farmville's black town council members. Tonight, he wears a Farm-ville High School Eagles football booster's cap.

"So what was it like?" I ask.

"It left a mark that will never go away," he says, as he passes out a pair of red bowling shoes. Chuck wasn't a bad student, but he wasn't a good one either. He went to the catch-as-catch-can classes while the schools were closed and doesn't remember thinking much about it. After the schools reopened, he didn't take his education very seriously, and when he got back from the military and tried to go to junior college, he discovered he was way behind. Yes, he says, it was his own fault for not knuckling down in school, but some of it had to be those years that he missed. Today, Chuck says, Farmville still has deep race problems. Whites rarely patronize black merchants, he says, and once a white business hires one black, that's it. "But it seems like it's gotten better and is getting better in this town," Chuck says. He works mostly with college and high school kids who come into the rec center, and they seem not to notice that he's black, which amazes him. Young men and women, black and white, ask him for advice about intimate personal problems. One white girl even asked him what she should do about her parents' objections to her dating a black man. (Chuck's advice: "Maybe you better leave him alone.") He says, "It's just really different today."

The other men and women I talk with, all in their thirties, agree that race in Farmville is better—better but with a long way to go. And Phyllis Tillerson, Theresa Clark, Donnie Gresby, and Beau Lee surprise me when they say they didn't suffer academically, as Chuck Reid did. They all have good jobs today—a bank employee, a professor at Longwood, an administrator at West Virginia State College, a professor at North Carolina A&T State University. They all knew people like Chuck Reid—brothers, sisters, friends who fell behind in school and never caught up. They are still angry about that. But for themselves, well, things worked out fine. Of all their stories, I find Beau Lee's the most touching. He is a tall, gentle man, thirty-four years old, with a doctorate and a teaching job at North Carolina A&T. In first grade, he was sent off to a family of strangers in Washington, D.C. Although the family was wonderful, six-year-old Beau was deeply hurt and confused by the move. When his parents visited one Sunday, he threw a tantrum at dinner to see who would discipline him—his real parents or his new parents.

"Looking back," he says, "it must have been hard on my folks." When the schools finally reopened, nobody had any idea what grades the black children should enter, so they were tested. Beau tested as a genius—and a public-relations-minded school official leaked the information to *McCall's* magazine to prove that Prince Edward's black kids deserved access to good schools, that they were not inferior to whites. The national publicity landed Beau in upstate New York at a school for gifted children. He eventually graduated from Cal Tech and then got his doctorate from North Carolina State. For Beau, Prince Edward's shame opened a whole new world.

"Do you have close white friends today?" I ask.

"Oh, yeah, but there are cultural differences." He says that when he failed his exams for his doctorate the first time he took the tests, he was devastated. He'd never failed at anything, and he was tempted to let himself think it was racism—a white school and faculty. But it wasn't true. And the people he turned to for consolation were all his white friends around the country. They could understand what he was going through, what it meant to him, because they'd been there.

But when his mother died—he was so close to her—it was his black friends with whom he grieved. It was they who knew him then. When it came time to decide where he'd teach, Beau passed up prestigious white schools for A&T, a historically black college. He was tired of black–white campus politics, of having his race always be an issue. He wanted to be appreciated and judged for what he knew and how well he could teach.

Beau falls silent for moment, and when he speaks his voice is nearly inaudible. "I'm all the time re-realizing what happened," he says of the school closing. He still thinks about those days a lot, about what makes people think they have the right to be on top with others on the bottom. The bank Beau used to patronize helped build Prince Edward Academy, a private school where nearly all the whites started attending while Beau and the other black kids were locked out. And when he'd go into that bank he'd think about that. "To me, it would show a fault in my character to think that I should be here and you should be there because I'm some color." He reaches out and touches my arm, my white skin, and then he touches his own dark-skinned arm. But most whites in Prince Edward, he says, were proud of what they'd done.

"What can you say?" Beau whispers. "They must really have something wrong with them to think they have the right. They're the sick ones. You just have to shake your head."

My last night in Farmville, I stop for a late dinner. As I eat my burger, I notice a short black man bopping around the place like he's just starting out working on a busy day, although it's near closing time.

"Where do you get your energy?" I ask.

"Man," he says, as if he's known me for years, "I been in here since this morning and ain't never stopped. But I like it. In the last few weeks I worked 150 hours here, and I got a part-time job in the morning a few days a week. I worked all my life, man. My daddy worked every day, on the railroad. My mama worked. My older brother quit school and helped so me and my sisters could stay in school. I owe 'em."

I tell him why I'm in town, whom I've talked to. He tells me his name, that he's in his mid-thirties. Without prompting, he begins: When it was time for him to go to first grade, the schools were already closed and his older brother had missed a couple of years.

But with him reaching school age, too, his parents rented a house in a nearby county, something they couldn't really afford to do. During the week, the family lived there, and the kids went to school. He says the closing didn't hurt him, but his older brother, who was a teenager, is another story. While out of school, he got a job, became an adult, and never went back. "There were lotsa guys like him," he says. "Me, I worked all the harder."

Then it hits me: *they all worked all the harder!* The people I've met all mentioned the casualties of the school war, the lost generation. But that isn't what happened to them, who were among the youngest of the children locked out. "That's it!" I say. "You were all determined to prove yourselves. In a crazy way, you all benefited. You decided to succeed." After the closing, after all their parents did for them, I say, nobody was ever going to tell him and the others they couldn't suceed.

"That's right!" he says. "So tell 'em I'm doin' fine."

The next morning, before I leave town, I decide to drive by the school Beau Lee had mentioned—Prince Edward Academy, the school that opened around the time the public schools closed. Almost all the county's white students had been attending there, and the academy became a national symbol of white resistance to school integration. A few years ago, the academy admitted its first black students, and it now has about a half-dozen. Prince Edward Academy is today like private schools everywhere—mostly white, with a smattering of black faces. Back at my home near Washington, D.C., liberal white lawyers, doctors, and politicians send their kids to such schools. Washington's schools—filled with poor black kids—just aren't good enough. This isn't seen as racism, but rather as dedication to superior education.

I'm not implying that a person who picks a private, mostly white school for his kids is racist. I've thought about it for my own kids plenty of times. So far, my wife and I have decided against it. But remember, Jesse Jackson didn't. He sent one of his sons to D.C.'s St. Albans prep school, which makes Prince Edward Academy look like a one-room schoolhouse. And if the public schools in my neighborhood were bad enough, I wouldn't blink at sending my kids to a private school. Neither would most parents—black or white—which is why so many blacks in American cities send their kids to Catholic schools.

After passing Farmville's only McDonald's on South Main, I turn at Putney Street and head down the hill. When I get to the academy, I notice that its driveway is an extension of Church Street, and I wonder how many of the school's students have wrestled with this moral irony. The academy has tennis courts and a swimming pool, but mostly it is a modest affair—no red-brick ivy-covered walls, but lean, utilitarian buildings. Before driving around the fifty-three-acre campus, I figure I'd better get permission. So I go into an open building and introduce myself to a man inside. I tell him about my trip, and we chat amiably. He tells me the school is integrated now, that as many as 15 of its 650 students will be black next year. He says Prince Edward now has minority scholarships. I tell him my theory about how Prince Edward Academy is today more like private schools everywhere. I ask about the SAT scores, and he proudly says the average was 970 last year, that the top 25 percent of the class scored more than 1,100, that all fifty-five of the academy's seniors are going on to college. But the man also says that Prince Edward Academy never did seek to keep blacks out, that none ever actually applied until recent years. He says that any qualified minority student could have attended the school even decades ago.

"You expect me to believe that?" I ask.

"I don't give a damn if you believe it or not."

From here, our conversation is all downhill. "We just want to be left alone to educate our children," he says, and he sounds suddenly very weary of it all. But a light also has seemed to go on in his head, and he threatens to take my tape recorder away from me. I make a beeline for the door. He reaches for my recorder and jostles with me for an instant. But his effort seems half-hearted and I think that he doesn't really want to do this. I slip out the door, and he follows, hollering for me to get off the academy's property, which I do, fast. With that, I've had enough of Farmville.

While waiting at the stoplight at Farmville's new Wal-Mart, I notice a policeman standing outside his car on the corner watching the traffic flow by. It strikes me that there was a time not long ago when my disagreement at the Prince Edward Academy could have brought me serious trouble. Somebody out there could have called the white police chief, who could have sent somebody from his all-white police force who could have hauled me in for something like trespassing, without a whimper of objection from anyone but me. But no more. Today one of Farmville's policemen is black. Black Virginia Governor Doug Wilder carried Prince Edward County last election. The Prince Edward Academy has black students. Mr. Doswell and Chuck Reid are town councilmen. And Mr. Doswell even sits on the county planning and zoning commission, which on occasion decides who will and who will not get rich. Today, powerful white people always think to say hello to Mr. Doswell when they pass him on the street. He believes they have come to like him. I believe it is also something more.

4

SHARECROPPERS AND CHEVROLETS

OXFORD, NORTH CAROLINA

Along the narrow North Carolina country road, high and arching plumes of water carrying a hundred dazzling rainbows revolve around the irrigation sprayers in the tobacco fields. In one field, I see the latest innovation in farm labor—seven Hispanic men. A cycle everlasting. People say that except for slavery there has been no worse, no more exploitive work than sharecropping. Looking at the seven men, who aren't sharecroppers but probably earn a few dollars an hour, I wonder if they would agree with that.

My destination this morning is Oxford, North Carolina, population 7,913. I'm headed there to learn about sharecropping through the eyes of its offspring. In the heart of northern Piedmont tobacco country, southeast of Farmville just below Virginia, the town of Oxford is the home of Charlotte and Zeke Hester. They're having a family picnic at their house this weekend, and I've been invited. Charlotte's father, a man named Joe Green, was a sharecropper—and the son and grandson of sharecroppers. He is still alive at age seventy, and so are his fifteen children, most of whom will be at the picnic.

Zeke meets me at the Beacon Express convenience store just inside Oxford. He's a short, wiry, muscle-bound man with a thick mustache that hangs over his upper lip. He wears a well-wetted Jheri curl. Friendly and relaxed, he asks if I'd like to meet his father-in-law before going to the picnic. On the way, he talks. He's forty-two, his wife is thirty-two. They have a ten-year-old daughter, Terilyn, who's an honor student in the fifth grade. Except for a few years in the military, Zeke has lived in Oxford all his life, as has Charlotte. They're doing well. Charlotte works as a hospital aide, and he's a shipping clerk at a clothing factory. Three evenings a week, he works as a clerk at the Beacon Express. On Monday, he and Charlotte are going to the bank to pay the last $800 on their $61,000 house. After that, except for payments on their '87 Nissan Maxima, the Hesters will be free and clear. Zeke is so proud, he could dance.

But Zeke turns serious now and says the better that life goes for him, the more his black friends seem envious and even angry. "Right now, with my job and my wife's job, we're outcasts, because we got goals," he says. "They call me all sorts of names." Blacks tell Zeke he's trying to be white, that he thinks he's a big shot. "That's what we're faced with," he says. "It's terrible. Blacks won't talk this way to whites, but a black friend of mine once said: 'I despise niggers.' That's what he told me: 'I despise niggers.' Well, now I see what he meant. We are a race very envious of each other.

"There are opportunities out there, but to make our black youth aware of them, you're beatin' a dead horse, because they don't want to do anything. And this burns me up because my girl is ten years old and it's frightful. When she gets to be a teenager what is she going to have to select from when it comes to males to be the head of a household? It's the 'system,' it's 'society.' But I can't blame the 'system' alone, because we're all livin' in the same 'system.' I could just go on talkin'. It's terrible. I'm really leanin' toward puttin' my girl in a private school just to separate her from this trash out there."

I am startled. "You'd put her in a white school?"

"I'm really leanin' toward that. It is terrible! You have to be black to see exactly what I'm talkin' about."

Zeke and I get to Joe Green's house, an old trailer in the countryside, with a huge, red-dirt garden behind it. We go inside, where Mr. Green is sitting in the living room on a wooden kitchen chair that's wired together at the lower cross beams. His legs are splayed, with four buckets of freshly picked string beans in front of him. He's a thin man with tight, gray hair and a baseball cap on his head. He wears green work pants and a green work shirt, unbuttoned, no shoes or socks. His feet are a working man's feet, with huge knots at the toe knuckles. He smiles and shakes my hand. He has only one tooth peeking out on the lower right side of his mouth, and he quickly explains that he's having his teeth pulled so he can get false ones. His were eaten up with decay.

On the couch nearby is another elderly black man. He's talking toward the television, which is running in the corner, and I cannot understand him. Mr. Green says to ignore him. I sit on the couch, but pretty soon the man is hollering so loudly a few inches behind my back, cursing and calling me a "white-assed motherfucker" and threatening to beat my butt, that I move to a chair where I can keep an eye on him. "Don't worry 'bout him," Mr. Green says calmly.

While snapping beans, Joe Green, with relentless cheerfulness, tells the story of his life. His first memories, he says fondly, are of "pickin' that cotton." They lived in whatever house the white farmer gave them. "You could count chickens under the house, man—one, two, three, four, five, six, seven," and he laughs. "You could look up and see the sun comin' up. We raised them hogs and raised them chickens. Every Sunday mornin' my mama said, 'Catch that chicken right there.' We'd clean 'im. So then the preacher'd come. You know what she give us children? The feets and the necks! Save the rest for the preacher! That's the way we come up." He laughs long and deep. "Old time, yeah, old time. *Hard!* I been raised hard all my life. You know anything about a mule?"

"No," I answer.

"You don't know anything 'bout no mule?" Mr. Green is flabbergasted that such a man exists. Joe Green went as far as the third grade, attending classes off and on. As a boy, he worked the tobacco fields pulling worms off the leaves for three cents a worm. Almost every year, Joe Green's father moved the family—a wife and fourteen children—to different white folks' farms for a slightly larger share of the tobacco he tended or for a better house or for a better monthly fee. By the time Joe Green was twelve, he was a full-fledged farmer, doing a man's work. At nineteen, he married his fourteen-year-old sweetheart, and they took their place in what seemed an ageless and immutable cycle. They had fifteen children, thirteen of them boys. This male brood made Joe Green a sought-after sharecropper, because with him came his sons, as if they, too, were mules. Like his daddy, Joe Green moved the family often. In his best years, in the late fifties and early sixties, he had a pretty decent house, a two-acre share that earned about $1,200 a year and a $25-a-month salary. But every year, when his profit came after harvest, Joe Green was still in debt to the landowner.

"Did you feel cheated?" I ask.

"No, I didn't feel like that. Everybody sharecropped then to make a livin'. The white man was supposed to get more 'cause he had the land. He had everything. And we didn't have anything. I thank white people. I love white people. If it wouldn't have been for the white people, we couldn't a made it." Finally, in 1966, with tobacco on bad times, Joe Green quit sharecropping and took a minimum-wage job in a brick factory.

Across the room on the sofa, the other elderly man has been getting louder. "You white motherfucker!" he bellows. "You come in here! I can't go in your goddamned house! You ol' white-assed motherfucker. I been mistreated all down the line. I know 'bout you, your race. Your race ain't shit! Why? You know why! Your race ain't shit, 'cause they always wantin' to damn that black man. Your race ain't worth a fuck!"

"Ignore him," Mr. Green says.

To tell the truth, I'm pondering which of these men is talking to me more honestly—the one who hates me or the one who loves me. Or if they're both talking honestly, telling different sides of the same truth.

"Have you always been so happy?" I ask Mr. Green.

"I been happy all my life," he answers. "But nothin's good as farming. I liked farming. I miss farming."

The picnic starts slowly. Zeke hooks up the stereo in his backyard, and his eleven-year-old nephew takes the microphone and raps out his own composition. When the real music starts, it's Digital Underground singing "The Humpty Dance," a bawdy rap with the line, "I once got busy in a Burger King bathroom." The yards are big and wooded in Zeke's neighborhood, and no one will complain about the noise. He has a three-bedroom brick house in a black neighborhood of such houses. On the grass along his driveway, the cars in Zeke's collection are posted like vigilant sentries: '75 Corvette, '49 Plymouth, '73 dune buggy, '84 Nissan pickup. Around the side of the house is his fifteen-foot motorboat. Charlotte has the charcoal grill fired up and the chicken and hot dogs cooking when her sister and brothers begin to arrive.

"Erving, come over here," Zeke says to Charlotte's brother. "I got someone I want you to meet." Erving and I shake hands and Zeke tells him what I'm doing. Erving is a big man, my age, with shoulders rounded from hard work, strong hands, and a calm, deliberate voice. He cocks his head, eyes me warily and asks, "So you like black people?"

I smile and say, "I got a black wife. Does that count?"

"Say wha!" Erving gasps. He puts an arm around my shoulder, smiles and with mock affection says, "You a brother!"

"Erving rebuilt my Vette engine," Zeke says. And for the next half-hour, as the dusk turns the sky a brilliant orange and cools another oven of a day, the three of us talk cars. Erving has eight classic cars. He works at a factory making roofing shingles, but cars are his love. He has had no training as a mechanic. It's just something he picked up. He's building a garage at his house now so he can run a little mechanic's business on the side. Erving mentions that he changes the oil in his cars every thousand miles, Zeke says he changes his oil every two thousand miles, I say I change my oil every three thousand, and we talk about what's best. We talk about how we now tune up our new cars every thirty thousand miles and about how back when we were teenagers, bopping around in clunkers, we had to tune those babies every ten thousand miles or they'd start coughing and wheezing like a dying man. We talk about the old two-ply tires and how they used to go flat about as regular as rain, bursting on little nails or shards of glass, and how the new steel-belted radials just won't go flat on anything. Erving mentions his '63 Chevy Impala.

"I used to have a '63 Impala," I say. "Red with black buckets. It had a, let's see, a 326-cube engine."

"A 327," Erving says, correcting me.

"That was a hot car," I say.

"It still is," he answers.

For these minutes, I'm lost in an illusion of my own creation, of my own narrow universe. For these minutes, I mistakenly believe that Erving, who is my age, and I share a cultural memory known in America as the teen years. It was the sixties, man! I had my car and

my summer job and my girlfriend, the high school baseball and basketball teams, Saturday nights hanging out in the McDonald's parking lot, trips to the beach. I had the suburbs. In this world, high
school was preschool for college. And of course, binding these experiences together, imbuing them with a special and artificial feeling of
adult freedom, was cars—wheels, man! Wheels!

"So you were a kid when your dad quit sharecropping?" I ask.

Erving is taken aback. "*Nooooooo!*" he says. "We started helpin'
sharecroppin' 'bout seven years old." Erving quit school in the ninth
grade, and when he was about sixteen he went to work with his
daddy in the brick factory. That is my wake-up call.

"We used to plant twelve, thirteen acres of tobacco," Erving says.
"And I mean nice tobacco. We rolled, man—me, Donald, Earl, Fletcher,
Larry, and Henry. We was all old enough to work the field. Back then
you used to have sons, 'cause if you didn't have no sons to work the
fields, they wouldn't want you. The white man got the daddy and the
kids. Shit, yeah! They called 'em 'points.' If your ass didn't go to work,
your ass was out. The white man would say, 'Joe, take your boys, go
down ta that field, and y'all take the middle outta this corn field, lap it,
put soda 'round it and then do this other field.'" In return, Erving says,
the kids got two pairs of clothes a year—one for Sunday, one for the rest.

I think to myself: Lyndon Johnson was president, the Beatles and
the Beach Boys were the rage along with white socks and penny
loafers. As Erving talks, the other brothers and sisters begin to gather
around us at the table.

"What was your life like?" I ask.

"It was hell," Erving says, and his low, calm voice raises an
octave in the saying. "It was hell, man!" Everybody mutters in agreement. I chuckle.

"Your father says it was the best time of his life."

"Yeah!" says Charlotte, angrily. "He got the money!"

"Get out!" says Erving. "He didn't have nothin'."

It turns out that the older boys in the Green family—those who
are over about thirty today—lived the early years of their lives, into
their twenties for several of them, as if it were 1930, even 1910. While
I was running for student council president in the 'burbs, they were
"bustin' the middle outta corn fields". They went to school a couple
days a week and fell hopelessly behind. They did tobacco. They
chopped and piled wood and put it in the shed. They shelled corn for

the geese. When it rained and they couldn't get the tractor and trailer into the field to bring out the corn, they walked the rows, threw the stalks in a pile, shucked it, bagged it, tied it with twine three times round, laid it on a mule sled, and drove the mule over to the tractor, where they moved the corn to the trailer before taking it to the shed.

"How old were you?" I ask.

Erving thinks a moment. "'Bout eleven."

"Did you feel like slaves?"

"What could you do?" he asks.

"Your daddy wishes he could have kept farming."

There is pained laughter all around.

"So the white man made a lot of money," I say, "your daddy made a little money, and you got two pairs of clothes each year?"

"Right!" Erving hollers, his anger finally rising. *"And we got to slop the hogs, feed the hogs, get up all the damned corn, shuck it. . ."* Then, as quickly as his ire flashed, Erving's temper recedes, his voice trails off, and he sits shaking his head at the memory of it all. He says calmly, "That's the way it was."

I must remind myself: Erving and I are the same age.

While everyone is getting ready to eat, Zeke leans over and whispers that he'd like to show me something. It's nearly dark now, but we hop in the car and drive to what Zeke calls Oxford's "black orphanage." He explains that the orphanage, now called the Central Children's Home of North Carolina, will take white children, but that they rarely end up there, because across town is the privately funded Oxford Orphanage, operated by the Grand Lodge of Ancient, Free and Accepted Masons, which takes no black children.

The black orphanage is located on a sprawling, wooded campus, and today it houses about eighty foster children. It's a complex of aging, red-brick buildings that reminds me of an old Mickey Rooney orphan flick. When Zeke was a boy, living with his mother nearby and attending the black public elementary school that was then on the orphanage grounds, there were hundreds of orphans. We walk across the crackling gravel of the driveway, with the sound of a local church choir singing the word "Amen" in beautiful, elongated reprises inside the orphanage's gymnasium, to a large clearing in the trees. It was here, Zeke says, that the old school, a huge two-story brick building, once stood.

In the enveloping darkness, Zeke points to the right side of the building he still sees in his mind, to the second floor, where the sixth-grade class used to be. Then he points over the front doors, where the seventh-grade class met. And then, finally, to the lunchroom, where the country kids—including his wife and her brothers and sister—sat quietly while the other kids ate. The Greens, Zeke says, didn't have the four cents each a day to buy a carton of milk or the penny for cookies. Erving and Henry were a few years behind Zeke, but he can still remember them, how out of place and uncomfortable they looked in school. And he remembers two of Erving's older brothers to whom he caught up and eventually passed in school. "You know what the teachers would do with them?" Zeke asks. "They would put them in one row, ignore them, and teach the rest of us. That's what they did. It wasn't right."

I say, "Maybe that's why blacks envy and resent you, Zeke, someone who has done well. So many people never got a chance."

Zeke nods his head. "I know it is, man," he says quietly. "I know it is. But I've got my little girl to think about."

5

"I'M TIRED OF TALKIN'"

GREENSBORO, NORTH CAROLINA

The streets of Greensboro, North Carolina, are empty early the next morning, Sunday. It was here, at the F.W. Woolworth's, that the modern lunch-counter sit-in movement took off in 1960. Within weeks, it had swept through the South. Only one of the four North Carolina A&T State University freshmen who launched that movement remains in Greensboro today, and I'm here to visit him. He's David Richmond, forty-nine years old and out of work.

I've never been to Greensboro before, but I know it must look different than it did thirty years ago. A city of 183,521 people, Greensboro today has a real skyline, with modern buildings that tower into the morning's hazy sky. Once downtown, though, I see that plenty of

Greensboro's aging, masonry one-story buildings remain, tucked like old photos between the new pages of glass and steel. Driving slowly, I notice a boarded-up movie house: "Ce-ter Th–er," the marquee reads. I'm nearly past the block when I see the Woolworth's across the street. At 8:30 in the morning, mine is the only car around so I pull a U-turn and park.

Woolworth's is closed on Sundays, and from beneath the marquee across the street—in the absence of people, cars, trucks, birds, even a breeze—the store and the whole street seem like a museum, or maybe a back-lot movie set. The first floor of Woolworth's has been updated with some kind of pseudomarble, but the second floor is still as it should be: gray concrete decorated at intervals with what look to be Greek-style vases. On the sidewalk in front of the store is a brass inlay bearing the footprints of the four men who asked for a meal and began a revolution. A plaque reads: "Four who dared." The prints are smudged with blue because last winter someone spray-painted "KKK" across the brass plate.

·When I turn to leave, I see that a solitary old black man has appeared across the street and is peering into the window of Lane Drug. I walk over to talk with him. He's short and strong, hunched badly at the waist. He's wearing a worn red polo shirt with the top button fastened tightly. His maroon knit slacks are held together at the fly with a safety pin. His light-blue straw dress hat is stained with the sweat of many wearings. His shoes are cracked and torn at the seams. Except for a thin, expert mustache, he is clean shaven. This man tells me that he is seventy-four and has lived in Greensboro all his life. He never married nor had children. He's checking the price on the seven-inch fans in the window. He asks if I can read the tag.

"It's $7.78," I say.

The old man wants to know this because he complained so much about the god-awful heat in his rented room this summer that a man at the snack bar where he often eats gave him a new seven-inch fan. He's trying to figure out how much the man paid for it.

"I noticed Woolworth's is on sale for $11.88," I say.

"Well, that's it then, that's the one," the old man says with sudden confidence, "'cause that's where he got it, Woolworth's." The old man speaks quickly with a deep voice, bobbing his head and spiking the air with his right hand. I think that he might have done a little boxing in his day. He looks me directly in the eye and stands very close, where I can see the yellow teeth in the back of his mouth and smell his old-man breath. I tell him I'm here to visit the Woolworth's where the sit-ins began, and I ask him what he remembers of those days.

"Quite a bit."

"Was it exciting?"

"It was high time somethin' happened. It just oughta happened way 'fore it did." The old man worked as a freight handler in a cotton mill in those days, and as a black man he was paid less than white men doing the same work. But he never came to any of the hundreds of demonstrations that took place here over the years, because he was afraid for his job and his life. "If it hadn't been for them boys, it'd still be like it was." He suddenly laughs: "Ya know, I bet I ain't got down to eat at Woolworth's five times." He seems to enjoy that, as if it is some kind of justice anyway.

"What was it like then?"

"I'm gonna break it down like it was. White people were just against us and we hadn't never done nothin' to 'em, and I always wondered why they did that, but that's the way it was. We were afraid to speak, 'cause, see here, you might think I'm lyin', but walkin' up and down this town, if a white woman was walkin' in front of me and a white man was walkin' behind me, I better be careful how I'm lookin'. He gets me for reckless eyeballin'! You know what I'm talkin' 'bout? 'You're lookin' too hard!' And here's what I say now: the white man has used our women, worked 'em in the kitchen, and got what he wanted, too. Ya know what I mean? He wanted what he wanted, and if she wouldn't do it, well, he couldn't use her no more. But if I even look at a white woman, they ready to do that number on me! That heaved me up, made me a little bit hot. I think if a woman want a man, I don't see where another man be ready to shoot him or have him electrocuted for it."

"Is it different today?"

"Well, yes, night and day," the old man says, bobbing his head, spiking the air, and still breathing into my face. "But I'd say there's a whole lotta white people still don't want their kids involved with blacks, 'specially it's a girl. They think they better'n blacks. They don't show it, but so many of 'em still hate the daylights outta ya. And in the next hundred or a thousand years, it'll never change."

* * *

David Richmond and I eat breakfast at Woolworth's the next morning. Or rather I eat breakfast. He drinks coffee and smokes cigarettes. I don't think he looks healthy. He says that he's lost fifteen pounds recently, and he's so emaciated that I wonder if he's ill. He says no, he has always had trouble keeping his weight up. His doctor has him on a high-calorie diet right now. David has long, bony fingers that tremble slightly when he puts a cigarette to his mouth, and he has a disconcerting way of looking away when he talks. His thinning hair is cut short and his beard is like a shadow on his dark skin. It does not take long to realize that David Richmond, who will be fifty soon, is a burdened man.

The lunch counter we sit at is pretty much preserved the way it was when David was the last of the four young men to sit down and ask for service as a crowd of Monday afternoon customers looked on in silent astonishment. At the counter, which today runs in a series of horseshoe shapes rather than a straight line, sit about as many blacks as whites. A mirror decorates the wall behind the counter and signs announce the day's specials. There are both black and white waitresses in red-and-white uniforms. A friendly white waitress says, "Mornin', David," and brings him an ashtray before he has a chance to ask for one.

The first time David sat at this counter, he was terrified. Unlike so many other tactical maneuvers in the civil rights movement in the forties, fifties, and sixties, the sit-in here wasn't orchestrated by movement leaders. But there was talk of sit-ins—called "sit-downs" then—in the air.

"Every night, we talked and talked," David says. But they told no one about their fantastic idea, because talk seemed about all they could muster. Then on January 31, 1960, one of the four, Frank McCain, said, "I'm tired of talkin'." After class the next day, the men—dressed in dark overcoats and ties and nice shirts—silently and fearfully walked the mile from campus to downtown. "It was the longest walk I ever took," David says. At the lunch counter, they ordered coffee and apple pie. The rest, really, is history. The event came and went quietly, with the four men leaving by the side door after Woolworth's closed. "We will be back," one of them said. It was over that quickly. There had been no outside agitators—only four men, little more than boys, who had acted alone. Their resolute action was like flipping a hot-switch of electric current through black America: the next day, dozens of students occupied the Woolworth's lunch counter. Soon hundreds were in the streets, with the sit-downs spreading to Greensboro's other segregated eateries. After two weeks and a bomb threat, Woolworth's closed its doors. Within that time, the sit-ins had spread across the South.

If ever there is proof that people suffer from injustice, it's when so many act in spontaneous concert because the time has simply come. Over the weeks, there were hecklers and water bombs dropped on demonstrators from the windows of Greensboro's King Cotton Hotel. (I wonder how many parents in Greensboro today proudly tell their children they once dropped water balloons on people who asked only to be served coffee and apple pie?) David was a hero, but never a leader, of the movement. At campus rallies, he was always onstage taking his bows. He was arrested about a hundred times from 1960 to 1963, and he was always proud of what he'd done, never embarrassed at the attention that came to him. "I don't know if I could ever do anything to top February 1, 1960," he says. Then, with an edge in his gentle voice, he adds, "I had accomplished one good thing in my life." I cannot tell if this is said with bitterness, cynicism, or resignation.

Life came to engulf David Richmond, as the opportunities that grew from the revolution he had helped foment seemed to pass him by. Today, while his three sit-in compatriots hold good jobs, David is looking for work, having lost the nursing home job from which he took home $243 every two weeks. Last week, he made $80 doing odd jobs. David doesn't seem to want sympathy. But it's impossible to sit here—with the black and white waitresses hustling behind the counter and the cash register jangling and black and white workmen bantering on the stools next to us—and not feel an abiding sadness for what has happened to David Richmond. His daddy was a cotton mill worker and his mother was a domestic. David has worked for as long as he can remember, always giving whatever he earned to the family.

David was always gentle and shy and quick to have his feelings hurt—sensitive, his mama called him. He remembers only once in his boyhood when the repository of his deep resentment and anger about race flashed. "The only whites I knew as a boy were those who came to the neighborhood as insurance men and bill collectors," David says. "I noticed that they all called my mother by her first name when nobody called my mother by her first name. And they always walked in the house without knocking. I can remember saying to myself, 'I will put a stop to this as soon as I'm big enough.' And I did. This guy walked in—I was about fourteen—and I grabbed him and he landed in the grass about three, four feet away. I told him, 'From now on, you call my mother "Mrs. Richmond," and do not come in this house unless you knock.' "

David never graduated from college. He married in his sophomore year and had a baby. He lasted three years at college and then quit. He started drinking heavily, chasing women, partying. His marriage ended in divorce. Over the years, he worked as a house painter and farmer, whatever came along. But he was unable to find a good job, a counseling or social work job of some sort. His alcoholism didn't help, but David's friend Hal Sieber, who worked for the Greensboro Chamber of Commerce then, remembers more than a few times when he was called as a reference for David and the potential employer would say, "Well, we don't want a troublemaker." David had earned a national reputation after the sit-ins, but in Greensboro, which the other sit-in leaders had left, that reputation wasn't necessarily an asset. A few years ago, David's second marriage failed and his parents and his older brother all died in a single year. He began drinking again.

"Is your trouble related to February 1, 1960?" I ask.

"It may or it may not be," David says. "It depends on how you look at it. It's depressing when you look at, say, a Joe McNeil, very successful, at Frank McCain and Ezell Blair. And you look at me. I'm sorta down on myself, really. I'll put it that way: I should have done better than this. But I'm glad for Joe and Frank and Ezell, I really am. I'm proud to see so many of my black friends doing so well. The more the merrier."

David—kind, gentle, sensitive David—sounds as if he really means this. He lights another cigarette, and I think about the new bind that blacks like him now face since they changed the world. "The injustices were once so clear," David says. "It's not like that anymore. There are so many intangibles." I think to myself that somewhere deep inside, David would like to believe that being black— being a black man who stood up to whites—is part of the reason for his life's disappointments. The old man I met in front of Woolworth's yesterday has believed all his life that if a black man gets too uppity, they—the whites—will get him. But that explanation, which made perfect sense in the old man's day, is harder and harder to accept. There are so many examples to the contrary, like Joe, Frank, and Ezell.

"You have to blame yourself for your failures," David says.

Neither of us speaks for moment, and then I say, "I wish it were true that the meek shall inherit the earth."

"Why is that?" David asks.

"Because then people like you would own nine-tenths of it."

An old friend of mine lives in a town a couple hours outside Greensboro, and tonight I stop by for a visit. He's a white man in his forties, a Southerner, a corporate executive. He's doing well, lives in a big house on the fairway of a prestigious country club. My friend is a good man. He gives time and money to local charities. He's no mossback, and I don't believe he has a racist bone in his body. Over beers, he asks me why the hell I'm on this trip. I give the short answer, saying whites today seem baffled about why blacks aren't more grateful for all the racial progress in America, that whites increasingly believe blacks are simply whining when they complain about discrimination and racism. I tell him that I hope to understand something about all this when I'm done. For the sake of my children. My friend seems baffled.

"I don't think whites think about it," he says finally. "What discrimination are you talking about?"

"Well, how many managers are at your company?"

"About fifty."

"How many are black?"

"None."

"Do many blacks belong to your country club?"

"I don't believe any have ever applied."

He is my friend, and I let this answer slide, although we both know it's hooey. His country club is well known for having no black members. My friend, an expert and avid golfer, belongs to a club that would not want me and my family as members.

"What I can't understand," I say, "is what the people who keep blacks out of clubs like this tell their children."

My friend seems miffed at this remark, because he has several children of his own. But he calmly mentions that, first, he does not determine membership at the club, he just plays golf. If it were up to him, anybody with the scratch could join. Second, he doubts that the subject of club discrimination ever comes up between parents and children. "This is not a particularly complicated subject, or even a very intellectual one," he says, rather sharply. But, he adds, the parents probably tell their children that people in private clubs have the right to associate with people like themselves. Like doctors enjoy being with doctors, and lawyers with lawyers, and, he supposes, plumbers with plumbers. "People with common interests."

"No rich black people like to play golf?" I ask.

As old friends, we are both careful not to offend too deeply. But I say that racial exclusion is different from lawyers and doctors, even plumbers, hanging out together, because it assumes that a person's race can predict a whole range of his attitudes and behaviors—and that blacks, by virtue of skin color, will not share the upper-middle-class traits and beliefs of a country club member. Black professionals in polo shirts driving Mercedes-Benzes abound these days, proving the theory dead wrong.

Finally, we let the subject drop. I like to think that my friend knows I'm correct about this, that he agrees it's morally indefensible for any club to exclude people on the basis of their race. He's a good man who simply doesn't think about what it might mean that his company has no black managers, what it might mean to belong to a club that takes no black members. He likes to play golf. But a while later, he says, "You know, one of the things that blew me away when I got here was when I'd be talking to somebody about how I was going to make a deal or maybe work on a civic project with some guy, and the person I was talking to would say, 'You know, he's Catholic.' I'd think, Yeah, he's Catholic. What's that got to do with it? So what? I just didn't know what he meant. See, all of a sudden, I was supposed to know something about a person because I'd been told he was Catholic, but I didn't know what it was I was supposed to know. It means nothing to me."

"When will it be like that with race?" I ask.

"I don't know," he says, and for the rest of the evening, we talk of work, wives, children, and old times.

6

A GIRL NAMED CLOVER

YORK, SOUTH CAROLINA

She hooked me from the first line: "They dressed me in white for my daddy's funeral." Who could put down a book with that first line? Apparently, a lot of people couldn't, because Dori Sanders's first novel, *Clover*, named after its ten-year-old heroine, was considered the most successful literary debut of the year. *Clover* is an easy read, and just 183 pages, but its subject isn't so easy: Clover's widowed daddy, a black grade school principal in a rural South Carolina town a lot like York, the author's hometown, marries a well-educated white woman from up North. He's killed in an accident hours after their wedding, and Clover—a sassy, clear-eyed girl—is left with her new white stepmother, to the shock and disgust of her black country relatives who run a family peach orchard and roadside produce stand.

A few miles north of York—the real York, with 6,709 souls and located just below North Carolina in central South Carolina—the fact and fiction of *Clover* start to blur as the signs appear: PEACHES. All kinds of signs—from hand-scrawled to expertly blocked and lettered; signs painted in black, red, and green; signs permanently posted and signs tacked up for the season. People think of Georgia as the peach state, but South Carolina, with its sand and red-clay soil is also ideal for growing the fruit.

A mile north of York on narrow U.S. Route 321 is the sign I'm looking for: SANDERS PEACHES AND PRODUCE. It's a small enough sign, but one of those that is expertly blocked and lettered. Beneath it is a peck of peaches, their ripe, reddish sides carefully exposed and their basket nicely decorated with green leaves from the orchard. Like an offering held up on prayerful hands, the peaches sit atop a lean tree-stump pedestal. In the clearing to the right, naked to the merciless sun, is a small wood-post and tin-roof produce stand framed by an orchard of thick, squat peach trees heading off into the rising, then sloping, distance. At the counter will be Dori Sanders, novelist and true-life peach farmer.

When I introduce myself to Dori, whom I recognize from her book-jacket photo, she doesn't so much scream as sing her welcome: "*Ohhh, WaltHarrington, WaltHarrington, WaltHarrington is here!*" The woman is seriously giddy, and she throws her hands in the air and spins her body in tiny circles, as the dust at her feet erupts in puffs with each rounded step. Folks look over. I wave and smile. They nod, lift a hand, and go back to pawing the Crowder peas or the Blue Lake string beans. Just as I am used to my eccentric aunt Doris, these people are used to Dori Sanders.

It's afternoon and the white wooden tables beneath the Sanders's stand are pretty bare—a dozen pecks of peaches, a few handfuls of peas, beans, and okra, some pathetic new potatoes, no more corn. The heat has withered the vegetable crop this year, and a February freeze and a hailstorm last Sunday have eviscerated the harvest of early Georgia Belle peaches, the only peach ripe this early in the summer. So plenty of people are looking to buy what's left. As they do, Dori talks . . . and talks. Like a radio announcer trained to say a lot in little time, she sucks quick, assertive breaths between cascading sentences, the whole while waving her hands and commenting with wide eyes, puckered lips, a pinched nose. The remark you hear most about her is: "Dori? Oh, she's a character!"

This afternoon, she wears a tan straw hat with its rim turned up all around, a white crew-neck T-shirt, skin-tight jeans, anonymous tennis shoes, and white gym socks with blue and yellow rings at the top, pulled up over her pants almost to her knees. Her book jacket claims she is fifty-five, although she confides that she is older. Looking closely at Dori, I think that she is of no identifiable age, somewhere between thirty-five and sixty. For one, she's pretty, with young skin and a young smile. For another, she's strong, with shoulders and thighs well packed, a taut stomach. She's got the look of somebody who works on the Nautilus, although work is the only Nautilus Dori has pressed during however many years she's been around.

I find an empty log-stump stool in the shade of the stand, out of the ninety-seven-degree sun, and sit down. Dori's customers are about equally split between black and white, and she seems not to change for any of them. She hugs and kisses those she knows well, fusses over those she doesn't. Almost everyone has heard about her book. Just today, she has sold a box of them, complete with autograph and inscription: "Thanks for visiting the Sanders' Peach Shed."

Dori Sanders is a celebrity. For god's sake, Walt Disney has bought the movie rights! All of which amazes people who for decades knew Dori as that goofy lady who sold the best peaches in York County.

It's hard to see in Dori Sanders the woman who wrote her book, which is set in the present-day New South where racism is tempered and the legal caste division between black and white is gone. *Clover* is filled with insights about the way blacks view whites, insights that blacks rarely share with whites. Most revealed are the black women, those who had already picked out a local black girl as the new wife for Clover's widowed daddy and who were outraged when he instead selected a "Miss Uppity-class" white woman from the North. One black woman says that Clover's new white stepmother, Sara Kate, is epileptic—must be if she couldn't get a white man to marry her. Clover's aunt Everleen reminds Clover to always compliment Sara Kate's cooking: "You know how white women are. They want you to brag on 'em all the time." To these women, Sara Kate is a strange creature. A commercial artist with a master's degree, she wears white to her husband's funeral. She will not allow plastic flowers on his grave. She can't cook grits.

For some reason, Dori Sanders—middle-aged, living in York and working at the family peach stand all her life—knew that the blacks who populate her novel didn't understand that Sara Kate wasn't only being "white," but she was being Northern, educated, and upper-middle-class. For some reason, Dori knew that race is often a stand-in, an easy fall guy, for these other, deeper explanations. Little Clover, living with Sara Kate while being bombarded with the biases and stereotypes of her black relatives, slowly comes to understand this. In the end, *Clover* is a hopeful novel.

At 4 P.M., Dori closes up. We agree to meet in the orchard at 6:30 tomorrow morning to pick peaches. That evening, what I can't figure out is how the Dori Sanders I met earlier could be the Dori Sanders who wrote *Clover*. In York, at the peach shed, where did she learn the things she taught Clover?

At six in the morning it's already sixty-nine degrees. At this still hour, the peach orchard has a cool, fragrant scent. It smells like peaches taste, as if you could take a bite out of the air. Dori is different this morning. She doesn't talk incessantly, and when she does it is without the pace of a pinball careering around its board. Her sentences are deliberate and each word is pronounced clearly and individually, with a tone of archness and formality. I ask about this, and she explains that when she was a girl on the farm, number eight of ten children, they called her Miss Thu-thu because she had a lisp. So when she was alone, she'd talk to herself in slow, enunciated syllables: "soda-bi-car-bo-nate." Today, when she talks quickly, she's often covering up for words she can't pronounce. And when she talks slowly, she must consciously pronounce each word. This is like owning a car with only two speeds, and it explains something about Dori.

I ask Dori why she sometimes talks so much and acts so silly. "They calls me the talker," she says, laughing. "They say I talk in my sleep, but I don't. My daddy always said, 'Be friendly and show your best side, always turn the peach pretty side up. Make it look pretty, put a leaf in the basket.' I've been livin' here all my life, and I can't change, especially now, after my book. If I do, people will say, 'She's gotten uppity.' People think that if Dori wrote a book, anybody can. I let them think that. And once I open the peach shed, I don't close my mouth till I close the peach shed. When you've done something all your life, come from an old family, your outlook on life is totally different, you're not out to prove anything, you're confident."

Finally, I tell her that it's hard for me to see in her the same woman who wrote her book. Dori laughs again and says that later she will show me the Sanders family farm, and I will understand.

By 7:30, the sun is up and burning fire through the morning mist. By 8:30, the sky is perfectly clear and blue, and I can see now why there's a crayon named Carolina blue. Dori, with me hauling the baskets, picks nineteen pecks of peaches. Her brother Orestus arrives from the family vegetable farm nearby with a bushel and a peck of peas, two pecks of okra, a handful of Silver Queen corn, tomatoes, yellow squash and cucumbers, and a batch of pathetically small, drought-dwarfed new potatoes. He and Dori decorate the tables, pretty side up.

The heart of the original Sanders homestead is in a speck of a town named Filbert, on Holly Road, just northwest of the produce stand. After the early morning rush of customers has passed, Dori and I climb into her old Ford Custom truck, with its mask of South Carolina dust. We drive a mile up Holly, where Dori pulls off onto a tractor road that meanders through fifty acres of peach orchards, vegeta-

bles, watermelon, and cantaloupe patches. Altogether, the Sanders
family owns 150 acres. We come to the end of the tour at the site of
Dori's old family house. It burned to the ground twenty-five years
ago, but through the thick foliage the red-brick chimney still rises and
the huge 150-gallon water tower still peaks through the woods, sagging atop spindly legs. Dori sits on a bench spanning two log stumps,
and I sit on the grass.

"No wonder I can tell stories," she says, taking off her sunglasses
and spinning them absently between her fingers. She is speaking
slowly now, thoughtfully. "I lived here all my life. I had my play-
house right there under those trees. I worked hard all my life. You
talk about hard work? Honey, let me tell you, I milked cows at four in
the morning and then worked in the field till I couldn't see how to
work anymore in the field. But you see, it was our land. My daddy
was an elementary school teacher and he bought his first land in 1916,
before he was even married, for two thousand dollars. My daddy was
tall, six-something, an imposing figure, the son of a sharecropper. He
was articulate to a fault and respected. We're talking about a black
man who bought eighty-one acres of land before he even married,
we're talking 1916. We're talking about a man ahead of his time. He
had a library, with Poe and Shakespeare. He loved symphonies. I
never thought we weren't in control of our lives. I never thought I'd
have to clean houses. There was always the land, with its sense of
permanence and pride. This is mine! You can feel it, let me tell you.

"I saw black bitterness. Most of my friends' parents were sharecroppers. I heard people complaining about not getting a fair share of
crop after harvest. My father would always say, 'Well, maybe you
should buy yourself a little land.' I felt sorry that they had to live that
way, but I could never say a white man came up to me and said, 'Boy,
gonna pop corn today!' My daddy didn't become bitter or angry
about things. He just did things. When I was a little girl, I jammed a
pair of scissors into my eye, right there. And there was an ophthalmologist in our county who didn't take coloreds, but he was the only
ophthalmologist. So my father marched me into his office and said to
the nurse, 'I must see the doctor immediately. My daughter has a serious eye injury. *I must see him now!*' Well, the nurse about blew right
up, but she got the doctor, and the doctor treated my eye.

"I remember once in school, they had a scale model of my
daddy's farm built—the thirteen-room house with dormer windows,

three big ones across the front, trees on the hill, all the buildings. It was exhibited in schools all around the county: Here is the Sanders farm. Well, on the road home one day a girlfriend said to me, 'You think you're somethin'. You think you're rich.' It hurt me and I went home and told my father. My daddy said, 'You're little friend says *you* think you're rich. Well, maybe *she* thinks you're rich. Don't be upset with her.' The next day I went right out and waved to her, and she never said another word.

"When I was on the book tour, one young black woman asked me, 'How can you feel kindly toward people, whites, who will come in and take your land, 'cause that's what happened to me. They came in and took my daddy's land.' The only thing I could say was, 'They didn't take my land.' How could I have that feeling? I have sad feelings for her, but I cannot say I hate whites because they took my land when they didn't. The land my daddy bought, I farm and live on today. I think we should realize that not every black person was a sharecropper. I wasn't. Why should I have to apologize for it?

"Do you know that the greatest differences that divide people are not skin color? Cultural differences, culinary differences, especially rich and poor differences. I know because I saw this as a girl. I set out to write a book about how people can live and get along together well. You have a white woman and a black girl facing problems of their very own. The only thing they shared was their loss and their grief. Will the little things that divide them become so insurmountable that they won't be able to handle them? The little differences that don't matter, like food and culture and education. Do you know that Southerners like their corn firm and Northerners like their corn tender? What does that matter?"

She pauses as if she is done, and I can now see in Dori Sanders, peach farmer, the woman who wrote *Clover*. I say, "Everybody here seems to love that you are a celebrity. But do any of them ever talk about what you're *saying* in your book?"

"They want to know who this character is in real life and who that character is, and is it about our town? They never get into anything that's psychologically deep. They don't deal with that."

"Do they understand that through little Clover you are criticizing their own racial biases?"

"Ironically, they don't. They say, 'Yes, that's the way it is!' The people around here know all this. This is York, really."

7

WHEN WE WERE YOUNG

COLUMBIA, SOUTH CAROLINA

I dug out my old college freshman yearbook before I left home a few weeks ago and looked for a picture of Jim Green. I found him seated among the members of the Organization for Black Cultural Inclusion. He's got his skinny, six-foot-three body sitting stiffly in a wooden chair. His arms are crossed at their wrists on his lap, and his long legs are bent with his right ankle resting on his left knee. He's wearing a turtleneck sweater and a long African-style necklace. He has a blank expression on his dark, handsome face, but even today I think I detect the hint of a smirk. I can't quite tell, but he seems to have a mustache and a little goatee. He definitely has a short, unruly Afro.

It was 1968. Race riots had torched America's cities, the Black Panthers were calling for a revolution, and the nonviolence of the murdered Martin Luther King, Jr., was being contested by those who said blacks should no longer turn the other cheek. In pursuit of black equality, Malcolm X had threatened violence, and even at backwater Blackburn College, with five hundred kids in rural Carlinville, Illinois, race had become a raging issue.

I had the misfortune, or maybe the fortune, to draw a room next to the one occupied by the leading campus black radical, Davill Armstrong, with whom Jim Green spent a lot of time. I think I can safely say I was something of a loudmouth in those days. I enjoyed arguing about anything and everything that might get a rise out of somebody, and I gravitated to the late-night bull sessions in Davill's room. I thought this was fun. I don't remember exactly what we talked about, but whatever it was I quickly got labeled a racist and was uninvited to the sessions. Jim Green and other blacks later refused to play on the dormitory basketball team with me, and I spent my college years marked as a racist.

Today Jim Green is a sergeant in the army. He's on leave in Columbia, South Carolina, smack in the middle of the state, visiting his mother in the home where he grew up, and I have been invited for dinner. I find the small brick house in a nice, working-class black neighborhood of Columbia. Jim's mother opens the door and, with the kind of hospitality I've become used to on this trip, greets me as if I were a visiting dignitary. It turns out the Greens are having a party and the living room is filled with folks, all black. Jim, too, seems glad to see me. Naturally, he's still tall, but I doubt that anyone would call him skinny anymore. And, like me, he no longer has the luxury of deciding how he'll grow his hair since much of it has fallen out. He shakes my hand, lets loose the same distrustful laugh he had as a youth, and says hello.

I'm ushered into a room where a huge dinner of homemade chicken and fixings is steaming on the table. During dinner, the women at the table say little, but Jim and his cousin, a man who is about our age, talk plenty—and both at once. With humor, Jim tells stories about what a jerk I was in college, while Jim's cousin keeps asking me how much I figure he's going to charge me for the meal I'm eating. "What you think it's worth?" he asks, "'cause you gonna have ta pay or you ain't leavin'." Eating chicken and following the banter—Jim's sentences that begin before his cousin's end and vice versa—I realize I've learned a few things since my days in Davill's room. For one, I'm comfortable in conversations like this. I've learned to tell people like Jim's cousin, "You don't think I'm gonna pay for a meal if I gotta sit next to you to eat it." For another, I've learned that in freewheeling conversation with blacks I must listen not only for the conversation's harmony, but for its melody—for not only its content, but its rhythm.

I learned this mostly on hunting trips with my wife's father, Alex, his brother Bobby, and their friend Carl. For years I could not follow their conversations. I'd be listening for whole sentences and thoughts to arrive in straight lines, as they do in the pages of a book, but they kept rolling over each other, without punctuation. I would chide myself for remembering the way Amos and Andy used to answer each other's sentences before they were completed, but the similarity was unmistakable. Over many years, though, I learned to open my ears and to hear more than one speaker and one idea at time, while still following the flow of the conversation, much like a symphony conductor must hear the flute and oboe and violin each individually, while at the same time hearing the entire orchestra.

Eventually, I realized that Alex, Bobby, and Carl were speaking a different language, a conversational language—an "in concert" language, if you will—that I too could learn if I'd hang around long enough to get educated. Long after that, I read that linguists believe the African language traditions that arrived in America were indeed conversational, free-form, and that these traditions deeply affected black English. It wasn't until I saw Spike Lee's *Do the Right Thing* a few years ago, with its three male characters sitting in front of a red wall in the street and bantering back and forth, finishing each other's sentences—like Alex, Bobby, Carl, and, yes, Amos and Andy—that I realized this tradition could be depicted with both humor *and* respect. "Amos 'n' Andy" was a racist depiction, not because there was no truth in the portrait, but because it lacked knowledge, affection, and appreciation.

Anyway, I'm comfortable tonight at Jim Green's table. After dinner, the women excuse themselves and Jim's cousin says he's going to take a nap. "It's a fifteen-minute thing," he says, smiling broadly. "All niggers do it." He seems to relish trying to shock me, reminding me how white I am.

"Go to bed!" Jim says, laughing and following his cousin out of the room. I'm pouring Jim and myself another glass of jug chablis, when he returns with his old Blackburn College yearbooks. With a forearm, Jim sweeps the dirty plates and silverware away from the space before me, slides over his chair and opens the book for 1968, our freshman year.

"Goddamn, old home week!" I say.

"He was my Big Brother freshman year," Jim says, pointing to the picture of a young black man. "I couldn't stand the guy. If I saw him today I wouldn't talk to him. You know they burned a cross on his damned door in the dorm and he laughed about it." He points to another black man. "Remember him? He married a white girl. He flunked out. Used to read all the damned time about Malcolm X. He didn't do any damned school work. He flunked out readin' the wrong shit!" Jim laughs and shakes his head at, I suppose, the very idea of what it is like to be young.

"Ohhh!" I say, pointing to a white girl I'd dated.

"I went out with her, too," Jim says. "I never slept with her, but I went out with her." I nod, knowing exactly the hormonal nostalgia he is just now feeling.

I point to the picture of a geeky-looking white guy. "He was such an asshole!"

"I couldn't stand him," Jim says. "Nobody liked him, nobody! I always thought he was the guy who used to slide the racist stuff under our door."

"Racist stuff?" I ask, suddenly serious, suddenly reminded once again that whites and blacks may walk through the same rooms in life, but inevitably they see different details in the decor. "What racist stuff?"

"'Nigger go home,' stuff like that. People'd put these little notes under our door and then run down the damned hall." He points to a white professor I had liked. "He was a racist."

"He was?"

"He told me once that he didn't think blacks should be at Blackburn. My favorite teacher was Harold Ziegler."

"Harold Ziegler?" I say, shocked. "He was terrible!"

"He used to have Davill and me over to his house. He had one of the best personal African art collections I've ever seen."

"*Harold Ziegler?*"

"Yes! He couldn't teach history worth a damn, but he'd lived in Africa and China for twenty years. Davill and I would go to his house on Sundays and he'd show us slides. His wife would cook and we'd drink wine. He identified with us. He'd lived all over the world and he realized how narrow Carlinville was." Then, with sudden solemnity, Jim points to a picture: "Davill."

Davill Armstrong: firebrand, genius, angry young man. A doctor in Houston today. Jim laughs and says, "I guess the statute of limitations has run out by now," and he then tells me that he and Davill and a few others, including a white friend, had sneaked out one night and broken the windows in the home of a college dean they believed was racist. Jim cut his hand badly on that mission and had to be taken to a hospital in St. Louis to be stitched up. On another late-night guerrilla assault, they smashed and destroyed the scientific experiment of a professor they also considered racist. Today these acts sound pretty juvenile, but in 1968 the young men viewed them as political statements: Be fair to blacks or pay the price. They were never caught.

I say, "I remember Davill as being more handsome."

"No," Jim says, laughing. "And when you visit him, tell 'im I said he's still ugly."

I ask, "So what didn't you like about me?"

"You were arrogant, cocky, and naive."

"I remember going in Davill's room and having great fun arguing about race. It was like an intellectual salon."

"Not to us. I can't remember the specifics, but you were very smart and persistent. We felt as though you were ridiculing us. And several days after a session with you, we started getting notes under our doors calling us names and troublemakers."

"You thought I'd do that?"

"Why not? We didn't know you. Then an anonymous essay came out in the campus paper about how all the little red and black ants had gotten along until one red ant stirred up trouble, and the whole colony was destroyed. Davill was supposed to be the red ant. This came out after you started coming into the room."

"So that's what happened," I say, realizing for the first time that more than my refusal to sign the black's clubhouse petition was at play. "I had no idea. For twenty years I've thought about what happened. Looking back, I really believed then that good-hearted people could ignore race and that it would go away, disappear. Naive is just the right word."

"I think we all understand things today we didn't then," says Jim. "From growing up here in the South, where whites and blacks mingle, we are used to dealing with each other, like it or not. That wasn't true in the Midwest, where you whites were never around blacks. They're stuck off somewhere. I felt as if you people weren't sincere, that the students and the faculty didn't want us there, except to play basketball."

"How do you think race is different today?"

"People are more tolerant of blacks, accepting. Whites have realized that blacks will treat them well, but whites still hold certain stereotypes about blacks that aren't true—that we are a violent people or that we are easily satisfied in life. Young blacks don't think 'race' as quickly as we did, and there's less hostility toward whites for a lot of them. But young, inner-city blacks are very hostile. Rap music expresses their anger, but people aren't listening. Even affluent blacks don't want to listen, 'cause those niggers out there are embarrassing 'em.

"But to be straight, I deal with a lot of kids in the army, and, as a whole, white kids are better prepared emotionally than black kids. White kids will listen to you. They are purposeful. Black females are like that too. But black males are less mature, more playful and disruptive." Many of them, Jim says, are obsessed with athletics and fashion, use poor grammar, and are rude.

"It pisses me off anytime I see a young black person wasted, dead, or incarcerated. And they're saying, 'The white person incarcerated me.' No, the white person didn't incarcerate you. Look what you've done! You didn't even commit your crimes against white people, but mostly black people. To blame the oppressor for everything saps you," Jim says, echoing my father-in-law's older, less radical philosophy of life and making me wonder if Jim has gotten older or wiser or both. "It makes you so angry that you can't achieve anything."

"Are you optimistic about the future?"

"It's frightening to think about."

"Must whites still be threatened out of their racism?"

"That's obvious. Yes."

Jim and I continue to talk late into the evening, but mostly about the small things, what has happened to people we knew, families, careers. When it's finally time for me to go, I say thank you to Jim's mother and good-bye to Jim's cousin, who is now very much awake on the couch in the living room. He cannot resist one last shot: "So how much you payin'?"

"Now, don't forget," Jim says as I leave. "When you see Davill, tell 'im I said he's still ugly."

"It was good to see you."

"Yeah, it really was."

And I think that this time we both mean it.

8

HARD COP, HARD TALK

CHARLESTON, SOUTH CAROLINA

When it comes to using filthy language, Charleston Police Chief Reuben Greenberg has got to be among the world-class champions. The old man in Joe Green's trailer in Oxford, North Carolina, might be a match for him, but my guess is that Chief Greenberg would take him on points for creative usage. "Can't anybody outcuss me!" the chief says, and then he proceeds to defend his claim for the next several hours as we tool around Charleston in his cruiser.

Charleston, on the Atlantic Ocean halfway down the South Carolina coast, is a beautiful city: quaint yet urbane, filled with tourists and elegant little waterfront shops, bookstores, horse-drawn carriages, museums, and tours of old houses. Once a jewel of the South, Charleston is today a struggling city of 80,414 people, about 40 percent of whom are black. Of those blacks, about 15 percent live in squat and unquaint public housing projects. Charleston was unique in the Old South, because most of its craftsmen were free blacks who had successfully pushed white craftsmen out of business. But in those days, Charleston was also a major slave market, and it was the Confederate firing on Fort Sumter in Charleston Harbor in 1861 that launched the Civil War.

Heading out on Columbus Street toward a northeast Charleston neighborhood that was once an open-air drug market, Chief Greenberg—a short, balding, crew-cut, forty-seven-year-old man with an emergent paunch and an aggressive staccato voice—is about as far from "Old Charleston" as you can get. For one, he was educated at Berkeley in the sixties. For another, he's Jewish. For another, he's black. But the people of Charleston have forgiven him his lack of pedigree, because Chief Greenberg's law enforcement strategy is credited with slashing the city's reported crimes nearly in half. For this, Reuben Greenberg has won national accolades and worshipful treatment in that journal of middle American inspiration, *Reader's Digest*.

Curious about what the nation's number one black crime fighter thinks about race and crime in America, I've come to talk with him. I quickly discover that with Chief Greenberg, who wears not a police uniform but a blue blazer and conservative tie, I don't have to talk much, only listen. "Unless you de-racialize crime," he says, "you're going to give criminals liberal allies they don't deserve." He suddenly spins the steering wheel to the right and brings us to the curb at the Quick Stop Grocery and Fish Market, a tiny cinder-block store in an old, gray neighborhood at the corner of Columbus and Aiken Streets. "The greatest enemy blacks ever had is white liberals. The philosophy is that it's not the criminal's fault, it's society's. I approach it from the exact opposite. I zero in on the individual."

With that, Chief Greenberg is out of the car and striding toward a bent old black man in a worn baseball cap and dingy T-shirt who's sweeping the sidewalk in front of the Quick Stop.

"Hello, how you doin'?" the chief says, reaching out and clasping the flabbergasted man's hand in a he-man shake.

"Doin' good," the old man says, softly.

"You have no idea how glad I am seeing you out sweepin' up." The chief doesn't wait for another reply, but heads for the Quick Stop's front door. The dozen or so young men milling around lower their heads and slide east and west.

"Mornin'," Chief Greenberg says with authority.

"Mornin'."

"Mornin'."

"Mornin'," come the mumbled replies.

Inside, the decidedly older men playing the Miss America pinball machine aren't at all ambivalent about the surprise visit, and several holler, "Hello, chief!" and gather round.

"I just wanted to tell you how glad I am you've got someone out cleaning up the street in front of your place," he tells the black woman behind the meat cooler. "Good work," he says, and flies back outside, back into his car, back on his way. The whole bit seems a little theatrical, but Chief Greenberg insists that such theatrics are all part of reminding decent, law-abiding people and the "bums"—the thieves and muggers—that Reuben Greenberg and his cops are the ones who own Charleston's streets.

To do good police work, Chief Greenberg says as we pull away, you have to understand how things work from the inside out. Take a little store like that. He nods back over his right shoulder. "The owner is usually of two minds about the guys hanging around the place. You see, if you run 'em off, you're losin' customers 'cause all the wine that's bought is bought out of them, all the beer that's bought is bought out of them. On the other hand, they also keep other customers away because they're hanging out." But the everpresent crowd also keeps robberies down. "So store owners don't know which way to go, which is in their best corporate interest, you might say. See what I'm sayin'? You gotta see it from the inside out."

Seeing it from the inside out is what Reuben Greenberg does best. Years ago, he decided that arresting drug dealers was a waste of time because they were back on the streets the next day. So he stationed uniformed officers about forty feet away from a suspected dealer on the street corner. The cop just stood there. If the dealer moved, the cop moved. If the dealer switched corners, the cop switched corners. "Nobody would touch him, buy anything, or even say hello," Chief Greenberg says, smirking. That dealer's business was dead.

When a known drug dealer once complained to police that suburban youths were being mugged in one city neighborhood, the police discovered that the youths were being robbed before they could buy drugs, cutting into the dealer's business. Chief Greenberg liked that idea so much he had his police begin stopping suspected drug customers for minor traffic violations, taking their names and addresses and snapping their photos. Sometimes the camera lacked film. But the intimidation worked. Over a period of years, Charleston's drug dealers moved off the streets and into houses and bars— and out to the suburbs. Deciding that my job on this tour is to pose the "white liberal" questions, I ask, "Doesn't that just move the problem?"

"Who gives a fuck?" the chief growls. Let cops in the suburbs take the same hard-line posture, he says, and then we'd make some real progress against the drug thugs. Again and again, Chief Greenberg has looked at crime—and its racially tinged politics—from the inside out. Black chain gangs cleaning streets in white neighborhoods had long been a fixture of Charleston life, so Chief Greenberg sent chain gangs of mostly white prisoners into black neighborhoods. He also sent well-known black drug dealers, often the idols of young black street kids, back into their own neighborhoods to sweep the streets in jail threads. His message: "The wages of sin are death." He says that about 40 percent of crime in the country is committed by men on parole and that one study found the average parolee committed 187 crimes a year. So he assigned a cop full-time to oppose every parole application for felons who committed their crimes in Charleston and who were convicted of armed robbery, sexual or aggravated assault, or burglary. The officer took victims and families of victims along to testify. Last year, Chief Greenberg boasts, 90 percent of those parole applicants, most of whom are black, were rejected.

Playing my part again, I ask what he thinks about people who complain that black men have a far better chance of going to prison than white men who commit the same crimes.

"I wish it were a 100 percent better chance!" he snaps. "When I look in a jail and see a lot of blacks in there, I think of all the sons of bitches out there who are still ripping off people in the black community. See, the reason I'm supported by hardworking black people is because I'm the only one who ever gave a shit whether they could walk down the street." He says the liberals at their suburban cocktail parties complaining about crime in the ghetto don't care. "When we say 'burglaries are down,' you know what that means?" he asks. "It means burglaries are down in the *black* community, because that's where the burglaries are. Most of the criminals who prey on blacks are other blacks. I say there ain't enough in jail. Let 'em serve right to the last day. I wouldn't let you change into your civilian clothes before ten minutes before you walk out."

Again seeing it from the inside out. . . . In the early eighties, with crime in Charleston's public housing projects soaring, Chief Greenberg assigned an officer to check the criminal records of families applying for public housing. Those with serious records were rejected. Since then, crime in Charleston's public housing has fallen every year. Last year, in its 1,652 public units with 6,500 residents, only four rapes, one robbery, and forty-six aggravated assaults were reported. Only eighteen arrests were made for narcotics violations.

"What about folks who couldn't find a place to live?" I ask.

"Fuck 'em!" Chief Greenberg says again. He tells his officers that if they want to be popular, they should have become firemen. "What about the poor people who never did anything to anybody?" he asks. What about the respectable poor? In Charleston today, he says, the fact that a person's address is in public housing presumes he has no criminal record. "Think about that. You're giving public housing to people for whom it was meant, people with the same values you and I have, but they just don't have money—as opposed to armed robbers, rapists, and all the other criminals."

For a couple more hours, it goes on like this, with Chief Greenberg driving and lecturing, me listening. He takes me to a new police precinct he had located in the center of one of the roughest black neighborhoods in Charleston. He stops to see if workmen have yet gotten the air-conditioning on one of his police buses pumping strong enough to beat the one-hundred-degree heat.

"I was a typical Berkeley graduate," he says more calmly now.

"You thought all criminals were victims of environment?" I ask.

"Exactly."

"What did you learn as a probation officer?"

"That it didn't work. They said go out and get jobs for these guys so they won't have to be thieves, right? I went out and did that and the sons of bitches didn't want the jobs. They said, 'Two weeks' vacation a year? Nine to five? Gotta come in every day?'" A parolee told him he could easily steal $1,000 to $2,500 from a tourist's purse, and then added, "I got more money in five minutes than you'll have in two or three paychecks."

"Were you shocked?" I ask.

"Yeah, I was, to tell you the truth. I found out they made a calculated business decision: they didn't mind going to the county jail if they lived the way they wanted the rest of the time. Their jobs were to go out and rip people off. I don't believe any black youth needs to knock down a poor black woman on the street, snatch her purse, and, when she tries to hold onto it, kick her in the head, in order for him to eat. That's bullshit! Fuck 'im! If he wants tennis shoes, go out and get a job. There are people who are lazy, low-down, good-for-nothin' sons of bitches who break into people's houses for no reason other than that!"

We drive through a poor black neighborhood of small, single-family homes and come to a house that's being renovated by what look to be dozens of college-age kids, all wearing work clothes and boots and carpenter's belts, carrying shingles and two-by-fours in every imaginable direction. It looks more like a party than a work site. A big sign proclaims HABITAT FOR HUMANITY, which is a national group that rebuilds poor people's houses for next to nothing. Chief Greenberg stops and stares quietly at the scene before driving on.

"Notice they're all white?" he asks. He points to a crowd of young black men hanging out on a nearby street corner. "Now, look at these bums here. You'd think they would come out and help."

Struck by the deep anger in his voice, I ask what a good white liberal would ask, "What do you say to those who say talking like you talk is a form of racial self-hatred?"

Quickly, the edge comes back in Chief Greenberg's voice. "I don't have any self-hatred. I'm just. . . " And then he stops, shakes his head, looks out the window and sighs with exasperation. When he speaks, his voice is calm again. He says many of the problems of black America are endemic. "Let me give you an example. When I go into a neighborhood and I see all the wine bottles and whiskey bottles and Kentucky Fried Chicken boxes and Burger King wrappers, and they are talking about how the white folks won't fix up their little houses, I say, 'I wish they'd do a lot better, but why would they wanta fix these places up? You're obviously very happy with the way it is. Because it ain't no white man who came down here throwin' these wine bottles out, this paper and trash. No white man did that.'

"I say forget about the forty acres, forget about the mule. There ain't gonna be no fuckin' forty acres! It's been a hundred and twenty-five years since the Civil War. The only fuckin' thing you're gonna get is what you work for yourself.

"We don't want to do that. We don't want to make sacrifices. It's a whole philosophical outlook. We get complaints every night about noise around schools. You know what the kids are fuckin' doin'? They're bouncin' a fuckin' basketball at two o'clock in the morning and yelling. I tell 'em, 'If you wanta do something that's gonna do you some good, get a fuckin' book and crack that son of a bitch at two o'clock in the morning. You got a better chance of being elected to Congress than you do going to the NBA.'

"It's insane! You never hear me talk about fortune or luck. I say 'Fuck fortune!' Not any fuckin' fortune was the reason I went to college. I had to cut grass and work in a cafeteria. I had to do papers and read books about Kant and Hegel and Socrates and Sophocles. The reason that guy's a doctor over there wasn't because of good fuckin' luck. It was because of hard fuckin' work! Fortune is buying a ticket to the lottery and hoping you win.

"Sure, discrimination exists. I know for a fact that blacks don't have equal opportunity, but neither do Koreans, Cambodians, or Vietnamese. But that doesn't mean all is lost. If you're Jewish there's certain clubs you can't belong to, but you can't let that permeate your whole life."

The culture of poor people—black and white—is just different, he says. "Poor people say they don't have money for medical insurance. But every time fuckin' James Brown comes to town, they got money to buy a thirty-dollar fuckin' ticket." Chief Greenberg says he used to teach college and he knew black kids who dropped out for lack of money, only to go home and find the old man driving a new Cadillac. I'm a little stunned by this last remark and I must show it, because Chief Greenberg looks at me, waiting for a response. "If a white guy said that he'd get run out of town as a racist," I say.

"Oh, but it's true!' Chief Greenberg says. "People don't wanta hear that shit!" See, you don't go begging wearing a new suit, he says. So black leaders put on their old suits and tell whites things are just as terrible for the black man as they ever were. Even worse! "But let me tell you what's happening. We're in a bad situation. When you tell black kids that things are worse than ever, they say, 'You mean after Martin Luther King was assassinated? He died for nothing? After the little girls in the Birmingham church were bombed? After Rosa Parks stood up on the bus? After Goodman, Schwerner, and Chaney, Medgar Evers, the Reverend Reeb? After all these people died? You mean all was in vain? We're worse off than we were?!'" With a black head of the Joint Chiefs of Staff, a black governor of Virginia, eight thousand black elected officials in the United States, eight of ten mayors in the biggest cities? Blacks are worse off? And their leaders answer, 'Yes.'

"It's discouraging to people," Chief Greenberg says. "It's discouraging to a lot of whites as well. They say, 'After all that effort, hell, I'm tired!' It discourages people from going on."

I ask, "Is it also not true?"

"That's right, it's not true. What year do we want to go back to? Which year was so goddamned good? Is it going to be 1619 when the first slaves were dropped off in Virginia? Is it 1865, or 1930, when blacks were being lynched?"

Chief Greenberg wants to make one last check on the air-conditioning in his bus, so we head to the police garage where he discovers that the A.C. is pumping now. But he notices that a small light that should be illuminating the bus steps is not working. He lies down on the macadam, slides under the bus, finds that the light isn't even wired up, and orders it fixed before the bus travels another mile. After that, we head over to his office, which is a small, Spartan place with only a few plaques on the walls and a handful of mementos on the shelves. I'm just about to leave, saying thanks and good-bye, when a policeman knocks and enters with a sheaf of paperwork. He reminds the chief that tomorrow the department will testify against another Charleston convict up for parole. Chief Greenberg smiles, extends his right arm, makes a tightly clinched fist, palm up—and violently jerks it into the air in the universal gesture of "Shove it up your ass!" With that gesture for tomorrow's parole seeker, Chief Greenberg smiles grimly.

I say, "You won't win any popularity contests."

"If I wanted to be popular, I wouldn't be a cop."

"You'd be a fireman?"

"I'd be a fireman."

I am a long time mulling the words of Reuben Greenberg, which is no surprise. My destination this afternoon is St. Helena Island, located two hours south of Charleston in the tidal salt marsh islands off lower coastal South Carolina. For several hundred years, a hybrid African American language known as Gullah has persisted there, and I'm going to visit a native Gullah-speaking family. As I drive, the scenery on two-lane U.S. Route 17 alternates between vast panoramas of blue sky above low-swaying, knife-stemmed marsh grass and dense walls of spindly pines that climb overhead into a dense canopy against the deadening sun. Thought comes easier in such a setting.

So, what to make of Reuben Greenberg? As a white person, I just don't hear that kind of talk, although I now know a lot of blacks share his view. "Blacks won't talk this way to whites, but. . . ," Zeke Hester had said. Like family members who can insult each other freely but won't let an outsider do it, blacks rarely criticize blacks to whites. They circle the wagons.

But wait, if black people often privately share some version of Reuben Greenberg's beliefs, isn't that something whites should know? Isn't it possible that white racism *and* the self-defeating values and behavior of some blacks can both be undermining black America? And if blacks believe this, is it racist for me as a white man to believe it? Or is Reuben Greenberg a racist too?

9

AT HOME AND FREE, FINALLY

ST. HELENA ISLAND, SOUTH CAROLINA

Bad news: the Gullah family I've come to St. Helena to live with for the next few days has changed its mind, decided not to see me. No explanation is given and none is expected. I was a little sur-

prised they had agreed in the first place. The black people of the South
Carolina and Georgia Sea Islands have always been private, distrustful of outsiders, especially the *buckra*, the white man. For nearly a century, they've been studied and catalogued, their culture poked and
prodded by anthropologists and curious tourists hoping to see, perhaps, a barefoot boy casting a fishing net from an old flat-bottomed
boat, or a woman in a West African head wrap sitting cross-legged
and weaving a basket of palmetto butts, or, most coveted, an old man,
a native Gullah speaker, telling the story of, say, Brier Rabbit in the old
talk: "One time Buh Rabbit gone tuh de Lawd fuh git mo' ecknowl-
edge, mo' wisdom. En' de Lawd tell Buh Rabbit. . . "

For nearly a century, the Gullah people have been treated like living artifacts, and who can blame them for snubbing one more nosy
visitor? Anyway, it's too late to seek out another family, so I drive out
from the mainland's Beaufort—a franchise heaven of a little town
with a McDonald's, Wendy's, Burger King, Hardee's, and Kentucky
Fried Chicken—over Cowan Creek and to St. Helena, which is still
relatively unspoiled. I'm looking for Penn Center, whose director,
Emory Campbell, had helped me locate a Gullah family. Penn Center,
which serves the Sea Islands' poor residents and preserves the memory of its culture through its museum, is the descendant of Penn
School, located on St. Helena in 1862 to serve the island's ten thousand newly freed blacks.

I find Penn Center on narrow Land's End Road amid a forest of
giant live oaks—those groaning and ominous monster trees indigenous to the southern lowlands and laden with their drooping wigs of
crusty Spanish moss. In the early evening light the shadowy glen in
which the center's old white stucco buildings sit seems to resemble
the very place where Ichabod Crane must have met the headless
horseman. A quiet, creepy place. Nobody's around this late so I walk
the grounds—past Brick Baptist Church, built for white masters by
black slaves in 1855 and inherited by them during the Civil War. It
was in Brick Church that poet John Greenleaf Whittier's "St. Helena
Hymn" was first sung on Christmas in 1862:

> *Oh, none in all the world before*
> *Were ever glad as we!*
> *We're free on Carolina's shore,*
> *We're all at home and free.*

On past Benezet Hall to the tower containing the huge brass bell which was cast in the image of the Philadelphia liberty bell and which, like Whittier's poem, was enthroned during the Civil War in celebration of a soon-to-be-aborted liberty. On past Cope Hall, where Martin Luther King, Jr., and his aides made plans for the historic 1963 March on Washington.

On and on, the place is alive with history. I knew none of this when I decided to visit a Gullah family. I knew only that on the Sea Islands had emerged a distinct African American creole language called Gullah, a blend of English and the languages of West Africa. Because of the severe isolation of the islands, accessible only by boat, that language—with its beautiful singsong West African rhythm, its missing conjunctions and uninflected verbs—had lived on into the fifties, when new bridges from the mainland to the major Sea Islands had brought a rush of whites seeking waterfront homes.

But in Charleston yesterday I'd stopped and picked up *When Roots Die,* a recent book by African American anthropologist Patricia Jones-Jackson, who spent nine years working among the Gullah people. The original Gullah language—born of Mandinka, Ewe, Igbo, Yoruba, and Gidzi—contained thousands of Africanisms, many of which have entered mainstream English: *goober* for 'peanut', *biddy* for 'chicken', *tote* for 'carry'. Such Africanisms, their derivations often lost, also live on today in the wider African American culture. For instance, I've even heard my own wife and her mother, unbeknownst to them, use Gullah-rooted references. My wife, when asking for a second cup of coffee, says, "Put some hot on it"—as do traditional Gullah speakers. And her mother laughingly describes the entertaining stories of my father-in-law as "lies"—just as Gullah speakers fondly describe their culture's "tall tales" as "lies." All of this is beautiful and fascinating to us today. But until recently, Gullah speakers were seen simply as ignorant. Even the Penn School's teachers, who often arrived from the North brimming with idealism, told their Gullah students that anyone who spoke the language was ignorant.

In the glen of live oaks, it's nearly dusk now and the hot air is thick with the marshlands' brackish salt fragrance. As I head back to my car, I think that this quiet, creepy place is a kind of hallowed ground for the Gullah people, for all African Americans really—hal-

lowed by all they created and all they endured. The fading shadows
of the glen's monster trees, with their groaning branches and their
eerie wigs of dangling Spanish moss, are like the shadows of a history lost and now born again.

Beaufort has a waterfront that's redone in that quaint, affluent style—
expensive restaurants in aging red-brick buildings, an art boutique, a
gourmet ice cream shop. I stop at one of the restaurants and strike up a
conversation with a young man at the table next to me. He's seventeen,
a Beaufort native home for the summer from private school. He asks
why I'm in town, and I tell him I'm here to meet some Gullah people.

"What's Gullah?" he asks. The boy has never heard of the Gullah
language or culture. He also doesn't know a single black person in
his home county, which is about one-third black. I ask if he knows
Mom's Restaurant, for many years a famous local eatery serving the
traditional Gullah foods of rice, shrimp, gravy, and soup. "Yes," he
says, "it's a place where truck drivers eat." He has never been there.
"I went to private school, to camp in the summers, and off to sec-
ondary school," he explains without defensiveness. "When I was
home, I spent a lot of time at the yacht club. It does have a few black
members, but I don't know them."

The next day, I have no better luck finding a Gullah family, although
it's not the fault of Penn Center director Emory Campbell, a forty-
eight-year-old black man with, I think, a Gullah lilt that occasionally rises in his voice. He calls people all over the island, but
nobody is interested. Knowing that Emory is trying his damnedest,
I go off to Port Royal, on the mainland, to find the famous Mom's
Restaurant. When I get there I discover that Mom's is defunct, its
building now inhabited by a video store and surrounded by a Pizza
Hut, Burger King, and Kentucky Fried Chicken. Out of frustration, I
decide to track down Mom herself. After a lot of asking around, I
find her little brown house down a long, dry dirt road off Land's
End on St. Helena. Leaning against her fence, as if in tribute, is the
huge block-lettered sign that once announced her restaurant:
MOM'S. Mom, a sturdy and healthy-looking woman, answers the
door with a spatula in her hand. She's cooking right now and clearly
doesn't want to talk to a stranger. From up on her porch, with the
screen door pushed only slightly ajar, she says she closed down a

year ago, that she couldn't compete with all the new restaurants.

"Are there any places like yours left?" I ask.

Mom puzzles for a moment, then waves her spatula and says, with a rich, Gullah intonation, "They all gahne now."

Back at Penn Center, Emory Campbell tells me sorry, but he can't find a Gullah family who will agree to take me in. I guess I look pretty disappointed, because after a moment he invites me to dinner at his home on nearby Hilton Head Island, where, he says, his own Gullah family has lived for six generations. I quickly accept, thinking that Mark Twain may have been right and that circumstances are suddenly doing the planning for me.

Hilton Head's Gullah world fell to invasion long ago, after the bridge to the mainland went up in the fifties. Today Hilton Head's land-scaped main drag is a wall of restaurants, golf courses, and hotels, and I wonder if Emory lives in one of the huge houses scattered along the fairways. At Spanish Wells Road, taking Emory's direc-tions, I go south, and suddenly it's a different world—no landscap-ing, only dense woods, teeming marshes, more live oaks and dan-gling Spanish moss. No fairway mansions, but plenty of mobile homes. There's a wrecking garage and a parking lot full of junk cars. Like it or not, Spanish Wells is a taste of the old Hilton Head.

Emory's home, which sits just off the road in the woods, is a little one-story house painted a pleasant dark blue. It looks positively sub-urban. Emory's wife, Emma, answers the door and ushers me into the kitchen, where Emory, fork at the ready, is keeping guard over a cast-iron skillet sizzling with whiting fish, their black eyes still bulging. Ochieng (pronounced O-che-ing), the Campbells' twenty-year-old son, home from Tuskegee Institute, and Ayoka (pronounced I-yo-ka), their sixteen-year-old daughter, are setting the big table in the dining room. They look as preppie as kids come. Emma, relaxed and smiling, tosses the salad, pulls the Gullah dish of rice, shrimp, and vegetables from the oven, and mixes the homemade lemonade. Emory hands me a beer, a Schaefer.

"Hey, that's my beer," I say. "My neighbor makes fun of me, but I like it—for $7.05 a case." Unwittingly, I've struck a chord, because the whole family suddenly roars with laughter.

"Emory takes it to parties!" says Emma, with a tone of exasper-ated pride. "Nobody will drink it! He brings it home!"

"I'm sorry!" Emory intones, with dramatic exaggeration. "I take *my* beer! A 12-pack is $3.49. That's why it's *my* beer."

Everybody laughs, but Emory laughs the hardest, and it's clear that he and his family are used to such merriment. Leaning against the refrigerator, my can of Schaefer in hand, I look closely at Emory for the first time. He's taller than I had realized, maybe six-foot-three or -four. His short, natural hair and neat mustache have nearly turned gray. He wears a red-plaid short-sleeved shirt, blue cotton pants, and old tennis shoes. He's lanky, but still strong, with wide shoulders, long powerful arms, and large, expressive hands that often wave and gesture in slow, eloquent motions around his head as he speaks. When he begins to laugh, he uses those dexterous hands again, covering his mouth and lowering his head at the first sign of a chuckle. Then, throwing his arms high in the air as if the humor is too powerful for strong muscles to contain, he laughs from down deep in his chest, wholeheartedly. It's easy to like Emory Campbell. By the time we sit down to eat, his sister, Regina, his brother, Herbert, and his sister-in-law, Allyne, have arrived. It's a wild crowd.

"So he come ta hear de Gullah," Herbert says, exaggerating the old Gullah cadence. "He come de right place, eh?"

Amid the laughter, Emory adds, "Let we go now."

Then he turns serious and begins. He can remember only about five white families from when he was growing up on Hilton Head in the forties, although he knows there were more. The island was over-whelmingly Gullah. He grew up on Spanish Wells Road, right over there, he says, pointing out the window to the south where a small clapboard house once stood. He figures he had, oh, 150 relatives ("Everyone was a cousin!") living along this road alone. His father was a laborer who worked in Savannah for weeks at a stretch until he was disabled and collected $45 a month in disability pay for the rest of his life. His mother worked at one of the island's first resort hotels as a maid, earning $20 a week. Emory worked there, too, as a youth, from 6 A.M. to midnight for $4 a day plus meals. The sixth of twelve children, he couldn't go to school one year until well into the fall because the family couldn't afford shoes.

As a boy Emory knew nothing of white people—and nothing of Jim Crow or discrimination. In the fourth grade he even got in an argument with an older cousin who said whites were more powerful than blacks in the United States. Emory was incredulous: this couldn't be. On Hilton Head whites were ridiculed and laughed at, harassed if they came around. After grade school, when he and the other island kids—along with the few island white kids—rode the ferry to the segregated mainland schools, he learned differently. Children with even a trace of Gullah accent were upbraided by their black teachers. "The teachers beat you to death for speaking Gullah," he says. Yet back home, if a child didn't speak Gullah, his family believed he was trying to be uppity. So all Gullah kids learned two languages—one for home, one for the *buckra*. Emory learned better than most and graduated valedictorian of his class. He became the first member of his family to go to college—Georgia State University—and then graduate school at Tufts University, where he met Emma. They lived there for seven years.

He abandoned his Gullah roots. Discovering that even blacks looked down on his heritage, he came to be embarrassed by it. Many people believed Emory's accent was West Indian, and he often let them believe that. He told people he was from Savannah. He used his beautiful Gullah language mostly to entertain friends at parties, telling quaint, funny, faintly derisive stories about his Gullah past. But one day in the sixties, Emory was driving out in the Boston suburbs when he realized that these people commuted hours each day just to live on a tiny piece of green. It struck him that he already had that piece of green back home on Hilton Head, and he began to lay plans to return home, which he did in 1971.

I ask, "Why's everybody so nostalgic about the old days, if it was so grim that you all left?"

"Because we have lost the freedom of choice," Emory says.

"The freedom to be poor?"

"Yes. Then you could live within your poverty without dictation. You could use the rivers and streams for income and food. Now you can hardly get to them, plus they're filled with motor boats. The freedom of choice is gone."

"And it wasn't grim!" says Herbert, as everyone laughs in agreement and the entire tone of the room changes.

"Everybody was kinfolk," says Emory, cheerfully.

"Everybody was a parent," adds Herbert. "And anyone had the right to punish you at any time."

"Or lie on you!" Emory interjects. "Those old folks would *lie!* They'd say, 'Oh, yeah, I saw him throw that brick at that cow.' Or, 'I saw him in my melon patch.' If you denied it, mother'd say, 'What you calling Mrs. Jones? A liar?'"

"No jury trial!" says Herbert, and the laughter around the table is loud and constant.

Life was great fun, Emory says. "We played baseball, wrapped a can up in a rag. Our mother would even play. She'd hit and we'd have to run the bases. She wouldn't run."

"How long did she bat?" I ask.

"As long as she wanted!" says Emory.

The only whites were the judges, the government people, and those running the oyster factories, says Herbert, although some couldn't read. "Grandfather taught one white man to read and write."

"And they made him a judge!" roars Emory, laughing. "My grandfather told the old stories. Remember the one about the rabbit who stole the butter?" A round of "Oh, yeahs" rises forth. "Boy, we used to tell those stories so vividly." In the old story, the rabbit stole the butter, but nobody knew for sure if he was the thief, so the rabbit and the rat were sent out to sleep in the sun. The rabbit woke up sweating the butter, all right, but quickly rubbed it on the sleeping rat, who got blamed.

"All those stories were about life," says Herbert.

"People always used to say, 'That'll tell who ate the butter,'" says Emory. The moral was: "If you're right, you better keep your eyes open," Emory says. "Don't fall asleep, 'cause people are gonna blame you for things you didn't do."

"Remember the juke joint?" asks Herbert.

"Oh, yeah!" Emory explains that next door to the Campbell house Rufus had a "juke house," complete with jukebox and liquor. "Played Fats Domino, 'Please Don't Leave Me,'" says Emory, who stops to sing the title stanza. "But Rufus didn't have electricity, so a cord ran through the woods from our house. If it got too loud and happy over there, we'd pull the cord!" The word *juke*, he tells me, is actually a Gullah word for 'unruly'. "We never talked about white people at all, weren't even curious about them."

"They used to be rough on white people," says Herbert.

"Black people too, if they were 'fereigners,'" Emory adds.

"Outsiders," explains Herbert.

It used to take twenty years for a newcomer to be accepted, but not anymore, Emory says. "Not now. The population has switched so much that *we* feel like the outsiders now." Today only a tenth of Hilton Head's 23,694 people are black. Most black people here still despise the term *Gullah*, Emory says. It goes back to Penn School: "People came regularly looking for 'Gullah niggers' to write about and have speak, and the missionaries sanctioned such research." Today, there's still a stigma in most Gullah people's minds about being called *Gullah*. "We were all taught that Gullah was an ignorant language," Emory says. To tell the truth, even he didn't know anything about the so-called Gullah culture until recently. Even his kids grew up embarrassed by it. "They laughed every time the old man talked," he says.

"It was white scholars who convinced me differently. It wasn't until two years ago, when the president of Sierra Leone visited from Africa that I really accepted the truth of my heritage. Because I spoke to him in Gullah, and he spoke back to me in Gullah." And for the first time, Emory knew it truly was his language. Then he went to Sierra Leone, and he felt as if he were home, from the desperate rural poverty, to the extended family—in one village, he saw a woman ordering fifteen children around—to the form and pattern of speech, to the rice and seafood. They even poured their soup over their rice, like Emory does. And their sense of humor! Emory says blacks laugh at things whites don't find funny. "Somebody's girlfriend dumps him, man, that's hilarious!" The Africans bantered like this, too.

"Do you feel different after learning all this?" I ask.

"Oh, a whole lot better," Emory says. "I can explain myself. I can explain myself to myself. I realize why I am who I am. Why I eat the food I do. Why I like rice. Our folks came here and reached back and used their knowledge to survive. The soup, the rice, the okra, the shrimp. That's who I am!"

I ask Emory's children, neither of whom speak Gullah, "Has knowing this changed you?"

"I go to school and brag about being Gullah," says Ochieng.

"Me too," says Ayoka.

"I tell ya," Emory says, now laughing again. "They have a lot better chance than I had at Georgia State. Called me a 'Carolina rice eater.'" Emory then leans back in his chair, raises his long arms in one of his slow, eloquent motions, and gets serious: "It's good they can look backward and forward to know from whence they came. I couldn't. Not for a long time, and it hurt."

As everyone at the table nods in agreement, I think again of Whittier's poem:

> *Oh, none in all the world before*
> *Were ever glad as we!*
> *We're free on Carolina's shore,*
> *We're all at home and free.*

So many different kinds of freedom. So long in coming.

1 0

BURN, BABY, BURN

DARIEN, GEORGIA

It's fitting that I should leave Hilton Head for Darien, because it was also from near Hilton Head in the spring of 1863 that the black Union soldiers of the Fifty-fourth Massachusetts regiment left port bound for battle. When they arrived in Darien, then a fading town on Georgia's Atlantic coast, an embittered and profiteering white commanding officer ordered them to loot and burn the town. Darien was deserted at the time and of no strategic importance, and its incineration ranked as one of the Civil War's more gratuitously destructive acts—and as the symbol of a harsh and fearful black vengeance exacted against former white masters. The event was recently made both famous and infamous by its depiction in the Oscar Award-winning movie *Glory*, which correctly portrayed the black soldiers of the Fifty-fourth and their white officer, Colonel Robert Gould Shaw, as reluctant torchbearers. Only a few buildings survived the inferno, and I'm curious about Darien today, about what has become of the town that burned.

Upon arriving, I am disappointed. Entering Darien—with 1,783 residents—on North Way I'm greeted by one of the ugliest four-lane commercial strips I've seen anywhere. It's filled with used-car dealerships, gas stations, quick-stores, a couple of worn-out motels. The new supermarket doesn't help much, and Darien's four-lane ambitions are, so far, sadly unfulfilled. The heart of town is quaint enough, with beautiful Victorian homes for the well-to-do and tidy clapboard homes for poorer folk. The waterfront along the Altamaha River, in antebellum times banked with warehouses for cotton, rice, and lumber, is peaceful and pretty. I arrive just as the rising tide and a hot, whipping wind make the Altamaha appear to be flowing magically inland in lazy, swirling rivulets.

Tomorrow Chester DeVillars, the retired black principal of Darien's public elementary school, will show me around town, but this afternoon I'm on my own. Near the waterfront, I notice a tourist center and I stop. A white county official who happens to be in the building raves to me about the wonders of Darien. When he learns I'm from near Washington, D.C., the homicide capital of America, he assures me that violent crime isn't a problem in Darien. He can recall only one murder here in recent years. Offhandedly, he says, "Two nigger boys."

"What?" I ask.

Quite casually, the man then explains that it was these "two nigger boys" involved in the killing. He says this comfortably, as if I'm used to hearing people talk like this. I'm surprised that a man in so public a position would use such language, and I wonder if I'm supposed to feel safe knowing that Darien's single homicide was simply blacks killing one another. Or perhaps he meant to shock me. Or worse yet, perhaps he didn't know better.

"Ya seen the dig?" a woman asks.

"The *dig*?"

"Yeah, we got an archaeologist diggin' up the waterfront right next door. They found all sorts a stuff from the fire. You gotta see it 'fore you leave." Next door at the dig, which is shaded by still another of those massive live oaks, Mattie Gladstone, the archaeologist's assistant, gives me a tour. She's a short, sturdy, elderly white woman wearing turquoise pedal pushers, a navy-blue T-shirt, and a dark-blue bandanna around her gray hair. Dirty and sweating in the ninety-three-degree sun, she smiles and wipes her forehead with the back of her wrist, the only unmuddied spot available.

"They looted the whole town," she says, seeming excited at the chance to share her knowledge with someone. "Ledgers and documents, horses, cows, chickens, furniture, pianos, beds, dressers. They slaughtered the animals they couldn't take, and a few days later they could be smelled three miles away." Every structure in Darien except part of the Methodist Church, one small store, and one house was destroyed. Colonel Shaw and some of his black soldiers were sickened by it.

Waving to the open yard around us and the ten-by-six-foot hole where several equally dirty people are fingering through sections of earth cordoned off by twine, Mrs. Gladstone says, "This was a warehouse that burned." She walks me to the edge of a ten-foot cliff facing the river. I can see where the back wall of the warehouse was at the cliff's edge. From this ground, she and the others have dug roofing slate, door hinges, pipe stems, iron nails, almonds, watermelon seeds, charred beams, and an 1860 penny that dates it all.

As the fascinated and fascinating Mrs. Gladstone talks on, it suddenly strikes me that I'd like to touch a piece of the very wood that was charred on that Saturday afternoon, June 11, 1863, exactly 127 years ago. Unfortunately, she tells me, the beams have all been carted off for classification and study. "I'm sorry," Mrs. Gladstone says sympathetically, seeming to understand my peculiar wish for a more tactile sense of the history before me. Just then, I notice a piece of what looks to be darkened timber poking out from the dirt and stone rubble below us.

"What's that?" I ask, pointing.

Mrs. Gladstone descends a path around the edge of the wall to investigate, and I follow. She digs around with her hands for a few moments, and then pulls out the blackened object. "A piece we missed!" she says, delighted. I take the two-foot shard of wood in my hands. It's heavy and dense, probably Virginia heart pine, Mrs. Gladstone says. Though charred, it isn't crusty and brittle like newly burned wood, but hard and solid, like a fossilized bone. Dapples of resin can still be seen in the wood, and when I hold it close to my face to smell, the scent of tar and soot is still strong. Instinctively, I jerk back my head and squinch my nose. I can't explain why, but I think to myself that I'd like to take this relic home so that my own children can touch it, smell it, and squinch their noses at it—tactile history, a fossil that, like the Civil War and the freeing of slaves and the ravishing of their masters, embodies an exact moment of simultaneous creation and destruction.

"Take a small piece if you like," Mrs. Gladstone says.
I don't take it. As a relic, it's not mine to own.

It's early evening now, and I check into one of the worn-out motels
back on North Way. Next to my door, sitting on a masonry flower box
filled with white impatiens, I find a young black man laboring over a
large cardboard box brimming with whiting fish that he has just
begun to clean. He wears no shirt, no shoes, no socks; a fresh band-
aid rings his left big toe; and his black pants are caked with what
looks to be the gray mortar of a drywaller. Whatever his work, I
notice that the man wore a short-sleeved shirt while doing it today,
because patches of the goop are hardened up the length of his arms to
his biceps. Only the palms of his hands, washed by the bowels and
blood of the whiting, are clean of the mud. In the heat, the flies have
already found the day's catch.

"Dinner?" I ask, sitting on the flower box next to him.

"A surprise for my fiancée," he says in a voice that is low and
slow and steady. He looks straight into my eyes and smiles, but with
the kitchen knife in his right hand he continues to slice the back of a
fish, stick his thumb into the incision, pluck off the fish's head, slice
its pale belly, and scrape its innards into the white plastic bucket
between his legs. "Maybe we'll have a party. There's thirty-six
pounds here. Bought 'em from a guy for three dollars. I know somebody who'll keep 'em cold till I go home tomorrow night." Home is a
small Georgia town, a few hours west. The man tells me his name
and that his work isn't drywall but exterior stucco. For the last
month, he's been working in Darien, living here at the motel during
the week and driving home on weekends. He loves the job, has been
doing it for three months now. It's hard, tiring work, but the money's
good—as much as $500 a week after several years' experience.
"That's what I'm shootin' for," he says, adding that he has a black
supervisor and that he likes him. "A lot of black guys try to bring
down successful blacks. But I don't. That's what I'm workin' for, to
be where he is. I don't have patience for anybody who says, 'I can't
get ahead 'cause I'm a black man.'"

"You hear that a lot?" I ask.

"Not in straight out sayin' it. They say, 'Well, I'm not going to
work today.' They say, 'Live for the weekend.' I do *not* live for the
weekend! I once heard a black man say, 'Blacks get mad if they don't

get a check on Friday or have to work the weekend.' Well, how can you judge me that way, man? Why can't people just say, 'This is how *I* feel? I don't know how *you* feel. But this is how *I* feel.'?"

To be honest, I find this conversation strange. I haven't told the man why I'm in Darien. I've said nothing about black and white. I just sat down and race came up, as if the young man felt the need to immediately clear the air and define his respectability for a white man he has never met before, a white man who, for all he knows, might be a scumbag drug-runner who's never worked an honest day in his life. This is power I don't want, and I decide to change the subject, asking what it's like working in Darien.

"It's like they're still fightin' the Civil War!" he says. At the little greasy-spoon restaurant where he and his co-workers eat, he heard an old white waitress actually say to a young white waitress, "Go to the table, give 'em a menu and that's that." He believes the girl was afraid to serve a group of strange black men. "I believe it's what she's been taught: 'Blacks are wild and crazy, they this and they that, they don't show you no respect, they all the same.' Why should I hate you and don't even know you? I wanta work hard and get ahead, man! These people here are livin' in a dead zone that shouldn't even be no more. All that should be past. Why do I be good and get stabbed in the back all the time?" He hates it that people who don't even know him seem to think he's lazy or no good. "I hate that. I hate it!"

The man seems lost in his intensity. And as he talks and cuts and guts his fish, a dark, roiling, lightning-streaked sky blows rapidly toward us from the west. Soon, the wind is bending the palmetto trees along North Way to two o'clock, the grit from the parking lot is stinging my face, and a wind chime somewhere is clanging wildly. It gets so dark so fast that the street lights flick on. But no rain comes, the wind and lightning disappear, and in a matter of minutes the street lights flick off again. The whole time, the man cuts, guts, and talks. He tells this story: When he was twenty-four and in the army, he befriended a nerdy white recruit who needed help learning the ropes. One day, three white vets from New York were picking on the kid, and he rose to defend him. The three white vets then beat senseless the man sitting in front of me, pounded on him with a baseball bat, put him in the hospital for two months. "I went crazy," he says. "Hey, man, don't nobody care if you good or bad! It made me hate whites."

By now, the dogged relentlessness of the man's revelations to me, a stranger, has begun to amaze me. He seems to notice this in my face, but he mistakes my amazement for disbelief, because he says, "I got pictures of how I looked. I carry 'em everywhere I go." And for the first time since I sat down, he lays down his knife, goes into his room and returns with an old brown briefcase from which he pulls three colored photographs of his badly beaten face—one from the front, one from each side.

"Why do you carry them with you?" I ask.

"I sit back and look at 'em when people do things to me."

"Like what?"

"Like when people act like I'm not a person. After they hassled us at the dirty spoon, I came back and looked at 'em. I asked, 'What is wrong with me that people treat me like this?'"

"You! What is wrong with *them?*"

"I try to be nice no matter what the color is, man."

"Don't you think they're asses and sickos?"

"Yeah, well. . . ," he says, and his voice wanders away.

Now I understand. The young man is *not* convinced that *they*, we, me—whites—are the sickos. Why else would he have told me the things he did? Why else would he care what I thought? Sitting here on the flower box at Darien's worn-out motel as this man cuts and guts his fish, the beginning of Ralph Ellison's *Invisible Man*—the literary anthem for black Americans a half-century ago—comes to mind, and seems painfully modern: "I am invisible, understand, simply because people refuse to see me. Like the bodiless heads you see sometimes in circus sideshows, it is as though I have been surrounded by mirrors of hard, distorting glass. When they approach me they see only my surroundings, themselves, or figments of their imagination—indeed, everything and anything except me."

I say, "I wish it had stormed and cooled the air."

He says, "Yeah, well, it's been hotter."

For breakfast the next morning, I stop at Archie's, a little restaurant that's recommended by everybody as the best in town. It has been in Darien for decades, and back in the days of segregation blacks were served at tables in the rear. This morning, everybody eats together. At a table near mine, two white men eat bacon and eggs. Out of the blue, one of these men, old and fat and wearing bib overalls, says in his booming voice, "Yeah, he got so dirty he looked like a nigger." I look up to see the other man nodding casually and forking food into his mouth. Honest, I don't hear this kind of talk back home.

Chester E. DeVillars is seventy-six years old and has lived in Darien or its surrounding McIntosh County all his life. He was a teacher at the segregated black schools and principal of the black high school. After integration in 1969, he became principal of the elementary school. He retired a decade ago but remains a respected pillar of the community, among both blacks and whites. As he tools me around town in his long Lincoln, past the big Victorians in the white neighborhoods, the nice ranchers in the newer middle-class black neighborhoods, and the sagging shacks in the still desperately poor black parts of town, he talks about life in Darien before and life here today. Don't let anyone kid you, Mr. DeVillars says, life for blacks in Darien today is light years from what it was. It's not perfect, not by a mile, but it's gotten so much better in his lifetime that it seems almost like a miracle.

"Everybody just about as poor as everybody else in Darien," says Mr. DeVillars, who is a gray-haired, heavy-set man with an aristocratic bearing about him. The jobs are in Brunswick, about twenty miles south, or even in Savannah, about sixty miles north. The bottom fell out of small farming long ago, and most young people today leave town. In these ways Darien is no different from the rest of the rural South.

But it turns out that when it comes to race, Darien has been different for a long time. Blacks could always vote in McIntosh County, Mr. DeVillars says. They had to pay the poll tax, but they could vote. White politicians campaigned in the black neighborhoods, held picnics, passed out liquor, and blacks always had some say. Even in the darkest days of Southern terror against blacks, coastal Georgia was a bastion of relative enlightenment. Blacks were lynched by the scores throughout Georgia, historian W. Fitzhugh Brundage wrote this year in the *Georgia Historical Review,* but only a handful of lynchings occurred in the state's coastal region. The reason for this independence, Brundage argues, was found in the coastal region's economics. For one, the large number of rich rivers and streams provided food and livelihood free of charge. For another, the Civil War had caused the breakup of the region's massive slave-cultivated rice plantations and left the insect- and malaria-infested lowlands largely unusable to its former owners. Thus, many blacks cultivated the abandoned land, becoming self-sufficient and largely independent of white economic power.

Years after the South's coalition of working whites and owning aristocrats had "liberated" its governments from blacks in the 1870s, blacks continued to hold local county offices such as coroner and justice of the peace. A black state legislator was elected off and on until 1907. Writes historian Russell Duncan in *Freedom's Shore,* "Whites compromised with the black machine and race relations in McIntosh County became surprisingly moderate." In short, real black power created a modicum of real equality.

"But just like America," says Mr. DeVillars, "Darien was hypocritical. We claimed we had good race relations and we got along great." But whenever Mr. DeVillars's good white pastor friend came to visit his house in the early fifties, the police still would cruise past the house suspiciously. He also remembers that when he was a youth, a black man was found killed and castrated. It scared the hell out of Mr. DeVillars then. "That wouldn't happen now," he says. "Blacks would tear this town apart."

"What's it like now?" I ask.

"Things are a little bit better," Mr. DeVillars says. Blacks ousted the county's corrupt white sheriff years ago. Today, blacks work in the various government offices. A person can live in any neighborhood he wants. The superintendent of schools is a black woman, elected with white votes. People get along. "But we still have an undercurrent. I'll give you an example: Just this morning, a white gentleman met me downtown and we started talking about politics. He said, 'Well, I hope we can get together on this election.' I said, 'Yes, I hope so.' He said, 'You know, you have two fine black gentlemen running for office, but me and that third black fellow, we don't see eye-to-eye. It's a shame you got these two fine black gentlemen running and then you got one nigger running.' I said, 'Now, back at you. Do you realize that your white candidate once stood on the state Senate floor in Atlanta and said that all black men should be castrated?' He said, 'No, I didn't know that.' I said, 'I don't know if I need to hold that against him or vote for him and let it go.' I said, 'Now, just 'cause a man doesn't see eye-to-eye with you doesn't mean you have to call him a nigger.' He said, 'Well, I didn't mean any harm.' I said, 'No, no harm taken.'"

* * *

As I leave Darien, I stop at the Dairy Queen just outside town for a quick Grilled Chicken Deluxe before starting the long drive to Montgomery, Alabama. At a table across from me, I notice a young black man and a young white man chomping their Braziers and talking and laughing in the way only friends do. I introduce myself and explain my trip. The black man is a college student. The white man is headed off to college this fall. They've been friends for years.

"Young blacks and whites get along fine," says the black kid.

"Everybody and their brother is datin'," says the white kid.

"Blacks and whites?" I ask, dumbfounded. "In Darien?"

The young men laugh uproariously. It started about, oh, four years ago, they figure, when a boom in interracial dating hit the high school. Last school year, they estimate, maybe fifty interracial couples were dating, out of only four hundred students.

"Kids don't tell their parents," says the black kid, who adds that when parents find out it can get weird fast. One white girl's parents wouldn't let her leave the house alone when they found out she was dating a black guy. They drove her to school and picked her up every day. The guys think that's absolutely hilarious.

And I leave Darien in a very good mood.

1 1

SAVING THE DOOMED

MONTGOMERY, ALABAMA

I'm not an expert on religion, far from it. But somewhere along the way, I learned that in ancient Jewish legend there is told the story of the *lamedvovniks*, the thirty-six secret saints, the Righteous Men, who were said to live and work among us—always poor, unnoticed, and without glory, always unaware of their own perfection—and by whose purity God was said to judge all mankind. According to the legend, if a Righteous Man were ever discovered, he would deny his sanctity, disappear, and reappear—unknown and unknowing—in a distant place.

I don't believe in saints. I certainly don't believe in *lamedvovniks*. But over the years, I've sometimes thought about the idea of these secret ones living among us and realized that the yearning to understand what it means to be truly good was as mysterious to those who lived a thousand years ago as it is to us, with all our modern sophistication.

For the last few days, while visiting Bryan Stevenson in Montgomery, Alabama—where in 1955 Rosa Parks refused to move to the back of the bus and where Martin Luther King, Jr., pastored the Dexter Avenue Baptist Church—I've found myself thinking about the *lamedvovniks* once again. This morning Bryan—who is thirty-one, a lawyer, and a black man—is on the road out of Montgomery bound for Phenix City, a tiny Alabama town where Bryan's client George Daniel is locked in the Russell County jail awaiting execution for killing a policeman. Yesterday the court overturned Daniel's conviction and ordered that he be given a new trial.

That's what Bryan does: he files appeals. He's one of those much-maligned lawyers who clog the courts with petitions meant to postpone men's dates with the electric chair, gas chamber, or needle. He's one of the reasons countless politicians have called for limits on the number of court reviews for the condemned. He's one of the reasons that with nearly twenty-four hundred people on death row, fewer than two hundred have been executed since the Supreme Court declared the death penalty constitutional in 1976. Although 75 percent of Americans today favor the death penalty, including a majority of blacks, this thirst for final vengeance has gone mostly unquenched, partly because of Bryan Stevenson.

At the Russell County jail, an old stone building that resembles a medieval castle, Bryan and I are ushered into a small room where George Daniel is waiting. As Bryan tells him that he'll have a new trial—which might literally save George's life—the thin, thirty-four-year-old black man smiles blankly, squeezes his nose tightly, rocks his body gently and bounces his legs to some rapid, internal rhythm. He wears a white jail uniform that is filthy at the crotch. The last time Bryan visited George, his cell was dirty with his own urine. Court records show that at least once during his incarceration George Daniel ate his own feces and that he is mildly retarded. "I need cigarettes," he says finally. Bryan promises to get cigarettes, and George is led away.

How to figure Bryan Stevenson? A graduate of Harvard's law school and its John F. Kennedy School of Government, he's the director of the Alabama Capital Representation Resource Center, which is involved in some way with most of the 119 death row inmates in Alabama. Bryan earns $24,000 a year. While his Harvard class-mates—black and white—get rich, he defends penniless murderers. Even his parents, working people from rural Milton, Delaware, didn't always understand him. They used to say, "Take the money."

These days, the road is home to Bryan, a thin, athletic man, just shy of six feet, who was a soccer star in high school and college. He wears short, natural hair and a short beard, unstylish clothes, and clunky sunglasses. He talks so softly that I must sometimes strain to hear him. He has a soft voice and no discernible black accent. On the phone, prosecutors and defense attorneys who don't know him usu-ally assume he's white. Once, when Bryan suggested that a defense lawyer try to plead his client down from a death sentence charge to life without parole, the lawyer said, "Didn't I tell you, he's a nigger. Can't get a life plea for a nigger in this county."

"I have always felt," Bryan says, as we drive out of Phenix City and on toward Atlanta to visit another client, Roger Collins, who is on Georgia's death row, "that I could just as easily have ended up as one of the men I am defending. I've had friends, cousins who fell into trouble. It could have been me.

"The people who end up on death row are always poor, often black. And almost always they had bad lawyers—real estate lawyers who never handled a capital case and who had to be dragged scream-ing into the courtroom. In one case, the judge actually sent the defense lawyer out to sleep off a drunk. The Supreme Court declared it unconstitutional, but prosecutors in the South still keep blacks off capital juries by giving bogus reasons to strike them. In one rural Alabama county we found potential jurors labeled by the prosecutor as 'strong,' 'medium,' 'weak,' and 'black.' Why do I do what I do? How can anyone do anything else?"

Bryan grew up in rural southern Delaware. His mother, who migrated from Philadelphia through marriage to Bryan's father, had volunteered to put Bryan and his older brother in the all-white school even before integration was formally in place. She had only to look at the ramshackle schoolhouse that black children attended to know where her kids were going. "You are here to make a mark," she'd tell her two sons and daughter. "Otherwise you will be the mark." She insisted on perfect grammar, diction, and pronunciation. And there was one absolute rule: "I never want to hear that you can't do something because you're black. You can do anything you want."

Bryan's father, Howard, a native of southern Delaware, gave less incendiary advice. He had been the child of a prominent black mechanic in nearby Georgetown and had grown up playing with the children of the town's prominent whites. He was rarely mistreated by whites. In fact, because he dressed nattily—refusing to wear the jeans and overalls most Milton blacks then wore—it was more often blacks who insulted him, saying he was highfalutin. Howard's advice to his children was that most white people will treat you well if you treat them well. From his mother and father, Bryan received a singular message: whites are not to be feared.

The Stevenson kids all did well, went to college and graduate school. But Bryan was always the family darling. In his overwhelmingly white high school, he was president of the student council, a star athlete, and a straight-A student who graduated number one in his class. A self-taught musician, he also played organ and piano at the Prospect African Methodist Episcopal Church, where he learned to shift his tempo to the spontaneous outbursts of congregants as they "got happy" with the power of the Holy Spirit.

"I had the happiest childhood," Bryan says. "Years later, at Harvard, so many kids I met felt that if they hadn't gone to Andover and Harvard, their lives would be over." He smiles. "But I always figured that people with even zillions of dollars couldn't be happier than me. I had fights with the white kids on the bus. They'd call me 'nigger.' When they did integrate the schools, all the black kids were in 3-C. I was the only black kid in section A until junior high. The reason I always say I've never met a client whose life isn't worth saving is because they are like me, except they didn't get in 3-A. They were in 3-C.

"You know, my grandfather was murdered, stabbed dozens of times, in his own home in Philly. The killers pleaded to a low charge. I had a black friend raped on campus, but the case was never pursued. She was leaving town, had no family there to pressure the prosecutor. That's our justice. We overprosecute crimes against whites and underprosecute crimes against blacks, because whites have political power and blacks don't. I saw it in my own life long before I studied the death penalty.

"But when I did, and discovered that a man who murders a white has a 4.3 times greater chance of getting the death penalty in Georgia, I saw it as a symbol of all the race and poverty bias in our society. We're not yet capable of valuing the life of a black mother of four in the projects the same way we value the life of, say, the ex-president of Chevron. We're just not capable.

"Do you know that in Montgomery, I spent weeks looking for an apartment. On the phone, a man said, 'You don't sound black, but I ask everyone.' I lost all humility. I told one woman I was a lawyer with a Harvard degree. She said the apartment was $250. I put on a suit, but when she saw me her whole body sagged. She said the rent was $450. It's very demoralizing and debilitating. None of my Harvard degrees, my suits, meant anything next to my little black face. A lot of whites think of me as more like *them* than the *real* blacks. Well, that's wrong. Those black people *are* me."

At the Georgia Diagnostic and Classification Center, death row, Roger Collins is waiting in the visitors' room, a deep, narrow place with a wall of screened bars and a long row of empty stools. Roger stands to greet Bryan, takes away Bryan's clunky sunglasses and puts them on, hams it up. He is Bryan's age, thirty-one, handsome, with short hair and a close-cut beard. He is on death row for brutally murdering a woman thirteen years ago. Roger was eighteen, his accomplice twenty-five. Roger got death. His accomplice got life. Roger could get an execution date any day.

"I understood right from wrong," Roger says. "I did, yeah. It just started out one thing and ended up another. I've done some hellful things in my past." When he was thirteen, Roger says, he and his father would go to Florida from Georgia and rob places every weekend. His father, who eventually went to prison for murder, is out now, and he visited Roger a few weeks ago. "He said they went for the death sentence," Roger says, "and missed."

Bryan says, "It looks real good. Don't get down."

Roger says, almost to himself, "Ain't set no date."

Outside, back on the road, Bryan says, "I meet people like Roger every day. Their lives are a mess. Half of my clients have had somebody in their families murdered. They are always getting their electric turned off. Or they mention that their daughter has been in jail for six months, and, by the way, what should they do about it? They live at the margins of society, with no sense of control over their lives. We've given up trying to help them. To mention it is to be ridiculed as naive and weak." Bryan falls silent. Then he says, "I'm afraid they're going to kill Roger."

Bryan has yet another stop, this one several hours south of Montgomery in tiny Monroeville, Alabama, where he must talk to the family of his death row client Walter McMillian. "You know," he says, "when I go to a Harvard reunion or I run into an old classmate who's doing something he hates, these people act like I'm a priest, making such sacrifices for my condemned men. When people say I'm great, they aren't talking about me. They're talking about themselves, about what's missing in their lives." As Bryan and I cruise toward Monroeville in the fading evening sun, past cotton and cane and giant pecan trees, past the barren and beautiful countryside, past Alabama's Holman Prison and its death row, I think about the *lamed-vovniks* and that Bryan would understand why ancient legend required that they deny their goodness: to believe you are good, special, better than the rest, is to be neither good nor special.

"How important is your faith?" I ask.

"Church is not so important to me today," Bryan says, "but I still glory in the charisma and spontaneity of the black church, still love to play the piano for a person who stands and dances to the Spirit. It is restorative. A grandmother who stands up and says, 'I've lost my son and daughter in the fire, all my belongings, but I'm here with my grandson and we're gonna make it.' It is more restorative than praying with people who are thankful for their wealth. I must return to that well. If there's an afterlife, that's who it's for—those whose lives have been hellish and who've struggled to be better. That's who Christianity is for: the rejected, despised, and broken. And those are my clients."

It's dark when Bryan and I arrive in Monroeville and meet Walter McMillian's sister, niece, and nephew in the cold wind outside the IGA at Ollie's Corner. He brings them up to date, and then asks, "Is everything else going all right?"

"Did my daughter call you?" McMillian's sister asks.

"From Mobile, yes. I haven't had a chance to call back."

"They got her son for capital murder."

"Is that right?" Bryan says, masking his shock with studied calmness. "Have her call me. Make sure she tells him not to say anything to the police. Does he have an attorney?"

"No."

"Make sure she calls tonight."

"How late?"

"Anytime, anytime."

Back on the road, Bryan says, "It's probably too late."

Naturally, Bryan thinks first of the accused. But tonight I can't help thinking of the victim, for whom it's far too late, and I ask, "But what about the people your men kill? What about their husbands and wives, their kids? Don't these murderers deserve to die?"

Bryan thinks for a moment. "I feel worse for the families than I do my clients. It's the hardest thing. Maybe if the death penalty weren't so racist, I'd feel better about it. But for it to be imposed fairly would require us to have a wholly different society. I tell my clients, 'I don't care what you did, how awful it was. I don't believe you should be killed.'"

"It's not right to kill them back?" I ask.

"It's not right to kill them back."

Traveling Alabama with Bryan, I haven't gotten to see much of Montgomery. So before leaving town the next morning, I go to the Civil Rights Memorial at the Southern Poverty Law Center on North Hull Street in the heart of town. The memorial was designed by Maya Lin, the young architect who conceived the long, low, dark Vietnam Memorial in Washington. If anything, her Civil Rights Memorial is an even more elegant and brooding tribute to the dead. Etched in a large circular black granite table are the names of forty men, women, and children who died in the name of civil rights from 1954, the year the U.S. Supreme Court ordered the nation's schools desegregated, to April 4, 1968, the day Martin Luther King, Jr., was assassinated. Their names radiate like spokes on a wheel, and this morning a black man and his young son walk slowly and silently around the table. Water rises gently from the monument's center and washes seamlessly and soundlessly over the names into a pool below. On the black marble wall behind the table are Martin Luther King's words:

··· UNTIL JUSTICE ROLLS DOWN LIKE WATERS AND
RIGHTEOUSNESS LIKE A MIGHTY STREAM.

Beautiful words, although even decades after they were spoken, when the memorial was unveiled in 1988, whites in Montgomery protested and bomb threats were received.

A few of the martyred are famous to us today: Emmett Till, the fourteen-year-old boy murdered in Money, Mississippi, after he allegedly flirted with a white woman; Medgar Evers, leading an integration drive in Jackson, Mississippi, killed by a sniper; Addie Mae Collins, Denise McNair, Carole Robertson, and Cynthia Wesley, the four little girls killed in the bombing of Birmingham's Sixteenth Street Baptist Church. Others are less well known: Willie Edwards, Jr., forced by Klansmen in Montgomery to jump off a bridge; Louis Allen, killed after witnessing the murder of a civil rights worker in a town named, of all things, Liberty, Mississippi; Viola Gregg Liuzzo, a Detroit housewife killed by Klansmen as she drove demonstrators from Montgomery to Selma, Alabama.

Reading each name is like ringing a bell. And standing here with the black man and his son, I can feel only incomprehension, the same feeling I have when watching the grainy films of naked, hollow bodies piled high in the Nazi camps. Utter disbelief. I have an odd thought for a man who is an agnostic: *oh, let there be a hell!*

Hopelessness is a feeling I despise, however, and up the street and around the corner at the Dexter Avenue King Memorial Baptist Church, within sight of the Alabama statehouse where Confederate president Jefferson Davis gave his inaugural address, I find the antidote: Mrs. Pauline Wilson and her children. They are on a kind of pilgrimage from their hometown of Anniston, Alabama, a nearby city of 26,623 people, to visit the Civil Rights Memorial and the Dexter-King Church, where the Montgomery bus boycott was set in motion on December 1, 1955. The doors to the narrow red-brick church, with its tall white steeple, are locked this early in the morning. So the Wilsons pose for family snapshots on the church's steps under the bright sun in a nice breeze.

"The Civil Rights Memorial was our first stop today," says Mrs. Wilson, a cheerful, young-looking woman in her fifties. She wears her black hair long and straight down her back and carries a large canvas purse slung over her shoulder. "Things are a lot better today, that's for sure. Just look at my children." Then she proudly ticks off their achievements: Gregory, twenty-nine, a pediatrician who graduated from Johns Hopkins University; Stanly, twenty-eight, finishing his master's in chemistry; Gerald, twenty-six, working on his master's in business administration; Priscilla, twenty-three, just graduated from Tulane University; Anthony, twenty-two, studying mechanical engineering at MIT; Paulette, twenty, studying chemical engineering at the University of Alabama; and Kimberly, eighteen, bound for the University of Alabama this fall. "Is that seven?" Mrs. Wilson asks, looking around at her children and counting on her fingers. "Yes, seven. My husband, Clarence, is a minister and an educator, and he and I preached education." A round of laughter and "that's for sure" comes forth from the assembled children.

"I don't think we could have gotten to where we are today under segregation," says Gregory, the doctor. "But, looking back, so much had to do with my folks stressing education. Because when the opportunities started coming in the seventies, I was ready with the dreams to match. I went for it, and I can look back at my friends who didn't. Their dreams weren't as large as mine. That's the only thing I can put my finger on, because half of them were smart enough to go to college. But I believed nothing could stop me, while, after high school, they stopped dreaming."

"What about racism?" I ask.

"It's there, it permeates, there's no way you can get around it," says Gregory. "I knew that putting all those years and work into school and career were going to pay off in the future with dividends, but it's something we haven't comprehended as a race. You can't stop talking about racism or people will forget about it, but the emphasis now has got to be on taking advantage of opportunities that *are* there. Only then will people finally realize, 'Hey, it's possible, I can do it.'"

Fittingly, Mrs. Wilson, clearly a respected authority on the subject of black motivation and achievement, has the final word. "He's right," she says. "He's absolutely right."

1 2

KLAN COUNTRY, USA

PULASKI, TENNESSEE

The Ku Klux Klan was born in Pulaski, Tennessee, in 1865. For about a hundred years, white people there were more or less proud of that. But times have changed. Last year, the town went to court in a failed effort to keep the ragged, modern-day remnants of the Klan and its assorted allies from descending on Pulaski to celebrate the Klan's founding. When the day came, virtually every Pulaski business (almost all of which are owned by white people) closed its doors, turning the city's quaint downtown square into a ghost town occupied by only a gaggle of pro-Klan marchers and dozens of cops and reporters. Pulaski dubbed itself the City of Brotherhood, and Peter Jennings declared it America's "Citizen of the Week." In the PR business, this is called turning a liability into an asset.

No journey into black America is complete without a stop in Pulaski, a town of 7,895 people that sits in the lower middle of Tennessee about twenty miles above the Alabama state line in some of the most ruggedly beautiful forest and farmland in the South. I drive in on the David (not Davy) Crockett Highway, past parched fields of corn and hillsides dotted with grazing goats and hulking rolls of golden hay, past green mountainsides obscured by shimmering layers of mist, past the footloose clothing factories indigenous to this nonunionized countryside, past the Beans Creek Primitive Baptist Church, and the Jack Daniel's distillery. The sky is threatening rain this afternoon, but a lot of folks are out and about, although I see very few blacks. Unlike the Deep South, where the wide expanses of tillable land were believed to require mass slave labor and ended up creating huge black majorities, the mountainous landscape of Tennessee never acquired a large percentage of blacks. Today only 13 percent of Pulaski's Giles County and a quarter of Pulaski's population are black.

My destination is the Queen Ann Funeral Home, where I'm to meet James Brown, a sixty-two-year-old black man who has been Pulaski's reigning black radical for thirty-five years—ever since he returned from the Korean War and was nabbed by the town constable for drinking from the whites-only water fountain. Twenty years later, in 1972, after winning a federal lawsuit that required Pulaski to end its racially gerrymandered voting districts, Mr. Brown was elected to the county commission—the first black elected in Pulaski's Giles County since reconstruction.

After getting directions at the Bluebird Cafe just off Pulaski's downtown square, I find James Brown at the funeral home he owns with his wife, Anne, who is the descendant of a free black Pulaski carpenter named Gabriel McKissack, whose family members today are principals in the first black architectural firm in America, Nashville's McKissack, McKissack & Thompson. Mr. Brown's office is about the size of a big closet, and with its walls plastered with photos of everyone from John Kennedy to Jesse Jackson to Jerry Butler of the Impressions, the room feels even smaller. I wait as Mr. Brown sits behind his desk talking on the phone. He wears a gray checkered suit and a gray paisley tie, its clasp a replica of the Martin Luther King stamp put out by the U.S. Post Office. Even though Mr. Brown is seated, I can see that he is a large, tall man. He has an oval face and a shock of still-dark, full hair that he wears in, I think, an Afro. It's been so long since I've seen an Afro, I can't be sure.

Off the phone now, Mr. Brown says, "It's never changed. It's just a racist town. That 'brotherhood' here last year was a sham. You black and they white." Then he says harshly, "We haven't got no 'brotherhood' here." Mr. Brown runs off a list of examples: only two black policemen on Pulaski's force of twenty; no full-time black policemen on the surrounding Giles County force of fourteen. "Not one!" he says. Only one black assistant school principal in the whole county. The membership of the Lions Club and Kiwanis Club, the bank boards, and the county industrial development committee is almost all white. The local country club is nearly all white, except for memberships the city bought for use by its council members, one of whom is black and the head maintenance man at the courthouse. With bitterness, Mr. Brown says, "Black folks can't be nothin' here."

Reaching behind him, Mr. Brown retrieves an old King Edward cigar box from which he pulls the many missives he has received over the years: "The Klan is watching you," printed on business cards! He's found them on his front door, behind his windshield wipers, on his office door. After he was first elected in 1972, someone burned a cross in his yard. So all this brotherhood talk is hard for Mr. Brown to swallow. Everything blacks have won in Pulaski—city council seats, integrated public schools, even the integrated local hospital—has been won only after lawsuits or legal threats, he says, and that isn't brotherhood, it's power. Even most of the stores don't have blacks working in them, he says with a tone of sadness and disgust. He suggests I walk around the town square and see for myself.

A couple dozen stores fortify Pulaski's downtown square, which in its turn-of-the-century style is anchored at its center by a stately brick county courthouse boasting an eagle-topped cupola with clocks on four sides, one of which is a couple of minutes behind the others. The stores are mostly two-floor Victorian buildings dating from after the Civil War. They are nicely kept and painted in muted Victorian yellows, reds, and blues. I park in front of the Quality Stamps Redemption Center and am about to begin my employment census, when the rain starts falling torrentially in angled sheets from the north. It doesn't look as if it will let up soon, so I start in the rain, working my way around, stopping in every store that's open—places like Harwell & Son Hardware, Hunter & Smith Furniture, Reeves clothing, Beech & Co. men's clothing.

At 4 P.M. on a soggy summer afternoon, I find one black man behind the counter at the Gibson & Cardin Pharmacy and one black woman sewing clothes at the Sunshine Cleaners. That's it. Every other clerk I see is white. I'm soaked to the skin, and surprised. All through my travels, I've noticed that today stores everywhere—even in rural Farmville, York, and Darien—commonly employ blacks. Trying not to jump to conclusions, I decide to test my little-known Wal-Mart Racism Indicator Theory.

This isn't elaborate social science. Talcott Parsons, don't move over. But here's my theory: The percentage of black workers at any local Wal-Mart (which, in most places I've ever been to, employs numerous blacks if they're around to be employed) is directly correlated with that local community's attitudes on race. Armed with my theory, I head out to the new Wal-Mart Discount City west of town. Just inside the doors, I find five women working the checkout lines. All are white. Beyond them, I find two women stocking Right Guard deodorant. Both are white. A man is atop a large ladder hanging poster advertisements from the ceiling. He is white. Three women are stocking blue-jean skirts. All are white. A woman behind the jewelry counter is stocking sunglasses. She is white. One woman working near the dressing room is also white. Two women at the camera counter are white. The man in Sports is white. The woman in Wallpaper is white. The clerk in Garden Supplies is white. The one in Books is white. Finally, I see a black clerk. The final tally: whites, 19; blacks, 1.

You don't have to be Talcott Parsons to conclude that something beyond random selection is at work here. I wait for the black woman to finish with a customer, then I tell her about my trip and ask her why so few blacks work in Pulaski's Wal-Mart. "It's not because of prejudice, any overt prejudice," she says, looking around to be sure that no co-workers are near enough to hear. "It's more that people get hired at the store because they have a sister who worked here or somebody here has known their fathers. It's small-town. It's more the old-boy network."

"Do blacks apply?"

"Yes."

"Do they ever get hired?"

"They do if someone knows their families." She says the few blacks who do work at the Wal-Mart are in jobs of authority. "Number one is you have to be known," but that's true all over town, she says. It's even harder to get jobs in other businesses. "Things have improved," she says. "They have. Now black people work at the banks doing things besides cleaning the floors." The public schools at least have one black vice principal. "But it's slow. It's slow. Everybody in Pulaski gets along, which is weird. I don't think it's that whites want to keep blacks out of positions of authority as much as it is, 'Well, I never thought of that person doing that.'"

I ask, "Isn't the result the same?"

I must head north out of Pulaski for a few miles to Dunnavant's country grocery, turn right on Pigeon Roost Road, turn right over Pigeon Roost Creek, and then hang a sharp right onto the red-gravel City Dump Road to find the home of sixty-one-year-old Ella Mae Cheatham, famous in these parts for being the only black woman who takes black foster children into her home. In thirty-two years, Ms. Cheatham has been a foster mother to sixty-eight children.

"Where in the world are we?" I ask Ms. Cheatham, a short, round woman with dark gray hair cut close to her scalp. From where we stand on the porch of her little brick house, I see a panorama of trees and fields overgrown with white Queen Anne's lace and kudzu, which has grown so thick and high in the trees that the vines seem to be flowing down from above, like water, rather than growing up from below. "Now, this is the country," I say.

"Too many weeds!" calls a woman's voice from inside the house, where Ms. Cheatham's two adopted daughters and her granddaughter are waiting to talk with me. Lori is twenty-four; Laronda is twenty-one; Lisa, the granddaughter, is seventeen. Asleep in a nearby cradle is Roxanne, six months old and wearing a yellow dress and white socks that say "Mommy." Roxanne is number sixty-eight.

"You're the color of my son," I tell Laronda. "You're obviously a mixed-race girl."

"My mother was white," she says confidently.

"Well," I say, "what's life like for young blacks in Pulaski?"

"Ain't nothin' changed," says Ms. Cheatham, sounding a lot like Mr. Brown. She hesitates. "It's gotten a little better."

"Do the younger people get along?" I ask the girls. Ms. Cheatham didn't raise any shy offspring, and they all talk at once. I can't keep track of who's saying what so I give up and listen.

"If I walked around downtown with a white guy, everybody in Pulaski would know, like I committed a crime. Most people figure blacks should date blacks and whites should date whites."

I ask, "Is dating common between blacks and whites?"

"No, but a lot keep it secret."

I ask, "Is race always in the air?"

"Mostly."

"How?"

"'Nigger,' for one thing."

"You still hear that?"

"Oh, yeah!"

"That word is everywhere."

"'What you doin' with that nigger?'"

"'Nigger!'"

"'Look at that nigger!'"

"Me and you walkin' down the street: 'What is that white man doin' with that nigger?' You gonna hear it! They say it loud!"

I ask, "Only if you're with a white man?"

"No, sometimes just walkin' down the street."

"We have seen people ridin' down the road sayin', 'Nigger! Nigger! Nigger!'"

"I was goin' into my apartment one day and this girl opened her door and said, 'Nigger!' and closed it."

"Little white kids, nine and ten years old, say, 'Look, there's a nigger, Mama!'"

I ask, "Are you ever afraid for your safety?"

"No."

"Except when the Klan came, now that was a different story."

"When it snows down here, nobody goes out. And that's how it was for three days. The town was closed down."

"But at least they turned that Klan plaque around."

"The Klan plaque?" I ask.

"Yeah, on the building downtown where the Klan first started."

"The building is still standing?"

"Sure is, right downtown."

The sun is out and bright, but the rainwater still glistens on West Madison Street in front of the single-story Victorian building, its brick walls painted beige and its windows trimmed with blue-green shutters, where the Ku Klux Klan was founded as a young men's social club on December 24, 1865. Just as the young women had said, bolted to the front wall is a two-foot-square metal plaque, tarnished to a shade that matches the blue-green shutters, that is turned face toward the wall. I find some irony in the lawyer's shingle announcing that the building is today a public defender's office. The doors are locked and so I ask around town for the building's owner, who turns out to be Donald Massey, a local businessman who, I'm told, can often be found at the Highway 64 liquor store he owns just west of downtown Pulaski.

Sure enough, Don Massey is behind the counter, sitting on a tall, stiff-backed stool and rapidly fingering his calculator as he runs through an inventory list. He's a tall, thin man, at the upper edge of middle age, wearing a white pullover golf shirt and bright green pants. There's an air of confidence about him. When I tell him I'd like to talk about the Klan plaque, he stops calculating, straightens up, eyes me cautiously, and says nothing for a long moment, simply sits framed by the row of single-shot liquor bottles on the window sill behind him and the collection of half-pint Jack Daniel's bottles on the counter before him. He asks for my identification, which he studies carefully.

"Things got all out of proportion," he says finally. "Press people called me from California and New York." Mr. Massey says he bought the West Madison Street building about five years ago and remodeled it to serve as law offices for his son, who is the public defender for several nearby counties. The plaque had nothing to do with it, he says. Anyway, the building had always been "a point of interest, a rallying point," he says, for Klan members when they came to town. But it wasn't until the more militant Aryan Nation white supremacist organization held a rally in Pulaski that the town's leaders got worried.

"They came to me to see if I would take the plaque down," Mr. Massey says. "I thought about it and thought about it. Well, in some people's minds racism had nothing to do with it. Some people looked at it as a point of historical interest. A lot of people thought I shouldn't take it down, reasonable people."

This thinking is rooted in the belief that the original Klan, which began here and counted 550,000 members throughout the South within only a few years, emerged spontaneously—like a form of social protest—when Confederate veterans returned home to find not only their homes and towns destroyed but their communities in the grip of Northern military rule, carpetbaggers, "poor white trash," and newly empowered blacks—and themselves disenfranchised. The original Klan is supposed to have been a noble organization created to defend the South from lawlessness and military dictatorship. Intimidating blacks out of voting was only part of the Klan's mission—and was similar to the role of the carpetbaggers' Loyal leagues, which also set about to secretly manipulate the black vote. When the Klan was reconstituted in Atlanta in 1915, supposedly it became a disreputable and violent organization, preaching against not only blacks but also Catholics, Jews, foreigners, communists, and union members.

"I talked to people of all walks," Mr. Massey says. "Actually, opinion was about split. Some racist remarks were involved and some people who weren't racist were very indignant about not taking it down. They thought it was a part of history and that it should be left up, that we couldn't be proud of all our history, that if blacks took it the way they should, they could use it to spur themselves on, like the Jews use Auschwitz. But the majority of blacks didn't see it like that. The main thing people were offended by was the bias and brutality that it represented."

During the dispute about the plaque, Mr. Massey thought about the local white Presbyterian preacher, the Reverend Gary Kelly, who a few years ago had undertaken a one-man protest on the square against the Klan when it came to town. His lonely act had launched what eventually became the townwide boycott of the Klan activities. Yes, the town fathers were worried that if they didn't stand up to the

Klan, Pulaski would get a racist reputation that would keep big busi-
nesses away. But at least some of the sentiment, like that of Rev. Gary
Kelly, seemed to Mr. Massey also quite sincere, not just a sham, as
James Brown believed it was.

So Mr. Massey turned the plaque around. He got threatening
phone calls. "They'd say, 'Nigger lover,' and hang up." He lost a few
customers here at Highway 64 Liquors. But he also learned that local
black ministers had led their congregations in public prayer asking
God to keep him and his family safe, which touched him deeply. "In
my lifetime—I'm fifty—I've gone from riding the school bus in third,
fourth grade and passing black kids who had to walk to school." He
remembers turning his head so they wouldn't see him, he was so
embarrassed. "We've come from that. My whole family agreed we
should turn the plaque around as a symbol of turning our backs on
violence and, quite frankly, to challenge some of the people who were
so adamant about taking it down to hire blacks themselves, to put
their money where their mouths were. Some firms were pushing me
to take it down but had no blacks in executive positions."

"Did they hire any?" I ask.

Mr. Massey smiles wryly. "I'm not sure how many steps have
been taken for additional employment."

"Did they admit they had a problem?"

"They never did respond."

I've been told that the Union Bank on the corner of South Third and
West Madison downtown sells copies of a book about the black history of Pulaski and Giles County. So just before leaving town, I stop
by the bank to get one. The several workers I ask haven't heard of the
book and they scurry helpfully around the cavernous lobby to see if
anybody else has. It turns out, they haven't. No one around has heard
of it. While I wait, I notice only whites behind the many desks before
me. I look around at the long wall of tellers. Only whites. I look into
the executive offices. Only whites. Again, I take a census: whites, 23;
blacks, 0.

I know it will sound rude, but I ask the pleasant white woman
who has been helping me, "Do you have any black employees?"

She gives me a flat, consciously blank look. It strikes me that here
in the South she cannot know the direction from which my question
comes. Am I glad that I see no blacks? Or am I upset that I see no

blacks? She says calmly, "Yes, we have. We have a couple." After a dramatic pause, she adds, "And they're very nice people."

"I'm sure they are," I say, as I wonder at the depths from which the pleasant woman's last remark had come, wonder at the shadows to which she had responded without even being asked. If I had to guess, I'd say the woman was offended by my question and that, in her mind, she was standing up for her "couple" of black co-workers. That was decent of her. But this morning's employment tally still stands in the lobby of Pulaski's Union Bank: whites, 23; blacks, 0.

1 3

THE MUSIC MAN

FLORENCE, ALABAMA

Before I left my home, a friend gave me this advice: "Follow the music." By that, he meant that the passage of blacks through America is in many ways a passage of their music, jazz, in all its precursors and historical variations. Work-gang music, spirituals, gospel, barrelhouse, ragtime, stride, boogie-woogie, swing, bebop, cool bop, hard bop, soul, third-stream, avant-garde, fusion, and, of course, the blues. I haven't taken my friend's advice, because the undertaking is simply too great. I'm no musician—can't play a note—and the breadth of modern African American music is so sweeping and so profound, with each form defined by subtle changes in chord structures and sequences and altered melodies and harmonies, that I don't believe I could ever fully grasp it, much less explain it.

Yet jazz has been my music of choice at least since I left Jim Morrison, John Lennon, and Mick Jagger behind. Without a clue about the roots or methods of jazz, I have, over the last twenty years, accumulated recordings by Dinah Washington, Bessie Smith, Sarah Vaughan, Billie Holiday, Lena Horne, Jellyroll Morton, Scott Joplin, Muddy Waters, Robert Johnson, John Lee Hooker, Ella Fitzgerald, Duke Ellington, Louis Armstrong, John Coltrane, Thelonious Monk,

Charlie Parker ("Sounds like somebody bouncing on a whoopie cushion," says my eight-year-old son), Ornette Coleman (whose music really does sound like somebody bouncing on a whoopie cushion), B.B. King, Lionel Hampton, Miles Davis, Stanley Turrentine, Terence Blanchard, Wynton Marsalis, and others. Even my recordings of white musicians tend toward the jazzy—say, John Mayall and his white-boy blues, the ballads of Rosemary Clooney, the gravel-voiced, piano-bar poetry of Tom Waits.

The list may seem long, but to a jazz aficionado mine is a paltry collection. I'm an untrained listener, and jazz is my background music as I read or write or even clean the house. I've grown so accustomed to it that when I go to someone's home and they don't have jazz playing softly in the background, I find it momentarily strange. For whatever reasons of temperament, jazz music speaks to me— makes me tap my pen, whistle, brush an invisible drum—at the same time it relaxes me. Jazz reaches me in the way I imagine calliope music reaches marching elephants in the circus, unconsciously. I suppose I'm a lot like the other white folks who've always found their way to the black neighborhoods of New York, Baltimore, New Orleans, Chicago, Kansas City, or Memphis and plunked down the bucks that eventually made jazz profitable and downright Middle American.

That's where I stood when I ran across a 1955 autobiography of W. C. Handy, *Father of the Blues,* in a used bookstore in Charleston, the same place where I bought a book on Gullah culture. It's hard to go wrong for $2, so I bought it and discovered that Handy is called the Father of the Blues not only because of his remarkably popular hit songs "Memphis Blues" and "St. Louis Blues," both published just before World War I, but because he documented the rural, Southern, black roots of blues music, which is at the heart of much American music, including jazz and rock 'n' roll.

Unlike so many country blues musicians, W. C. Handy had formal musical training, and when he ended up traveling the South, particularly around Clarksdale, Mississippi (the town where the anthropologist in Williamsburg suggested I visit harmonica player Wade Walton), Handy became a kind of blues detective, collecting the lyrics and the music of roustabout and backwoods pickers. Handy was the son of a preacher and, like other respectable blacks, was at first repelled by the gritty, rough-edged, low-class, bawdy "blues." But he saw how people, like the circus elephants, *moved* when they heard the music, couldn't sit still. He knew a hot seller when he saw it.

I look up Handy's hometown of Florence, Alabama, on the map and see that the little city of 36,426 people sits just across the Tennessee line below Pulaski. So off I go. Handy described the town this way: "Where the Tennessee River, like a silver snake, winds her way through the red clay hills of Alabama, sits high on these hills my hometown, Florence." On the sunny morning when I arrive, Florence seems less a city on a hill and more a scene out of some old movie house newsreel. If its gray downtown could be suddenly filled with women wearing cotton house dresses and horn-rimmed glasses, with boxy black purses hanging on their forearms, it would seem that not a year had passed since 1947.

Out West College Street, in Florence's black neighborhood, I find the Handy Home and Museum. "I can remember where the cabin used to be. I grew up in Florence," says the museum's curator, a fifty-five-year-old black woman (she says she is too shy for me to mention her name). It's the middle of the week and I'm the museum's only visitor, so the curator gives me a personal tour. In 1873, Handy was born in this two-room log cabin that has been moved to this site and refurbished. Today, with its heavy poplar logs sealed with seams of clean white mortar, the place looks more like a ski lodge than a rough nineteenth-century cabin. The floor is wood instead of the hard-packed dirt of Handy's childhood. Nicely framed photos and paintings decorate the walls, two China plates hang above the heavy stone fireplace. The Handy cabin is history through sentimental eyes, and a faded photo in the museum foyer reveals a harsher vision: the cabin years ago when its original logs were covered with unpainted siding on the outside, its front porch and roof were sagging desperately, and a raggedy-ass ladder built from tree branches leaned against it in hopeful anticipation of repair.

The curator tells the story of Handy's life: his preacher father who believed that all but church music was the "devil's plaything"; the rebellious son who took formal music lessons and who could play about any instrument he picked up and who ran off at eighteen, riding freight trains and playing music for change. W. C. Handy lived down and out in St. Louis during the Panic of 1893, unable to find work, sleeping on the riverfront with an army of paupers. But his luck changed. Bands then were as plentiful as jukeboxes today, and Handy's musical talents eventually moved him through a series of decent gigs, finally landing him in Clarksdale. There he found the distinctive form and feeling of "the blues"—its twelve-measure strains and its repeated chorus lines, followed by a single line of elaboration:

> *Oh, the Kate's up the river, Stack O' Lee's in the ben',*
> *Oh, the Kate's up the river, Stack O' Lee's in the ben',*
> *And I ain't seen ma baby since I can't tell when.*

What made the music unique was the way musicians twisted the notes between major and minor scales to make them evoke the same emotions carried in their lyrics of work, love, and suffering and the sounds of the world as they knew it: train whistles, sledgehammers, howling animals, wailing women, cruel bosses. Handy heard this music made on everything from dime harmonicas to beat-up guitars to washboards. He, the trained musician, heard notes played that weren't technically possible. "Theory once had it that no instruments other than the violin family and slide trombone family are capable of perfect glissando," Handy wrote, referring to the sliding effect created by playing a series of tones in rapid succession. But clarinet players in Clarksdale, through "false fingering and incorrect lipping," did the impossible. "Had it not been for the mistakes of the ignorant and illiterate, Gershwin would not have been able to write a two-octave chromatic glissando clarinet passage for his 'Rhapsody in Blue.'"

Handy formalized what came to be called "blue notes"—the flattening of the third and seventh notes, which, in Handy's words, "suggest the typical slurs of the Negro voice." Of black music he wrote, "Whether in the cotton fields of the Delta or on the levee up St. Louis way it was always the same. Till then, however, I had never heard this slur used by a more sophisticated Negro, or by any white man." In 1914, in his famous "St. Louis Blues," Handy introduced the techniques full blown, along with hesitations in the melody to allow the singer or his audience time to fill in the gaps with shouts of "Oh, lawdy," "Oh, baby," or whatever. Handy's haunting lyrics were written in poor black Southern country dialect—"Got de St. Louis Blues jes as blue as ah can be, I loves dat man lak a school-boy loves his pie ... Lak a Kentucky Col'nel love his mint an' rye"—at a time when some black poets and authors had abandoned rough black dialect as an embarrassment to the race. But to Handy—and black Harlem Renaissance poets such as Langston Hughes and others who would follow in the twenties—that rough black dialect *was* the poetry. Overnight, "St. Louis Blues" became an international hit.

"I feel very, oh, I don't know, sentimental," the curator says, "because I am old enough to remember when W. C. Handy was still back in Florence. I remember when he came back in forty-nine to the Princess Theater on a Sunday afternoon. I remember I was in the tenth grade and we went to see him, the kids from my school. I remember he played the 'St. Louis Blues.'"

"Why did his life touch you?" I ask, suspecting that, once again, the conversation has turned to the intricacies of race.

"W. C. Handy was somebody special to us because he was born here. I always loved music and I'd think about him and all the obstacles he had to face. He was an inspiration."

After all, it had been Florence's prominent white band leader who had told Handy as a boy that he couldn't learn to play the coronet because his lips were too thick. When the curator was a girl, everything in Florence was segregated, and she remembers standing in line to buy items, waiting for all the whites to go first, realizing she was finally next, and then having another white walk to the counter in front of her. "That's the way it was. You just waited. You got tired of it. But I've put it behind me now. You have to. You can't carry it around." The woman's husband was in the air force, and they left Florence in the fifties and returned in 1971 to find that much in W. C. Handy's hometown had changed. The demeaning public segregation was gone and whites just seemed more friendly. For instance, when she had left, decades ago, a white person would never have called a black person "Mr." or "Mrs." By the time she returned, it was common.

"What is it like today?"

"There is a different feeling now, a warmth," the woman says, pausing to think. "It gives you a sense of, oh, I don't know, I'm going to say it gives you, well, a feeling that you belong."

That night, I go out for a bite and a beer at a lounge near my motel. The place is nearly empty and I sit at the bar with a few other folks, all white, and we end up chatting. After a while, a man asks me why

I'm in Florence, and I tell him. Suddenly, it's like I've turned a switch. For the next half-hour, the man names town after town in Alabama where governments have been taken over by "the niggers." The man likes Florence because, he says, the town keeps its "niggers" in control. "Used to be able to get a man to cut your grass," he says, perhaps getting to the heart of his dismay. "Now you can't get a man to cut your grass." I say very little and, finally, he thinks to ask just whose side I'm on, anyway—the whites or "the niggers." I don't answer and he lets the question pass. I try to change the subject.

"Leavin' tomorrow for Brighton, just past Birmingham," I say.

"Great!" the man roars sarcastically. "A wonderful town!" Turns out "the niggers" have taken over Brighton too. "Used to have a sheriff there who if a garage was broken into, he'd call in Eddie Joe and say, 'Eddie Joe, who broke into the garage?' Eddie Joe'd say, 'I don't know, sheriff.' And the sheriff would slap him up side the head and Eddie Joe'd say, 'Bobby did it! Bobby did it!' And the sheriff'd say, 'Okay, now you go bring 'im in.' The sheriff didn't even go pick 'im up! Sent out a nigger to bring 'im in! But since the niggers took over, they've had fights at city council meetings and police cars sittin' with flat tires and broken windows." Better watch it in Brighton, the man says, because there's always "cuttins and killins. It happens in all the towns the niggers take over. So watch yourself in Brighton. Don't stop at a stop sign. And keep your doors locked."

1 4

ALL THAT CUTTIN' AND KILLIN'

BRIGHTON, ALABAMA

For the first time on my trip, I am afraid. The man in Florence has put my every nerve on edge. And as I pull off the highway for Brighton the next day, which is rainy and ugly, I feel as if I'm driving into the worst neighborhood of Washington, D.C., or into Watts in Los Angeles. Off the highway, I stop at the Speedway gas station, which does little to calm me. The place looks like a junk-car convention. I see ancient Camaros, Firebirds, and Coupe de Villes. An old, rusty Oldsmobile Cutlass groans in towing another old, rusty Oldsmobile Cutlass, a towing chain jangling eerily on the macadam. A monstrous black man, his work clothes worn and greasy, rolls out of the lead Cutlass and lumbers back to the chain, gives it a hard tug. He puts $2 worth of gas in his car. Inside the Speedway's crowded convenience store, where I get a cup of coffee, I feel as if people are watching me. On the narrow road into Brighton, at noon, I lock my doors.

Downtown Brighton is a pit. Three little streets come together like spokes to a hub of tired single-story brick buildings. Many are empty and boarded up, others house a dry cleaners, a liquor store, a cut-rate drug store, a florist, a used clothing store, a used furniture store, a beauty parlor. A line of graffiti reads: "Fuck the police." A sad-looking man walks away from a gaggle of other sad-looking men, taps on my window and asks for a cigarette, which I don't have. In a field nearby, a junk car without an engine sits with its hood resting upside-down on its roof. A speed limit sign is defaced with a hand-scrawled pentagram, the symbol of Satan.

Ahead on Huntsville Avenue into Brighton, which sits on the Birmingham city border and has a population of 4,518, the landscape is much the same: boarded-up and burned-down houses, dilapidated places—some inhabited, some not—a junk yard, a mountain of old tires, piles of trash. At Donald Avenue, I see a sign for the Blue Gardenia Club and turn left toward my destination—the home of Loudelia and Printeris Cooke, an elderly couple who moved to Brighton in 1946 and raised nine children, all of whom went to college. Donald Avenue is a mess, too, with weed-enshrouded shacks on the right and another dilapidated place at the corner across from the Blue Gardenia, which, incongruously, is painted yellow. After Donald Avenue veers to the right and becomes Clay Street, next to still another abandoned house I find the Cooke home.

To my surprise, it's a nice little house with yellow siding. Its front is guarded by two thirty-foot pine trees and terraced with green, orange, and white lilies, a thick Xavier bush, and bright-blooming yellow dahlias, on which a bumblebee is lunching. Along the side of the house are more flowers, blue carnations, and more shrubs. In the rear are two plum trees and two peach trees, their fruit spread out rotting on the ground and hanging heavy from overladen limbs. The bees are feasting.

"With the children gone, we just don't take in the fruit anymore," says Mrs. Cooke, as we walk around the back yard. I ask the name of the purple flowers blooming around the house. "Oh, I been takin' care of flowers so long," she says, waving off my question with a expressive flick of her wrist, "I can grow 'em without knowing their names." Mrs. Cooke is a thin, pretty, seventy-one-year-old woman with short, straight hair. She's dressed nicely in a navy-blue polka-dot dress with padded shoulders, high-heeled shoes, and a gold necklace and gold bracelet. Mr. Cooke, who's tall and erect at age seventy-two, is less formal, wearing a white short-sleeved shirt and soft denim slacks splattered with paint. We walk around to the front screened-in porch and sit down to talk. The ugly day has turned bright and muggy now, and Mr. Cooke flicks on the big oscillating fan.

"Brighton was nice when we moved in," says Mr. Cooke, his voice slow and soft and heavy with Southern drawl. As he talks, he has a habit of gently rubbing his left hand on his forehead.

"It's gone down," says Mrs. Cooke.

"A lotta houses just stayed empty when people died out."

"'Bout all the children went to college and left."

The story of the Cookes is the story of an industrial era in America that is well past. Mr. and Mrs. Cooke met in the forties in a church in the country about an hour outside Birmingham. Their fathers were sharecroppers. The Cookes married and already had two children when they moved to town. In 1946, Mr. Cooke took a job pushing a dolly at a nearby brick factory, where he stayed for forty years and four months, until he retired. They bought this house for $2,500. The steel mills were booming in those days and the black men of Brighton had work. They held the lesser jobs, no doubt, but still the money was good. Most of the men's wives, like Mrs. Cooke, were homemakers who never did domestic work in white people's homes. The Cookes' lives played out in Brighton at the segregated but solid neighborhood schools and at the Friendship Baptist Church, where Mr. Cooke is still a deacon, Mrs. Cooke was the music director, and the kids spent most of their spare time.

I ask, "Whatever made you think you could raise nine kids who'd all go off and do well?"

"Church on Sunday, no hanging out," says Mrs. Cooke.

"We never had no trouble," says Mr. Cooke.

Life in comfortable, working-class Brighton could be—as in relatively well-off neighborhoods everywhere—somewhat isolated from the world. The drama and terror of the historic civil rights battles in Birmingham, with mass protests organized by Martin Luther King from the balcony of the A.G. Gaston Motel; the 1961 Mother's Day mob assault on the Freedom Riders; the fire hoses and the police dogs; Public Safety Commissioner Bull Connor drawing a line and daring the demonstrators to cross, which they did, with violent consequences; and the Klan bombing of Birmingham's Sixteenth Street Baptist Church and the deaths of four innocent little black girls—all this more or less passed the Cookes by.

"I don't remember much about it," says Mr. Cooke.

"It never did reach out here," says Mrs. Cooke.

"Did you think it was good that it happened?"

"My mother taught us, 'Don't you ever bow down to anybody!'" says Mrs. Cooke. "Now, we never did no marchin'. I didn't allow my children out on that. To get out there in the street and march, I never saw no sense in that." I think to myself that perhaps Mrs. Cooke missed the point of the civil rights movement, but she then explains what she means. "I'd a had to pack me a pistol so it was good for me to stay home."

"What did you think when the church was bombed?"

"I hated that," says Mrs. Cooke, her voice cracking. "That hurt me in the heart."

"The hatred?"

"That's what got to me. I couldn't understand it."

"Did you ever hate whites like that?"

"Oh, no, I didn't hate the white man. But killin' four little girls. That's what really got me. I didn't know nobody was that mean. All the little children cried."

"How did integration change your lives?"

"Well, it was a lot better," says Mr. Cooke. "Even out at the plant, they used to have black and white showers."

"What kinda silly junk was that?" asks Mrs. Cooke, laughing. "That's their stuff. I know how to handle it."

"How?"

Abruptly, Mrs. Cooke says, "I never quit smilin', but if you don't like standin' beside me, you're welcome to go."

"There were some old heads at the plant who never took another shower after it changed," says Mr. Cooke.

"They went home dirty?" I ask.

"Yeah."

"And they were welcome to?" I ask.

"Right!" says Mrs. Cooke.

We have been talking a long time now. I've seen pictures of the Cooke children at various ages, I've gotten a tour of the house and Clay Street. The sun is beginning to soften outside the screened-in porch behind Mr. Cooke, but he'd still like to show me around Brighton. So we hop in my car. With Mr. Cooke as my guide, I discover that Brighton has a lot of well-kept homes. The shacks and burned-out houses are real enough, but, like a child who awakens from fearful night shadows in the morning, they seem less ominous now. Even on Huntsville Avenue, I see that only about a third of the houses are really badly dilapidated and that a good third are downright nice. For many of the falling-down homes, Mr. Cooke knows the specific person involved and the specific story of how each house came to be in disrepair. Knowing, for instance, that Mr. Smith died and that his daughter let an elderly aunt live in the place for years until she too died somehow makes a house seem less a public nuisance. And I see that Brighton has little churches tucked in block after block. Mr. Cooke takes me inside his Friendship Baptist Church, a modern red-brick building that seats hundreds. New wall-to-wall carpet has just been laid, and the sanctuary has that unmistakable scent.

"You still read the Bible at worship?"

"They let me read whenever I want," Mr. Cooke says, proudly.

We continue our drive around town and Mr. Cooke says, "I never thought of Brighton as a place where I had to be scared of crime." Every once in a while, there's a shooting, he says, but not every day like in Birmingham, and usually it's in downtown Brighton over drugs. "A lotta things you hear about Brighton don't be true. It ain't never been no bad place like the man described to you." Take the house next door to him, Mr. Cooke says. It's been getting bad since the man who owned it got old and moved out more than a decade ago. But it's only been real bad since the renter left three or four years ago. "Just ain't nobody to move back in these places," Mr. Cooke says, because the kids all moved north to find better jobs. Or, like his son Larry, when things opened up, they moved out to suburban Fairfield or Mayfield, to nice new houses. And when the area's steel mills began closing five to ten years ago, a lot of Brighton men lost their jobs or were forced into early retirement. "The younger ones who ain't moved outta Brighton are findin' any kinda job they can," Mr. Cooke says, "which usually don't pay anywhere near what they used to be gettin'."

Mr. Cooke's tour is done. At dusk, I take him home. Mrs. Cooke is outside sweeping her front steps, which already look clean to me. Several neighbors, one of whom is an elementary school teacher, are standing out on Clay Street, chatting. Lights are just coming on in the houses along the road. The moist, fragrant smell of foliage is in the air, the night bugs are just awakening, and up the street a man has his hose out and is watering a patch of flowers. Funny how unfrightening Brighton seems now. I think of the fear I had this morning, and I remind myself that poor people usually drive old cars—as my father the milkman once did. I remind myself that a monstrous man in an Oldsmobile Cutlass towing an Oldsmobile Cutlass has probably bought the second car for spare parts, for frugality. I remind myself that his clothes are worn and greasy because he works hard. I remind myself that there are bums mooching cigarettes back home, and that while Brighton is a hard-luck town, not everyone in Brighton is a hard-luck case. Finally, I remind myself how different a place looks from the inside—and how insidious an evil notion can be.

Am I wearing a white sheet over my head or what? Once again, this time while catching dinner at a fast food joint on the other side of Birmingham, it happens. One table in front of me and to my left three young black men are eating. One table in front of me and to my right an older white man, maybe sixty, is eating. I'm absently munching my coleslaw and chicken fingers when the black men get up and leave. Instantly, the white man looks right at me, like we're beer-hall buddies, and says, "Them nigger boys were talkin' 'bout Shoal Creek Country Club." He snickers viciously. "They don't even know where it is. It's in Shelby County. They think it's in Jefferson County." The man is talking about the controversy now raging over the PGA golf championship, which is scheduled to be held soon at nearby Shoal Creek Country Club. After the club's founder recently mentioned that his club had no black members because "that's just not done in Birmingham," a firestorm erupted. Blacks, led by a black Birmingham minister, threatened to picket the tournament, and Toyota, IBM, and Anheuser-Busch pulled their sponsorships.

The man continues: "They ain't got no niggers up there, and they don't take no niggers up there. It's just like that all over the country. They got neighborhoods in Chicago where the only niggers they got is during the day when they got deliveries to make. At night, they don't let niggers in."

For a good ten minutes, he talks. I nod with no expression, and study him carefully. He's wearing pastel green slacks and a white short-sleeved shirt, white socks, and white buck shoes. He's tall and lean and a little hunched, bald with his remaining gray hair clipped short. As he talks, with increasing emotion, he rips his chicken off the bones and tears it into little pieces. He then tears his biscuit into little pieces and, as if tossing a salad, jumbles the chicken and biscuit pieces together with his fingers. He puts the box in a bag, wraps the bones in a napkin for the trash. During this ritual, he must use the word "nigger" a hundred times. The "niggers" have ruined every-thing they've touched. The poor white people of Shelby County already had to sell their homes and move out of Birmingham to get away from the "niggers." "And now here come the niggers again!" He says the "nigger preacher" getting ready to picket Shoal Creek convinced the "nigger councilman" from Birmingham to join him because he wants to run against Birmingham's "nigger mayor."

Finally, I send a signal: "Yeah, blacks are upset."

The man looks at me with hesitation. With one word—"black" instead of "nigger"—I've stopped the man's harangue. When he begins again his voice is softer, more plaintive. "They opened the schools to the blacks but all the whites moved out, and so the schools are still black." I look around the restaurant and see only the old man and a half-dozen blacks working behind the counter. I decide to push harder. "Well, I think blacks should be able to join what they want. Private clubs use public sewers, they use public water, they've got taxpayer-backed electricity running to them, they've got public liquor licenses. My wife is black and I think its an outrage." Now, it is the old man's turn to hide behind a mask of no expression. He says, "Well, you'd feel different." He gets up, picks up his bag of mulched chicken and biscuit, and walks out the door without saying another word or even glancing at me.

I suppose he has just resigned me from the white race.

1 5

DOWN ON THE FARM

EPES, ALABAMA

To call Epes a town would be an exaggeration. There's a post office the size of a family garage. A few old houses, the Leon & Laura Styes grocery store, painted white with turquoise trim, a similarly turquoise-trimmed gas station I'd swear is too ramshackle to be standing, and a sagging shed that has its walls, its boarded-up windows, even its tin roof painted a dayglow fuchsia. Epes, sitting about 125 miles southwest of Birmingham on the Mississippi border, is a town that seems to need bright paint. Past town, I head out Main Street, which quickly turns from macadam to deeply rutted gravel. I enter a woods, pass over a narrow bridge spanning a lime-rock creekbed as white as bone, and emerge on the blacktop of Cedar Hill Drive, which in a few miles will deliver me to the Federation of Southern Cooperatives, where I'm to meet Yvonne Hampton, a forty-nine-year-old woman who works there. She's going to introduce me to Sylvester Clark, a seventy-six-year-old black man who has farmed here all his life.

This piece of Alabama, depending on your outlook, is either God's Country or Nowhereville. Sumter County, where Epes is located, has only 16,174 people living in a space about the size of Connecticut. Seventy percent of those people are black, a lot are poor. Once, this was some of the roughest Jim Crow country in the South. At the green-and-white sign for the federation, I turn right over a cattle gap and follow the tire grooves that run like train tracks in the dirt through a forest and into a beautiful, sunny pasture, where the federation's several buildings sit a hundred yards in the distance. Crape myrtle bushes the color of the dayglow fuchsia shed in Epes line the driveway.

When I find Yvonne Hampton, a short, hefty woman with a Jheri-curl hairdo, she is scratching the hell out of her swollen left ankle, which has just been stung by a mud dauber. "Call me Yvonne," she says with a slow Southern drawl that is, thankfully, easily understandable to me because of Yvonne's crisp diction.

I've stopped being surprised at the speed with which great storms appear and disappear in the South. As Yvonne's Dodge truck heads farther up Cedar Hill Drive at seventy miles an hour, the white billowy clouds atop a picture-board expanse of green countryside go ominous just that fast, as if someone has whipped a dark blanket over a mountain of cotton in the sky. Suddenly, the wind—a howling hot wind, a tornado wind—starts yanking wood from the trees and sending it south. The rain is visible far away, and when we arrive at its edge we seem to crash through a solid wall. So loud is the rain on the truck that I can't hear the radio. Can't see ten feet.

"Quite a storm," I say.

"Oh, this isn't a bad storm," Yvonne says.

"What's a bad storm?"

"When the roof blows off your house."

Talking with Yvonne, I learn that the image I carry in my head, circa 1932, of poor black farmers living in barn-wood shacks deep in the hollers, eking out a living on clay soil, is passé. Today, almost all black small farmers—those with, say, fifty to a hundred acres—have second jobs or retirement incomes. They earn $1,000 to $4,000 a year from farming, plus they put meat, poultry, and vegetables on their tables year-round.

"Why bother for a thousand dollars?" I ask.

"If you don't have any money, a thousand dollars is a lot."

"But it's so much work. Why do people stay?"

"They live here. They have land here. Their family is here. I live a quarter mile from where I was born. My folks was farmers. I love it. I couldn't leave." But steadily, for a hundred years, black small farmers in America have been leaving the land more than twice as fast as white small farmers, who are also an endangered species. Black-owned farmland has fallen from fifteen million acres in 1910 to fewer than five million acres today. Black farmers were traditionally the poorest of the poor. Some were cheated out of their land through intimidation, and until the sixties they had little legal recourse. Many couldn't get bank loans when they needed them.

But perhaps the most noxious grab for black-owned land was the "partition sale." Many uneducated black farmers lacked formal wills, so when they died their land passed in proportional shares to all living heirs. That meant a grandson in, say, Chicago might own a twentieth of the farm. Real estate sleazes could look the man up and pay him, oh, $1,000 for his share. Once the real estate thugs owned an interest in the land, the law allowed them to demand that the entire farm be put up for sale to determine the market value of their paltry piece. Then they could grab the whole farm. And all perfectly legal.

"They stole thousands of acres that way," Yvonne says.

Alabama and other states have reformed their partition sale laws. But like so much to do with race in America, reform was too late for many, and the bitterness runs deep. Hardly a day goes by that Yvonne doesn't hear some resentful young black mention that "the white man" stole his daddy's land. As late as the sixties, Yvonne says, there was a partition sale every month in Sumter County.

The rain stops as suddenly as it started and the sun is out when Yvonne takes an unscheduled stop to say hello to an old black man she notices sitting on his front porch as we drive past. He's reading a 1951 edition of *Practical Carpentry*. He speaks to Yvonne, but his accent is so thick, I can't understand a word. She translates: "He's getting ready to do some carpentry." Looking around at the place, he has one big job ahead of him. Anyway, we sit on the porch—me in the squeaking swing next to a large box of empty beer cans—and Yvonne and the man talk. The only sentence I understand from him in the next ten minutes is, "I born in three one." Then Yvonne tells this joke: The Lord calls the devil on the phone and asks, "Got a minute?" The devil says, "Hold on." When the devil gets back on the phone, he says, sorry, but he's got an emergency in hell. The devil says, "Some niggers done went down there, put the fire out and got a darn air conditioner." The man roars with laughter. Yvonne roars with laughter. They laugh so hard, they must wipe tears from their eyes. They stop laughing. Then they start laughing again. For several minutes, they do this. I smile, pretending to see the humor. After we leave, I ask Yvonne what was so funny about her joke. She starts laughing again.

"Oh, we just always makin' bad situations good."

We meet Mr. Clark near his farmland and follow his truck through a foot-deep swamp of red-dirt mud, down a narrow dirt path to the hundred acres of pasture he rents for his thirty head of Holsteins. Mr. Clark is seventy-six and bald, but with the face and body of a man twenty-five years younger. He wears a black shirt that's spattered with something, maybe white paint, and worn blue jeans. He carries a feed bag. We take up seats on the protruding roots beneath a century-old red oak, and the cows amble over and encircle us like statues, bringing with them the smell of fresh urine. Fortunately, the storm has left behind a strong breeze.

"I do all the tending to 'em—spray 'em, feed 'em," Mr. Clark says in a deep, clear voice. "I do everything. Been farmin' all my days, 'bout sixty years. I was born right here in Epes, 1914. That's a long time ago. I can tell you a lot, all of it hard. I missed education in my life, can't write, just make my mark. I went ta the field at age eleven, in 1925. It was rough! Them old people didn't have no eight hours." "It was sun-up to sun-down—cain ta cain't!" From the time you can see at dawn to the time you can't see at night. "I remember my mother, she would carry us babies out ta the field and the moon be shinin' bright, she'd be so early.

"Those days, we wasn't treated good as a good dog is ta peoples now. Whites was just that bad! Up here in Geiger, used ta hang colored peoples. Come git your child outta bed and beat 'im and you couldn't say nothin'! Always inside, you had ta be a little 'fraid, 'cause you let it out you know somebody gonna kick ya. I have seen white people slap children and you couldn't say nothin'. This black boy went 'round old man Nelson's house and made water, and Nelson's wife said the boy was shakin' his privates at her. And that old man hit him and from that day, he know I don't like 'im.

"It wasn't no one white man, 'cause all of 'em was just alike. I worked on the railroad from eighteen years old, and they would cuss you, call you everything but child a God. Everything! Son a bitch. Everything! Call your mama motherfucker! Then they would slip 'round and make your girlfriend have 'em. I know a white man would take a girl down in the field and force her ta have it. And told that stuff to all us 'fore he died! 'That old girl yonder, I used ta have her many days. Used ta carry her out in the field and push her over.' I told 'im, 'You lucky she wasn't mine. I'd a killed you or you'd a killed me.'

"But God-time have changed it, brother. They say the bottom rail come ta the top 'fore the end a time, and I have lived ta see colored peoples get more a their rights. It a hundred times better, but it a long ways from equal. And I don't never believe it ever gonna be equal. But I do know if these children go ta school and get a good education, it *will* be better. It hurts me ta see black children outta school. See, I missed it. I ain't got no schoolin', nothin'. The black man today, he can't put this on the white man no more. There is a part *you* got ta do! These few cows up here, I feed these cows 'fore I feed myself, every mornin'. I comes up here 'round five-thirty, see, gets outta my bed. When you got somethin', you got ta tend to it, if it ain't but one."

I ask, "Are young blacks tending to it?"

"They ain't in a lotta ways. A heap of us is layin' down. A heap a whites have changed, said, 'I'm sorry.' These young white people today are nice. You don't have no trouble outta them. The Lord done changed it. All the white done did to the black and we still climbin'! They done killed us, done took from us, done beat us, done had our women. And we still movin'! I may be dead, but we gonna get over one a these days.

"My three boys finished college. People were lookin' for 'em ta come home, 'cause I was a poor man. You know what? I was fifty-some years old before I owned a car. I used ta walk. I bought my house and it was a hundred years old, and I was payin' for it. People thought I was bein' cute, thought I shoulda had a car. I wanted me a home and my children in school. White man in the forties tried to get me ta take my boys outta school ta do his field. I said, 'I don't take my boys outta school for my own field.' I didn't have no more trouble with him. Whites give me credit for that. The white man, you watch him, he'll just 'bout go naked to keep his boy in school, 'cause he *know* that what it take.

"A lotta blacks wanted ta see my boys drop outta college. Jealous and evil-hearted. I'm 'bout the onlyest black in Epes got his kids through college. My boy said to me, 'Daddy, you done somethin' ain't nobody in Epes, black or white, ever done: You got three kids in college.' And they all come through this old man. I was a hard hustle! Every year, the Lord give me some peas in my little pea patch, rain or no, 'cause I gets up outta my bed and plants and works. And that's what some blacks hate me for."

Mr. Clark stops talking. He is done. What is there for me to say in the face of his pride and strength and eloquence? Mr. Clark is a poet and I am speechless.

I return to the mundane: "What are those white spots all over your shirt?"

"Don't know," Mr. Clark says, looking down and pulling on his shirt for a better look. "Can't say."

"You been fryin' corn?" Yvonne asks.

"That's it!" Mr. Clark says. "Wife's outta town, and I fried me up some corn. Ya know how that is, splatters."

"I do," says Yvonne. "I do."

16

WHERE THE OLD SOUTH STILL LIVES?

NATCHEZ, MISSISSIPPI

I don't suppose Mammy's Cupboard was what the civic-boosting sloganeers of Natchez had in mind when they dubbed their town of 19,460 people as the place "where the Old South still lives." They meant the more than one hundred grand antebellum homes that dot the Natchez countryside. They meant the downtown homes of the long-dead planter class, the white-pillared churches, the high-bluff waterfront overlooking the Mississippi River just above Louisiana, the steamboats docked at the old Under the Hill neighborhood of Natchez. They meant magnolia trees and mint juleps.

But driving into Natchez on old U.S. Route 61, it's Mammy's Cupboard that greets me first. Picture this: a massive statue—twenty-eight feet high—of a black woman dressed like Aunt Jemima, wearing a red scarf, a white blouse, and a red hoopskirt that actually houses a restaurant. I must stop, go inside, marvel.

"I went in Mammy's," I later tell Ora Frazier.

"Oh, Lord!" she says, laughing. "You should've seen her years ago! They've dressed her up, used to be *very* black. She left a bitter taste in black people's mouths for a long time."

"Can't image why."

Ora Frazier, who is fifty-six, flashes a wide smile, the kind I saw in Yvonne Hampton when she told her joke about the blacks who air-conditioned hell. Mrs. Frazier whispers that black folks in Natchez say, "Well, white people are eatin' under Mammy's dress." This time, I get the joke and we both laugh well.

We're standing in Natchez's riverfront park, a long, narrow strip of grass and aged trees running the length of downtown Natchez and sitting a couple hundred feet above a wide Mississippi River that comes and goes as far as I can see. We've met at the town's historical marker set up in memory of Richard Wright, the black novelist whose books *Native Son* and *Black Boy* portrayed the anguish of growing up black in America before World War II.

I remember reading *Black Boy* after my college years and realizing—far too late to help me with my black dormitory mate Jim Green—that although I might live in the same world as a black man we do not see the same world. For the first time, I realized that the lives of blacks and whites cross in space and time but not in perception, not unlike the different ways that, say, Jews, Christians, and Moslems perceive the same Holy Land. I know this is a simple, mundane insight, but it forever changed the way I thought about blacks, whites, and myself. Richard Wright made me see for the first time that blacks lived every day of their lives as if in land occupied by invaders, and that this made them profoundly different from me.

In *Black Boy*, Wright wrote: "The hostility of the whites had become so deeply implanted in my mind and feelings that it had lost direct connection with the daily environment in which I lived; and my reactions to this hostility fed upon itself. Tension would set in at the mere mention of whites and a vast complex of emotions, involving the whole of my personality, would be aroused. . . . I had never in my life been abused by whites, but I had already become as conditioned to their existence as though I had been the victim of a thousand lynchings."

These words were written more than fifty years ago. But if my journey so far has taught me anything, it is that after all the changes and, yes, the progress, black distrust of whites still runs so deep for so many real reasons that it's yet up to me, up to whites, to prove we aren't the people blacks must assume we are. Does an Israeli assume a newly met Palestinian can be trusted? Does a judge hear without skepticism the alibi of a criminal? Does a father teach his young daughter to trust every nice man she meets on the street? No. I first began to think this way about race from Richard Wright. Out of respect and curiosity, I've come to visit his hometown.

Ora Frazier is an amateur historian and one of the movers behind getting Wright's riverfront marker placed just last summer. Mrs. Frazier has lived in Natchez for thirty-two years. It was her husband Joe Lester Frazier's hometown, and they moved back after college to become teachers in the area's black schools. They lived through school integration. Today Mrs. Frazier is a high school guidance counselor and Mr. Frazier, a former teacher and elementary school principal, is a school district administrator.

"Natchez is thick with black history," says Mrs. Frazier, a short, petite woman in casual slacks and a flowered blouse. "And it's coming out now because of time and a change in attitude, black and white." The mix of power in Natchez has changed. Today, the police chief is black and two blacks sit on the city council. And young whites, she says, just aren't as worried about "prettying up" history as were their parents. For years, whites wrote blacks out of Natchez's plantation tours and its tourist festival plays and musicals—in the same way that Colonial Williamsburg air-brushed blacks out of its history. But as at Colonial Williamsburg, some blacks in Natchez were silent partners in this omission; to them, black history—like Mammy's Cupboard—was a humiliation best ignored.

"We used to have a black gospel choir that sang every spring for the thousands of tourists who come to town from all over the country to tour the antebellum homes," Mrs. Frazier says. It's called the Spring Pilgrimage, big business for Natchez. But since the civil rights movement, blacks had refused to take part, wouldn't sing for the white folks. "This spring, for the first time in almost twenty years, we agreed to do it, if we could write our own story." Plenty of blacks complained. "They didn't think we should be showin' off for white people. They said, 'Everybody knows about slavery and I don't think we need to be tellin' people about it.' I've got a tape of it. Like to see it?"

Mrs. Frazier lives in a nice brick rancher on a quiet street in Natchez. Her husband, Joe Lester—a big, balding fifty-six-year-old man with a mustache and a gentle manner—roots around for the tape, apologizes ahead of time for his blurry camera work, and pops it in the VCR. While he does this, I look around the living room and see three portraits of the Black Madonna with baby Jesus and a collection of pictures depicting Christ's crucifixion with black disciples in African dress.

When it is finally on the TV screen, the Spring Pilgrimage show, "A Southern Road to Freedom," is a stunning performance—a blend of gospel music, song, dance, and storytelling. "Go Down Moses," "Amazing Grace," and "Swing Low, Sweet Chariot" interspersed with the stories of Natchez's antebellum blacks: Ibrahima, born in 1762 the son of a Fulbe empire king in Timbuktu, Africa, and sold into slavery by enemies at age twenty-six. The story of Queen Victoria and Aaron Jackson, former slaves who became prosperous, respected middle-class blacks after the Civil War. The story of John R. Lynch, a slave from Natchez's Taconey Plantation who became a Mississippi delegate and a U.S. congressman, as well as the owner of his own publishing company, the president of the Capitol Savings Bank of Washington, D.C., and the paymaster of the U.S. Army.

"Somebody, black or white, cried every night," Mrs. Frazier says of the two hundred or so Natchez residents and tourists who packed the show three nights a week for four weeks. "One or two whites came up to me and said, 'I am so sorry. I am so sorry.' Many people said they were so glad they had come and seen the other side. They said, 'This is great. This is good.'"

I ask, "What did it feel like to see that show?"

"Really," Mr. Frazier says, "I felt proud."

"It made me think that life has genuinely changed," Mrs. Frazier says. "We have a long way to go, but it has changed."

The Fraziers would like to show me around Natchez, take me to meet the daughter of Queen Victoria and Aaron Jackson, a 105-year-old woman named Annie Fields who still lives in the house her parents built in 1887, take me past the house where it's believed Richard Wright once lived with his mother.

"People have told us that Richard Wright lived here about 1912 or 13, sometime before 1917," Mrs. Frazier says, as we arrive at 20 East Woodlawn Street. "We believe maybe his grandmother lived next door after she left the Traveler's Rest Plantation." Wright's boyhood home is an ancient, little clapboard house with scabbing white paint and a rusted tin roof. A cozy picket fence runs the length of the front yard, and only the shiny aluminum screen door seems to mark the passage of nearly a century.

"Did his books ring true to you?" I ask Mr. Frazier.

Even in his day, growing up in the forties, Mr. Frazier says, a black boy walked carefully. "Mothers told their sons to always say, 'Yes, sir,' to a white man. And never get upset about anything said to you by a white. And don't pay any attention to white girls. Mothers had to teach this fear to their sons. The fear of going into certain neighborhoods, of speaking your mind. I didn't understand why. They were just rules." Later, he understood.

We find Annie Fields in her bed, a big double bed in the middle of a large sunny room. Although she's blind, the color in her eyes gone flat, she lies facing the bright window, resting between perfectly white sheets. Only her small head and the tips of her fingers peek out from the ocean of white, and she looks as if she is about to disappear into the door of heaven. Her face, amazingly, is smooth and unwrinkled.

"Hello, Nanny, how you doin'?" Mrs. Frazier asks.

"Fine, how you doin'?" Mrs. Fields answers, firm and clear.

"Pretty good, Nanny. I have a man here I want to meet you."

"My name is Annie Fields. I'm one hundred and five."

"Lord," I say, "you were born in 1885."

"Eighty-four. I'll be one hundred and six in November."

"She's been in this house since she was two years old," says Mrs. Fields's sixty-four-year-old granddaughter Dorothy Gibson, who lives with Mrs. Fields and cares for her.

"Course, I married and moved out," Annie Fields says softly, "but I came back." The Fraziers and Mrs. Fields talk for a few minutes, but she is drifting off to sleep and we soon retire to the living room, where Mr. Frazier asks Dorothy Gibson if she would mind showing me "the pouch." She leaves the room and returns with a small, aged blue-and-beige gingham pouch about the size of a boy's marble bag. I think to myself that when Mrs. Fields and the pouch were young together its beige was probably white. "You are honored to view this," Mr. Frazier says, quite seriously. "She doesn't take these out for anybody. They're too fragile."

From the gingham pouch, Dorothy Gibson gingerly removes onto the coffee table a cache of decaying yellow documents and a photograph of Mrs. Fields's mother, Queen Victoria Jackson, who was beautiful with dark skin and green eyes, and, in this picture, beautifully dressed in a long dark skirt and fine white blouse. As the Spring Pilgrimage presentation had said, Mrs. Fields's family was relatively affluent. Her father, Aaron, was a gardener, which was a good job in 1880. From the gingham pouch also comes a list of the building materials used for the house in which we sit: $861.81 for materials and land; $3 to dig the outhouse; $43.20 for the 6,150 bricks; $29.75 for the 8,500 shingles. Also in the pouch is a document dated July 17, 1895, Certificate No. 415.790, from the U.S. Department of the Interior that awarded Queen Victoria Jackson a pension as the wife of a Civil War Veteran. Aaron Jackson had served in the C90th Regiment New York Voluntary Infantry.

After the pouch is put away, Ms. Gibson asks, "Did you see Grandma Nanny's skin? It's so soft, and her hair, it's still not white, but dark gray. Nowadays, she talks and talks to people who are long dead, as if they were alive. Mr. Leon Stewart will be helping her gather greens. I'd say, 'Mr. Stewart isn't here, Nanny.' And she'd say, 'Yes, he is. Don't you see 'im? Right over there.' Every time I fix mustard greens, it reminds her of her mother. When she goes off, she talks about getting back home to her mother, who is eighty-six and at home alone. Her mother died at age eighty-six in 1927. Sometimes she'll go off for twenty-four hours without sleeping. We'll say, 'Nanny's got company in there.'"

"Quite a journey," I say.

"Yes, it is," Ms. Gibson says. "That's what it is."

The Fraziers have one more person they'd like me to meet, Denise Ford, who was once Mr. Frazier's secretary when he was a grade school principal. "Her father was Wharlest Jackson," Mr. Frazier says. "He was blown up in his truck back in the sixties, after he applied for a foreman's job at the Armstrong Rubber plant."

"Where do I know that name?" I ask.

"Don't know," says Mr. Frazier.

"Is he on the Civil Rights Memorial in Montgomery?"

"Yes, that's him."

Denise Ford, who is thirty-three, was a young girl when her father was murdered on February 27, 1967. He had punched out at work at 8:01 P.M. and driven up Natchez's Brenham Avenue and then along Minor Street almost to North Pine, which is now Martin Luther King Jr. Street, when the bomb blew. Despite a $35,000 reward, no one was ever arrested in the slaying, not to this day. Jackson was thirty-seven years old, married, with five children. After all these years, Denise's eyes water when she talks about her father.

"Nobody else would go after the promotion, so he did," she says. "He never got it. He died instantly."

"Do you think of your father as a hero?" I ask

"No, not really, just Daddy."

"Everyone else does," Mr. Frazier says.

"It boggles the mind," I say, "to think that somewhere in this little town are the one, two, or three people who did this, and they've kept it a secret. And that you may, at some point, have had a conversation with the murderer himself on the street, or gotten your car repaired by him."

Denise raises an eyebrow, shrugs. "Having Daddy's name put on the Civil Rights Memorial was the best gift they could have given," she says. "His name had just died down and nobody seemed to talk about or remember what he had done. The service at the memorial was overwhelming. *Amazing* is the word I would use. You know, I didn't know until I saw the pictures that so many killed were white. We all reminisced over what had happened to each of us—to our fathers, our brothers, our sisters. It was amazing." In twenty years, Denise had never really put her father to rest until that day at the memorial.

"After the service," Mr. Frazier says, "the white teachers and administrators at school asked, 'Is that *our* Denise? Was that *her* father?' A couple of white teachers had told me that they didn't understand why she seemed so bitter. White teachers thought Denise wasn't as kind and helpful to them as she was to black teachers. After the service, one said, 'I don't know if I'd be even as pleasant as she is.' It changed a lot of them. They felt self-conscious around her for a long time."

"As if they shared in the guilt?" I ask.

"It was like they wanted to say, 'I'm sorry,'" Denise says. "I had several whites come to me and tell me that."

"Did it help?"

"It did. Yes, it did."

"It was a sad, awful thing," Mr. Frazier says, "but Wharlest Jackson didn't die in vain. The blacks closed this town down. It took a year, but things never were the same after the bombing." Blacks armed themselves and patrolled the streets and guarded their leaders' houses. A lot of black churches had been burned before the bombing, but very few afterward. "It was like Watts: It really pulled people together. The movement started—boycotts, picketing—and some whites finally spoke up. Today, some of the young whites are truly changed." Here, Mr. Frazier hesitates. "But so many fled the schools with integration and went to the private academies. I can't help but think *they* still don't like blacks."

At 8:30 the next morning, Sunday, church day in Natchez, I stop at the Bellemont Laundromat before leaving town. It's a beat-up joint in a little strip shopping center next to Big Joes (no possessive apostrophe) Ribs, just up the road from Mammy's Cupboard. Half the fluorescent light tubes are burned out, the TV is disconnected, the three garbage cans are full. I'm alone in the place, putting my washed clothes in the dryer when the phone rings—and rings and rings. I know it's not for this itinerant, and I don't answer. But just after it stops ringing, a young white woman walks in with curtains to wash and nods hello.

"I think your husband was trying to reach you," I say. "The phone was just ringing off the hook."

"Nope, ain't married. Prob'ly some nigger."

I try to hide my incredulity. "What?"

"Yep, prob'ly some nigger."

"Ah, OK." What to say? From what depths did this woman make the link between my casual remark and her answer? Through what synaptic (or social) glitch did she see a connection? She looks so "normal," in shorts and a T-shirt. She's driving a sensible American car. But she's from another planet. Scotty, beam her up!

"What ya doin' here?" she asks.

"Just traveling the country. Where you work?"

"I'm a teacher."

I think of Mr. Frazier's last remark. "Where?"

The woman names one of the region's many private white schools. In a few minutes, when her curtains are sloshing in the washer, she says a pleasant good-bye and goes out to her sensible American car to read the paper. I study her through the window: She looks so *normal*. No wonder that, fifty years after Richard Wright, I, we, whites must each day still prove that we are not her.

1 7

THE HOUSE WHERE MARTIN WEPT

MARKS, MISSISSIPPI

In the midst of field after field of flat farmland demarcated by distant tree lines that separate red-flowered cotton plants, stumpy soy beans, and stalks of rice that roll in the breeze like the waves of a bright green sea, Marks, Mississippi, is a brief footnote in history. Only weeks before his assassination in 1968, Martin Luther King, Jr., visited the town's poor black Cotton Street neighborhood and was so moved by the destitution he saw that he cried. Marks became "the town where Martin wept."

I'm headed to Clarksdale, the Mississippi Delta town where blues music was born, to visit Wade Walton, the barber and harmonica player recommended to me back in Williamsburg, Virginia. I'm hoping to have some fun. But Marks is on the way, so when I see the sign that says WELCOME TO MARKS, I stop at Holmans Amoco for directions. I make the few turns necessary to find Cotton Street, a beaten lane surrounded by some of the roughest-looking houses I've ever seen—shotgun shacks with rusty tin roofs, shanties with barn-wood siding cracked to the weather, places built haphazardly with cast-off lumber. I turn onto the gravel path that is Sims Street and follow it a short distance until it disappears into a field of tall weeds. To my right, shrouded in undergrowth, is what's left of the house where local legend says Martin wept.

It's a tiny green-roofed shack, abandoned and twisting in different directions as if it can't decide which way to fall. The gray asbestos siding has risen with the distortion, the window mullions have popped their eyes, the front porch has collapsed at one end, and the brick chimney has tilted. When Martin Luther King came to the Cotton Street neighborhood, he visited many homes, and this one on Sims was no better or worse. But the neighborhood often flooded after heavy rains, and that day the end of Sims Street was a lake. King got to the house by small boat, and there he found a family living as if on an island in the floodwaters, an island of poverty amid an American sea of plenty. He cried.

The front door to the house is hanging off its hinges today, and, while wondering just what kind of snakes populate the Mississippi Delta, I push it aside and walk in. The three rooms of the house are revealed in shards of light that cast through the naked windows and the holes in the roof. Once my eyes have adjusted, I can see that no one has lived here, I hope, for a long time. A fragment of ratty green carpet covers a piece of the floor. Hunks of cheap paneling are falling off the walls and ceiling and their newspaper-insulation innards have settled around the room. Doors have fallen backwards, wasps fly everywhere, and red paint has been splattered on a remaining white wall. In the sweltering Mississippi heat, the whole place has the humid, claustrophobic smell of water-rotting wood. But if you swept up the trash, chased out the wasps, and painted the walls, this house wouldn't be much worse than some of the others in the neighborhood.

Across the street, at a sagging clapboard house, I talk to Bertha Lee Turner, a short and thick eighty-one-year-old black woman in a crisply clean white house dress and white go-ahead slippers. She lived here when King visited, although she wasn't home that day. "It's worser now than it's ever been," Ms. Turner says. She points to the floodwater line a couple feet above her foundation. "It gets higher and higher every year." Of the shack across the road, she says, "That house wasn't in that bad a shape. That house was a *good* house."

I ask, "Are things better since Martin came?"

"I think so. They get food stamps and lots of 'em on the welfare. I think it's better. They ain't workin' hard like they used ta. They used ta have ta chop cotton, pick cotton. I know'd I was poor. We poor yet, ain't we? I'm poor now."

At one of the many other shanty houses in the neighborhood are seven black children laughing and running, playing in a dirt yard. A stagnant canal of cloudy green septic water reeks at their feet. They stop and stand stiffly when I introduce myself. I ask if they know that Martin Luther King once visited their neighborhood. They stare at the ground, kick the dirt for a long moment, until an older boy, a boy in high school, speaks up confidently. "He fell to his knees and cried at that house over there."

I ask, "You got any good white friends?"

"Skateboard friends," a different boy says.

"Do you go visit them?"

"Sometimes."

"You ever invite them to your house?"

A long silence. "They don't know how ta get here."

Then the confident boy speaks again. "Maybe they won't like our neighborhood. The way we live."

"What way is that?"

"Floodwater, tin houses, stuff like that."

"Is it that they wouldn't like the way you live or do you not want them to *see* the way you live?"

Another long pause, until the confident boy speaks. "We don't want them ta *see* the way we live."

"It's embarrassing to you?"

"Yeah."

"Do the white kids live this way?"

"No! Brick houses, big *fine* houses, sidewalks."

"What do you think when you visit them?"

He hesitates. "Why couldn't we live in houses like theirs?"

"And why can't you?"

"Our parents didn't have the right educations."

"How do you do in school?"

"Straight-A work."

"What do you want to be?"

"An architect."

"Where do you want to go to college?"

"Harvard. Or Yale."

His answer catches me off guard, and I feel simultaneously glad for his ambition and saddened at the long odds he faces. More than twenty years after Martin Luther King wept on this street, I can think of nothing to say except, "I wish you the best."

1 8

WHERE THE BLUES WERE BORN

CLARKSDALE, MISSISSIPPI

Just for kicks, I pop in a Robert Johnson tape and head for the intersection of Route 61 and Highway 49, where the renowned thirties bluesman is supposed to have sold his soul to the devil in return for the demonic secrets of guitar picking. The roads meet in Clarksdale, the little Mississippi Delta city of 19,717 folks about an hour south of Memphis and a few minutes east of the Mississippi River, where in the last century the most dispossessed of Americans created the hard-edged, brutally honest, wailing, shouting, crying music that has shaped American music since, especially jazz and rock 'n' roll. As I've said before, I can't play a note, but I've always loved the blues. And I now have a theory about why that is, about why the blues so capture white imaginations.

It struck me in Montgomery, Alabama, when Bryan Stevenson, the black Harvard law school graduate working for next to nothing to save men from execution, told me that people who call him a hero are really bemoaning what's missing in their own lives: commitment, passion, and sacrifice. That is the secret of the blues. Affluence and respectability demand a propriety that keeps us always looking over our shoulders for the judgments of others. And as modern folk, we've also become so adept at intellectualizing life that too often we aren't living life but merely thinking about living life. Enter into this void the blues, as symbol and evidence—as symbol because their unmediated emotion reminds us of what's missing in our lives, and as evidence because for all our advantages, we modern folks didn't, couldn't, make the blues.

Famed British rock 'n' roller Eric Clapton, who with Cream recorded a version of Robert Johnson's "Cross Road Blues" in which Johnson supposedly reveals his deal with Satan, displays these dual sentiments in the liner notes to the Columbia Records collection of Johnson's songs: "All the music I'd heard up till that time seemed to be structured in some way for recording. What struck me about the Robert Johnson album was that it seemed like he wasn't playing for an audience at all... he was just playing for himself.... He was true, absolutely, to his own vision.... I know when I first heard it, it called to me in my confusion, it seemed to echo something that I had always felt."

The word for it is *authentic*. That's Robert Johnson and that's the blues. They are a cry of the soul, without slippage between intellect and emotion. A blues guitar is not a guitar but an extension of the human voice. The human voice is not a human voice but an evocation of the spirit. The blues are ancient intuition standing against modern analysis. As the old blues musicians say, you don't play the blues, you live the blues.

At the intersection of Route 61 and Highway 49, I find gas stations, convenience stores, and Abe's barbecue. Not exactly the image I had in mind. But sixty years ago this corner was country, and because it was known locally as "the crossroads," it has come to be thought of as the place where Johnson cut his apocryphal devil's deal. Robert Johnson, with a guitar that is a voice and a voice that is an evocation of the spirit, told it this way:

> I went to the crossroad
> fell down on my knees.
> Asked the Lord above "Have mercy
> save poor Bob, if you please."

. . . You can run
tell my friend-boy Willie Brown
Lord, that I'm standin' at the crossroad, babe
I believe I'm sinkin' down.

The next morning, I find Wade Walton at his barber shop. He's a short, thin man with a frown that seems set on his face. He has a full mustache, large glasses beneath high, dark brows, and thick natural hair. He wears burnt-orange slacks, a white short-sleeved shirt, a small black bow tie, a black belt, black leather shoes, and white socks. A pack of Kool cigarettes shows through his left breast pocket. He nods hello when I introduce myself and then goes back to running the clippers over the head of a boy in the swiveling barber's chair. By the window, an old man sits quietly while a black kitten on the sill behind him dabs playfully at the man's gray hair.

Wade knew I was coming, but for more than an hour it's clear he's ignoring me. Won't look at me, answers my few questions with a gruff yes or no. Not knowing what to make of this icy hello, I sit back and examine his shop, which is filled with the scents of male tonics and powders. It's in a cinder-block building maybe fifteen feet wide, maybe fifty feet long. The inside of the shop is painted white with bright blue trim that matches the bright blue floor. Wade uses only about a third of the space, and the rest of the tunnel-shaped room runs off into shadows at the far end. On the wall are a newspaper clipping about the day Wade was inducted into the Clarksdale Hall of Fame and an autographed drawing of electric-bluesman B.B. King, who's from nearby Itta Bena, Mississippi. High on the wall, placed prominently above the mirrors, is a framed photograph of Wade Walton playing his harmonica.

I'm beginning to think my visit is a bust, when I say, "Don R. Hill told me I had to visit Wade Walton." At that, Wade turns off his clippers and looks over at me with a changed expression, with a wide smile. He nearly runs across the room, shakes my hand, squeezes my shoulder. "You're a friend of Don R. Hill," he says. "Why didn't ya say so?"

"Ah, well, we're not *close* friends," I say, not wanting to lie but also not wanting to tell Wade that I met Don Hill for only about ten minutes while on my visit to Colonial Williamsburg. Wade goes on to tell me that Don R. Hill is one of the finest men he's ever known, that

Don R. Hill, a white man who is today an anthropologist, and a friend came to Clarksdale in 1958 to record local blues musicians. The three of them went out to the infamous Parchman Farm state prison and asked for permission to record the songs of black inmates. The request got Don Hill and his friend run out of Mississippi by the state police. But a few years later, Don still helped Wade record his first and only album, "The Blues of Wade Walton: Shake 'Em on Down."

"So what do you wanta know?" Wade asks.

Born in 1923, Wade was the sixteenth of seventeen children. His father was a sharecropper—as was nearly everybody, black or white, who didn't own land in the South of those days. They lived out on the Head Plantation, which was near Parchman Farm. As a boy, Wade worked on the plantation like everyone else. But on Sundays, he danced and sang for the Parchman convicts, who'd toss nickels as his reward. By the time Wade was a teenager, he was playing the guitar and harmonica for tips. He went to barber school and in 1943 opened shop in Clarksdale's black neighborhood. During the day, Wade cut the hair of musicians such as Sonny Boy Williams and Ike Turner, later of Ike and Tina Turner fame. At night, he played the juke joints in Clarksdale and surrounding Coahoma County, which boasted dozens of great blues players, including Robert Johnson, Charlie Patton, Arthur "Big Boy" Crudup, Muddy Waters, Howlin' Wolf, Elmore James, Junior Parker, and John Lee Hooker.

It's no accident that Mississippi also boasted more sharecroppers than any state in the nation. The life of the sharecropper was deplorable: dawn-to-dusk hours, wooden shacks for houses, constant indebtedness to the plantation owners. But half the South's sharecroppers were also white, and they didn't create blues music. What's supposed to have made the difference were the indignities of racism and the musical and religious traditions of Africa and African Americans: the intense emotionalism of black religion, the call-and-response of preacher and congregation, the spontaneity and improvisation of black religion and music, and the belief that the world, awful as it is, must be seen and described with blunt honesty. All these things made the blues.

I ask Wade, "Why didn't you leave Clarksdale and become a professional like everybody else?"

"I didn't wanta sleep in a suitcase," Wade says as he cuts the head of hair that the kitten was just pawing. He had a wife and family he wouldn't leave behind. "They said I coulda been a star in the music business, but I loved barberin' too well." He laughs, saying that he played some wild joints as a young man. "But I wouldn't ever go in a place where I couldn't get back to be in the barber shop the next day." Wade knew Muddy Waters and Howlin' Wolf, and he even vaguely remembers Charlie Patton, who is believed to have been a teacher to Robert Johnson. Wade clicks off a few of the bluesmen with whom he's jammed—John Lee Hooker, Frank Frost, Junior Parker, Big Jack Johnson.

For the next few hours, Wade cuts hair, stops occasionally to play his mesmerizing harmonica, and tells stories. There was the time B.B. King was playing a little road house in Indianola when Howlin' Wolf walked in. Naturally, B.B. asked him to sing. Well, Howlin' Wolf was depressed that night, and he sang so sad and so low that he "tore that house up," Wade says. "I'll never forget the number he did: 'Oh shake it for me, baby, oh shake it for me, oh shake, little baby, shake it like a willow tree.' Oh, man! *Good God!*"

Wade tells about the time in 1937 when the great blues singer Bessie Smith was in a car accident outside town and died in a segregated black clinic in Clarksdale. He tells about the plantation owner who let one of his black sharecroppers cuss him out in front of a white friend, who said, "I wouldn't take that from no nigger." The plantation owner said, "I takes that cursin'. That nigger makes seventy-five bales a cotton a year. And I takes that, too."

I ask, "But why did the music show up here?"

"You put it like this," Wade says. "It's the Cotton Belt and years back there were a lotta black sharecroppers on the white farms. Some a them didn't earn nothin'. There wasn't too much recreation and people lived way out in the country, and they found their ways of havin' their fun. They made corn whiskey. They made their fun and they made their own music."

An older black man who is waiting for a haircut says, "Music was another language. They sang the blues from way down here." He points to his heart, closes his eyes, squinches his face, and cuts loose in a booming baritone: "I suuuuuuuure wanta seeee my baaaby." He claps his hands, laughs, and sings the line again. "I suuuuuuuure wanta seeee my baaaby." Then he says, "You got ambivalent feelings, sad feelings and good feelings." Like the joke about the plantation owner taking the black man's cussing as well as his cotton, the blues are serious and humorous at once. "The music brings out good feel-ings *and* bad feelings," the man says. "It wasn't just music. They lived it. The stuff white men used ta do, call you niggers and mess with our women. You wanta hear the truth? You wanta get down to it? The blues was our way to release the pressure." He sings another line, this one from a Muddy Waters song, "An*ooo*ther mule is ki*iic*kin' in my st*aaa*ll." He says, "He's not talkin' 'bout a mule. He's talkin' 'bout another man havin' his woman." And the man sings, "E*eeeeee*vil, *eeeeee*vil's in m*yyyyyy* home."

Another older black man who is also waiting for a haircut says, "They was a lotta cotton raised on sharecropper's backs. I remember doin' thirty-six bales a cotton and clearin' one hundred dollars." He laughs deeply. "It wasn't no sharecroppin', 'cause there wasn't no share." But Wade interrupts, saying that the blues grew from more than just the evils of sharecropping and racism.

"You gotta play the blues from love, not hate," he says. "See, kids today don't know how ta *love*. My mama made me go ta Sunday school, shoes or no shoes. They don't make children go ta Sunday school no more." The blues didn't come about just because black peo-ple were poor and mistreated, Wade believes, the blues came about because of the way black people *reacted* to being poor and mistreated. The secret to black blues, Wade says, is that blacks in the delta didn't let themselves be eaten up by hatred. And that love—or that refusal to hate, anyway—is the soul of the music. A black kid can be poor and mistreated in Chicago, but if he's only angry, not feeling good and bad, love and hate, he'll never sing the blues.

Wade says, "You gotta *love* people to play the blues."

A young black man, twenty-two years old, has been waiting for Wade to give him a modern-day fade haircut and listening quietly. When he ascends to the swivel chair, I ask, "What about you?"

Hesitantly, he says, "I just can't *feel* the blues."

"What music do you like?"

"Pop, R&B, rap. Stevie Wonder. Bobby Brown."

I ask, "Do the blues sound like cotton-picker music to you?"

"Some of it do." Everyone is quiet and the young man says, "I like B.B. King. He's the grandfather of the blues."

I say, "He's more like the grandson, isn't he?" And over the buzz of his fade-cutting clippers, Wade nods.

Wade Walton then does me a great honor. He has only one copy of the album he recorded thirty years ago, but he lets me borrow it and take it to the Coahoma County Library for listening. It's a wonderful album, with guitar and harmonica songs titled "Big Fat Mamma," "Choo Choo De Shoo Shoo," and "Rock Me, Mamma" (and Wade doesn't mean in the cradle, baby). But on side two, I come to it—"Parchman Farm"—a Wade Walton guitar ballad about the time he, Don R. Hill, and Don's friend went to Parchman Farm prison, now renamed the State Penitentiary at Parchman, and asked to record the blues songs of its black prisoners.

In the years soon after the men's visit in 1958, Parchman became infamous for its brutality and corruption. Inmates were regularly beaten and even killed by armed guards. The hellhole was finally reformed in the seventies. But what an ironic revenge Wade Walton exacted for his mistreatment at Parchman: with a guitar that intones evil, he immortalizes Parchman's "Mr. Harpole" in a way nobody wants to be remembered. Wade has Mr. Harpole—who was Bill Harpole, Parchman's superintendent from 1956 to 1960 and later a Mississippi state senator—tell Don R. Hill and his friend they "should have known better than to come in here with a nigger." Harpole tells Wade, "Boy, if you knowed like I know, you'd be out of here runnin'," which Wade was, lickety-split. In blues tradition, Wade's "Parchman Farm" is both serious and funny. Back at the barber shop, where Wade gives me a quick trim around the ears, I say, "You got even with Mr. Harpole." Wade smiles.

"By the way," I ask, "why are we white people so interested in how you black folks came to sing the blues anyway?"

"It looks like it's because whatever we did, we did it outta nothin'," Wade says. "We've taken zero and went ta a hundred, where you started at fifty and went ta ninety." We both laugh. It is a good bluesman's answer: serious and funny.

That night at my motel, I see a basketball court out back, borrow a ball at the front desk, and go out to shoot some hoops. After a few minutes, I notice a white boy, probably nine or ten years old, my son's age, staring at me from the sidelines.

"You wanta shoot some baskets?"

"Yeah."

"You any good?"

"Yeah, I'm real good. I play with niggers."

Well, here we go again. But I'm finally getting the knack of this Southern white etiquette among perfect strangers, and I'm speechless for only an instant. "You go to school with 'em?"

"No, no, no," the boy says with distaste. "But I live by a bunch of 'em. They go ta nigger school, public nigger school."

"Where do you go to school?"

He names a private academy, and then asks, "Can you dunk?"

"Not even close."

"Just about every short nigger I know can dunk."

"Is that so?"

After a few minutes, the boy says, "Nice meetin' ya," tosses me the ball, and runs off, and I try to think of him as Wade Walton might. The boy's prejudice is sickening, makes me sad and angry. But it's also hilarious, because it makes him and others like him, North and South, sound so dumb. It makes him the joke—and he doesn't even know it! I want to scream, cry, and laugh at once. I do understand better: This boy will never sing the blues, but he's certainly one of the reasons we still have the blues.

1 9

A DIFFERENT MEASURING ROD

TUNICA COUNTY, MISSISSIPPI

On the way to visit a poor man who lives in the poorest county in America, I see a small, white, flat-roofed, concrete building in need of paint along the edge of Route 61, the famous two-lane road that runs just east of the Mississippi River from New Orleans to Thunder Bay in Canada. It was once a main roadway exit for the earliest of the five million blacks who, with the start of World War II, eventually abandoned the South for good factory jobs and relative freedom in the North. The road is still surrounded by vast expanses of cotton, but today that cotton is tended not by an army of black pickers but by men on tractors, five of which are this morning pulling through the distant field like giant turtles in a race, leaving red-dust tails hanging behind them on a blue horizon.

The man I'm going to visit, Virgil Fleming, drives a tractor for $4.50 an hour. He's one of the lucky ones. Since the 1940s, farm mechanization has forced Tunica's blacks north and west and left Tunica County with the fallout. Today, more than half of Tunica's black residents, who make up three-quarters of the county's 8,164 people, live in poverty, and the single major source of income is government transfer payments to the poor—this in a county with more than two hundred farm operations with products valued at more than $41 million and a reputed population of more than thirty-five millionaires.

On the front of the small concrete building on the edge of Route 61, I notice a rough, hand-written sign that is emblematic of the region's hardscrabble existence:

> J+JOLDFASHIONCOOKINGANDGROC
> ERIES.BREAKFAST.HOTLUNCHE S.

At Virgil Fleming's place in the Tunica County countryside, living is as make-do as that hand-scrawled sign. I find Virgil's spread in a small enclave of rough houses and trailers. His two trailers—the little one a traveler on wheels and the bigger one a house model—are connected, and an unpainted plywood porch has been added. A small stream of septic-clouded water runs along the road that fronts the property. Virgil's land, which he rents for $30 a month, is cordoned off with a sagging, leaning, unpainted fence. He has a big garden and corrals that hold his chickens, hogs, and ducks. There's a tin-roofed shed with a Hula-Hoop on top of it, a basketball rim that sags almost perpendicular to the ground, a pile of old tires, a crowd of rusted barrels, and an old sink lying on the ground. All of it is atop a yard of hard dirt.

Virgil Fleming, a tall, strong man who wears blue work pants and an untucked work shirt, greets me at the door. Once inside the compact house trailer, he looks even taller and stronger. At age fifty-eight, he has an unruly shock of still-dark hair, a booming voice, a great smile. When he motions me to the couch, I notice that the index finger is missing from his left hand. The tiny living room where we sit has brown panel walls decorated with framed photos of the thirteen children Virgil and his wife are raising—ages seventeen years to nine months. Three of the kids are from his previous marriage, five are from her first marriage, and five are her grandchildren. Home today are Mrs. Fleming and ten of the kids. With all of us and the couch, chairs, coffee table, end table, TV, and VCR, the room is snug. The place isn't exactly tidy, but it's clean and the air smells of dish soap. It's a few minutes before I notice the cockroach climbing up the wall behind Mr. Fleming. Then the cockroach on the floor between his legs. Then on the floor by the legs of one of Virgil Fleming's little girls, who pushes it away with her right foot. Then on the walls around the room, on the pictures, the TV, the coffee table. Mrs. Fleming sprays Black Flag all the time, but those cockroaches are tough.

"So where are you from?" I ask Mr. Fleming.

Virgil Fleming was born only about five miles west of here, and his father was a sharecropper. "He was a sharecropper like me," Mr. Fleming says in a confident, expansive voice. "We was *po', po', po'!*" he says, laughing deeply. "It was fearsome! It was horrible! Man, I come up *hard!* I started ta work when I was seven years old. I pulled worms for 'bout two hundred choppers."

"Choppers?" I ask.

"Cotton choppers! From cain ta cain't. My pay was $2 a week for five days, and I got 15 cents outta that. That was my allowance. I bought candy and bologna. I stayed in school long enough ta learn how ta spell *winky.*"

"To spell *what?*" I ask.

"Winky. W-I-N-K-Y. Winky."

"What's *winky?*"

"That was the marking on the back of the book. The name 'Winky.' That's the only schoolin' I had."

"How did white people treat you?"

"Hmmmmm," Mr. Fleming says, tilting his head and eyeing me carefully. "They treated ya, hmmmmm, they treated ya just about like you would treat a dog that you didn't care anything about." At this, he roars with dark laughter. "If you were workin' for Mr. Tom over here, Mr. Charlie'd say, 'You don't have ta put up with that stuff.' Well, he'd treat you a little better. And you'd ease on down the line like that from one ta the other, and they'd treat ya a little bit better, git a little more money, talk to ya mo' better. But them rough ones, them there guys what believed in that whuppin', and you be workin' and he got the horse in your back and you choppin' cotton and he put that horse in your back and push."

"The horse?" I ask.

"Yeah, they had them horses trained!" And Mr. Fleming laughs again. "You think that's a joke, but that's true."

Then the subject changes. "See, long as you honored them white folks—'Yasuh, boss'— and tipped your hat, you was their nigger. He come ta you and ask you somethin' or another about a brother, and you told 'im, you was his nigger. But what you was doin', you wasn't doin' nothin' but white mouthin', tattlin'.'"

But no matter how much "Yasuhin'" a black man or woman did, when they got back to their homes, they lashed out. "They'd say everything! And they'd send one a us children out ta see was any a them listen'. You stayed out there and watched." Inside, he says, the grown-ups would say, "'Oh, Mr. So and So, I'll tell you one thing, I feel like takin' a stick and beatin' his god-damned brains out!' What was it the cooks used ta say? They'd spit in the food." He laughs again. "My mama was cookin' for old man Forrest. Mama was cookin' for him and raised his little children, and the food that mama would spit in, she wouldn't give ta the children. Or they'd put a pinch a snuff in. They called themselves gettin' back at 'em." Mr. Fleming, who has been enjoying this story, suddenly stops laughing and turns serious. "But they couldn't get back at them folks, unh-unh, no way." He shakes his head somberly. "Life was hell! They 'lowed ya ta go out on a Saturday and play ball on a Sunday, but be there Monday mornin'! They had the M's wrote up on the wall: 'Meet My Mule Monday Morning, Motherfucker.'" He roars with laughter.

"*No!*" I say.

He repeats, "'Meet My Mule Monday Morning, Motherfucker.'"

Mr. Fleming sharecropped until he was twenty-two years old. But he never went into debt to the plantation owners like so many others who had to steal away at night to go north to escape their creditors. "Let's just lay it on the line: I made a lotta corn whiskey. That was the only way." In the early fifties, Mr. Fleming hitched a ride on Route 61 with some men who'd come to buy bootleg whiskey. He found a job in a Memphis steel mill and was eventually transferred to Buffalo, New York, where he worked in a steel mill making $13.65 an hour. "I felt like I had stepped outta hell into heaven," he says. "I was treated like a king and I got king's pay. They approached me as 'Mr. Fleming'—and that's the men that run the plant! People in the North, they more civilized than these here Southerners. They just don't know how ta treat people, white or black. In the North you could go anywhere you wanted. If you wanted ta sit down and order a steak, you could sit down and order a steak. They treated you with respect, because your money was green." But after ten years, Mr. Fleming had the factory accident that cost him his left index finger.

"That added up to thirty-seven thousand five hundred and fifty-one dollars and thirty-seven cents," he says. "I can remember that to the penny till the day I die."

Mr. Fleming moved back South and eventually returned to Tunica. I ask how it had changed. "Just as much as midnight and day," he says. "It was just different all the way around. Couldn't nobody compel you ta work no mo'. But back then they could compel you ta work whether you was sick or wasn't sick. You walked the street with a necktie, the boss man or some a them other white guys would choke you ta death with your own necktie. I'm tellin' ya like it was: 'Nigger, you s'posed ta be in the field workin'!' It's done changed a whole lot. It gettin' better and better every year. They treats ya like men nowadays."

Nowadays Mr. Fleming works nine hours a day driving a tractor, a nice tractor with a radio and cassette player. He earns about $8,000 a year and gets unemployment pay during the cold winter months when he's out of work. He also puts food on the table by net fishing the creeks for buffalo, carp, and catfish. During my conversation with Mr. Fleming, the ten children have been remarkably polite. The baby has cried only occasionally, and the others have sat quietly and listened intently, got up and made hot dogs for dinner, offered me one, eaten, and then put the dirty dishes in the sink. "What do you hope for your children?" I ask.

"I hope they get a education as best they can and get themselves a decent job," Mr. Fleming says.

"How are they doing in school?"

Two of the Flemings' teenaged girls moan, and I can see that this is something the Fleming family has discussed before. Mr. Fleming says they're doing "fair." But this is in a Tunica County school system that ranks near the bottom of Mississippi's school districts in expenditures per student. The Tunica public schools are virtually all black, with the county's few hundred white students attending private school.

"What do you want to do with your lives?" I ask the girls.

"I wanta be a cosmetologist and a secretary," one says.

"A cosmetologist and a doctor," says the other.

Just then, before I can ask about the girls' ambitions, I notice that each has her initial inscribed on a gold front tooth. "You girls have designer teeth!" I say. Proudly, Mr. Fleming announces, "They cost ninety-nine dollars each."

I ask the girls, "Do you feel poor?"

"I do," says one girl. "I wanta have some real expensive clothes, like cost a hundred and some dollars. You know, fashion designer clothes. The real thing."

"I want a diamond ring on my finger," says the other.

I ask, "Do you know people who live better than you?"

The girls think for a moment but can come up with no one, until they think of one girl who has extra money from her part-time job at a store in Tunica. One girl says, "She dress fashion."

The other says, "We poor."

Mr. Fleming laughs at that, too. "I really think I'm just as rich as the man what got the money," he says. "The Lord allowed me to have my health and strength and I got some a what I want. Got a lot full a pigs, chickens, ducks. We was raisin' geese, but my wife got mad at 'em and killed 'em." They picked twenty-eight bushels of peas out of the garden, and butter beans, tomatoes, okra, corn, and sweet potatoes. "I feel like I'm doin' my share," Mr. Fleming says. "Whether they satisfied or ain't satisfied, I feel great."

After a few hours of talking, I say good-bye. And as I head for Little Rock, Arkansas, to visit a young black honors graduate of the city high school it took federal and Arkansas national guard troops to integrate in 1957, I marvel at how little it has taken to make Mr. Fleming feel proud, how far an ounce of human dignity can go. And I think of something Jesse Jackson once told me: "You have a different measuring rod comin' from the bottom up." I finally understand what he meant.

Now, as an aside, this next thing is embarrassing to admit. But for the rest of the drive, I can't shake the feeling—the tickling, tingling sensation—that cockroaches, an army of cockroaches, are climbing up my legs inside my pants. And tonight, at the motel, before I pack my dirty clothes in a plastic bag, I violently shake out everything, not wanting to take any Black Flag-resistant critters with me.

2 0

THE BEST AND THE BRIGHTEST

LITTLE ROCK, ARKANSAS

On the way to Little Rock, I stop in one of those gas station–convenience store combos to fill my tank and grab a sandwich and a cup of coffee. I'm the only customer in the place, and when the cashier—a short, fat, black woman about twenty-five years old—gives me my change, I realize I've got a pocket of silver and a wad of dollar bills. I ask if she can give me $1 bills for three dollars in change, which she does with a "harumph." While she's doing this, I also ask for two $5 bills for ten ones. She slams the register drawer closed and tosses the three ones on the counter.

"I can't be openin' up the cash register just ta give you change!" the woman snaps in a high-pitched whine.

"Why not?"

"I just can't be doin' it!"

Now, this isn't the first time I've been treated brusquely by black sales folks on this trip or in life. Rarely is anything this blunt said, but more than occasionally an air of surliness seems to be lurking just beneath the surface. I always ignore it, even pretend it isn't happening. I know that minimum-wage jobs in gas stations, hamburger joints, and car washes are crap jobs. I know people get sick of obnoxious patrons. But this lady's too much, and all my anger, frustration, and resentment—not about this woman but about the buried images I carry in my head about people like this woman—burst forth.

What happened to "The customer is always right" and "Service with a smile"? What about respect and efficiency and pride in your work? What about some decency toward *me*? All these things flash in my mind. And for an instant, knowing that this woman is poor and uneducated can't outweigh that she's rude and lazy. For an instant, from my own depths, she isn't an individual, she's all poor black people. I can feel it. I think of my black hunting buddy, Howard, back in Glasgow, Kentucky. He had said that once while listening to two young white men harmlessly talk about basketball, a thread seemed to be pulled in his brain and a collage of past racial indignities flashed before him. It's like that for me, only mine is a white man's thread. And for an instant, my hard-earned empathy evaporates, and I hate and fear all this sorry woman represents. I think: Some people deserve to be poor!

I say, "Great service, lady. You're gonna go far in life with that attitude." As soon as I've said this, I regret it, realizing how mean and classbound was the retort, how I had instinctively pulled social rank by aiming for the bull's-eye of this woman's dead-end job and, by inference, her dead-end life.

"I don't care!" she hollers. "I can't be openin' up just ta give you change." She crosses her arms and stands seething. She has exercised her power, such as it is. Back on the road, calmed down, I remember a white motel clerk in Mississippi who'd been at least as rude when I told her she'd double-billed me for $27 in long-distance calls. "Don't be tryin' ta get away with that!" she'd shouted. The woman ticked me off, but she didn't set me off, didn't pull a thread. She stood for only one belligerent old lady. That she was white never entered my mind.

Karama Neal is an eighteen-year-old girl-woman who graduated among the top of her class last year at Little Rock's Central High School, where in 1957 President Eisenhower sent troops of the 101st Airborne Division to protect nine black kids who were integrating the school. Today, about 60 percent of Central's 1,660 kids are African American. Yet black students still make up only a tenth of Central's academic honors classes, and as a group their academic achievement is only half that of white students. Of sixteen National Merit semifinalists in Karama's class, she was the only African American.

This summer, Karama is back at her mother's house after a year at the elite Swarthmore College outside Philadelphia, where she'll return in a few weeks. She has agreed to show me around Central, introduce me to its principal, and get together a group of Central's former black students for me to meet.

When Karama and I get to Central, I'm reminded of my visit to South Carolina's Gullah territory of St. Helena's Island, where the beautiful Brick Baptist Church was built for whites but inherited by blacks. That's also true of Central High: In 1927, the white folks of Little Rock would never have built this grand, neo-Gothic brick castle if they'd known black kids would someday inherit it. What black school in the South had arched windows atop oak doors; life-size statues representing ambition, personality, opportunity, and preparation; and a balcony garden in full bloom?

Karama takes me through Central's front doors and down its hallways like she owns the place. In a way, she does. The girl got only two B's in all of high school! One was a typing class, the other a so-called world history class that she protested because it taught almost no African history. She was on the student council and in the Honor Society, as well as being an Arkansas National Achievement Scholar. On the side, she tutored kids at her church. She's no virtuoso, but she plays piano and violin.

In short, Karama has everything going for her that the Fleming daughters in Tunica have going against them. Karama doesn't "dress fashion"—unless it's the African dashikis or head wraps she occasionally wears on her tall, lean body. She has no expensive hip-hop hairdo. Not long ago, inspired by an old photo of Isaac Hayes, she shaved her head, which has grown out about an eighth of an inch now. She couldn't care less about jewelry, although she does wear dangling Africanesque adornments on her ears. Karama is a post-post–civil rights generation African American. She revels in being black, flaunts it just a bit, but speaks Standard English, savors learning, judges whites and blacks as people, has white and black friends. She has never dated a white man, but she would—if he were "special," if he were decent and humane and also had firsthand knowledge of "the minority experience," though not necessarily the African American experience. To be decent isn't enough, Karama believes, because even decent white people can't understand what it is to be black in America without knowing what it is like to live as an outsider in a hostile world. White people can't only think their way to this knowledge, she believes, they must also feel their way.

Like many of the other black kids in Central's honors program, Karama isn't from a poor family. Her mother is an insurance claims adjuster with a college degree. Her father is a lawyer. Karama grew up in her mother's house. She went to a Montessori school from age two to age eight. Her mother took her to museums and the opera. She insisted on Karama speaking straight English. At age six, Karama began piano. When Karama was about eight years old, her mother moved from a poorer black neighborhood to an overwhelmingly white, middle-income neighborhood to find stable families and less crime.

Karama's mother, who is forty-nine, had been a black radical in the sixties, and she taught Karama African American history and literature. When "Roots" appeared on TV and the grade school kids called the dark-skinned Karama "the African," her mother told her that Africans were beautiful. By high school, the lessons had taken root, and Karama was a straight-A student who refused to drink Coca-Cola because of that company's investments in South Africa.

Karama was accepted at Princeton but chose Swarthmore because a close friend of her mother's went there. The place costs $22,000 a year, although $14,000 of that is covered by loans or scholarships. Swarthmore has been a culture shock for Karama, but not a racial culture shock. "I don't think I was ever really aware of *class*," she says. By this Karama means *social class* and all it can entail: money, wide experience, superior education, confidence, arrogance, myopia, and condescension. Karama has seen the white, upper-middle-class liberal mind-set up close in too many of her fellow Swarthmore students, and she has been appalled.

"All the cafeteria and housekeeping people are black for all these white students," she says. "Many of the kids treat them poorly." She has seen white students eat a pizza in their room on Friday night and put the empty box outside their door for the maid to clean up Monday morning. "They can't walk those extra steps to the trash cans," Karama says, amazed. "Or they spill popcorn all over the hall and don't clean it up." Karama once saw a white student in the cafeteria go to the kitchen and ask for milk for his breakfast cereal. When a black kitchen worker told him the milkman hadn't delivered yet that morning, the white student threw the bowl of cereal in the black man's face. "They would never call me a nigger," Karama says. "I mean, I'm at *Swarthmore*. The housekeepers are niggers to them." But only two generations earlier, Karama's grandmother was a housekeeper who stayed in the maid's quarters at a rich person's house and virtually raised her employer's children. She visited her own children, including Karama's mother, on weekends.

"If I ever heard anybody talk about my grandmother like they talk about the housekeepers, I would hit them," she says. "Swarthmore has this attitude of being totally, totally liberal in every way. It's hypocritical. They think they're really liberal and so accepting of everybody. Well, you can't call yourself liberal and accepting if you can only accept somebody as long as they go to Swarthmore College. But if they occasionally break a verb, then they're automatically lesser human beings." As Karama talks, I think of the rude cashier in the convenience store. I tell Karama about the woman and ask if the workers at Swarthmore often act surly and short-tempered, if they exude resentment, if perhaps the white students are also reacting to these signals. Karama says yes, some workers do act that way. Yes, she has even heard white students ask each other why the help can't be more cheerful.

I ask, "Why are you more understanding?"

"If I had to put up with them," says Karama, who has become friends with some of the Swarthmore workers and attends one of their churches on Sundays, "I'd be annoyed too, real annoyed."

I ask Karama how, if she earns her planned doctorate in biology and becomes successful herself, she will keep her children or her children's children from taking wealth, privilege, and housekeepers for granted, and she tells me a story. "This is strange, but when I get into a public bathroom stall, if I have long pants on, every time, I think, 'Right now, no one knows I'm black.'" Others in the bathroom can see only her shoes and her pants slumped at her ankles. That moment, Karama says, is literally the only time she can think of when people aren't judging her in some way by her race. As long as that's true, she says, African Americans of all incomes will know what it means to be an outsider looking in.

Karama goes off to find Central's principal, and I think to myself that so many well-to-do Americans believe the nation is doing people like Karama a favor by paying much of their way through college, cutting them in for a piece of the action. In truth, it's America that desperately needs the Karama Neals, black and white, of this world, the kids who can still touch the sensations of what it's like to be poor and struggling. And nobody needs people like Karama more than the people at places like Swarthmore, those encumbered with generations of privilege, those who disproportionately run this country and who claim to speak for it. Without the Karama Neals, they haven't got a clue.

* * *

Principal John L. Hickman, Jr., is thirty-five years old and beginning his first full school year as Central's principal this September. He's a former military man—short, bald, demanding, unforgiving—and cut from the same mold as Charleston police chief Reuben Greenberg. Too many black kids self-destruct, and John Hickman believes he knows why. So in his school, there will be no gold chains, cocked caps, no, "Yo, man!" hollered in the halls. He says he'll do what white principals have been afraid to do: make Central's black kids, 40 percent of whom are poor, check the jive, hipster, rap-man street culture at the arched doorways. "'Hey look, Fred,'" he says, talking to a hypothetical black student, "'that stuff you got on is a pile of crap. You oughta take that stuff off and let me educate you.' Instead, we're drawing back and afraid to say it."

Mr. Hickman makes no apologies for being a proponent of middle-class values, language, and standards of behavior. "That's what's going to allow them to achieve in the mainstream world," he says. White teachers afraid of black kids and charges of racism and black parents afraid that white teachers might actually be racists have conspired to let black kids coast through school too often. It's the dirty secret of integrated education: black teachers, Mr. Hickman says, had an authoritarian way about them because black culture is more authoritarian than middle-class white culture. "Here comes jive Johnny, and a black teacher would kick him in the ass! But Mrs. So and So from white America sees Johnny and he's six-foot-one, two-forty, and he's gettin' loud and so she takes a step back and leaves him alone. 'If you don't say anything to me, I won't say anything to you.'" And she'll pass him on. "Now this has been done for generations."

It's time, Mr. Hickman says, for blacks to confront their self-defeating subculture head-on and stop glorifying it with stylistic mimicry. Maybe Spike Lee can get away with wearing Air Jordans and Malcolm X hats to the office, but most blacks can't. "It hurts me to see a kid and he's got five gold chains and all these rings and all these earrings and his hat turned to the side and his crazy-lookin' walk. And his English is a third grader's vocabulary. You have to do something for that kid. And what you have to hope is that he doesn't infect the other kids.

"I want black kids to see that while they're actin' a fool, white kids are learnin'! You're here fussin' and cussin', walkin' up and down here actin' crazy, and they're in those honors classes doin' their lessons, because their moms and dads are sayin', 'You're gonna be a doctor, you're gonna be a lawyer. Just stay away from the niggers. They wanta fight and fuss and tear it up, you'll be all right.' That's what hurts me about our kids, when you hear 2 Live Crew talkin' about 'me so horny' or a guy like Eazy-E sayin' there's nothin' in life but bitches and whores and money. *This is real!* We gotta take a very strong role."

Karama has been quiet during Mr. Hickman's proclamations, which are too harsh for her taste. She believes kids can do well in school and still like rap music, wear cocked hats. Maybe Mr. Hickman is right that the last chance for a lot of Central's hard-luck kids is his kind of shock therapy, but nobody should forget that the white students who are doing so well at Central often come from the affluent Pleasant Valley neighborhood of Little Rock.

At Swarthmore, Karama has seen the power of privileged birth, and she knows its dynamics are at work at Central too. Even most of the black kids in her high school honors classes came from solid families with decent incomes. And tonight at Karama's house, a little brick home on a quiet suburban cul de sac, I meet four such kids, all of whom are in college. The affluent family of one student is paying for his college, but three of the students are getting substantial financial aid. Their parents make, say, $25,000 a year. All the students say they know their high school grades and SAT scores didn't have to be as high as those of white kids to win college admission and financial help. All say they feel resentment from white students over this. All say they resent that resentment.

"I think it's gotten worse for blacks," says one student.

I say, "You have a full scholarship. How's it worse for you?"

"It's a full scholarship to a school I didn't want to go to." The Ivy League school the student preferred offered no money.

I ask, "Is that racism?"

"No," the student admits, because the Ivy League school accepted him in the first place only because he is black.

"Me, myself," says another student, "I don't want to be accepted because I'm black." This comment comes from a person who has just said he got a college scholarship because he *is* black.

I ask, "So why didn't you turn down the money?"

"I'm not stupid enough to turn it down."

I ask, "So why the bit about wanting to do it 'on my own'?"

At that, the kids talk heatedly about how black people have been historically deprived of opportunity and education and that blacks deserve a leg up because of this mistreatment. I agree, but I also share another idea: colleges give preferential treatment to the children of alumni, and especially to the children of alumni who are big donors. They give preferential treatment to athletes, who are sometimes admitted even if they don't know how to read. Once jocks are in school, they're often given unfair breaks on their grades. The Ivy League was for generations famous for its "gentlemen's C," which meant simply that the dumb or unmotivated sons of prominent parents were simply passed through college. Even today, perhaps the application of a dull child of a congressman has some smidgen of an advantage over that of a bright Iowa farm boy. Not to mention that influential people have forever been giving jobs to each other's kids. "It doesn't bother these people," I say. "Why does it bother you?"

No one answers the question directly, but one student says racism today has gone underground, which is why it's worse than ever. Frankly, I'm tired of hearing this. "Come on!" I say. "You'd rather have been in a ramshackle school without books instead of honors classes at Central? You'd rather step off the sidewalk when whites passed? You'd rather say 'Yasuh, boss'?"

"At least you knew where you stood."

I say, "So what? You stood at the bottom."

"It's just how you *feel* about the situation."

I say, "It's not just how you *feel*. It's also a question of looking at the reality of twenty-five years ago and not just going, 'Oh, poor me. I'm even more oppressed.'"

In 1963, three civil rights workers were murdered a few hundred miles from here in Philadelphia, Mississippi, with the help of the police. Blacks were terrorized and humiliated right here in Little Rock. "You think it's worse? You, with a scholarship because you're black? You, who got accepted into the Ivy League because you're black? You think you're worse off than migrant workers or poor

Appalachian whites or an unemployed Italian kid in New York? Come on!"

"But you always have to watch your back."

I say, "Don't you think whites have to watch their backs? You think whites competing for a single lawyer's job or scholarship are nice to each other? They're ruthless."

"But people don't say, 'He got the job because he's black.'"

"No, they say he got the job because he went to the right school, or because his dad's a good friend of the chairman of the board, or because he wore the right suit."

"You can go out and buy a new suit," a student says. "You can't change the fact that you're black."

"And women can't change their sex," I say sharply. I'm not just playing the devil's advocate with these kids. I'm genuinely miffed. I see before me young people who are being helped along because enough folks in society, black and white, banded together to get the clout to give them a few breaks, and they seem to spend their time bemoaning the troubles that these new opportunities have created. But I know this is an ailment of youth, and I change the subject, asking how often they hear black kids complain that they'll not be able to accomplish this or that because whites won't let them. One student says he hears it a lot from a certain type of guy—usually somebody who hasn't worked hard in school, somebody from a poor family. Then the conversation takes a weird turn, as the young people begin to talk about the kids from the public housing projects who wear expensive Guess jeans, while they must wear no-brand clothing, how people on welfare seem to live better than their own working families. A tirade ensues.

"I see their grocery bags!"

"T-bone steak!"

"The little measly jobs that I have, they take my taxes out and give it to this person who isn't workin'. And this person is livin' better than I am—off *my* money!"

"They live better than people workin', sometimes twelve and thirteen hours a day."

"They'll start on welfare with one kid and end up on welfare after eighteen years with ten kids."

"The more kids the more money."

"But they're not spendin' it on their kids, but themselves and their boyfriend."

After quite a while of this, I say, "If a white person had said all this, you'd be screaming, 'Racism! Racism!' Right?"

Silence.

"Am I right?"

"Probably," one student offers.

"It's like if your sister calls you stupid, you won't get mad," says one student. "But if somebody you don't know calls you stupid, you'll get mad."

Says another, "White people would say *all* black people do that. Whereas, we're talking about *real* people."

I say, "But *all* poor people don't have kids to get welfare."

"But we live with the people. We *know* it exists."

"How is it different if you say it than if I say it?"

"Whites put on this air that this is just *you*," says one of the students. "*We* don't have these problems—whites on welfare, teenaged pregnancy. It's just *you*—and it's *all* of you." Everyone nods in agreement, and I see now what these accomplished young blacks are outraged and resentful about. It's not only that so many African Americans still live in the difficult straits these college students unsympathetically describe, but that the white brush of prejudice that tars such disrespectable people also tars them.

Karama has said almost nothing the whole evening. After the students leave, she says she doesn't agree with much of what they said. She's even a little embarrassed for them. But one thing is true: when black people are critical of black people, they're often saying something different than when white people level the same criticisms. Whites are too often like me, when I momentarily flashed and saw all poor blacks in the face of one rude, lazy woman. It isn't only that accomplished blacks are tarred by this blindness, Karama believes, but that it keeps blacks and whites from finding common ground to talk about some very sad truths.

This Karama Neal is a wise girl-woman.

2 1

THE LAST MAN WHO REMEMBERS

LITTLE RIVER COUNTY, ARKANSAS

Last year in Washington, D.C., the National Archives had an exhibit titled "American Voices: Two Hundred Years of Speaking Out." It was a collection of letters written to presidents of the United States asking for help—a woman seeking a second-hand coat, Native Americans seeking to remain in their homelands, physicists seeking to stop their country from using the nuclear bomb. Among these petitions was a handwritten letter to President McKinley dated June 5, 1899, from an Arkansas man named Henry Johnson. The letter didn't say if Mr. Johnson was white or black. He wrote: "The leaders in the mob that killed twenty colored men in April '99 in Little River County, Arkansas, were John Sanders, Jim Sanders, Eli Britt, John Hawkins." No record of a reply from President McKinley exists, but it's unlikely that Mr. Johnson found relief from the White House. President McKinley was a Union general during the Civil War, but he was also a staunchly conservative Ohio Republican.

Mr. Johnson's letter intrigued me, but not because it slowed the onslaught of black lynchings, 3,447 of which are known to have occurred from 1882 to 1982 (although 82 percent of those lynchings occurred in the South, states such as Indiana and Pennsylvania also had lynchings, and only the New England states are untainted). Mr. Johnson's letter intrigued me in the way bluesman Wade Walton's "Parchman Farm" song about Mr. Harpole intrigued me: the song and the letter reached out across generations to lay responsibility, they named names. How could those four white men of Little River County, imbued with the sentiments of their isolated time and place, ever have imagined that almost a century later Henry Johnson's unrequited act of putting pen to paper would forever mark them as barbarians? How could they have known that of all the thousands of men who committed murder under the cover of mob anonymity, their names would be recorded and remembered?

I'm ready to head home for a rest after ten thousand miles on the road, but Little River County, which borders Texas and Oklahoma in southwestern Arkansas, is too close to pass by, and the lynching of blacks is too much a part of the South's dark lore to ignore.

What to make of the South? Perhaps it's because I've heard so much about the "New South" over the years that I'm surprised at the racist remarks I've heard from white people—total strangers—all across the Deep South, where many white folks obviously figured my skin would safely predict my attitudes. I can count on one hand the number of times I've heard the word "nigger" used by whites in, oh, the last ten years. After a few months in the South, I'd need a calculator to keep score. Yet, from my wife's own family in Kentucky, to the Cookes in Alabama, to the Fraziers in Mississippi, to many more, the changes of the last several decades have been so striking that few black people I met believe life for them and their children is not far better. What struck me is that most people I met focused less on how white people may really *feel* about them privately and more on how white people actually *treat* them today compared to yesterday. And that is with far greater overt respect. I have one regret about my time in the South: Several of my planned visits with poor people in big southern cities—Atlanta, Memphis, New Orleans—didn't work out for one reason or another. Maybe these people would have felt differently.

As I'm about to leave the region, I take with me one overarching thought: The awful old days *are not* ancient history. They are barely past. In Burkesville, Kentucky, Nell has never been acknowledged by her white brother. It has been only about a decade since Colonial Williamsburg's officials believed they could ease black history into their telling. Today, Chester DeVillars can still go to breakfast in Darien, Georgia, and have a white man calmly tell him that he can't vote for that "nigger" running for political office. And worst of all, the daughter of Wharlest Jackson, only thirty-three years old, must live without her murdered father every day of her life—knowing his killers are still at large. As a white man, I never really knew how much I was asking black people to put behind them when I said, "Trust me. I am different."

I spend the night in Texarkana, Texas, which is big enough to have motels, and head for Little River County just after dawn. When I cross the Red River into Arkansas and Little River, near where the lynchings supposedly took place, I see that the bottom land has been recently flooded. The season's lost wheat crop is stubble and the ground is poisoned with the flood's red-sand leavings.

From Arkansas State Historian John Ferguson in Little Rock I've collected copies of articles in the *Daily Texarkanian* and the *Arkansas Gazette* that reported the Little River lynchings, which actually occurred in late March of 1899. By the time word of the murders reached Henry Johnson, the number of men lynched had apparently been multiplied by rumor from the seven reported in the newspapers to the twenty reported by Mr. Johnson. Headlines in the *Arkansas Gazette* on March 24, 1899, blared:

SEVEN NEGRO MEN LYNCHED
Wildest Excitement Prevails in Little River County

BLACKS PLOT RACE WAR
Thirty-three Negroes Implicated in the Plot

ALL MAY BE KILLED
Negroes Run Down and Murdered One at a Time

That pretty much tells the story as whites saw it. From the ancient newspaper accounts, it seems that a black man named General Duckett, age unreported, shot and killed a wealthy white planter named James A. Stockton. None of the ten articles gives any explanation for why Duckett killed Stockton, other than a rather vague report that Stockton's murder was supposed to touch off a race war as it was plotted by Duckett and his band of alleged conspirators. "Friendly Negroes of the white people," as one article described them, revealed the supposed race-war scheme after Stockton's killing. After several days of hiding out in the bottom lands of the Red River through which I'm now driving, Duckett turned himself in to sheriff John Johnson. While in transport to jail in nearby Richmond, the sheriff was reportedly overtaken by a band of men, a gambit commonly used in lynchings to protect local lawmen from charges of conspiring with the mob. The men took Duckett, hanged him, and riddled his body with bullets at 12:35 P.M. on March 21. In the next few days, whites tracked down Duckett's alleged partners and sympathizers and murdered them—Edward Goodwin, Adam King, Joe King, and three brothers, Joe, Ben, and Moses Jones.

Goodwin was shot and probably hung. His body was found at
the mouth of Mud Creek, just across the Red River in Texas. The
Jones brothers, who had split up to make their escape, were captured
and lynched. Joe King, who was said to have remarked that planter
Stockton should have been killed sooner, refused to give up his gun
to whites. He was taken to the woods and whipped. The next morning, his body was found hanging from the same tree used to lynch
Duckett, along with the body of Moses Jones, whose crime was that
his wife had cooked food for Duckett while in hiding. Edward Goodwin was lynched because he supposedly took that food to Duckett.
One article notes that blacks were leaving Little River County for
Texarkana by the wagon load. The *Nashville News* reported local fears
that Little River would lose its black labor supply if the violence continued, and quoted a planter saying, "The Negro who attends to his
own business is as safe in Little River County as elsewhere." No
irony intended, I'm sure.

Later articles reported that Little River citizens were outraged
over press stories about the murders: "It is high time that our people
were taking steps to stop all such injurious lies being sent broad-cast
over the country." White folks in Little River seemed more upset
about redressing harm to their county's reputation than they did
redressing the massacre.

So that's the story from long-buried newspaper files, as it was
reported in 1899. With the help of an amateur historian in Little River
County, I discover that local legend holds that after General Duckett's
surrender he was taken to what was then the George Plantation,
located a few miles southwest of the little town of Foreman, which
even today has only 1,267 residents. It was supposedly from there
that the sheriff set out, only to be overtaken by the mob. I head out
Arkansas Route 108 from Foreman and turn left onto what's called
the Hawkins lateral, a narrow red-gravel road. Henry Johnson's letter
to the President claimed that a John Hawkins was among the leaders
of the mob.

Just off Hawkins lateral, near where Walnut Bayou and French
Creek cross, is the black Alfred French Cemetery. My hope is that I'll
find the grave of General Duckett or one of the other murdered men
in this old cemetery located so near where three of them were
lynched. I find the graveyard, which only recently was beneath the
floodwaters of the Red River. This morning, it's quiet and serene, a

flat, grassy meadow in a wood of pecan, oak, and bois d'arc trees. A few minutes after my arrival, in the cool morning air, the birds start up again as I walk among the graves. The name *Duckett*, like the name *Hawkins*, is common in Little River County, and I find the graves of Frank Duckett, Lucy Duckett, Charley Duckett, Mary Duckett—but no General Duckett, and no Edward Goodwin, Adam King, Joe King, or Joe, Ben, or Moses Jones.

So I ask around Foreman and learn that only one person might still have a memory of the lynchings—John French, a black man who grew up in the vicinity of the Alfred French Cemetery. In the afternoon, I find Mr. French sitting on the wooden porch swing in front of his small white house on the outskirts of Foreman. He has just returned from the road with his mail, and it sits on his lap unopened. Mr. French is ninety-six years old. He stands when I introduce myself and walks off the gray floor of his porch onto the grass. He's a short, fit man. He wears worn blue-jean overalls and a light blue tank top underneath them, which exposes still-strong, broad shoulders. His posture is erect and not even a century of living has yet worn away all of his body's muscles. His head is bald and he is clean shaven. Only his mouth, which recedes slightly, and his eyes, the right one nearly closed and the left one vacant, seem to betray his longevity. As he speaks, he looks straight ahead, and his voice is weak and gravelly. But his mind is strong and clear.

"I know'd a lotta lynchin's went on in those days," he says.

I ask, "What year were you born, sir?"

"Eighteen ninety four."

"You would have been five years old. He supposedly killed a man named James Stockton, a planter."

"General Duckett?" Mr. French says, almost whispering and twisting his mouth and forehead in thought. "That's right! I remember that. Yes, I remember when that happened, know exactly where it was. That man, they hanged that man down on the Hawkins place, where that old big pecan tree was down there. Yes, sir, I was big enough to know about it. I didn't 'member so much about the hanging, but I know the lynchin' went on. That same man, I remember him comin' by my home." It turns out that Mr. French's family lived only about a mile from where the hanging took place.

"Come by of a home one mornin' 'fore day and asked Papa about goin' somewhere, and Papa told 'im he just didn't know. And he said, 'Well, I'll go somewhere,' and he went on and they caught him that morning. Caught 'im! I think the man had a double-barreled shotgun when he left. On Hawkins farm, that's right. We called it the Hawkins place. That's where they hanged him. I know that. It was a big old tree. They done cut it down now." He says the tree was beyond the cemetery, just across the bridge where Walnut Bayou and French Creek cross. I take out the list of names mentioned in Henry Johnson's letter and read them out loud: John Sanders, Jim Sanders, Eli Britt, John Hawkins. "Do you recognize those names?"

"Yes, I knew all a them," Mr. French says. "I didn't know much about 'em, just knew their names and knew where they lived."

I ask, "What did you think about them?"

"I didn't think nothin' good."

"Did you ever talk to any of these men?"

"Yes, sir, I talked to all of 'em. They was nice to me."

"Did you know they were the men who did it?"

"That's just what the people said."

It's hot in the afternoon sun and Mr. French's bald head has broken out in beads of glistening sweat, and he seems suddenly tired. I extend my arm to shake his hand good-bye, but he stands motionless, still looking straight ahead. He seems to sense the silence in the air and laughs. "Were you tryin' ta shake my hand?" He says that he is blind in his left eye and nearly blind in his right. He extends his right arm. When I shake his hand, it is wan and weightless in mine, and I'm glad I found him before it was too late, before he was gone. Let the letter of Henry Johnson and the memory of John French immortalize these names: John Sanders, Jim Sanders, Eli Britt, John Hawkins.

JOURNEY
TWO

UP NORTH

1

"MISS COOKE, SHE'S MEEEAN!"

WASHINGTON, D.C.

Nellie Cooke has the power to change lives.

It is not a gift of providence, this power, but a result of work and pride and affection. It is the power of priests and football coaches. It also is the power of good teachers, and that is what Nellie Cooke is, a good teacher. She laughs and says she is the best schoolteacher in Washington. On some days, Nellie almost believes it—when she has looked into the eyes of some junior-high child and seen that child lost in whatever Nellie Cooke was saying, maybe something about pronouns or plots, but more likely something about life, about how to make it against the long odds her poor and black city kids face. A child might be listening so intently that he's leaning awkwardly on his elbow, not realizing that his arm is about to slip off his desk, or he might not have blinked for a long time. That's when Nellie knows that she has reached that child, that she is getting through, that he will remember this moment—a moment Nellie is creating simultaneously for a youngster looking ahead and for herself looking back, a moment that is present, past, and future all at once.

I met Nellie Cooke's parents when I was in Brighton, Alabama, the little black town outside Birmingham where I visited Loudelia and Printeris Cooke, the elderly couple of remarkable strength and dignity. They had raised nine decent, hardworking children, all of whom went to college on Printeris's brick-factory-worker paycheck. I wondered: What kind of children did this triumphant old couple raise? Nellie Cooke is the answer. I found her at Shaw Junior High School, located in one of Washington's poorest neighborhoods. Since the turn of the century, nearly seven million blacks have moved "up North" from the South. Nellie and six of her brothers and sisters landed in Washington, each helping the next with money, food, and a bed until they were on their feet.

I live near Washington, and it's nice to go home to my wife and kids after spending the days in Nellie's classroom. I've got the same luxury while visiting other folks in Washington—four teenaged boys with whom I meet to shoot baskets and talk about their lives; Jesse Jackson, whom I accompany around Washington; a grandmother whose life is falling apart and the dedicated social worker who's trying to save her.

Being in my hometown is a nice reprieve. But from here, it'll be back to the road: Spike Lee in Manhattan; an old crippled woman in Detroit; a murderer in East St. Louis; a millionaire in Chicago; the first black man I ever knew in Ford Heights, Illinois; a favorite black fiction writer in Iowa City—with all the surprises and people along the way.

Nellie Cooke hit Washington as a short, Afro-adorned woman of twenty-four, a southern girl naive about the hard side of the city. She'd never heard the word *ghetto*. Mama and Daddy Cooke, who had insisted that their children steer clear of the historic demonstrations in nearby Birmingham in the sixties, had always sheltered Nellie, who was the baby of the family. So the city shocked, angered, even repelled her, and the job scared her. At Shaw, she discovered the great urban ills: kids living with one parent or grandparent, kids roaming the streets at night, kids whose folks worked long, tiring hours, kids who hadn't known the joy of learning. But Nellie was always a good student and she became her own best pupil, reaching back into her own life to little Brighton, Alabama, for guidance.

She remembered her high school principal, Mr. Brown, walking into her classroom and asking her teacher, "What are you teaching?" The teacher answered, "Gerunds," and Mr. Brown turned to the class, pointer in hand, and said, "A verbal noun that ends in i-n-g." Nellie remembered her high school English teacher, Mr. Crawford, who always smelled of exotic cologne. Nellie could still see Mr. Crawford as he walked up to her one day while she was flirting with some boy. "Why are you wasting your time?" he demanded. "You could be reading a book."

Nellie recalled these as moments of mastery, and she remembered them as gifts, which it was her turn to repay. Now, almost twenty years after coming to Washington, Nellie Cooke is a legend at Shaw Junior High, which isn't at all like the frightening stereotype of a city school with unruly, dangerous kids running wild in the hallways. At Shaw, I discover, kids' shoelaces have to be tied, boys can't wear jogging suits, girls can't wear jewelry in their hair, shirts have to be tucked in, and littering the halls is punishable by death or dismemberment. The place is as clean as a hospital. New kids barely have time to get a locker before somebody has clued them in: "Don't mess with Miss Cooke, she's *meeean!*" The sight of her short, strong legs striding across that blue carpet, her arms swaying confidently, her shoulders straight, her clothes hip, her gold bracelets and watch and earrings and necklace flashing, her Jheri curls glistening, her little widow's peak giving her just a hint of cool—well, she cuts a pretty impressive figure. She is just the kind of teacher Little Rock's Central High principal said black students need.

The kids call her "Miss Cooke," and over the years she has come to call herself the same. Or "Mizz Cooke" if she is angry at some child for goofing off, or lying about losing his homework, or saying "Washin'ton" instead of "Washington." She will say, "*Mizz* Cooke didn't hear you right, did she? I don't want to hear dialect!" You're not going to not get hired because you're black, she'll say, but because you can't speak English! When Miss Cooke gets rolling like this, gets *meeean,* the kids in her second-period eighth-grade honors English class squirm.

But the Shaw kids love her. Maybe not right away, but eventually. When Rokeya landed in Miss Cooke's English class, for instance, she freaked, told her counselor she had to get out: Miss Cooke was too *meeean!* She made Rokeya wipe off her thick burgundy lipstick. She smacked William's leg with a yardstick. She took Shed's old English folder, shook all the papers onto the floor, and ripped it to pieces because it was too raggedy. Rokeya figured, man, this lady's crazy! But no luck. They made Rokeya stay. Today, Rokeya says, "I love Miss Cooke. Miss Cooke is like a second mother to me. I mean she is the *best*. I never want to leave Miss Cooke."

Her English class dismissed, Miss Cooke sits at a child's desk and we talk. "I'm not stupid," she says. "I know I can't just preach to them. I have to teach. But I'm saying we know what's best for our black kids. We can save them. Honey, look who saved us! I tell them that on those slave ships, the strongest survived. The blood running through our veins is the strongest. These children and the lives they live were all new to me. I came to Shaw, then I saw it—children who, for whatever reason, their attendance was poor. You couldn't be defeated by it, you had to work around it. This is a calling, like being a minister. All my teachers were people who cared, they were people who disciplined. This is where I get it. I remember Brighton High. I will never forget. You never, ever forget. These black people shaped my life.

"Sometimes, even I think, 'What is *wrong* with these people?' And I say, 'You can do better.' Well, maybe they can't. Sometimes, I go down a street and all of a sudden I see one of my children in a doorway. I say to myself, 'God, this kid lives here?' Then I see him differently when he's in that chair. That child is doing wonderfully well. Take some Rhodes scholar and put him in that doorway at age four and see what happens.

"I teach the kids what I think they need to get along in life. I know it works. I know children I have touched. They aren't selling drugs. They went to college. They work for the city. They work in the checkout line at Giant. Or they are the manager of a supermarket. They work every day. That's what it's all about. I rail at the system. Then I think about those children, and I know what I have to do—take care of those kids! I'm not running a popularity contest. The things I say to those kids, I've earned. Baby, they know I'm here! We have normal, sweet, little, contained, sheltered kids. They want, they need, they love, they hate, they cry. They can read. They can do it all. We're not just whistlin' in the dark. We change lives."

While teaching English, race and racism are never far from Nellie Cooke's mind, because all Shaw's kids—bright or dumb—must eventually navigate America's white waters—in college and careers, every time they watch TV or read a paper, rent an apartment, or apply for a loan. "I know what they are feeling," Nellie says. She remembers, for instance, that as a girl she'd sit and stare at a picture of Jesus hanging on the wall of her home, a picture I have seen in her parents' house in Alabama. In it, he is light-skinned and blond, blue-eyed. As a girl, Nellie wondered how that Jesus could ever care about her, a little black girl. Finally, she asked her daddy, a man with a ninth-grade education. He sat her down and said that Christ had been born in the Middle East and that people in the Middle East aren't blond. Of the picture, he said, "Jesus won't look like that."

"I can't describe it," Nellie says today. "I just felt better, and I've carried that moment with me all these years."

Back in her classroom the next morning, Miss Cooke lectures on literary terms and the plot structure of an Edgar Allen Poe short story. She goes through rising action, climax, falling action, theme, mood, tone, characterization. How do we explain the weaving of a plot? Well, think of it this way: "Everything you do in life from birth to death, you're weaving a plot. You hope to reach a goal, become a doctor. You have to work toward that. So all these days you don't do your homework, you're weaving a plot. And then you tell me, 'I want to be a brain surgeon.' But you don't do your homework! I just pray to God that I never, ever, as a little old lady, walk into a hospital and look up and see you."

The class is laughing now.

"Oh, Lord! I have to go under the knife with you? But you're developing all these things right now. Think of all the elements of a short story in terms of your own life. What kind of person are you developing here? In terms of characterization, you are weaving that plot right now. If you are stubborn at thirteen, you're going to be stubborn at thirty-two. You have to work on getting rid of these things. What's the *tone* of your life? What's the *mood* from day to day? The elements of a short story—relate them to your life. Weave a plot that's going to take you in some direction."

Nellie Cooke is on a roll. Never, ever does she miss a chance to teach her message: Life begun at the bottom is treacherous but winnable. Racism and disadvantage are real, she tells her students, but you gotta ignore that, kids! Too much sympathy is pity, and pity will drain you. The fable of the tortoise and the hare, that's what some of you are like, she says, thinking you can win the race without effort, like Mr. Hare. But there isn't time for that. Too many temptations, too few second chances. So shoot for the moon, she says, because you might just land on the roof-top. "At least that's what my teachers taught me."

2

OF HOOPS AND DREAMS

SHAW NEIGHBORHOOD, WASHINGTON, D.C.

The alley court unfolds before Fred and Chez, Bryan and Derrick like a hot blacktop dance floor beneath a noontime sun, steam rising off the dirtied macadam and mingling with the power and beauty and grace of boyhood dreams. The alley court is a place of refuge, of gliding and dunking pirouettes, of young men watching themselves, judging themselves, proving themselves, distracting themselves with balls and baskets, with hope. The alley court is the fade-away hook, the look-away pass, the fantasy of the perfect game, the perfect life, Magic and Isiah and Michael, played against a squat cityscape of boarded windows and rusted bedsprings, of mediocre grades and bounded experience, of race. The alley court is boundless ambition, boundless illusion.

Two years ago, Fred and Chez, Bryan and Derrick took an old orange basketball rim and dug out a gray, splintered rectangle of plywood backboard from a pile of junk. Then, with eight-inch spikes, they nailed that sucker to a telephone pole behind Fred's house in the alley just off Third and P streets in Washington, a neighborhood most people, black or white, wouldn't want to be lost in after dark. The corner at Third and P is one of Washington's minor drug markets, and a while back a young man was killed right on the boys' alley basketball court. The police lights were glaring red in the rainy darkness when Fred's grandmother went out to make sure she didn't know the dead boy. She didn't.

I'm here to play basketball with these boys—young men, really— and to talk with them about their lives, hopes, and ambitions. Fred, Chez, Bryan, and Derrick are good kids. They go to church. They're not crack heads or drug dealers. They haven't made girls pregnant. They all live with their mothers or grandmothers. Their moms all have solid, if modest, jobs—a sergeant in the National Guard, an editorial assistant at the National Defense University, a secretary, a prison guard. The boys all hope to go to college. These guys are far more typical of America's black city youth, far more typical of the kids Nellie Cooke teaches, than the muggers and the drug dealers of suburban lore. They're kids with traditional American dreams who would rather be out of trouble than in trouble, kids who want a piece of the pie.

Twenty-five years ago, I was a decent basketball player, and on my visits to the alley court, I can play a good fifteen minutes at full tilt and not embarrass myself. After that I must sit down and watch and listen and ask questions. Playing basketball with teenagers is a heart-attack sport for aging, overweight jocks, and I'd like to be around for a few more seasons. The basketball hoop is hung exactly eight feet, two inches from the ground, for dunkability. Fred, Chez, and Derrick, who are sixteen, and Bryan, who is seventeen, are circling one another on this hot noon the way they always do before a game, territorially—rolling shoulders, stretching thighs, shaking arms like dangling rubber bands, grittin' each other with the evil-eye stare. Serious, stylized, NBA stuff. Like snakes shedding skins, they peel off T-shirts and hang them on the black skeleton of a dead car in the right front court. Lay-ups, jumpers, footwork fancies—and, pretty soon, a young, sweet, glistening moisture encases their lean bodies, for a moment, before the deluge of sweat and the game begin.

The game is called "33," in which each man is his own team, up to the winning score of 33. All against all, one for one. Get the ball and score, and it's your ball again, until you miss and someone else snatches the rebound. It's a flashy city game, one I never played as a boy in the suburbs. It's a game of offense, not defense, a game for Michael Jordans, not plodders of the pass-pass-shoot variety. The sun has dried the blacktop from the morning storm, and a pale yellow butterfly dances in celebration. The sky has gone blue-blue. But no one but me has noticed.

"Damn!" Bryan howls joyfully as he sinks a twenty-footer, drawing first blood. But then Derrick grabs the ball and pops five in a row. "Damn!" Bryan howls again, without joy.

I've talked with each of these boys privately about their lives, and I've talked with all of them together again and again. I've talked with all their mothers and with Derrick's stepfather. None of the boys lives with his natural father.

Chez's parents split up soon after he was born. After that, his mother married a man who treated her roughly. Chez remembers going into the kitchen one night during a scuffle when he was about three years old and threatening to hit the man with a lamp. He still fantasizes about visiting this man, motioning for him to lean forward and then crushing his nose, his teeth, his face with a baseball bat. "I'm thinkin' about it now," Chez told me. "I hate him." After that man, his mother got involved with a man Chez liked. Chez thinks of this man as his father. It angered him when they split up, though Chez didn't talk about it. He felt better when he saw the man on the street with his new wife. Chez thought, "My mom's prettier."

The stories of Fred, Bryan, and Derrick are different but the same. Fred's mother and father split up when Fred was a child, and Fred saw his dad only rarely. Yet when they were reunited for a while recently, Fred stopped sassing his mother and started doing his homework. Then his father stopped coming round, and Fred went back to his old ways. Bryan's mother and father split up when he was four. His mother then married a man Bryan thinks of as his dad. They are divorced now, but Bryan's stepfather still visits him often, and they are friends. He has promised to buy Bryan a car after he graduates from high school. Only Derrick, whose natural father left when he was seven, has a man at home. Derrick likes his stepfather, is proud he's a policeman. No, Derrick says, he doesn't think about his natural father, doesn't even remember when he left.

Even among themselves, the boys insist they rarely talk about their dads. "Nobody don't talk about their fathers," said Chez. But when I asked Fred privately why a man would abandon his children, he got quiet, his eyes watered, and he looked away to wipe them. "I don't know why," he said sharply, angrily. "I don't think about it." Bryan didn't volunteer the information, but his mother told me that he was devastated by her divorce from his stepfather. I asked Bryan about this, and he said that the divorce had made him think about how he has now been twice abandoned by a father. Bryan said, "I don't like to think about it." Yet when I asked the boys to recall their favorite memories from childhood, each mentioned something he had done with his natural father or the man he thinks of as his father: going to buy Jiffy Pop popcorn, learning to ride a bike, shooting baskets on a Sunday morning.

I asked Fred, "What's your favorite memory?"

"Bein' with my father. Just bein' with my father."

I asked Chez, "What kind of man do you admire?"

"A man who doesn't hit his wife and who takes care of his children. A nice, warm and gentle man."

Other than the alley court, there's not a lot going on at Third and P. The guys swim at the nearby Dunbar High School pool or they hang out at the rec center. Or they go to the corner and buy a Coke or a frozen-fruit Turbo Pop from the Asian woman behind the bullet-proof window. Or they watch TV. Or play Nintendo. Or listen to "Niggas With Attitude." They don't read books. None could recall a favorite book, except Bryan, who mentioned that he enjoyed *Green Eggs and Ham* by Dr. Seuss. No, the big excitement comes when the guys take a bus to Georgetown, one of Washington's wealthy white neighborhoods. In Georgetown, the boys catch a movie or hang out. Fred was in Esprit, a clothing store, a while back and when he left, a white rent-a-cop stopped him and searched his bag. She didn't even apologize when she found nothing stolen.

I asked Fred, "Was that racism?"

Fred looked perplexed. "What's racism?"

The boys don't believe there's much racism left in America. "Old people who think they know everything" still believe there's racism, Bryan said. "People who lived back at the time of slavery." Each of them said he has never experienced racism personally. Well, except that time they took the subway to White Flint Mall, one of Washington's upscale suburban shopping centers, and were asked to leave Toys R Us, although a bunch of white kids were also browsing inside. "Because we're black, they thought we were gonna steal somethin'," Derrick says. But, he adds, the guys later discovered that a kid with them *did* steal something from Toys R Us that day. Says Derrick, "That was stupid, man."

On the court, the game of 33 is still going hot and heavy.

"Stop, man!" Fred suddenly hollers angrily.

"My ball!" Chez demands.

"What you mean?" snaps Fred.

Bryan, as if mediating the dispute, walks to the black skeleton of the dead car where I am sitting and sits down. "It's too hot, man, too hot." The others follow, grabbing their shirts and wiping their faces and chests and pits and shoulders. I notice for the first time that they are truly handsome kids. Their clear-skinned faces are made prominent by the fashionable hairstyle of the day, the taper—a buzz cut that leaves only a shadow of hair on their heads. Fred, with elegant dark skin and muscles that are defined and edged, is the oldest-looking. Derrick, taut and lanky, is open-faced and wide-eyed. Because of his soft, raspy voice, they call him Froggie. Bryan is lean, deliberate, and boyish. He's the oldest, but sometimes looks like a younger brother. They call him Gucci, after the Gucci hat he often wears. Chez, the most popular with the girls, is wiry and impish, bursting with intensity.

After my many visits, the boys have gotten used to my odd questions. I ask Derrick, "What do whites think of blacks?"

He looks around blankly for a moment, and then says, "That we always cause trouble and that we use drugs and can't ever do nothin' for ourselves. We always need them to help us. They think we're violent, that the only time we ain't doin' bad is when we asleep. A white person in our neighborhood walks fast with his face ahead and doesn't look either way. It makes me angry. It makes us want to mess with them."

I ask Fred, "Are whites and blacks different?"

"Blacks are better at sports. Whites got more money and better jobs. They keep their jobs longer. They ain't as violent as blacks. They know how to handle things. If the boss jumps on 'em, they don't say anything. Blacks wanta fight. White's just chill out. That's how they keep jobs. I'm tryin' to learn to control that. But I sometimes think about how black people always had to say, 'Yes, sir! Yes, sir!' I do my best to prove I ain't like that."

I ask Chez, "Do you act differently around whites?"

"Yes, I try to act more like a gentleman, act smarter. I act proper, say 'Excuse me' and 'Thank you' a lot more often. That's how white people act."

Says Derrick, "I quiet down a little bit and don't talk loud and act crazy, so they don't get all jumpy and call the police."

I ask Derrick, "Where do you want to live as a grown-up?"

"I'll live in a half-white, half-black neighborhood. I just figure an all-black neighborhood will be bad."

I ask Fred, "Ever wonder what it would be like to be white?"

"If I was white, I wouldn't feel comfortable in black places. I wouldn't be wantin' to go around blacks. Some blacks I know don't like whites. They'll do stupid stuff, jump 'em and try to hurt 'em. They think about how white people used to treat black people."

I ask Bryan, "Why do some whites and blacks hate each other?"

"I don't know." He pauses. "If you go into a bar full of white people and you sit down, all they're gonna do is look at you."

I ask, "Why?"

"I don't know. I don't like to think about it."

Fred and Chez, Bryan and Derrick are of a single cultural mind, and they share this fantasy: Their team is down one point with seconds left in the NBA finals. The ball is in-bounded to one of them, depending on who is doing the fantasizing. Each shoots, each scores, each wins the game. The boys dream this dream, even though none of them plays on his school basketball team. It is a fantasy that drives their mothers nuts. Fred's mom got so upset about her son's obsession with basketball that she once wrote Doug Williams, the Washington Redskins former Super Bowl MVP black quarterback. He wrote back and told Fred that only one of ten thousand athletes makes it to the pros and that school is the road to success. But the boys all know this, at least in their heads. Every day—literally, every day—Fred's mother tells Fred that school, not sports, will be his ticket. The other mothers are almost as insistent.

I ask, "How important is education?"

"To hear my mother," says Derrick, "it's very important."

Yet the boys rarely study, and they all say that if they were rich, they'd quit school. Their public high school grades are mediocre. Bryan believes it's nerds who get As, but then adds wistfully that it's also nerds who will probably get the best jobs later. None of the guys lacks for great aspirations beyond basketball stardom. Bryan wants to be a TV sports announcer, Fred an electrical engineer, Chez a doctor, Derrick a mathematician or a computer expert. But they seem not to have a clue about how long and hard is the educational road for such careers. Not a clue that, as Nellie Cooke tells her class, they are already writing the plot for their failure or success. What strikes me about Fred and Chez, Bryan and Derrick is that they don't enjoy learning for the sake of learning. To them, reading and studying aren't ends in themselves—they are hurdles, means to the end of money and the things money can buy.

I ask, "Why does a person want a good job?"

"Money and nice things," says Bryan, who adds that he someday wants a house on the beach, a boat, and a Mercedes. None of the guys say people want good jobs to make them feel better about themselves or to contribute more to society. They don't believe people with big-shot jobs are respected more because they have worked so hard for so long, because of their importance to society or because of their naked power to get things done.

I ask, "Why are these people respected?"

"They got all that money," Bryan says.

There's truth in Bryan's cynical view. But at an age when kids can't see past the next date or zit on their chin, when a job search seems light years away, is this attitude enough to keep them focused on arduous schoolwork for four years of high school, four years of college, and years of graduate school? Especially if the exhilaration of solving an algebraic equation or the joy of suddenly understanding a Chekhov story can't compare to the power and glory of a single, beautiful, dancing, gliding pirouette through nine extended arms and a wall of hard bodies?

But, unknown to their mothers, the boys' basketball dream is quite consciously practical, keeping their minds off the other choices offered city boys—namely, using or selling drugs. "I avoid being in trouble by playin' basketball," Fred says bluntly. "Basketball, basket-ball! We play it all the time. I like playin', but as long as I'm playin' basketball, I'm also doin' somethin' positive." The boys each say they don't sell drugs, but it's also clear that these good kids don't look down on people who do sell drugs. To them, drug dealers are making a living—a good living.

I ask, "Are drugs ever a temptation?"

"Not usin' them," says Chez. "But sellin', yes. I was thinkin' about all that money, gettin' a truck and stuff."

"What kind of person sells drugs?"

"A person who needs the money," says Chez.

"Do you worry about getting mixed up with drugs?"

"Yeah, I worry about it," Fred says, again bluntly. "If I can't get a job." Fred worries about it enough that every night, when he says his prayers, he asks God to, please, not let him get hooked up with drugs, please, let him make it through.

Cooled down now, the boys must finish their game of 33. Derrick, who imagines he plays like the Los Angeles Lakers' James Worthy, has just scored point number 30, and a single three-pointer will clinch the game for him. But Chez, who imagines he plays like the Detroit Pistons' Joe Dumars, grabs the rebound and dunks. Fred, who imagines he plays like the Lakers' Magic Johnson, hits a shot, then another, making the score: Fred 31, Derrick 30, Chez 30, and Bryan 2. From the skeleton of the dead car, I watch and remember when I asked Chez the other day what he thought would eventually happen to him and his friends. He pondered for a moment and then said confidently, "We all gonna make it. Bryan's gonna make it because his whole family's behind him. Derrick's gonna make it because his mom and dad want him to. I'm gonna make it because my mom'll kill me if I don't. I'm gonna play in the NBA and be a doctor. Fred's gonna be an electrical engineer. Derrick's gonna do somethin' with computers. Bryan'll be a sports announcer on TV. Yeah, we all gonna make it."

The final play: Derrick shoots a three-pointer, misses . . . Chez 'bounds, passes up the dunk for a three-pointer, misses . . . Derrick 'bounds, misses . . . Fred 'bounds, dribbles behind his back, blows the lay-up . . . Chez 'bounds, dribbles backcourt, rises in the air, hangs, flicks a three-pointer—and *scores!* Wins! Yes, Chez wins, although from my perch on the black skeleton of the dead car, I can't help thinking that for these four good kids, four good friends, the game has just begun.

3

FACES IN THE CROWD

WASHINGTON, D.C.

The difference is in their faces. When Jesse Jackson, who now lives in Washington, speaks to the crowds, white supporters are enthusiastic, clapping and cheering. But blacks are different. It is in their faces. They are reverent. Their eyes are wide and their hearts are open. They have the look of kids who have touched the mitt of Will Clark or Rickey Henderson. They have the look of people on the Old Time Gospel Hour, as if they have just seen a miracle. I noticed this in Jesse Jackson's audience during the Democratic convention, the way Jackson seemed not to be speaking to blacks in the crowd, but through them, as if he were their medium, not their leader. Republicans don't look this way over George Bush. Democrats don't look this way over anybody. No, Catholics look this way over the Pope.

In some way I don't understand, black Americans see a Jesse Jackson that whites don't see. So for a few days, I follow Jesse around Washington, riding with him in his black Lincoln as he makes appearances at Taft Junior High School, Shiloh Baptist Church, and on the streets of Washington. I take names of people in the crowds along the way, get their addresses, arrange to visit their homes.

Marsha McDowell is late getting home to her rented Northeast Washington apartment and the man inside doesn't invite me in. So I sit in my car at dusk on the narrow side street where she lives and wait, noticing that black women suddenly begin appearing in the street and calling their children into their houses, glancing over at me as they do. It strikes me that a white man sitting in his car in this neighborhood attracts the same kind of prejudiced reaction that a black man sitting in his car in a white neighborhood would attract. People pass by for a good hour, and just about everybody seems to notice me. Finally, I give up and track Marsha down the next week at Taft Junior High, where she is a clerk in the principal's office. The neighborhood around Taft in Northeast Washington is one of the many black middle-class enclaves in the city that are invisible to whites. It's a nice neighborhood of small brick homes and tree-graced streets, where the yards and bushes sport haircuts and the porches wear welcome mats.

It was at Taft Junior High where I saw Marsha, who is thirty-two, meet Jesse Jackson. She didn't get to hear much of his talk, because she had to answer the school phones while everybody else was off in the auditorium. But still, she came away inspired. I ask why, and she tells a story.

Marsha was in junior high in rural North Carolina the year they integrated the white schools. It was rough going. The white kids said, "We don't want you niggers in our school." This baffled young Marsha, because in old black tradition her mother had always protected her from that particular slur by telling her that a "nigger" was "an ignorant person." So Marsha, a smart girl and good student, couldn't understand why the whites kept calling her ignorant. She laughs at the memory. Well, that first year she sat behind a white girl named

Elizabeth whose father was well-to-do. Marsha marveled at Elizabeth's long blond hair. "It was like gold," she says. For almost a year, Elizabeth refused to return Marsha's daily hello. Then one day, Marsha walked into the girls' bathroom and found a white girl and a gang of her friends threatening to beat up Elizabeth over some disputed boyfriend.

"If you hit her," Marsha said, "I'll have every black kid in this school on your behind." The white girls retreated. Elizabeth quietly thanked Marsha and walked out. But later, Elizabeth offered to help Marsha, whose grades were slipping under the pressure of her new school, with her homework. The girls became friends, at least friends after a fashion. They never visited each other's homes, never double-dated, but—for that time and place—they were friends, walking the halls together, talking, sometimes meeting at night at local hangouts. Marsha's grades went back up. "It wasn't the help," she says. "It was having a friend."

Life has been hard on Marsha. She went to college, dropped out, moved to Washington, and is now raising two children as a single mother. She landed on welfare for a year. But finally she got a decent job and went back to college. She hopes to graduate next year. Marsha says that poor people, black people at the bottom, have got to believe in themselves more deeply than people at the top, black or white. People at the bottom can't focus on the reality of their lives, they must look out and away, they must be inspired, because only a fool or an inspired person can believe in themselves when they are desperately poor.

That, she says, is the message she hears Jesse preach. So many blacks are successful today: Hollywood stars, athletes, politicians. But where are they? Marsha wants to know. They aren't preaching at Taft. When Jesse ran for president, Marsha says, it amazed and inspired her. Not only because he did it, but because he got all those Iowa farmers—those white Iowa farmers—to vote for him. Like her friendship with Elizabeth, it gave her hope.

At Washington's Shiloh Baptist Church, in the crowd of elderly black women wearing necklaces of pearls, handsome dresses, and hats of reds and greens and the younger black women wearing necklaces of gold and fashionably broad-shouldered suits, sixty-four-year-old Clarice Harvey stands out to me. She's beautiful and elegant in her black skirt, white blouse, gold jacket, and gold-and-black hat studded with rhinestones. I notice that she beams like a lantern through Jesse's sermon on everything from drugs to faith to Republicans to the way his mama used to sweep clean the hard dirt in front of his boyhood South Carolina house.

A few days later, I find Mrs. Harvey's house in Washington amid a neighborhood of public housing projects. It's a pretty barren place, and Mrs. Harvey, now a widow, lives here alone in her spotless home, with her furniture kept good-as-new by their clear plastic covers. Her walls are filled with pictures of her deceased husband and their two sons. I tell her it was her stunning gold-and-black hat that made me notice her at Shiloh last Sunday. She tells me that she made it herself to match the outfit she wore. What Mrs. Harvey says she admires most about Jesse Jackson is his praise of the old values: study hard, work hard, stay straight, do your best, obey the law, love your family, love the Lord—and a good life will most likely come your way.

Mrs. Harvey was raised by an aunt in rural Buckingham, Virginia. Even as a little girl, she was a domestic who worked for her room and board. But she grew up and did what a generation of country blacks did—she moved to the city, met her husband, who was a tailor, and together they bought this little house. The now-deteriorated neighborhood was country when they moved here thirty-five years ago: no stores, no buses, and no public housing. The schools were good and Mrs. Harvey's boys excelled.

"I never had a problem with either of them," she says. "I had to go to nobody's jail to get them out. This was my hope and my dream: that my children would finish high school and go to college and finish college and become productive, good people. I'm blessed and I'm not ashamed to say it. I'm proud of them, very proud." When the projects came and the schools started going to hell, Mrs. Harvey fought ceaselessly to get and keep her sons in Washington's better public schools. The rules could be damned. "It was my children's welfare," she says. Charles graduated from Howard University. James, as a junior-high student, won a scholarship to Putney, a small, elite prep school in Vermont. "It was unbelievable," Mrs. Harvey says, recalling her first visit to the campus. "A school up on a hill with all-white clapboard buildings."

"What about Jesse Jackson?" I ask.

Joe Green,
Oxford, North Carolina.

Dori Sanders, York, South Carolina.

Virgil Fleming and family, Tunica County, Mississippi.

Bertha Lee Turner,
Marks, Mississippi.

James Brown, Pulaski, Tennessee.

John French,
Little River County, Arkansas.

Bienville Kees, Boley, Oklahoma.

Henry "Pee Wee" Hampton, Minneapolis, Minnesota.

Davill Armstrong,
Houston, Texas.

Charles Burnett, View Park, California.

Dolores Robinson,
Beverly Hills, California.

Sharon Richardson Jones,
Oakland, California.

Ishmael Reed,
Oakland, California.

John Langston Gwaltney, Lacomb, Oregon.

Mrs. Harvey takes a deep breath and says that as a little girl in elementary school, she remembers thinking to herself about how all the presidents had been white. She remembers thinking that blacks weren't allowed even to run for president. Jesse Jackson, she says with satisfaction, has ensured that no black children in elementary school today will ever have the same thought. "The main thing was that he didn't give up," Mrs. Harvey says. "He got knocked down, but the victory is in gettin' up. I admire him for where he's come from and where he's going. He tells people they can elevate themselves out of the ghetto, and I know they can."

Finally, on the way out the door, I ask, "By the way, what ever happened to your son James after Putney?"

"James," Mrs. Harvey says. "Oh, he graduated from Yale."

At the corner of Sixth and L streets, it looks as if Samuel Farmer's face might fall off. There he is, working with the road crew patching the street when the Lincoln stops at the light, the window rolls down, and the hand comes poking out. Sam leans down, unimpressed, until he sees the face—the face of Jesse Jackson. Sam sputters unintelligibly, wipes his hand and shakes.

A few days later, I visit Sam Farmer, who is fifty years old, at his girlfriend's apartment in one of Washington's most notorious housing projects, Stanton Terrace. It's a place of two-story brick buildings, many of them with neither windows nor residents. It's daytime but the streets and dirt yards are nearly empty—of bikes, barbecues, and children playing, except for a few boys who are accompanying their own rap music compositions on miscellaneous pots and pans. Sam Farmer answers the door, glances both ways furtively and says that he always checks to his left and to his right for suspicious characters whenever he opens the door.

"Oh, man!" he says joyously after the door bolts are closed behind us. "I met Jesse Jackson! I met Jesse Jackson! I never got a chance to meet important people." He pauses. "You know what I mean, not a man like me." Sam Farmer has lived in Washington since precisely 5 P.M., June 3, 1956, when he stepped off a Baltimore-bound beer truck he'd hitched a ride on from Dillon, South Carolina, where he'd grown up in a shack with kerosene lamps and no electricity. "We was dirt-poor sharecroppers. We raised everything and had no money. We plowed from sunup to sundown for three dollars a day.

We worked for the *man*—the man with the plantation." Sam's mother died when he was seven. He never knew his daddy. His brother raised him. He got enough schooling to read and write, though some of his brothers didn't.

At seventeen, Sam figured he'd had enough. One of his brothers lived in Washington, so Sam went there with no job, no suit, two pairs of shoes, and $6 in his pocket. In a week, he had a construction job earning $12.50 a day. With his first paycheck, he strutted down to the old District Credit Clothing on Seventh Street NW, put down a fin on a $50 suit, and was suddenly a man about town. Sam got married, unmarried. He had eight kids. For twenty-three years, he worked a jackhammer, until his insides were so jumbled that he seemed to spend more time at the doctor than he did on the job. Now he patches roads, which is seasonal work, and he worries about losing his health completely and being unable to work at all. A while back he tried to get a job unloading trucks and they said he needed a high school diploma. Sam Farmer twice voted for Jesse Jackson for president. If Jackson ran for dog catcher, Sam would vote for him.

"When he ran for president, I really got into it," Sam says. "A black man running for president!" He watched every minute of the Democratic National Convention at which Jesse spoke on national TV, every minute. "Somethin' hit me," Sam says proudly. "I sat and really cheered." It was just such a long leap from his childhood to Jesse standing on that podium. Sam is quiet for a moment, then leans forward in his chair and says that his grown sons tell him that if they had lived in the segregated South of Sam's youth, they would never have put up with it. They'd have fought back. Sam shakes his head. "They just don't know. They just don't know."

I ask, "What does Jesse Jackson stand for to you?"

Says Sam Farmer, "I got a son, seven years old."

4

THE CLIENT AND THE CASEWORKER

LANDOVER HILLS, MARYLAND

Shirley is the client. Jackie is the caseworker.
They were united a year ago on Tuesday afternoon, March 6, after the life of Shirley Rogers was routed Jackie Jordan's way via the usual, groaning channels of the poverty system. Shirley, who is fifty-five, was about to be evicted from her rented house in the nearby Maryland suburbs of Washington. Jackie, who is forty, was and still is what they call an intensive family services specialist. There aren't many like Jackie in the welfare system. Jackie works in one of two pilot programs in America aimed at giving social workers the time and flexibility to actually make a difference in their clients' lives. Most social workers are buried in clients they see only in the office, nine to five. They don't have time to know their clients as people. Likewise, their clients don't have time to know them—or, what's more important, to trust them.

So Jackie is a rare breed. At any given moment, she'll have only a half-dozen clients whom she might see two, three, four times a week, night or day. She'll go to their homes or their jobs, talk to their children, their spouses. She'll dog her clients, lobby for them with other social agencies. For as long as six months, she'll try to win their trust, sort out the grab bag of woes in their lives, devise a strategy of attack, and then charm, threaten, embarrass or frighten them into deciding to change their lives.

I sought out Jackie and Shirley, both of whom are black, because so many white people—not to mention the black college students in Little Rock—seem to believe that too many lazy black folks are sitting at home living high on the hog off welfare. I wanted to look at one welfare case to learn something about the human and bureaucratic complexity that faces social welfare workers and recipients. So I talked with Jackie and Shirley again and again, alone and together, collecting and correlating their intricate stories about how changing the life of one lost and struggling person is quite possible and at the same time nearly impossible. I didn't really do anything with Jackie and Shirley—didn't pick peaches, didn't walk the back forty, didn't attend classes or play basketball. All I did was listen. This is their story.

MARCH 9, A YEAR AGO Shirley is too busy to see Jackie, at least that's what she has told her. Truth is, Shirley is sick of Meddling Millies like Jackie Jordan, the prissy pests from this or that welfare agency, with their prying questions, empty promises, and hints that they don't believe half of what Shirley tells them. Where's the beef for Shirley, who is a short, large, somber-faced woman who, except at funerals and weddings, wears no-brand sweat suits, summer or winter. No, Shirley tells Jackie, Sorry, just can't make it, won't be home, gotta work today. But Jackie is sweetly persistent, saying that she will stop by the group home where Shirley works as a cook and housekeeper.

Shirley's fall to poverty has been so swift that she almost can't believe it. For eleven years, she'd been off welfare, working at the Lt. Joseph P. Kennedy Institute for the disabled, earning about $350 a week and loving every minute of it. Shirley taught ceramics classes at night and coached the floor hockey team. A year before Jackie's visit, Shirley might have pinched herself to be sure that her life wasn't a dream. For four years, she'd lived in a big rented house with her working son, who has sickle-cell anemia, his wife, and their three children; her working daughter, her four children, and her longtime male companion, who also worked; and another grown daughter, Jonnie, who is paralyzed on one side and suffering from lupus and sickle-cell. It was a lot of personalities to balance, all right, but with several people working at low-paying jobs and Jonnie's social security disability income, there was money for the $685-a-month rent, and some frills.

Then, *crash!* Shirley's working son moved out with his family to get a place of their own. Another son got hurt, lost his job, and moved into the house without any income. Then Shirley's working daughter and her companion moved out, leaving a teenage daughter with Shirley. All Shirley had left were her wages and Jonnie's disability income—to buy food and necessities for herself, Jonnie, her unemployed son, and her granddaughter. To top it all off, three of her grandkids had landed in foster care, and Shirley was struggling to win the right to care for them. All in a year!

On the first day Jackie visits Shirley at work, Jackie is impressed.

Although Shirley is abrupt, she's smart and articulate. She's also very proud, aloof, with a kind of defiant nobility. The toughness is a good sign. Jackie has learned that the best candidates for climbing up and out are people who take responsibility upon themselves, rather than blame society, racism, or bad breaks for their predicament—even if society, racism, and bad breaks are to blame. The illusion of power can create the reality of power. Another good sign is that the home where Shirley works as the housekeeper is spotlessly clean. "If you want to do something," Shirley finally tells Jackie, "then bring groceries." Shirley is down to cereal, milk, potatoes, and mulligan stew, a simmered mix of anything on the shelves—say, Spam, rice, spaghetti, peas, carrots, macaroni, and ketchup.

When Jackie leaves, Shirley figures it's the last she'll see of that pretty debutante, with her beauty-shop hair, dangling earrings, and fancy clothes. But that evening, Jackie arrives with bags of groceries. Shirley is shocked: somebody has finally delivered.

Jackie Jordan simply will not go away. She knows that the more little things she can do, the more Shirley will trust her on the big things. Jackie visits Shirley at least twice a week, calls her on the phone even more often. She knows that she must position herself between Shirley and the social service workers and agencies that Shirley sees as the enemy—as cold, uncaring bureaucrats. There's more truth in Shirley's caricature of Jackie's colleagues than Jackie likes to admit.

But even after only a few months on the job, Jackie understands what the system does to her colleagues. Nearly every day, a client disappoints you—lies to you, promises to do something and doesn't. They oversleep for a sick child's doctor appointment that you've fought to set up. *They oversleep!* Cynicism sweeps over you as the only defense. And just like Shirley can no longer allow herself to get her hopes up over the promises of social workers, social workers can no longer allow themselves to get their hopes up over the promises of clients. You just stop believing in the possibility of redemption. But Jackie's job is different. As an antidote to the cynicism, she can actually see people's lives get better. She's actually paid to do what all social workers ought to be able to do: take the time to make a difference.

MARCH 23 First off, Shirley needs an affordable place to live. From Shirley's apartment to her job in the city is a two-and-a-half-hour commute by bus, and finding a home closer to work would be smart. But Shirley has her paralyzed daughter, Jonnie, in the suburban public medical system, and she's afraid to change to Washington. Jonnie is constantly in and out of the hospital, and Shirley figures there'd be some screwup in the transfer and Jonnie would end up without care in an emergency. She'd rather commute. So Jackie gets Shirley on the waiting list for several public housing projects in Maryland, and goes with her to the Glenarden Apartments, a recently renovated project, to fill out the applications. No regular apartments are available for months, but Glenarden has empty units for handicapped people, and Jonnie makes Shirley eligible. In only a few weeks, Glenarden officials have scheduled an inspection of Shirley's home to make sure she's a desirable tenant.

Shirley doesn't know it yet, but Jackie has an ulterior motive for trying to get her into Glenarden. It's now that Jackie must play the uncomfortable role of God. She has decided that it's time for Shirley's children, who range from twenty-six to thirty-five years old, to stop returning to Mama when things get tough. Jackie feels the same way about another person in Shirley's life, someone with a drug problem who is very close to Shirley and whom Shirley often helps out with a place to stay. Glenarden will not allow any of Shirley's adult relatives or friends or grown children except Jonnie to share Shirley's new apartment. So if Jackie can get Shirley into Glenarden, she won't have to persuade Shirley to stop housing her children because the problem will take care of itself.

Then the other shoe drops: Glenarden rejects Shirley, claiming she has an "unpleasant attitude" and that her house is unkempt. Jackie, baffled, swings into action. Somebody—Shirley suspects one of her children who doesn't want to be left behind if Shirley moves—had trashed Shirley's house, turned it upside down, just before the inspectors arrived. And Shirley—proud and disdainful of social workers—also hadn't acted sufficiently grateful for the chance to move into Glenarden, at least that's what Jackie concludes. Weeks go by and no public housing slot opens anywhere else, so Jackie goes back to Glenarden, hat in hand. She asks Shirley to cool out. She asks Glenarden officials to consider Shirley's fierce pride an asset, not a liability. She convinces them to inspect the group home where Shirley is the housekeeper, since it must pass strict cleanliness inspections.

Jackie goes out on a limb—she vouches for Shirley personally. This time, Shirley is approved. She can move to Glenarden in August.

MAY 9   Two months after they meet, Jackie Jordan begins formal counseling sessions with Shirley. At first, Shirley doesn't want to hear about—what does Jackie call it?—"codependency," about how she supposedly lets her kids take advantage of her because it proves she's needed. My, God, somebody in your family's in trouble, what do you tell them, sleep on the street?

But Shirley, who is a thinker, mulls Jackie's comments. She has come to trust Jackie, who is probably the best friend Shirley has had in years. She just isn't like all the others. She seems to actually respect Shirley. She's not condescending. And she has kept every promise. Jackie has given Shirley the gift of optimism. Folks outside the welfare "system" just wouldn't believe what it's usually like. Once, when Shirley called an agency to set up an appointment, a recorded message told her calls were only accepted after 2:30. But after 2:30 the lines were always busy. So Shirley took a day off work and went in. She was told that because she hadn't called ahead for an appointment nobody could see her. Jackie, ever since that day she dropped off those bags of groceries, has been different. So Shirley listens.

And, well, when Shirley thinks about it, she realizes that she has let people walk on her, especially men. And as her kids were growing up, she was racked with guilt about how she couldn't give them the nice things they wanted, about how she and her husband had divorced, leaving them without a father. Shirley even felt guilty that two of her children were born with the genetic disorder sickle-cell anemia, as if her genes had volition. Jackie had asked, "When are you going to be strong enough to kick your children out?" Shirley could never do that, but she now realizes that she must first think of her sick daughter, Jonnie, of the three grandkids in foster homes, and of the fourteen-year-old granddaughter she's raising, whom Shirley has just discovered is pregnant. Glenarden it is!

AUGUST 6   Moving day is less than a week off and Shirley isn't feeling good about it. Her still-unemployed son, a quiet and withdrawn man, seems hurt to be pushed out of the house. He disappears without a word. Meanwhile, Shirley is also deeply afraid for the person with the drug problem, who looks worse and worse, like a skeleton.

Amid this gloom, Jackie Jordan makes her play. She suspects that the person with the drug problem sees the bottom of the pit looming and knows Shirley won't be a fallback anymore. Jackie has purposely never talked to the person about drugs, but now she does. Indifference is the first response. But in just three days, with Jackie's lightning help, the person is registered, admitted, and moved into a one-year residential drug treatment program. Shirley doesn't even know about any of this until after it happens, but she believes that Jackie has saved a life.

DECEMBER 7   Jackie has been off Shirley's case for months now. But like old friends, they stay in touch. When Jackie visits just before Christmas, she discovers that Shirley has no money, no Christmas tree, and no presents for her children or grandchildren. Jonnie has been in the hospital so many days this year that Shirley has overdrawn her vacation time without realizing it. She had planned to use her last paycheck before Christmas for gifts, but now there will be no check. For months, Shirley has struggled to get her three grandkids out of foster homes, but she has gotten only one so far. In pursuit of the other two, she has found a day-care woman in her apartment building and has gotten the public voucher payments for the day care approved.

But she has to figure out a way to get home by 6:00 to pick up the kids. If she takes the first bus at 6:00 A.M. from the liquor store near her home and then transfers to four other buses before arriving at work, she still can't get there much before 8:30. That would mean she could leave work at 3:30, but the bus commute back would still often run her past 6:00 in the evening. Shirley could take the subway, but that would be an extra $4.60 a day, which would put her budget in the red and probably make the foster care folks say she can't afford to feed and clothe the grandkids so she can't have them.

In the meantime, Shirley's now-fifteen-year-old granddaughter has had her baby, who goes to the home of one of Shirley's daughters during the day. Jackie had gotten the granddaughter into a home-study program and then back in school, but recently the granddaughter has stopped going to school again. But right now, that helps Shirley, because when Jonnie is home from the hospital somebody has to be there to take care of her. Shirley has been on several waiting lists for months now to get Jonnie into some kind of day-care program. No luck so far.

She tells Jackie that Jonnie could die before she gets off the lousy waiting list. After her Christmas visit, Jackie puts out the word that Shirley needs help, and several agencies come through with Christmas gifts for the grandkids. Then, while Shirley is walking across the parking lot one night, she notices a little artificial Christmas tree in the trash and takes it home. She sprays it with disinfectant and decorates it. She takes a few dollars she's been hoarding and at the Dollar Store she buys three teddy bears, three Raggedy Ann dolls, crayons, a coloring book, and a thousand-piece puzzle. She'll have a little Christmas after all.

DECEMBER 25 Jackie takes the good things in her life less for granted these days, especially at Christmas. Her job is to change people's lives, but her job also has changed her life, which seems more fragile to her now. She thinks more about how each day could be the last best day of her life, how it can all change overnight. She still plans for the future, like any good Middle American, but she's less certain about it all.

Jackie sees so much more clearly the illusion of permanence, the illusion that she is in control of her life—illusions created by her stable upbringing, her college education, her good income. But believing these illusions has given her real power that people like Shirley don't have. The less experience her clients have had with the straight middle-class life, Jackie has come to believe, the longer are their odds of ever achieving it. Everyone says they want a steady job, a nice place to live, a stable and loving family. But for those who have never experienced these things, the ambitions are more like dreams than goals. People can describe the good life, but it is something akin to the way Jackie might describe what she'd do with a million dollars from the lottery. The talk is fantastic. People must first be able to imagine the real experience of middle-class lives before they can pursue them.

Jackie thinks of the time she was listening to a man play classical piano in an event at the mall. Standing there, she overheard a beautifully mannered little girl tell her mother, "Oh, listen, Mommy, he's playing Bach, and it's my favorite piece." The little girl wasn't being snotty. Bach was simply the world she knew, and that knowledge—and all the other kinds of knowledge that go with it—will matter in that girl's life, because she will not be able to imagine herself any other way. Her idea of herself will in some very real way create the person she will be. Things, Jackie has come to believe, are not all that money buys.

* * *

FEBRUARY 1 Two of Shirley's grandkids are still in foster care. Her son who had disappeared when she moved to Glenarden has turned up living in a shelter, and Shirley would like to help him. Her teenage granddaughter still needs to be gotten back in school. But worst of all, Jonnie has been in the hospital off and on for weeks, which means Shirley has had to find time to visit her every day. She has missed too much work again. And as if Jonnie's illness weren't enough, just a few days ago Shirley's son landed in the hospital with a sickle-cell crisis. He's home, but very weak.

When will it stop? Shirley wonders.

This morning Shirley is at work, has just gotten off the phone with Jackie, when the hospital calls: Jonnie is dead.

A WEEK AFTER THE FUNERAL Shirley gets a letter from some agency telling her that Jonnie has finally been placed in day care. Shirley calls the name on the letter: "She doesn't need you anymore," she says coldly. "She's dead." When Shirley tells Jackie that she has done this, Jackie simply nods. What is there to say?

5

BRYAN'S SECRET

MILTON, DELAWARE

Way back in Alabama I met Bryan Stevenson, the young Harvard Law School graduate who defends men sentenced to death. Bryan is so decent a man that he reminded me of the legend of the *lamedvovniks*, the Righteous Men of ancient Jewish lore. The people I visited in Washington—Nellie Cooke and her students, the city boys with their grand dreams and limited savvy, Shirley struggling to stay a step ahead of disaster, the men and women inspired by the prideful image of Jesse Jackson—have made me think of the future—and how difficult it is to look ahead with confidence and optimism if your day-to-day life isn't an affirmation of those qualities. Bryan Stevenson, from an average family in a backwater town, has been so successful, always so confident and optimistic, that I'm curious about whence he came. So on a beautiful sunny afternoon, I leave Washington and drive across the Chesapeake Bay Bridge, through the swaying farmlands of Maryland's Eastern Shore and into tiny Milton in rural southern Delaware. I find Bryan's childhood home, a little white ranch house on county Route 319, and his father, Howard, a short, trim man with dark gray hair and black plastic glasses. Right off, he takes me to the Prospect African Methodist Episcopal Church on Railroad Avenue, past the road signs riddled with bullet holes, past Vern's Used Furniture.

It's a small, not so sturdy, white clapboard church about the size of some living rooms I've seen. The sanctuary is adorned with bright flowers, a cloth rendering of the Last Supper, and a piano and an organ, much like the ones Bryan once played here two, three nights a week and all day on Sundays. The church, with its vaguely musty aroma, is the very image of the tiny churches that dot rural America. Let me tell you, it's a damn sure long way from Prospect AME to Harvard Law. I am marveling at this when I notice that Bryan's father is standing before the little altar, framed by the bright flowers and the Last Supper rendering, lost in thought. He shakes his head, looks around at the empty sanctuary, and says wistfully, "Bryan used to set me on fire when he prayed out loud." Bryan never wanted to be a preacher, he says, but boy, oh, boy, he could preach to make your backbone shiver. And when that boy played "Swing Low, Sweet Chariot" on the organ your soul turned inward, as Howard's seems to do now, just thinking about it. As for myself, I can't help thinking about my Unitarian church, where one hot hymn is Mozart's Sonata K. 333, second movement.

Howard was raised in this ramshackle little church and has forever been a practicing believer in Pentecostalism—with its emotional and sublime encounters with the Holy Spirit, people who go off in cathartic spells and talk in what is gibberish to nonbelievers but what are tongues to the faithful. Pentecostalism was a backwoods faith that moved to America's cities with poor Southern blacks and Appalachian whites in the early twentieth century. It was a faith that softened the migrants' landing—the faith that Pulitzer Prize–winning black novelist James Baldwin immortalized in *Go Tell It on the Mountain*. In the sixties, Pentecostalism burst forth into the American middle class as the charismatic movement, which abandoned the more gaudy, snake-handler, Holy Roller trappings of the old faith and made this dressed-up, college-educated Pentecostalism part of main-line Protestant and Catholic faiths.

Traditionally, Pentecostalism was a faith of the poor, uprooted, and dispossessed. Howard Stevenson is no dressed-up charismatic. He's an old-fashioned Pentecostal. His wife, from a white-gloved Philadelphia Baptist church, hadn't realized this when they married, not until she saw Howard go off in the Spirit—"get happy" with the Holy Ghost. Oh, God, she was mortified! Howard laughs when he tells the story, adding that she didn't want her children to fall victim to his hick religion.

Back at the house, I say, "I remember Bryan telling me that you and Mrs. Stevenson didn't understand why he works for practically nothing until just recently. What did he mean?"

Without hesitation, Howard jumps up from the couch and dashes to the television. He roots around in a cabinet full of videotapes and pops one in the VCR. "This was last April," he says. "Bryan spoke to the national youth conference of the AME Church." In a few moments, Bryan, all grainy, comes on the screen. And for half an hour he talks, starting slowly and then, moved by the power of his own words and emotions, quickly. He says that we execute the retarded, the young, and the mentally ill. He says that we execute men for killing whites far more often than we do for killing blacks. He tells of the defense lawyer who was drunk, and of the blacks who are so often struck from murder juries by white prosecutors. He talks of the judge who said of a convicted man's parents, "Since the nig-gers are here, maybe we can go ahead with the sentencing phase." Then Bryan says, "It's not enough to see and deal with these things from a humanistic perspective. You've got to have a spiritual commit-ment. So many talk that talk, but they don't walk that walk. We've got to be prepared to pay the cost of what it means to save our souls." He quotes the Bible—Matthew 25:34-45: "Then the King will say to those at his right hand, 'Come O blessed of my Father, inherit the kingdom prepared for you from the foundation of the world, for I was hungry and you gave me food; I was thirsty and you gave me drink; I was a stranger and you welcomed me; I was naked and you clothed me; I was sick and you visited me; I was in prison and you came to me. . . . Truly, I say to you, as you did it to one of the best of these my brethren, you did it to me.' "

Bryan's audience is roaring. His voice rising, he says, "I wouldn't exchange what I'm doing for anything. I feel the pleasure of God."

Howard gets up quietly, rewinds the tape. Tears are in his eyes. "I didn't understand his faith until this talk," the father says of the son. "He never talked about himself, ever."

Sadly, Bryan's mother, Alice, is in the hospital being treated for a life-threatening illness, and Howard and I go to visit. Her lean, elegant body and handsome face are the image of her son, as are her slow deliberate mannerisms, perfect diction, and clear, accentless voice. She sits in a robe in a chair next to her bed, illuminated by a single lamp. Seeming tired, she closes her eyes as she speaks. "I told him he was not going to live in the sticks all his life. Please do not be satisfied." She opens her eyes and laughs. "Sometimes I think he listened too well. He is so far away. I miss him so. Did Howard tell you we didn't understand him until April of this year when we heard him speak?"

"I watched the tape," I say.

"He never talked about himself, you know. Me, I've been a money-grubber all my life. But now that I've been sick, I see that Bryan is right. Really, what are we here for? We're here to help one another. That's it." After a pause, she says, "You know, a college friend of Bryan's once asked me, quite seriously, 'Could Bryan be an angel?' Sometimes I wonder. He was just the nicest child. He ate whatever I cooked and said it was the best food he'd ever eaten. If I was in a bad mood, he was always the first to notice it. He'd say, 'You all right, Mom?'"

Howard says, almost casually, "The Lord touched him."

"What does that mean?" I ask.

And Alice tells this story: When Bryan was thirteen, in a hot little Pentecostal church in Camden, Delaware, where she'd taken the Prospect youth choir to sing, "Bryan went off in the Spirit. He got happy. He danced." I ask what that means, and Alice and Howard chuckle at my naïveté.

"It is to be in a realm of complete and absolute joy," Alice says, although that day, Alice—not yet a Pentecostal believer—didn't feel joy. "I cried because I never wanted that to happen to Bryan. I didn't want him to be a backwoods cultist Christian. He broke out in a sweat, completely physically immersed, and the Spirit took him over. I held him, hugged him and cried. But this was my child, my darling, my flesh. I knew there was no falseness in him. So I knew this was a real gift from God. I stopped turning my nose up at it as something only ignorant people did." And looking out the kitchen window one morning soon after, watching the sun rise, Alice Stevenson was suddenly overwhelmed with the presence of God. "That feeling," she says, "can't be put into words."

Perhaps not, but I remember that James Baldwin seems to have come very close in the final passages of *Go Tell It on the Mountain*. I try to imagine a young Bryan Stevenson as Baldwin's character John, try to imagine how transforming must have been his experience, whether spiritual or psychological, whether rooted in the love of God, or the love of family, or both. Baldwin wrote: "And something moved in John's body which was not John. He was invaded, set at naught, possessed. This power had struck John, in the head or in the heart. . . . The center of the whole earth shifted, making of space a sheer void and a mockery of order, and balance, and time. Nothing remained: all was swallowed up in chaos. . . . His Aunt Florence came and took him in her arms. . . . 'You fight the good fight,' she said. . . . 'Don't you get weary, and don't you get scared. Because I *know* the Lord's done laid His hands on you.'

'Yes,' he said, weeping, 'yes. I'm going to serve the Lord.' "

Finally, I understand Bryan Stevenson.

6

THE SOUL OF SOUL

HARLEM, NEW YORK CITY

She's not nervous. Well, maybe a little. One butterfly hovering, darting in her stomach, just one. At least that's the way Stephanie Burrous thinks about whatever it is she's feeling this instant, as she peers out at the fifteen hundred howling, raging, clapping, jeering, cheering people just beyond the glittering red-velvet Chinese curtain to her right.

Maybe one butterfly, as she waits to take the stage at Harlem's Apollo Theatre on its famed Wednesday evening amateur night. From her perch among the cords and cables, pulleys and paraphernalia of the theater, she can see into the front rows to the left of the stage. The seats are filled with black people, mostly young and hip, coolsters. She wonders if this is good. It was a mostly white audience that put her over a few weeks ago on her twenty-second birthday, cheering her to a spot in tonight's quarterfinals of the Amateur of the Year competition. But there's no use wondering. Gospel music isn't any Apollo crowd's favorite listening. The Apollo has been a breeding ground for just about every wave of popular music to hit America in the last half-century—blues, jazz, swing, bebop, doo-wop, rhythm and blues, rock 'n' roll, soul, rap. But it has never been a bastion of gospel, and Stephanie knows it.

I'm here because after my visit with bluesman Wade Walton in Clarksdale, Mississippi, and with Bryan Stevenson's parents in Milton, Delaware, I want to know more about how the deep emotional, intuitive faith of African Americans is connected to black music. Stephanie understands that connection. She understands that folks don't have to speak Italian to love opera. She believes the Apollo audience, which often mercilessly boos contestants off the stage, cannot boo her, because "He" would not let that happen, not after that Sunday a year ago in the shaking, quaking, baking storefront church back home in Washington, D.C. That morning, Stephanie was hit so hard with the Holy Ghost that she saw white light and was transported from the room—to where, she doesn't know.

No, they won't boo. Stephanie smiles a tense, shy smile. She crosses her arms and stands slightly hunched, her left leg forward, her body's weight resting back on her right foot. She wears a black leather skirt and black blouse. Her hair is curled tight and moistened to a sheen. Her right front tooth is outlined in gold in the shape of a heart. Her body carries a light scent of baby powder. Her gold-rimmed glasses sit low on the bridge of her nose and she nudges them up with an index finger. She takes them off and wipes her eyes, a little perspiration.

I met Stephanie "Cookie" Burrous in Washington, D.C., one Sunday morning at the House of the Lord, where she was to sing, and I arranged to go with her to the Apollo. Until a few years ago, from age sixteen, she'd been singing with a local gospel group, the Melodyaires, and performing in black churches and at gospel shows up and down the East Coast. She sang in what's called an "anointed" style— a churchy, preaching style in the fashion of the old black pulpit. She wasn't contemporary, not melodic or soothing, and her favorite songs were wailing, old-time revival tunes. She was good. She knew it. And she had expected more, faster. So Stephanie decided to sell out. She knew that everybody from Dionne Warwick to Ray Charles to Aretha Franklin to Sam Cooke had begun their rhythm and blues careers after years of singing gospel, and Stephanie figured she'd do the same. She quit the Melodyaires and began practicing top 40 R&B songs, Anita Baker and Whitney Houston songs. She did demo tapes and sent them out to record companies. She stopped going to church regularly. Her motives were simple: money and fame.

But nothing broke. No record companies called. Friends kept telling her to go up to the Apollo's amateur night and she agreed, but kept putting it off, drifting—and afraid of being booed. She felt more and more empty, more and more like those photographs of spacemen floating weightless, tethered only tenuously to a mother ship.

Then one Sunday morning, Stephanie, her mother, and her sister were driving home from a friend's church when they heard gospel singing. Not fancy, prettified gospel singing, but raw and undisciplined, genuine gospel singing—the tearful nasal voices, the spontaneous cries of "Praise the Lord," the jangling tambourines. Gospel music as authentic as the washboard, harmonica blues of the Mississippi Delta. They stopped and found the House of the Lord of the Apostolic Faith. Its sanctuary was a little larger than a suburban garage, its pews were folding chairs, its flickering lights were fluorescent, its altar cross was rough wood. But none of this fazed Stephanie, who'd spent her whole life worshiping in unadorned Pentecostal churches like the House of the Lord. Stephanie liked the little church, but in her spaceman's drift, she went back only occasionally. Too lazy, too lost.

Then came November 25th a year ago, a mild, sunny Sunday. Stephanie really wanted to go to the House of the Lord that day. She just had a feeling. When she got to church, it was buzzing with the hum of people singing and dancing, clapping, praising God. She wasn't singing that day. She was playing the drums, just bopping along, when suddenly she began to cry. She felt sorry and happy at once—sorry she'd lost direction but happy that she was now feeling sorry. She felt what Clarksdale's Wade Walton had described as the duality of the blues—the good and the bad at once. Suddenly, she found herself standing before the congregation, with people crowding around her praying, singing, and proclaiming the glow on her face. But that is all Stephanie remembers, because at that instant she was gone, touched by the lightning of the Holy Ghost in the ancient way of Saul. As her jubilant fellow congregants wept and cried "Hallelujah!" and anointed the forehead of the body she had left behind, Stephanie was off with God in the white light, free of sin.

From that day, no more R&B. "I can't put my all into rhythm and blues," Stephanie says. "I *can* put my all into gospel." Now when Stephanie sings her gospel, it's like a prayer. No, it is not the same feeling she felt when the lightning struck, nothing could be as intense as touching God himself. But, she believes, it is somehow similar, somehow connected to the place where the mysterious human soul resides, where God dwells in all people.

Tonight at the Apollo, onstage and lit by a row of yellow stage lights on the left and right, Stephanie clasps the microphone in her right hand, bends her knees, twists her back slightly down and to her right, closes her eyes. With a millisecond of dramatic hesitation, she lets it rip in a low, deep, hoarse register—the blare of a trumpet, the boom of a cannon, the blast of an alarm:

> *Ama*AAAzii*IIIng Graa*AAA*aaa*AAAAAA*ce*
> *shall alwa*AaA*ys bee*EEee*EEee*EE |
> *MY-MY-MY-MY-MY-MY-MY-MY-MY* soOoOong of
> prai*AlaiAlai*se. . . .

Like a brass band on the Fourth of July.

That quickly, with the opening lyrics of "He Looked Beyond My Faults and Saw My Needs," Stephanie has broken a cardinal rule of gospel persuasion: start out slowly, let the emotions of joy and redemption and deliverance simmer before they boil, save something for a soaring finale. But not tonight. From word one, Stephanie dives deep into her chest, makes a guttural instrument of her throat, and rolls and riffs and vibrates. Blasted back in their seats, stunned, the Apollo crowd is silent, as if they've just taken a bucket of ice water in the face.

What this silence means is still unclear, but Stephanie figured she had no choice. A sixteen-year-old gospel-singing sensation had preceded her on stage tonight, and the girl had brought the Apollo to its

feet. At that moment, Stephanie resolved that there could be no simmer before the boil tonight.

Usually, when Stephanie sings, she feels the music as it comes out
of her, and slowly that feeling starts to swell and take over, empower
her. Singing is so deeply connected to her lifetime in the church, to
the feelings touched in her by the emotional waterfall of spiritual
conversion—her own and the hundreds of others she has wit-
nessed—that when she sings these feelings are rubbed and mingled
and finally loosed within her. At her music's deepest, she can forget
the audience is even there, and she can sing not so much to herself
but as if there were no distinction between her mind, her body, and
her emotions, as if she were not so much singing as breathing. Odd,
but it is when she most forgets her audience that her audience is most
touched. But it can take a few bars or verses for Stephanie to travel to
that private place—a place inexplicably similar to where she traveled
when she was struck by the Holy Ghost and, for those moments,
became totally devoid of vainglorious self-consciousness, totally
within and without herself at once. Singing at her best, Stephanie
feels as if she's sitting on the back porch of heaven. From the first
note tonight, it's where she must be.

So that's how she plays it. From her twisting crouch, amid the
audience's shocked silence, bathed in white spotlights on the darkened stage, she flings her left arm behind her, fingers and hand
extended and contorted and jerking, her face a mask of intensity. She
takes a few steps to center stage, and wails:

> *I do noOOot knOOOOOooOOOOoOoOow*
> *just why He caAAAme*
> *to-*wOo-wOo-wOo-wOo-wOo-wOowOo *loOoOove me so. . . .*

With each ornamented syllable and rhythmic somersault, spines quiver.
The ice-water shock passes. The folks at the Apollo may not speak Italian, but they sure love opera. And before Stephanie is past the first
stanza, they're howling, screaming, hooting, already on their feet.

One man hollers, "Sing it, girl!"

The Apollo talent scout who discovered Stephanie had tried to
convince her not to sing old-fashioned gospel songs at the Apollo.
Why not go with a more up-tempo, rhythm-and-bluesy gospel song?
But Stephanie was no longer willing to sell out. Since that Sunday

morning in November, her music has changed. After the lightning, her singing seemed deeper and people seemed to feel it more. And Stephanie, well, it sounds strange to say, but she sometimes feels as if she isn't in the room, as if she's pure essence singing only for the joy and wonderment of it. "I feel like I'm singing a song, but I'm not really down here singing a song," she says, still mystified by the sensation. "It's like I'm somewhere else and the Spirit just takes over." Just before going onstage, she had said, "I may not win, but they won't boo me."

Indeed, they are not booing.

All around the theater, people are rising in waves, clapping, rejoining Hallelujah!, hollering and hooting joyously. Stephanie is saving nothing for a finale. Her eyes are still closed, the veins on her neck are swollen, her glasses have slipped down her nose. She glistens golden with sweat, on fire, holding notes and riffing the scales, for five, ten, fifteen seconds:

*JesuUUUUus die*IEIE*ed for me*EEEE*eeee*EEEE*eeee. . . .*

Stephanie launched her song so intensely, it's hard to imagine what can be left in the small woman to bring it home, but she finds it:

How*OOW*-Ah-Ah-Ah-Ah-Ah-Ah-Ah-Ah *maAArvelo*UUUUUU-
UUUUUU-uh-ah-uh-ah-uh-ah-*us,*
*that gra*AaAaAaAa*ce that ca*AA*ught my fa*AA*lling*
*so*OoOoOoOo*ul.*

She snaps off the song's last note, drops her arms limply to her sides, and returns her attention to the audience, which has gone berserk. Stephanie is always her own worst critic, but standing in the wings, with her fellow Apollo aspirants congratulating her, Stephanie is serene and confident. She says, "I think it was right."

It will be hours before the night is done, before all the singers, dancers, and acrobats have done their thing, for better or worse, and the night's winners are chosen by the crowd's applause. So I wander upstairs to the dressing rooms to find Ralph Cooper, Sr., the frail old man who still emcees the first half of every Apollo Amateur Night and who founded the event fifty-five years ago.

Ralph Cooper, like so many black entertainers of his era, is a man who should be a legend, and I want to meet him. He was one of America's first R&B disc jockeys. He convinced a former Cotton Club chorus line girl named Lena Horne to come out of retirement to costar in one of his films. But perhaps his most singular claim to fame was his discovery of Billie Holiday singing at Hot Cha's spaghetti restaurant in Harlem. Ralph Cooper brought her to the Apollo stage at a time when the young woman knew only two songs.

In his memoir, *Amateur Night at the Apollo,* Ralph Cooper recites the Apollo's remarkable pedigree: Billie Holiday, Sarah Vaughan, Ella Fitzgerald, Duke Ellington, James Brown, Miles Davis, Charlie Parker, Earl "Fatha" Hines, Fats Waller, Billy Eckstine, Bessie Smith, Louis Armstrong, Count Basie, Louis Jordan, Fats Domino, Bo Diddley, Chuck Berry, Lionel Hampton, Gladys Knight, Stevie Wonder, Dionne Warwick, Aretha Franklin, Ray Charles, Sam Cooke, Patti LaBelle, Diana Ross, Michael Jackson, Little Richard, Smokey Robinson, Luther Vandross . . . to name a few.

But Ralph Cooper also recites the litany of offenses committed against America's great black artists—people recognized worldwide for shaping everything from big band swing to rock 'n' roll to disco to rap. Until very recently, their creations were often stolen or bought for a song. The jazz age anthem, the Charleston, was penned by Jimmy Johnson, the great stride piano player. Ever heard of him? Harlem was called "Swing Pan Alley" long before Benny Goodman became the King of Swing, hiring the great black swing composer Fletcher Henderson to write his arrangements. Ralph Cooper tells again the story of Memphis record executive Sam Phillips, who said, "If I could find a white man who had the Negro sound and the Negro feel, I could make a million dollars." He did.

The first songs Elvis Presley ever recorded—for his mother, the story goes—were ballads by the Ink Spots. Later, Elvis not only recorded the songs of black artist Otis Blackwell—"Don't Be Cruel" and "All Shook Up"—but his managers insisted Elvis even be given first writing credit. The list of Elvis's songs written and first performed by blacks is astounding. It includes "Lawdy Miss Clawdy" and "Hound Dog." Later, Bill Haley, Jerry Lee Lewis, Pat Boone, Tony Bennett, the Beatles, the Rolling Stones, the Doors, Led Zeppelin, Cream, Ten Years After, and even Megadeth recorded the songs of black artists. By the time of Megadeth, anyway, the black contribution to rock 'n' roll had been well documented, if little appreciated by the average white guy whistling "Don't Be Cruel" while walking his golden retriever in the suburbs.

I find Ralph Cooper upstairs in the dressing room, sitting on the couch. He looks very old up close, his eyes haggard and wandering, his hands trembling. But his memory is sharp. "When Billie came out at Hot Cha's and walked up on that little stage and sang 'Them There Eyes,' I knew," he says, recounting the story of his discovery of Billie Holiday. At the Apollo the next night, she sang the only two songs she knew—"Them There Eyes" and "When the Moon Turns Green"—and the crowd went wild. Ralph Cooper told the audience she'd learn a couple more songs and be back again, but some guy in the audience yelled, "Let her sing 'em again, Coop!" And so she did. "That was the first and last time I'd ever heard tell of a thing like that," he says.

I tell Ralph Cooper that I'm at the Apollo with Stephanie Burrous, the young woman who sang "He Looked Beyond My Faults" earlier tonight, and that I'm interested in how the spirit of her faith enlivens, deepens her music. That, says Ralph Cooper, is the secret to it all. That's why he was never worried about having enough good talent to fill the stage every Wednesday night for fifty-five years. Harlem and black America are filled with churches, and it is in those churches that blacks learn to feel, to experience their music in a way that whites don't. Ralph Cooper says blacks came to dominate and define the entertainment style in America because they were so much more in touch with their emotions, so much more able to dive into themselves, to lose themselves in their music. Because of their African and American religious traditions, blacks are in much closer touch with the intuitive side of their lives, in church and out, which is why whites often seem stiff and formal, cold and uncaring to them.

"They all came out of the church," Ralph Cooper says of the great black entertainers—Bessie Smith, Ella Fitzgerald, Ethel Waters, Sarah Vaughan, Aretha Franklin, Sam Cooke, James Brown, Whitney Houston, Patti LaBelle. Even those who didn't stand at the front of the church and sing still got a heavy dose of the spirit back in the pews. "That's where they got the *soul*, the feeling, the excitement—from the church," he says. "Very few just walked up to the microphone and started singing. If you turn your back today and listen to many white entertainers, you'll think they're black. They have adopted that black style, that soul styling, which comes from the church. It's the feeling, the *feeling*."

Back downstairs, at about midnight, the audience speaks: Stephanie ties for third and earns a spot in the year's semifinal Amateur of the Year competition. At that contest, Stephanie will not finish among the winners. But packing up the van to go home tonight, outside the theater's 126th Street stage door, under the Harlem street lights, with rap music pouring from a black Saab parked with its doors open, with hordes of vendors still hawking caps and ties, pears and apples just around the corner on African Square, Stephanie is a very happy woman. "I gave it my all," she says. "I thought it was good. I felt close to God. I never feel that way when I sing R&B. Gospel is me."

For her, the feeling is reward enough.

7

WHAT MAKES SPIKE DIFFERENT?

MANHATTAN, NEW YORK CITY

SCENE 1, BLACK-AND-WHITE, *FILM NOIR*

Gritty and urban, realistic and surreal at once, its characters, whites and blacks, talk in offbeat and cynical asides, in tangential remarks that often elicit no response, followed by long, long silences that nobody finds uncomfortable. The word "motherfucker" is said often and easily. In Manhattan's Sound One, Studio D, the light is vague and pale, making people's faces, including that of filmmaker Spike Lee, washed and colorless within an already washed and colorless black and gray room thick with a cigarette haze, which everyone has been breathing for eight weeks now during the arduous sound mixing for Lee's next flick.

Beyond these real-life characters, on the huge theater screen, rolls a splotchy black-and-white rough-cut of a film about fictional characters, Spike Lee characters, black and white characters, all with an equally gritty, offbeat, cynical, and urban way. They, too, say the word "motherfucker" often and easily.

Title this scene: Black & White & Spike all over.

For this private showing, I've got a front-row seat next to Spike, who at age thirty-four is already America's black film eminence. A dozen or so film editors, technicians, and music and sound experts also are sprawled around the dark room in the few rows of comfortable, cushioned seats or in the wheeled chairs down by the twenty-foot-long bank of buttons and knobs that can instantly put in the "sssplatt" of a foot in a puddle or suck out the "rrEEEEEE" of a police car's siren. For five days I'll sit, watch, and listen.

Spike is working on his fifth film, *Jungle Fever*, which must be finished next week. I'm here because his first films—*She's Gotta Have It*, *School Daze*, *Do the Right Thing*, and *Mo' Better Blues*—turned my head, and America's. Spike Lee's movies are filled with ideas and characters and language that rarely made it to the screen until he came along. They spotlight the buried realm of racial language, style, and belief that so many blacks and whites prefer to ignore. They poke and prod whites and blacks for their prejudices, portray irresponsible black characters no white moviemaker would dare create, portray human and humane black characters no white moviemaker would know enough to create. They even wrestle with the taboo topic of black-on-black prejudice and tackle the silent rift between poor and affluent blacks, which I have encountered again and again in my travels.

Spike Lee has taken flak from everybody—blacks who believe he's playing to white stereotypes, whites who think he's an anti-white bigot, blacks who think he glorifies "bougie Negroes," whites who think he endorses violence against whites. As for myself, I think he's a daring moviemaker raising issues that must be raised if this "race thing" is going to get better. I want to know what makes him different, what makes him able to see and portray what so many ignore.

SCENE 2, STUDIO D

Stevie Wonder's R&B classic "Livin' for the City" ("A boy is born/ in hard-time Mississippi. . . ") has been blasting during a stunning scene in *Jungle Fever*—the affluent black architect, Flipper, is searching for Gator, his crack-head brother, through the streets of Harlem and into a crack den that is reminiscent of the battlefield hospital scene in *Gone With the Wind,* although the casualties of this war aren't soldiers.

Spike is slouched in his chair, with his glasses sitting on the tip of his nose, his black Malcolm X cap (publicity for his next movie) pulled down to his eyebrows, his feet and their black-and-red Air Jordans propped up on the table. He wears a diamond earring in his left lobe. Suddenly, the music ends before the film stops and Stevie Wonder himself, who has been sitting beyond the iridescent bank of sound-mixing equipment, stands up in the darkness, his face white-lit by the movie projector, his sunglasses glinting and his shadow looming like a giant against the screen. He smooths his beard with a brush, spreads his arms like unfurling wings and sways in that way he does.

"Sounds good," he says softly. "I'm done."

Stevie Wonder has contributed nine songs to the *Jungle Fever* sound-track, and Spike is solicitous in his good-byes, especially compared with the curt way he can treat people, including me. But the next day, on the phone, when Stevie wants one of his songs to replace Frank Sinatra's "Hello, Young Lovers," which plays while three Italian men beat up their friend for dating a black woman, Spike is more like himself.

"No, no, no," he says, and suggests another scene for Stevie's song. He waits, rubbing his eyes, while Stevie talks on the other end of the line. Then he says, "It's either that or I'm gonna bite." No joke, Spike Lee has the balls to kill a Stevie Wonder song. "Call me back," Spike says. When Stevie calls back, Spike is again solicitous. Stevie has agreed.

Spike Lee comes from a long line of accomplished people, on both sides of his family. He grew up in New York, but his Daddy's family was from Snowhill, Alabama, a town so small it isn't in the Rand McNally Road Atlas index. Spike's great-grandfather graduated from Tuskegee Institute and become a convert to Booker T. Washington's philosophy of black self-sufficiency. In 1893, he founded the Snowhill Institute, a black private high school, at a place and time when there were even few black public high schools. Spike's great-grandmother was a European-trained musician who played Chopin and Brahms while her children sat on the floor reading Grimm's fairy tales. As children, Spike and his three younger brothers and his younger sister were told again and again the family legend of Big Mike and Phoebe, the great-great-great Lee grandparents from South Carolina who'd been separated under slavery—until Big Mike bought his freedom and walked to Alabama to find his wife and children. They were taught to be proud of their slave ancestry.

Spike's father, Bill Lee, was an intensely independent man who as a jazz musician refused to play commercial jingles. He attended the elite black Morehouse College in Atlanta, where he met Spike's mother, Jackie Shelton, who was attending the prestigious black women's school, Spelman College. Her own mother had attended Spelman; her father, Morehouse. But in those days, even college didn't guarantee blacks professional jobs, and Jackie's father was a postal clerk—who spent his free time reading French poetry in the original. Like Bill Lee, Jackie Shelton, who died in 1977, had a streak of raging independence.

Jackie Shelton's mother—Spike's grandmother, Zimmie Shelton—who is eighty-four, had foresight. She thought it ludicrous that there were different Atlanta finishing schools for dark- and light-skinned black girls—a theme that would later appear in Spike's movies—and she searched the stores for brown dolls for her daughter. She also saw to it that Jackie was immersed in the history and literature of black America. Years later, Jackie would teach African American literature and read her own children the works of black writers such as Zora Neale Hurston, whom Spike would later quote in the preface to *She's Gotta Have It*. Long before it became hip, Jackie Lee wore bold, bright pinks and purples and big, funky shoes, and she braided her hair in cornrows and beads, after styles she'd seen in books about Africa. She even braided the hair of her daughter, actress Joie Lee, who can remember that it was not whites but blacks—ignorant of African styles then—who made fun of their hair, perhaps reminded of the pickaninny braids of stereotypes past. But Jackie taught her children never to be embarrassed by what people thought.

Spike's a lot like his mother, a lot like his father. A double whammy.

SCENE 3, STUDIO D

From the Spike Lee slouch, he studies the *Jungle Fever* scene in which the Italian father beats the hell out of his daughter for having an affair with a black man. The father is hitting her wildly, whipping her with his belt, bellowing, "A fuckin' nigger! A nigger! What kind of woman are you? I didn't raise you to be with no nigger! I'd rather you be a mass murderer or a child molester!" It is a brutal, awful, hateful scene, and I cringe even after its tenth, fifteenth, twentieth run. The Italian father says "black motherfucker" like he's pulling a trigger.

"Ya know," Spike says in that tangential way, "Italians curse almost as well as blacks."

It's a short ride on the D train from Manhattan over the river to the Fort Greene neighborhood of Brooklyn, and I take a morning away from the sound studio to make the trek. Spike Lee grew up in Fort Greene and he has stayed there, where his Forty Acres and a Mule Filmworks is located and where he lives in a rented apartment just up the street from his father, who still lives in the house where Spike was raised. The business district at DeKalb Avenue and Bond Street outside the train station looks like a stage set out of the fifties, with its old squat brick-and-masonry buildings housing a Jackpot Discount and Wertheimer's ("We Sell For Less"). The faces on the crowded, sunny street are black and Hispanic and Asian. I hear snatches of Spanish and Arabic go past quickly, and a man on the corner with a battery-powered loudspeaker is yelling something indecipherable about Louis Farrakhan.

A few blocks up DeKalb, past the Soul Fashion clothing store and across from Fort Greene Park, where much of *She's Gotta Have It* was filmed, is Spike's Joint, a boutique filled with Spike Lee T-shirts and jackets (as pricey as $375), posters and pins. The neighborhood is different here. Well-scrubbed black and white women with their babies in strollers are standing on the street corner chatting, and the huge, four-story brownstones that line the side streets have clearly been refurbished. Fort Greene is often referred to as a "renaissance" neighborhood, filled with young African American movers and shakers besides Spike, including jazz musician Branford Marsalis, rap group Public Enemy's executive producer Bill Stephney, and an army of other black entertainment producers, lawyers, and artists.

Earl Smith, an old friend of Spike's from New York's John Dewey public high school and now the manager of Spike's Joint, isn't what you'd call a mover or a shaker. He grew up in the projects on Coney Island and was working for the YMCA when he ran into Spike on the

train ten years out of high school. As Spike did with just about everybody he knew in those days, he asked Earl to invest in *She's Gotta
Have It*, then only a shoestring dream girl.

"I'm gonna make the movie," Spike said.

"OK, sure, Spike, like I'm gonna build a rocket ship," Earl
thought. But Spike convinced him, and though Earl's girlfriend, now
his wife, thought he was nuts, Earl gave Spike $8,500—his life sav-
ings. In return, Earl won Spike's loyalty and a profit handsome
enough to buy his own refurbished four-story brownstone.

I ask Earl, "So knowing Spike changed your life?"

"It did," he says, as he walks up Washington Park, the wide and
tree-lined street of elegant old homes facing Fort Greene Park. It is
the street where Spike grew up. "When I visited Spike's house, that
was the first time I'd ever seen a brownstone."

"Any brownstones in Coney Island?" I ask.

"*Nooo!* It was bungalows and projects, nothin' but projects. So I'm
lookin' at these high ceilings in Spike's house, and I'm goin', 'Spike
we could put a basketball court in here.' And I'm seein' pianos and
an upright bass. I used to say, 'Man, I wanta come here!' I used to
show it off like it was *my* house!" Earl stops to laugh. It wasn't that
his family was poor. His dad had a good post office job. But living on
Coney Island—surrounded by working-class families like his own or
worse—Earl hadn't seen the possibilities.

As kids, Earl never saw the serious side of Spike, who wasn't a
leader in school, who never talked politics or race, Martin Luther
King or Malcolm X. The only incident that Earl recalls that seems significant when he looks back was the time Spike asked Earl to stop
calling a very dark-skinned girl in the neighborhood by her street-
imposed nickname, "Bosko"—after the black Looney Tunes caricature. At the time, Earl didn't think of Spike's request as a political act.
He had asked Spike, "Why, man, you like her?" Earl shakes his head.
"I just didn't think about it. I don't know why, but I always talked to
light girls. My wife is light. All the guys used to say, 'I want the light-
skin. I want the red-bone.'"

"The red-bone?" I ask.

"That's old, man. The red-bone, the light-skinned. I've heard people say, 'I wanta marry a light-skinned black or a Puerto Rican,
because I don't want my baby to be dark.' They just think it's prettier.
Such nice curly hair. I just never thought about it until *School Daze*

came out. Now I hear people talkin' 'bout it all the time. A girl asked me, 'Is that your wife?' I said, 'Yeah.' She said, 'I knew you didn't like dark girls.' She didn't even know me. Spike put all that out there, man."

By now, Earl has completed the grand, iconographic tour of Spike's neighborhood—the T & T Food Mart, where Spike buys his breakfast and listens for snippets of Italian dialogue for his movies; the Lopez Grocery Store, where Spike used to buy potato chips and candy when he was a kid; and the Baskin-Robbins where Spike worked in high school to earn money for Knicks tickets. The ice cream parlor is on Flatbush Avenue, inspiration for the name of the Flatbush brothers, the skinflint Jewish club managers in *Mo' Better Blues*. The world as Spike knew it.

"What about your brownstone?" I ask. "Is it decorated like Spike's house was as a kid?"

Earl smiles with mild embarrassment. "Almost," he says, explaining that the first thing he did after moving in was reverse the dining room and a bedroom. "I put 'em like Spike had 'em," he says. "I always told Spike, 'I'm gonna get a house like your father's. I'm gonna get a house like your father's.' I don't think Spike remembers that."

One of the few people Spike Lee talks with about the big questions raised in his movies—about things other than sports and music—is Lisa Jones, who writes for the *Village Voice* and who is the daughter of famed African American poet and dramatist Amiri Baraka, who has derided Spike for being a "bougie Negro," meaning that Spike has the artistic sensibility of a rich man, out of touch with the real black America. Lisa Jones was a student at Yale, where she met one of Spike's younger brothers, also a student at that aged bastion of the American Establishment—the alma mater of George Bush and William F. Buckley, Jr.

"I see Spike as part of the post–civil rights cultural movement," Lisa says. "For so many of us in the post–civil rights generation, the urge has been to fuse self-help and the fight against racism together into one. Take a stand against prejudice, but to blacks say, 'You have to be responsible for your destinies.'" The great issue of her generation, she says, is "the fusing of assimilation and separatism. How will they be balanced?" In other words, how can young blacks go to Yale, be journalists, doctors, lawyers, rich and famous moviemakers, and still be and feel black? Bougie or not, it's obviously a question many African Americans have had to face as the system has opened up for them. I hope a lot more will face it in the future. Spike's movies, and his life, posit an answer.

Spike has revealed a dirty little secret of African American life: prosperous and educated blacks have often been embarrassed by the style, language, and mannerisms of poor blacks, and as they've moved up the ladder they have often jettisoned the walk, the talk, and the cool, jazzy African American style that Spike has repeatedly captured in his films. For some, it is a distancing from their own people, but for many it is a matter of going along to get along. Spike says, for instance, that *Jungle Fever*'s black architect from Harlem, Flipper, works at an all-white firm and that his Standard English at work is strained and controlled. It's when he's with his friend Cyrus, a high school teacher played by Spike, that he is himself again—jiving and cursing, talking joyfully in the language and style of Harlem.

"W. E. B. Du Bois always talked about the duality of a black person here in America," Spike tells me. "You're an African and at the same time you're living in America. And Flipper, he has one world up in Harlem, and in his other world he's deep inside white corporate America. And that schizophrenia, that screws you up. You got to keep doing this tap dance between these two different worlds. That's given a lot of black men high blood pressure over the years. I just want to put out the question: Is it worth it to kill yourself? How much are we gonna do to be accepted?"

Accepted, that is, by whites.

The classic example of a black person trapped between his cultural tastes and the white world, Spike says, is the black who'd die before being seen eating watermelon at an office picnic. Even if he loves watermelon. That person is paying too high a price. Spike Lee eats watermelon at the office picnic. And in his films, he has mimicked his own life by creating characters—jazz musician Bleek Gilliam in *Mo' Better Blues* and Flipper and his wife and her friends in *Jungle Fever*—who are both affluent and black, people who talk black, act black, and think black but who are also educated, sophisticated, and successful.

"The old civil rights movement was to show white people that we're just as good as you," says Spike. "My generation, we didn't have to fight that battle. My concern is not to show white America that we're human beings, we're people." His concern is to show blacks as they are, whether whites like it or not. So Spike's affluent black characters work hard, collect art, and live well—but they also curse and jive, play the dozens, have riotous sex, and use the "invariant *be.*" And they be proud of it!

But as John Hickman, the principal at Little Rock's Central High School, said, people like Spike Lee, people who've already made it, can flaunt their hipster style and get away with it, because they already have acquired the middle-class skills they need to get ahead. Says Spike's friend and jazz musician Branford Marsalis: "I grew up middle class and most of the rich white kids I knew thought the world was theirs to lose. I grew up that way and so did Spike. To paraphrase Jesse Jackson, he was *somebody.* He didn't have to be told." In short, Spike Lee didn't get his black pride from his first high school African American history class, and it shows in his confidence and his immunity to attacks from both blacks and whites. He displays no compensatory black bravado.

Spike Lee is not embarrassed in any single way to be African American, and he'd never feel "less black" for criticizing black people. He doesn't believe it reflects "negatively" on his race to portray the drug addict son, Gator, in all his grisly horror. Nor is he afraid to describe simultaneously the humanity in that wreck of a man. Spike isn't afraid to admit that young black men use the word "motherfucker" about as often as George Bush says "golly." He isn't afraid to announce that light-skinned blacks often look down on dark-skinned blacks, even if it gives more ammunition to white racists. And he isn't afraid to portray black street-corner philosophers who would seem dangerously similar to Amos and Andy if it weren't for the affection with which they are portrayed. There's a kind of racial imperialism about all of this, of course, because it implies that successful blacks who speak Standard English and don't honor street jive are somehow less black—you know, Uncle Toms. I've no doubt that Spike believes this.

"See, what it all comes back to is that they think all this stuff will be used against black people to do further damage," he says of his films and their black critics. "That this will solidify all the negative portrayals. But I think that is outweighed by the good that could come from discussing these things. I mean, you cannot hide the fact that millions of black kids are being born out of wedlock. We gotta stop worrying about what white people think. I mean whites aren't killing black people. The cops, they're doing their part, but it's black people killing black people all across the country. We won't be able to turn anything around if we don't address these things."

I ask, "It's head-in-the-sand stuff you object to?"

"Always."

FINAL SCENE, STUDIO D

The film is being rewound and everybody's sitting in the dim light, more relaxed than usual. On my last afternoon here I have the same sensation I had on my first morning—that Spike, his friends, and his co-workers are making movies about people who are themselves, that the humor, camaraderie, and anguish on the screen isn't a fiction but a reflection. It is in their bones—people looking into a mirror looking into a mirror. Terence Blanchard, the twenty-nine-year-old trumpet-playing sensation who has written the score for *Jungle Fever*, is here. He grew up in New Orleans, where he picked up a trumpet at sixteen and by eighteen was playing with Lionel Hampton and then with the famed Art Blakey and the Jazz Messengers. Now he has his own group and several albums.

The conversation here at Stage D, as Branford Marsalis had described both jazz music and Spike's movies to me, moves not in the form of "a concrete sequential" but "a random abstract." Not on a straight, but on a circuitous path:

Says film editor Sam Pollard: "Man, one a my best friends was a drummer and he loved Art Blakey. Had the album with Blakey, Horace Silver, Clifford Brown, and Lou Donaldson."

"That's a *bad* album," says Terence.

"He wore that poor record out!" says Sam, laughing.

"Blakey always talked about Clifford," Terence says, slipping into a deep, slow, gravel voice to quote Blakey: "'That Dude's like such a nice cat. I knew he wasn't gonna last too long. The Lord had to take him. He was too good to be on this earth.'"

After a silence, Terence says: "The Knicks are like a college team."

Spike: "Remember the old days when Dr. J had that funny Afro way out over his head?"

They laugh, stomp the floor, slap their knees.

Terence: "That's how they learned to do them shots! They were tryin' to miss their hair!"

More laughter.

Spike: "Dr. J, he got old quick, man. Larry Bird was killin' 'im! Remember that fight they had? Bird was tauntin' 'im: 'I'm gonna give you fifty tonight!' Dr. J took a swing at 'im!"

More laughter.

"Be glad you're in music, Terence."

"Yeah, I just gotta worry 'bout guys like John Coltrane."

Uproarious laughter.

Spike: "Yeah, they haven't made the tough West Coast swing yet. Tough schedule! Sonny Rollins, John Coltrane, Johnny Hodges! Three nights in a row! We win one a those games, we'll be happy!"

More uproarious laughter and the slapping of knees.

But then comes *Jungle Fever*'s crowning scene with the crack-head Gator, who has manipulated, deceived, and pained his mother, who will always take him back no matter what awful thing he has done. Suddenly, Terence gets serious. He talks about how an uncle of his had two wives—one in New Orleans and one in Texas. The man never had a job. "But my grandmother, she would always take 'im in. He would do all kinds a shit to the house, try to get me to do junk, man. Whatever he did, man, no matter, she loved the guy."

The room falls silent and Terence coughs uncomfortably.

Suddenly, Spike pierces the silence with the seamless intertwining of art and life: "You always liked Flipper better!"

And the uproarious laughter begins again.

8

LUNCH WITH THE JAZZMAN

MANHATTAN, NEW YORK CITY

On his "Black Pearl" album cover, with his trumpet lit in a heavenly glow, Terence Blanchard wears a cool blue suit with a wide, rounding lapel and a sharp, blue-streaked yellow tie knotted over one of those dapper collar pins. At Sound One all week, he has worn old jeans, a baggy shirt, and untied Nike high-tops. I don't think he has shaved all week. But if his real style is out of sync with his jazzman image, his personality has matched his trumpet playing perfectly, running from poignant to funny to raucous. On my last day in the studio, Terence and I head out for lunch at a little Mexican cafeteria he knows a few blocks away on 50th Street, walking through the light rain and the hollering cabbies and honking BMWs with someplace to go.

"I saw *She's Gotta Have It*, and I thought, Man, I wanta be a part of what Spike Lee's doin'," Terence says. The movie portrayed an unmarried black woman who had three lovers. It was steamy as hell, which shocked Terence. Most blacks are so afraid that whites already think they're sex-crazed maniacs, he says, that they'd never portray black sexuality so candidly. They're so afraid of what's called "playing into white stereotypes" that they won't be honest about themselves. "I thought it was daring as shit," he says.

Terence played trumpet with Branford Marsalis in Spike's second movie, *School Daze*, which parodied the triviality of black college life and exposed the color prejudice of light-skinned blacks. For writing the *Jungle Fever* score, Terence's manager wanted a lot more money than Spike was paying. But Terence intervened, saying money wasn't the issue. "It's a film I'll be able to show my grandchildren." Soon he'll start work on the score for Spike's next film about the life of Malcolm X.

Even as a kid, Terence wanted to be a jazzman. His folks had more classical ambitions for him, and Terence took piano from age five through high school and hated it. But the musical phrasing and composition he learned playing piano put Terence light years ahead when at sixteen he began the trumpet. Eventually, Terence became friends with Wynton and Branford Marsalis, who with their father, Ellis, were about to single-handedly revitalize American jazz. "My father wanted to be an opera singer, but he never got the chance," says Terence sadly. "He sang in the Harlem Harmony Kings, an a cappella group. It was 1932. He's seventy-seven today."

"What about your mother?" I ask.

"She wanted me to be a classical pianist," Terence says. He and his family went to a highbrow black church in New Orleans that was attended by black doctors and lawyers and the black school superintendent. As Spike has pointed out in movie after movie, as I've learned on my travels, the status hierarchy in black America has been as strong and class-bound as any in the white world. "All the old ladies wanted me to be a classical musician. Even after I made my first jazz album, they said, 'Oh, that's nice, but you keep up your classics.' They were so worried about being respectable. There's a hell of a lot of denial about their past, about their history, and a certain amount of wanting to be respected by another faction of American culture"—meaning whites. "And it's sad, it's really sad. My father never graduated high school, and every year he would never win the church's Father of the Year Award. Even after I'd played with Lionel Hampton and Art Blakey, done the music for Spike's films."

"He was too lowbrow?"

"Yeah," Terence says, pausing. "When I was a kid, I told my father, 'I wanta be like you.' He said, 'No, you wanta be better than me. You wanta make a living and not be looked down upon by any man.'"

Terence went north to the Rutgers University jazz department at eighteen because he believed the real jazz action was in New York City. He was only at school a week when one of his instructors, who played with jazz great Lionel Hampton's group, invited him to go along on a gig to Philly. During warm-ups on stage, Hampton said, "Let me hear ya play a blues." The next week, Terence was on the road with Lionel Hampton. A year later, he joined the renowned Art Blakey and the Jazz Messengers, where Wynton Marsalis had played and where Art Blakey had become famous for training young jazz musicians. After a few years, Terence went out on his own.

"You have to study," he says. "You have to know what Dizzy Gillespie or Charlie Parker or Clifford Brown did, because you see how one may have grown out of the other. . . . You can't lie. There are times when I've heard my records and thought I played very well. And then I'd hear a Clifford Brown record and I'd say Damn! It would just blow me away. Art Blakey used to say, 'It's a tug-a-war between your heart and your mind.' The hardest thing is to keep my ego out of everything. It's like a basketball player who forces a shot. It's his ego taking over. You have to let it happen, let it go. My best performances with Art Blakey sometimes came when I was really tired and didn't have time to think about what was going on. I'm always analyzing things. And on those occasions when I was too tired to do that, I played my best. Those were the times I was relaxed and ideas would come to me and my ego wouldn't block them. Maurice André, the great classical solo trumpeter in Europe, once said that when he plays he sometimes gets the impression there's no trumpet. He feels like he's singing! I have yet to experience that. But when I listen to John Coltrane, I hear it."

I'm struck by how similar this description is to Stephanie Burrous's sense that when she sings at her best, she feels that she is not even doing the singing.

"What does being black have to do with it?" I ask.

"The harmonic side definitely comes from a European influence, but you can hear in the music, rhythmically, its origins in Africa. But I also hear a relationship to my experiences in life, hardships I've seen my relatives go through. And the spiritual influence. Take Coltrane's 'Love Supreme' album. I can't think of the song's name." He stops and sings to himself, "Bee-doe-bee-dee-dee-da-da," and then goes back to a common source of African American artistic intuition. "Whenever I used to hear that song, I always thought of church. I was raised in the church. I thought I was crazy until I came to find out that was an important part of Coltrane's background, although the song's not theoretically derived from that at all."

Like Branford Marsalis, Terence says Spike Lee's movies, which white critics often say bounce from vaguely connected scene to scene, reflect the nonlinear African American sensibility of jazz. I mention that the flow of conversation in Spike's movies reminds me of those I hear among my father-in-law and his friends—not straight ahead, but circular conversations that have complicated subtexts and reprises, a kind of "in concert" language.

"Now think about the music," Terence says. "The music is exactly the same way. When you listen to Bach, isn't everything really in place? When you listen to Duke Ellington, aren't there tons of ideas going on at the same time? That's the same difference between you and your white friends talking one at a time and your father-in-law and his friends with somebody sayin' somethin' and all of a sudden it's like a rally. Or when I listen to Duke, I hear things that my father talked about—workin' in a gas station and giving gas and havin' white people rub his hair."

"You mean like, 'Good job, boy'?"

"Yeah, yeah. I remember one time when I was playing with

Lionel Hampton in New Orleans and we were playin' at the Fair-mont Hotel in the prestigious Blue Room, and I brought my family. While we were walkin' up the front steps, my father started to cry. I said, 'Man, what's wrong?' I grew up understanding what racism was but I had never experienced it to any depth. My father said, 'You don't understand. I used to work in this hotel, but I never walked through the front door. I always had to go through the back. To go from that to walkin' through the front door to see my son play in the Blue Room is just a little overwhelming.'

"By the experiences of my generation being different, the music will be different. Things change. You have to accept that. But I'm still pessimistic about race. On the surface, it's better. But when you dig down into the roots, I don't see any progress."

I am, frankly, amazed. I'm talking to a twenty-nine-year-old black man who has already probably made more money than his father earned in his entire life. He says his worst experiences with racism were being called "nigger" as a child, being mistaken for a potential mugger when not dressed up, and being asked to leave a gymnasium at a private college in Buffalo, New York, where he and some black friends were exercising without permission.

"You think your father would agree?"

Terence takes a moment. "No, he wouldn't agree." But racism has gone from physical discrimination, he says, to psychological, sublimi-nal discrimination. "In a lotta ways, I think it's worse." He says that many successful blacks are still being robbed of their black heritage by trying to fit into a white middle-class mold. Again, we are back to the themes of Spike Lee's movies, the themes that Lisa Jones identi-fied as the great issue for her generation of affluent blacks—how to balance assimilation and separatism.

"They wanta be like Flipper?" I ask.

"Yeah. But even worse are the Gators," Terence says, referring to Flipper's angry, self-destructive, crack-head brother. The Gators, he says, are so afraid of becoming white that they become literal stereo-types of the black loser. He says guys like Gator are always saying, "Oh, you talkin' like a white boy."

"Are you accused of that?"

"Oh, definitely, because I'm not into commercial black music. I've heard ludicrous statements, man!" At Rutgers, the student jazz soci-ety once hosted the famed Kenny Barron, and some young, black woman stood up and yelled, "Stop playin' that white music!" She thought Motown was the authentic black music. "That was an eye-opening experience. Not having black people recognize my music, *their* music, is the most painful thing, man. I really couldn't believe that woman could possibly think that."

"Ignorance doesn't have a color," I say.

"Yeah," Terence says, "but we got a lot to learn."

9

OF SAINTS AND SURVIVORS

DETROIT, MICHIGAN

So this is what a saint looks like. Short, four feet ten inches tall, with ashen gray hair swept up tightly from her face and neck, braided into a coronet adorned with six yellow-tipped hairpins. Old, nearly seventy, with pains and maladies that cry out from head to chest to bowels to joints, pains that absolutely scream and howl at night in the calm and quiet of the bed. Misshapen, with a warped spine, a bony hump behind her right shoulder, a truncated torso, arms that dangle to her knees, and knuckles the size of small walnuts. Smiling, a wide and radiant smile that never looks tired or forced or feigned. Talking, always talking, as if she too might cease if the words ever stopped. Keeping busy, as in, "If you want a job done, give it to a busy person." Touching, as often as she senses that a person wants to be touched, on the forehead, the wrist, the chest, pressing gently until she can feel the tension and fear fade away. Joking, so filled with jokes and quick-liners that people await her morning arrival just to get ready, happy, and pumped up for the day.

It's hard work, this saint's life.

It's hard work, this being Fanniedell Peeples.

And the money, the money is lousy.

The neighborhood south of Brush Street and Mack Avenue in downtown Detroit looks as if aliens arrived last night and beamed up all

the human beings, leaving behind only their inanimate remains—
acre after acre of two-story apartment buildings, block after block of
huge, elegant, old brick homes. All hulking, empty, and abandoned. I
think of Beirut or Baghdad, bombed and broken. I think of the other
side of the moon—barren, rutted, and gaping. No wonder I see people who must come to this neighborhood from Michigan's affluent
suburbs and its little country burgs, who must come to Children's
Hospital of Michigan with their ailing boys and girls, glancing
around at the stoplights to check that their car doors are locked. No
wonder people are nervous about visiting the hospital after dark.
After the glamour of the Apollo Theatre and the excitement of Spike
Lee's studio, this place is quite a change, and I too am nervous, especially when I must walk past groups of teenage black guys who are
wandering the street in sharp tennis shoes, classy jackets, and cocked
caps, singing rap songs.

But to all of this, the old woman I have come to visit—Fanniedell
Peeples—is oblivious.

When I arrive at the Children's Hospital surgical unit first thing
in the morning, Fanniedell Peeples is telling the crowded waiting
room, "You may think that this is the ghetto. And you may be afraid.
But I am not afraid and this is not the ghetto to me. This is my home.
I live across the street." Fanniedell's accent and diction are very
proper, even arch. Her vowels are elegant and elongated. She does
not, for instance, say "ant" for "aunt." She says "auuunt." She rarely
uses contractions, and she slips in and out of street slang and dialect
only for humor and special effect. This morning, she has taken up a
strategic post in the center of the little beige waiting room, spread her
long arms like a graceful preacher, bowed her head, and spoken as if
onstage.

Three dozen people stop what they are doing. They look up from
magazines and over from Phil Donahue. A man about to run himself
a cup of coffee from the large silver pot stops in freeze-frame, left
hand holding his cup under the spout and right hand suspended
over the black lever, expectancy in his expression. Fanniedell knows
the look. Because just now, as their kids and grandkids are going
under the knife, the locked doors to these people's emotions are
thrown open, and it is written on their tentative and confused faces.
Fanniedell knows this moment like she knows her prayers.

Since 1983, when Fanniedell Peeples—"Peep," as she calls herself—first signed on as a volunteer at Children's Hospital, she has worked 4,244 hours. For free. The woman is frenetic. Today, she'll work in the surgical waiting room from 7:30 in the morning until four in the afternoon. In return, she'll get a free meal in the hospital cafeteria. Other days, she'll help with prayer services, push the library cart, give tours, or rock and cuddle sick or dying infants who have no one else. She lives in public housing and exists on $457 a month in social security. She's poor, old, and crippled, just getting by. She's also black, although this, she says, has always been the least of her worries.

It's a pretty average bunch in the surgical waiting room this morning. There's a woman whose fifteen-year-old son, a perfectly normal kid until three days ago, is undergoing his first chemotherapy treatment for leukemia. Just like that. There's a young couple sitting in the corner, staring straight ahead—Robert and Jacqueline Bruins, whose seven-week-old son, Robert Edward, is undergoing heart surgery. Since his birth, Robert had been at home, like any other baby. The Bruinses had gotten used to him. But if his heart isn't fixed, he will die.

For this gathering of hopeful and helpless people, Peep Peeples is the concierge. Anybody leaves, she writes it down. Anybody wants directions, she gives them. Anybody wants reassurance, she gives that, too, as in, "Dr. Canady is world famous." For this gathering of hopeful and helpless people, Peep is also the comedienne. She clears a circle around her, takes a deep breath, and kicks her leg high over her head, karate-style. People half her age marvel and say, "I can't even do that!" Her dexterity, the product of one of her many physical conditions, takes people's minds off their children for a moment. But it also serves another, deeper, goal. It is a weapon in Peep's war with those who look at her skinny, hunched body and think: That sad creature—how I pity her.

Peep loves to shock the bejesus out of 'em!

Peep's life began with grand dreams, which were all she lived on as a girl. Her mother died from an infection soon after her birth in 1921, and Peep remembers always believing that her older brothers blamed her for their mother's death. With her twisted spine, she was frail and sickly and she tired easily. The others resented having to pick up the slack. And when their father wasn't home, which was often, they'd lock her in the closet. They said she wasn't really their sister, that she was given to them by mistake at the hospital. They were tall and straight and good looking, and they told sister Fanniedell she was ugly.

Her old photographs prove this wasn't true. The protrusion on her shoulder was much less pronounced when Peep was young, and she was a sharp dresser, learning quickly to wear dresses that fell loosely from her shoulders, to hem them shorter on her left. She learned also never to wear earrings, which magnified the crooked tilt of her head. She had a pretty face, and, always, she had that beautiful smile. But at school, they called her the Hunchback of Notre Dame. The voice in Fanniedell's head told her that she was ugly, and she listened, was ashamed. For as long as she can recall, this was her fantasy: someday, the doctors would make her straight and symmetrical and then she'd marry a man as handsome as her father, and they would have six sons, all straight and tall.

Early on, Fanniedell decided she was two people: the ugly girl in the mirror with the "garbage can body" and the beautiful girl, the real girl, inside. "I decided this body was not me," she says. I'm struck by how similar Fanniedell's psychological distancing of herself from her misshapen and socially maligned body is to that of Maya Angelou's autobiographical character in *I Know Why the Caged Bird Sings*. Marguerite, the young black girl in Stamps, Arkansas, decides that her body is not really hers, that she's not really black, that she is a white girl mistakenly trapped in a black girl's body.

Marguerite learned from the white people around her to despise her own kind of "garbage can body." Peep learned to despise hers from *all* the people around her. Just as some African Americans try to be more white than whites, Peep decided she would be more normal than the normals.

"I couldn't do a lot of things," she says, "so I had to be able to talk and have a personality. It was my ticket out." Peep acquired an indomitable spirit and came to love being the girl people saw rising above her infirmities—not unlike the stories of blacks who are seen to have risen above the infirmity of black skin. Fanniedell was barely in grade school when her father died and she bounced from foster home to foster home. She was not mistreated so much as she was treated impersonally, like a guest. In time, the pain in her back became unbearable and she had the first of her fifteen operations, this one to fuse bones in her spine. She always saw great humor in that one of the bones the doctors used in her operation came from a white man. But her resolve never broke. She was a top student and won a scholarship to Missouri's historically black Lincoln University, where she graduated valedictorian of her class. She was named the student most likely to succeed and the Delta Sigma Theta sorority girl with "the personality smile."

"Normally," Peep says of her sorority sisters, "they wouldn't want *this*."

"What is *this*?" I ask.

"This body!" she says, with scorn.

After graduation, Fanniedell moved to Detroit because a girlfriend lived there. But again and again, her spine crashed. The last time, she ended up in a body cast that wrapped like a suit of armor from her head down to her knees. She had no money and no family and landed in a bad nursing home—one owned by black doctors—where the old people were lined up in beds an arm's reach away. Each morning, the attendants would casually check to see if anyone had died the night before. They'd say, "Hmmm, this one kicked the bucket," wrap the body in a sheet, and leave it until they had time to lug it away. When Fanniedell got out, she was bedridden and living on welfare. For about a decade, she was homebound. From her bed, she addressed envelopes for society balls and she worked for a phone answering service. Then, one day twenty years ago, she decided enough was enough. Fanniedell got out of bed, and she has not stopped since.

"Oh, I've seen racism," she says. "I've lived in little towns where the 1930s were like the 1880s, where nobody but blacks went to jail. And when the cock crowed, they were marched outside for a tin of grits and loaded on a wagon and taken out and worked all day with a black skullcap and a ball and chain. They laboriously crushed rocks to make gravel for uptown streets. I remember when stores wouldn't sell black women a dress if some white woman had already bought that one. I remember when only if you were 'light and bright' could you run the elevator.

"But bitterness is a cancer that will eat you up." She points at me. "You didn't flog my great-grandfather. And we didn't get free alone. A lot of whites helped. But black people don't want to admit that. They get mad when I say I've been treated equally bad by both black and white. It was *blacks* who discriminated against me for being mis-shapen, not whites. Truth is, most of the times people have gone out of their way to help me in my life, they were white. Now what if I went around hating all black people because so many of them have mistreated me? How would they like that?"

Back in the waiting room, Peep is talking to Robert and Jacqueline Bruins when the phone at her desk rings. Peep answers it, nods yes, yes, and hangs up. She walks around her desk to Jacqueline, who is now standing up stretching. She puts her hands on Jacqueline's shoulders and Jacqueline accepts them, relaxes her body.

"OK, now we're going to try and help you," Peep says slowly, calmly. "The nurse has called and the doctor wants to see you. Listen to what he says and don't fall apart. Be strong. You have to believe your baby's going to make it. He'll fight like hell, because he hasn't been here long enough to be thinking about blue jeans with a special label on 'em. He's for *real!*" She hugs Jacqueline, who is crying gently, and takes the couple into the quiet room. When the Bruinses come out after talking to the doctor, they tell Peep that Robert Edward's heart is being massaged. His condition is grave, but there's still hope. Peep ushers them back to the quiet room.

Fanniedell's phone rings: Robert Edward is dead.

By all accounts, Fanniedell Peeples should be dead too.

The chronicle of maladies that hangs over her bed at home in case an ambulance crew ever needs it runs a full page. Besides her curved spine, which causes constant pain from carrying the load of her body, she has arthritis and osteoporosis. Sometimes, the pain in her back is so bad that Peep imagines that the top half of her body is about to snap off from its bottom, that it will fall to the ground in two separate pieces, like a broken stick.

"I live with pain," she says flatly, as if she were talking about someone else. "I live with mental pain, physical pain. I have a Grand Canyon of emotional pain and scar tissue. The Peep who lives inside my head is lonely. But I love people, I love children more, and I love babies the most. They're not seeing this outer *thing*. A baby clings to you no matter what. They respond to love, caring, nurturing. This does something for them. But I didn't get this. If I had, I would be a different person. I wouldn't have this hard core. You know how you get a lump in your throat? I wouldn't have this lump of loneliness and pain down in my heart that persists even though I've tried to irradiate and shrink it.

"People are afraid of hospitals. Some parents cannot even be near their own dying child. They say they don't have taxi fare to the hospital, can't get off work till four. It's not my place to be judgmental. I sit with their child, and with each heartbeat, I wonder if it will be the last. Nothing bothers me. I've suffered too much. I'll even wrap the baby for transport to the morgue. It gets to everyone but me, so I can give what I never got. This keeps me alive. I have a need to prove that I am a human being, that I am alive, that I have a right to be on this earth. If that makes sense. Does that make sense?"

I nod. "Yeah, that makes sense."

At four in the afternoon, the surgeries are done and the waiting room is empty. I help Peep pack up her little pull-cart, tidy up the magazines, and toss out the dirtied styrofoam cups. She has one last mission: In the cafeteria, she finds Jacqueline Bruins, the woman whose baby died in surgery earlier today. It turns out that Jacqueline Bruins also has been searching the halls for Peep, and Jacqueline rushes to hug her. "You are a wise old lady."

"You be strong," Peep says.

It is advice Peep herself has always taken, as she has struggled with one kind of discrimination within another kind of discrimination. Tonight Peep is exhausted. As she heads slowly up the empty hospital hallway, she seems to me more hunched and shriveled, turned in upon herself. She's not smiling now, and at rest her face has gone old. Her hands look frail poking from the arms of her big overcoat, and her watch, hooked at the last notch on its black leather band, dangles like a loose bracelet on her tiny wrist. Her right shoulder, as ever, is hitched a bit above her left, and her head is angled vaguely forward over her shoulders, as if it were leading the way home. I think: This suffering and triumphant old woman . . . So this is what a survivor looks like.

10

"STILL FEELING KINDA SAD"

EAST DETROIT, MICHIGAN

Even in the rain, at nine in the morning, men are huddled on the street corners. Under the overcast sky the neighborhood looks drearier than usual, and there's no mistaking one of Detroit's most desperate human enclaves. The big old frame houses are falling down, porches are sagging, fences are broken, even the dogs are skinny, their eyes suspicious.

Michael Cross knows this neighborhood well, because as the director of the Detroit Urban League's Male Responsibility Program, one of only a handful of such efforts in the country, he visits it regularly on his way to the local elementary school, where 60 percent of the children's parents are drug users and most of the families are headed by mothers or grandmothers. Michael has a master's degree in social work from the University of Michigan. He's a short, lean, strong, tight-faced black man with a salt-and-pepper goatee, sharp clothes, and a quick, assertive, even domineering manner.

Michael tells black high school boys that unlike Spike Lee he will not use the word "motherfucker," because in slavery days the spirit of the strongest black males was often broken by being forced to have sex with their own mothers. He tells them he will not use the words "bitch" and "whore" to describe black women, because they degrade women who are already degraded enough by whites. Eddie Murphy aside, the word "ho" is not funny to him. He tells the boys he especially will not use the word "nigger," because it's the English and Irish corruption for the Portuguese word *negro*, for "black," from the Latin word *niger*. He tells them that all the times they've been told a "nigger" is an ignorant or uncouth person were only attempts to paper over that word's hateful meaning. After all, whites know exactly what a "nigger" is.

"To see African Americans smilin' and laughin' while their young children are dying is an atrocity," Michael says, as we drive through the neighborhood. "See that red house?" He points to a building that's a mess. "One of the greatest kids I ever worked with came outta that red house. Just look at it! I mean there's people living in there—alive!"

The public school is a beacon in this neighborhood. It's antiseptically clean, well lit, recently painted. Once a week Michael comes here to meet with the school's worst kids—those who are always in the office, cursing, fighting with other kids. School officials told me that they have been amazed at how dramatically even this limited attention has changed the boys' behavior. God knows Michigan needs the help. It has some of the most dismal statistics on black males anywhere in America. Last year only 6.5 percent were enrolled in public colleges or universities. Black males made up 6 percent of the nation's population, but they composed 57.5 percent of Michigan's prison population, 71 percent of its juvenile detention population, and 52 percent of its foster children. Most frightful of all, young black males between the ages of fifteen and twenty-four in Detroit's Wayne County had a greater chance of being murdered than those anywhere else in America. I called Michael Cross to talk about these things. A visit to this neighborhood, its school, and its boys was his answer.

He had asked, "What grade's your son in?"

"Third."

"OK, we'll do third graders."

"I'd like boys old enough to talk about their troubles."

Michael had laughed at that. "Don't worry."

This morning, ten third-grade boys are arrayed in a crescent of colorful plastic chairs before a green mobile blackboard in front of a lavender wall. They all have short-cropped hair, most wear jeans and tennis shoes and T-shirts. They're smiling and laughing and cutting up. It reminds me of my son's last birthday party. Over the months, they will talk about girls, drugs, sex, guns, discipline, fatherhood, health, black history, and respect. They'll also learn to shake hands the European American way, which many of these boys do not know. They'll learn that European Americans often expect children to show respect by looking directly into their faces when they are spoken to, which is different from African Americans, who often expect children to divert their eyes as a sign of respect. They'll also learn that all whites aren't bad, which many of them have already come to believe.

Michael has never met these boys. He introduces himself, says these meetings will be like membership in a secret club—nothing said here is to be gossiped about outside.

"Drugs?" Michael asks. "Ya know anybody who hits the pipe?"

Everybody talks at once. "I do." "I do." "I do."

I must remember: these boys are in third grade.

"I saw an old man on the street littin' it up," says one boy.

Michael asks, "'Littin'? Or 'lighting'?"

"Lightin' it up," the boy corrects.

"With my friend," says another boy, "I went in the backyard and seen three men stickin' needles in their arms. My friend said, 'They always do that.' I saw blood in the needle."

"I found a needle on the grass," says another boy. "We were wrestlin' near it. It had an orange top."

Michael asks, "Did you tell your mother so another person didn't come along and get stuck with that needle?"

"We told a lady and she scooped it up in a bag."

"A lady across the street," says still another boy, "took a needle and stuck herself right here." He touches the soft skin between his fingers. "When she pushed her hand, pus came out."

"You saw that happen?" Michael asks calmly.

The boy nods.

"That's where she had been putting the needle in," Michael explains, "and her hand got infected. Did she see you?"

"She didn't see me."

Michael asks, "How did you feel?"

"I felt sick. I was scared."

"What about guns and people getting killed?"

One boy says that up the street a man shot another man and then stuck a hypodermic needle in his eye. Another boy says the police came to a crack house near his home and shot down a booby trap and then arrested the people inside. That night, the boy took out the garbage and found a bag of cocaine hidden in the trash can.

"What did you do with it?" Michael asks.

"My auntie called the police."

Another boy says he once saw a man shoot someone in a park near his house and that the man then threatened to kill him and he ran away. He later saw the man on the street and he again threatened to kill him. The boy and his family then moved away from that neighborhood to this neighborhood. Several boys laugh out loud at this, and Michael sternly asks what is so funny. The boys lower their heads.

It's nearly time for Michael to leave. In fifteen minutes, he must give a speech to five hundred high school boys. But one boy at the end of the row has quietly sat with his hand held up through the conversation and Michael says, "We're gonna take time and listen." The boy looks straight ahead, at no one. He holds his chest with one hand and obsessively rubs his left eye with the other. He starts talking and the words pour out rapidly, but in a monotone. He talks to the air, and he doesn't stop for more than fifteen minutes. As he talks, he cries. Michael's speech to five hundred will have to wait.

One time on Friday afternoon my uncle asked my mama for some money, and she gave him $200, because she had a lotta money from the lottery. She said she'd give him another hundred when he came back, but that day he never came back. My brother went to a party and everybody knew at that party that my uncle's girlfriend was settin' him up. Then my aunt called my mom and told her they killed my uncle, and that's when my mom was pregnant, and they told my mama that they shot my uncle down there (the boy stops talking and touches his torso in four places) *and they had my mama cryin' and hysterical. They said he was in the morgue and his face was swollen and they had to put cotton around it. He was on the couch. The man had shot him once, but he wasn't dead. He shot 'im right here* (the boy again stops and points to his body). *My uncle fell and got back up to get his gun, but he was shot two times right here* (again pointing) *and the man kicked 'im in the head and said, "Get up, nigger!"* (the boy yells this) *"Why don't you do som'in' now!?" For the funeral, my family came from everywhere.*

The bell sounds to end the period, but Michael doesn't budge.
"When did this happen?"
"Last summer."
"Is this the first time you've talked about it?"
"A little bit with my mama."
"You still feel kinda sad about it, don't you?"
The boy nods, still looking at no one, still rubbing his eye.
"That's OK, you should. You loved your uncle."
The boy sits quietly for a moment and then says, "He used to come get us every day and take us to the park." Then he falls silent and stares straight ahead.

Later, on the ride out of this place, Michael says, "That little boy? That boy's gonna kill somebody someday. Now he'll get counseling.

He is so mad and so full of rage. And he's hurtin' *bad!* For him to cry in front of those guys—*ohh, man!*" It seems that Michael is almost in tears himself.

I ask, "Is there an answer to this?"

"Yes!" he says angrily. "People gotta know that this is deplorable and should not be going on and that these kids are hurting, suffering. They need *help!* Yeah, I'm angry! Look around you! Don't you think I should be angry?" These are *real* people, he says, and this is all they know. "What do you expect?" He spits out the words with contempt. Americans seem immune to sympathy, he says, don't want to hear that this kind of environment, *this place,* has consequences. Calming down, he says, "The experiences of the boy are in the father." Then he tells this story: When he was a boy his mother was unmarried, and the kids made fun of him for having no daddy. When Michael was thirteen, his mother married.

"I'll never forget the first time he called me his son," Michael says of his stepdad. "Nobody had ever said that to me. I was with him somewhere, and he introduced me to somebody. He said, 'This is my son.' I swear, it was like God had touched me. It was the most incredible feeling. I remember I couldn't talk. And he was looking at me, like, 'What's wrong with you?' It was just so *powerful,* so powerful. I'll never forget that moment. It was like I had started to live. Before that, I'd been in a state of suspended animation, and now I was alive. I was for real: I AM MY FATHER'S SON." He looks over at me. "Ya know what I mean?"

"Not really," I say, honestly. "My father was always there."

"Yeah, well, I know what these kids are goin' through."

1 1

TO BE FIRST A GREAT MUSICIAN

S Y M P H O N Y   H A L L ,   D E T R O I T ,   M I C H I G A N

I've got a feeling most of the people here tonight don't live in Detroit. Out of about 2,200 folks sitting beneath the chandeliers,

simulated gold leaf, and winged cherubs, I count six blacks—in a city
that's 75 percent black. But then, there's the evening's entertainment:
"Pops" arranger Richard Hayman conducting the Detroit Symphony
Orchestra in hits such as "I Love a Parade" and "Big Brass Band" and
the Dallas Brass sextet performing a tribute to Irving Berlin with its
grand finale, "God Bless America." Conductor Hayman strides
onstage in a glistening gold jacket, gold cummerbund, huge gold
medallion necklace—and green socks. He tells a bawdy joke about a
Catholic priest who can't get along without his martinis and his
rosary—that is, Rosary, his housekeeper! Get it? I think of what rap
star Ice Cube once said: "White people seem so corny." But the
crowd, well populated with sixtyish white women in pearls, roars its
approval in waves of laughter and applause.

On stage, buried off at the far right in the ninth bass chair, is
Richard Robinson. He's one of the symphony's two black musicians,
out of ninety-eight. He got his chair recently in an affirmative action
spectacle, after two black Michigan legislators threatened to block
$1.27 million in the orchestra's state-funded budget because of the
symphony's failure to hire more black musicians. Already under the
gun of a $5 million deficit, the symphony's players wisely voted to
hire Rick Robinson without the usual blind auditions, which
inevitably draw as many as a hundred hopeful classical musicians for
any single spot. Only about 1 percent of the competitors are usually
black. At twenty-five, Rick was already a substitute in the symphony
and he came with a long list of impressive credentials. But that got
buried in the flurry of debate that stretched from the local Detroit
papers to the front page of the *New York Times*. It seemed that no
occupation better symbolized the conflict between merit versus quota
hiring than Rick Robinson's ninth-chair bass seat.

During the first half of the show, I watch Rick from my balcony
seat. He's a tall, lean, muscular young man with a high-top natural
haircut. He's got a mustache and a stringy cool-cat goatee that hangs
à la Fu Manchu two inches from the bottom of his chin and balances
a high, open forehead. Like most good bass players, Rick has large,
strong hands and thumbs and long fingers that fly over the strings of
his 1819 Italian bass, with its deep brown finish broken and scarred
by spider webs of character-giving cracks. When he's not using his
right bow-hand tonight, Rick keeps fidgeting with his red tuxedo tie.
He just bought new shirts and can't get used to their fit. We met

briefly earlier today and every once in a while, his expressionless face casts a quick, wry smile and a raised eyebrow up to me. This "pops" stuff isn't music that needs Rick Robinson's undivided attention. It isn't the music he loves, the music he gets lost in. Tonight, it's a job. And after conductor Hayman's rousing harmonica rendition of "Mama Don't Allow It," Rick climbs the back steps and joins me for the intermission.

"Talk about a 'white' show," Rick says, smiling and eye-browing me again. "A brass band from Texas and a goofball."

Rick Robinson has always been odd man out in the white world of classical music. His father was an up-by-the-bootstraps man who grew up on a farm near Natchez, Mississippi, put himself through college, and became the assistant director of admissions at the University of Michigan. Rick's great-great-grandfather on his mother's side was the "March King of Augusta," conducting Sunday concerts in that Georgia city. Rick's maternal great-grandmother was a classical pianist, and his maternal grandmother studied violin at Oberlin College. His maternal grandfather was a surgeon. In those days, it was often tough even to find a teacher for a black child interested in classical music. Naturally, when you did, that teacher was white and you entered and left via the rear door.

Rick's mother studied piano as a girl, as did his older sister. His older brother played the cello and bass as a boy and was pronounced musically gifted in third grade—the age of the boys I met with Michael Cross. Rick's mother took his brother to a performance of the Detroit Symphony, scrimping to buy expensive seats so he could get a good view of the musicians. "But Mommy," he asked, "where are the colored people?" In 1963, there were none. Nobody in the symphony had spoken to the boy, nobody had discriminated against him, but he'd been excluded as surely as if Bull Connor had shown him the door. Rick's brother stopped playing the cello after that, and it is satisfying that thirty years later his little brother is on that stage.

By the time Rick began playing the bass as a boy, one black violinist had joined the Detroit orchestra. But for whatever reasons, Rick doesn't believe he ever noticed that. He cannot recall ever thinking to himself that the symphony was mostly white or ever doubting that his race might somehow exclude him. "I was closing my eyes," he says, closing his eyes. "I didn't care who was up there as long as it sounded good. To me, the music is more important." Rick's older siblings were far more race-conscious than Rick, having grown up in the sixties and the era of Black Power. In the Robinson home, strict Standard English was spoken, but Rick's older brother developed a hybrid speech that blended Standard and Black English. Rick, on the other hand, spoke like his parents, and often took ribbing from the kids in his predominantly black neighborhood. "Why you talk like that?" they'd ask. Rick saw himself standing between black and white worlds, and his dedication to classical music only intensified that feeling.

"Did you ever feel you didn't want to be black?"

"Not consciously, but I'm sure it existed on a subconscious level, just because so many things that I do are 'white.' And very often in the back of my mind I'm wondering if people would treat me differently were I white—and that I'll never know."

It was when Rick went off to the Interlochen Arts Academy on scholarship as a high school sophomore that he first recalls thinking, "Do I deserve what I earned or did I get it because I'm black?" During his years at the Cleveland Institute of Music and the New England Conservatory, this thought didn't exactly haunt Rick, but it always played at the fringes of his mind. When the Detroit Symphony job was offered to him, he hesitated, fearing that he and other black classical musicians would be stigmatized as not good enough to make it on their own. He'd done well for so young a musician in blind competitions, landing a substitute's job not only in Detroit but also with the Boston Symphony. He also won permanent chairs in the Portland, Maine, and Akron and Canton, Ohio, symphonies. But after the Detroit Symphony voted to accept Rick in lieu of formal auditions, he took the job—mainly because it meant a stable $50,000-a-year income.

He felt guilty and vowed to himself that he would work hard to prove he had deserved the job. His dilemma reminds me of children I've known from rich or well-connected families who feel guilty that they have had special opportunities over others. Like Rick, these people often work hard to prove they deserve their unequal advantage. But also like Rick, they rarely refuse the benefits of privilege. Everybody knows somebody who got started that way—from the daughter who takes over the family business to the plumber's son who inherits dad's union card. It strikes me as funny that so many commentators, black and white, mused that Rick's forced hiring "stigmatized" all

blacks as unable to compete head-to-head when I can't recall ever
seeing anybody argue that children of inherited privilege are stigmatized by those who pull rank for a job.

Anyway, Rick defended the symphony. He said he didn't believe it
was overt racism today that kept blacks off the nation's classical
orchestras, but rather the legacy of historical racism that had kept them
from taking up classical music. He was variously pilloried and
praised. Black Detroit mayor Coleman Young criticized Rick's remarks
and warned against "Uncle Toms" who will "sell their momma" for
money. But none of this being betwixt and between blacks and whites
was new to Rick Robinson.

"Do you feel alienated from black life?"

"Not alienated, but somehow removed. I feel an impatience. Like
Spike Lee says, people gotta wake up. We wallow in negative
imagery. But I also know it'd be a lot different if I grew up in
poverty." He says he thinks he understands what impact growing up
poor has on people. "But so does the white man. Everybody *thinks*
they understand." I think again of Michael Cross's boys. "I'm not a
mainstream black person. I'm mainstream 'new black thinking,' if
you will. I don't see anything wrong with seeming like what some
blacks have called an 'Uncle Tom.'" Rick says a real Uncle Tom—a
real sellout to his own race—is somebody who hawks drugs to kids
and his own mother. "But I worry about being called a 'Tom,'" he
says. "I don't hear it a lot, but I always think, 'It's comin', it's comin'!'
Say I'm waiting at the barber shop and I strike up a conversation
with the barber and he starts asking questions and I start defending
the orchestra. He'll say, 'Don't you think there should be more blacks
in there?' I say, 'Well, it depends. There aren't that many blacks
applying.' What I think he's thinking is, 'He's a Tom.'"

"Is he really thinking that?"

"What's important is that I *think* he's thinking that."

"Have you had to act 'white' in classical music?"

"No, in classical music, more than race distinctions it's class distinctions that make the rules. It's more the rich supporting the symphony and you have to cater to them to ensure success. You gotta
learn your salad fork from your dinner fork, otherwise people will
think less of you. It's not race, but class. To me, jazz is the American
classical music, because it only could have happened in this country."
Over the years, Rick has played jazz bass to make money. "I can lay it

down, but I'm not very good at jazz. Improvisation is hard. In classical music you don't have to improvise. Everything's written down. And that's what I enjoy: reinterpreting what's written down. Sure, you hear Beethoven's Fifth Symphony every time and you think it's the same. But to the *real* ear, with a *real* conductor, it's not the same."

"What is it about the music that touches you?"

"Ahhh, it's a power trip. I feel the way the music's going when it disappoints you, when it brings you to a great climax. Gustav Mahler in particular. You take it in your gut. The music and the emotion are one."

Simply put, Rick Robinson's life and ambitions and passions aren't about race. He doesn't want to find himself in his racial heritage. He wants to find himself in his music, which is not the music of most African Americans, some of whom are so insecure they see Rick's preference as a repudiation of them—at the same time African Americans are beginning to close the gap in classical entertainment. Each of the nation's symphony orchestras have only one to four black musicians, but black classical players are increasingly visible. The more prominent include composers T.J. Anderson, Anthony Davis, and Alvin Singleton; pianists André Watts and Leon Bates; conductors James DePreist and Isaiah Jackson; violinist Marcus Thompson; cellist Owen Young; and divas Kathleen Battle and Jessye Norman.

But for Rick Robinson, the American obsession with race is still distracting. I think of Beau Lee, the brilliant young black electrical engineering professor I met in Farmville, Virginia, who was so tired of the subtle but constant psychopolitical dramas he faced as one of a few blacks in white academia that he opted to teach at a predominantly black college. I suppose there are more than a few women who teach at women's colleges for the same kinds of reasons. Rick would like to live and work where race isn't always in the front of people's minds. He'd like to win an audition in Europe and live there, as have black American expatriates from Richard Wright to Josephine Baker to Paul Robeson. "Some people call that running away," Rick says, "but there are other things I want to do in my life, like music. I'm a very good musician, but I'd like to be a great musician."

As he said earlier, "To me, the music is more important."

After the intermission comes the Dallas Brass tribute to Irving Berlin. At first, I think it's meant as a parody of those sappy immigrant-

makes-good stories. But by the time we get to "In Your Easter Bonnet," I realize this is no joke. At the finale, with the sextet belting out
America's unofficial national anthem, "God Bless America," the nar-
rator says, in one of those melodramatic newsreel voices, "And if that
weren't enough, Irving Berlin proceeded to assign all royalties to the
Boy Scouts and Girl Scouts of America." The audience rises spontaneously and reverently sings along. I think again of Ice Cube: "White
people seem so corny."

1 2

NOBODY UNDER FORTY WORKS HERE

DAYTON, OHIO

On the road to visit an Ohio man who in 1953 became one of the
first blacks hired in a General Motors skilled trades training program, I notice a small car pulled off the highway far in the distance.
Suddenly, I see a bag of garbage fly out its window and land on the
roadside. I think, I bet they're black. It's an awful, reflexive, prejudiced thought and I hate it, kick myself, the instant it flashes to me.
I've never told anyone this, but over the years I've noticed that I see
more blacks than whites littering—gum wrappers, Coke cans. I hate
to even admit this because I think of it as a prejudice. But as I pass the
little blue Isuzu, I see that my reflex was correct—two young black
women are in the front seat and a young black man is in the rear.

Is it racism, the reflexive thought I have? Or reality? What do I do
when my prejudice is confirmed by blacks throwing bags of trash out
of a window? I remember a time when my children and I pulled into
a McDonald's drive-through and I was in a hurry. When we came to
the squawk box, I saw that the car in front of me had four black people in it. Again, in an instant, my mind made its unconscious calcula-
tion: We'll be sitting here forever while these people decide what to
order. I literally shook my head at the awfulness of that thought. My
God, my kids are half black! But then the kicker: we waited and
waited and waited. Each of the four people in the car ahead of us

leaned out the window and ordered individually. The order was changed several times. We sat and sat, and I again shook my head, this time at the conundrum that is race in America.

I knew that the buried sentiment that had made me predict that these people would be disorganized on the basis of race alone was wrong—bad, not nice, racist. I knew that there were other deeper reasons for their behavior, that race was only a stand-in for, as Rick Robinson understood, social class—or for education or individual stupidity or rudeness. But my prediction was right. Do I ignore that, pretend it away, and carry this affirmation of my prejudice deep within me?

I told my McDonald's story to a black friend. She furtively glanced around and whispered, "I might have thought the same thing." Now where do we stand? If it's racist for me as a white man to think that way, isn't it racist for her as a black woman to think that way also? But then my friend said that if she had pulled into McDonald's and seen four white teenage boys in the car, she might have thought much the same thing—they'll be goofing off, rude, oblivious to anybody else who might be in a hurry. Or if the car had been filled with four very fat people, she might have wondered if they'd be ordering so much food that it would take forever. These reactions too would be a kind of prejudice. But isn't it true that white teenage boys feeling their oats can be rude? Isn't it also true that fat people eat a lot of food? Sometimes, yes; all the time, no.

Just like the suburban whites taking their kids to Children's Hospital in Detroit, my friend said that she too will often think to lock her car doors when she's stopped at night on a city street where a horde of young black men are milling. The difference is that she knows black kids like those hanging out on that street, and she knows she needn't fear all of them, only a few. Because of the obvious—poverty, racism, broken homes, the sense that they don't belong anywhere or to anyone, lack of legitimate opportunity and plenty of illegitimate opportunity—it's probably true that more of these kids are dangerous than kids in the wealthy suburbs. But for my friend, the few do not translate into the many, because she sees each black face as an individual. At the McDonald's, she said, I might unconsciously have seen more than just four black people ahead of me. Perhaps they were driving an old, beat-up car. If the Cosby family in a Mercedes had been in front of me, she asked, would I have had the same reaction? The problem, she said, is that whites too often see race as explaining black behavior when the explanation often lies somewhere else entirely.

Just now, as I'm thinking about these things, Paul Harvey comes on the radio and reports that a new study has found that black families on the average watch TV far more than do white families. What does that mean? To the casual white listener it means that blacks spend a lot more time watching mindless drivel on the boob tube, that whites are smarter and more sophisticated. But in truth, Paul Harvey's report means nothing without factoring in different education levels for blacks and whites, since that's the best predictor of how much TV a person will watch, and there's a far greater percentage of blacks than whites who are poorly educated in America.

And what about other explanations? Remember all the black people who can easily carry on three conversations at once. Again and again, blacks have told me that black people are just plain louder than white people, that black people like noise. I think of my wife, who drove me crazy when we first married because she'd turn on the TV and the radio—and then read a book! I learned that her mother did the same thing. Yet my wife and her mother were better students than I ever was. In the quiet of my room, I never got past algebra, while my wife was doing her calculus in front of the TV. Even today, this (dare I say) cultural difference is a minor bone of contention, because I think our kids should go off to a quiet place to study, while she believes they can do it in the middle of everything, like she did. As trumpeter Terence Blanchard said, think of orderly classical music versus improvisational jazz. Think of Spike Lee's movies, with their complicated themes, subthemes, and jumbled sequences, versus the straight narratives of white filmmakers. Think of what jazz master Branford Marsalis called "the random abstract" as opposed to the "concrete sequential." And, finally, think of me trying to follow the overlapping and competing conversations of my father-in-law and his hunting buddies. Maybe those TVs are on but nobody's watching.

Maybe we've again mistaken one thing for another.

When I turn onto Third Street in West Dayton, just that fast, everybody's black, as are the neighborhood's symbols of mutual pride and desperation. There's Edwin C. Moses Boulevard (named after the Olympic sprinter), a used-furniture store, and a loan company

("Need Money Fast?"). The West Dayton Health Center is named after Dr. Charles R. Drew, the black physician who pioneered in using dried blood plasma instead of blood during medical operations. A forest of untrendy avocado and yellow refrigerators and stoves has taken root around the narrow building housing Ralph's Used Appliances.

But a few lefts and rights later, I come to Melbourne Avenue, which is lined with small bungalows brightly painted in white and green and yellow, with their yards neatly landscaped and mowed and American flags flying outside two of the houses. A football field's length ahead, at Melbourne's dead end, a white, steeple-peaked house sits facing Melbourne's homes like a castle overseeing lesser dwellings. This is the home of Raymond and Roberta Shackleford, and the view I'm seeing this moment is exactly the view they saw twenty-nine years ago on the Sunday they got lost while house hunting and made a wrong turn onto Melbourne. Roberta fell in love instantly, especially when they saw the hand-printed FOR SALE sign in the front yard. They paid $11,500 for the small two-bedroom house.

A few years earlier, this had been a white working-class neighborhood. Raymond's aunt had even worked as a housekeeper here. But by 1962, more than half the whites had left and soon almost all would be gone. The whites, whose homes were mostly paid off by then, moved at all costs when the blacks came.

Today, Melbourne is as nice as ever.

"Would you like a 7-Up?" Roberta asks as she ushers me into the living room. She's a short woman, fifty-five years old like her husband, and I can see in her face and her assured, relaxed manner that she was once beautiful and always confident.

"Sure, thanks."

"We're having spaghetti," she says.

"Spaghetti ain't what I asked for," says Raymond, as he shakes my hand, smiling and winking as he does.

"I forgot to get the liver," Roberta says, without apology.

"I'm glad you forgot," I say. "I hate liver."

Raymond laughs. "I don't think my kids have eaten liver since they left home. Only thing I won't eat is hominy grits. I like grits, but not hominy. I think we'll have grits today."

"No, dear," Roberta says, correcting him again. "Not today."

While dinner simmers, we sit down in the living room, which is filled with pictures of the Shacklefords' two sons and daughter and their one grandchild. Tucked into the room's nooks are a glass cabinet for Roberta's collection of owl statues and a glass cabinet for Raymond's Norman Rockwell figurine collection. Raymond is tall and thin with only a vague hairline remaining. He wears khaki pants and a Cincinnati Reds T-shirt. While Roberta is quiet and slow to talk, Raymond wastes no time.

"So why're you doin' this?" he asks.

"I guess it all started when I married a black woman."

I notice a quick glance fly between them, and I don't know what it means, although I think to myself that it probably means they disapprove. I let it pass.

Raymond says that his father, a sharecropper, and nine of his brothers and sisters migrated from Waxahachie, Texas, to Dayton in 1927. "For the rest of his life he dug ditches," Raymond says of his father. His parents later divorced, and Raymond, his siblings, and his mother returned to Texas and the Depression. His mother worked as a housekeeper for whites, and if she happened to fall ill there was no money and no food. Dinner was often "simple syrup"—sugar and water boiled to thickness and poured over bread.

"The depression was rough down there?" I ask.

"Yeah," Raymond says. "But the Depression, people see it as a period of time. I see it as a condition people are living in. There are people living in a depression right now. Just not as many. But, yeah, it was pretty rough." Raymond graduated from high school at sixteen, but the best job he could get was as a $35-a-week shipping clerk in a shoe store. So he packed up and came North to Dayton and his father. He quickly found a $40-a-week job at Ray's Department Store. Dayton, like the other Northern industrial cities, was the promised land for a young black man who'd grown up like many Southern black men of his time: trained from birth to fear white men and to avoid white women.

"I grew up scared," Raymond says, although he doesn't recall ever feeling resentful or angry about this. "To be angry about it would have meant being angry at my mother," he says. "She was doing what she thought was the right thing to keep me alive." On the other hand, Raymond had a sibling who was always angry about the injustices of race and who'd never "Yessum" whites, even though their mother sometimes whipped the child for the stubborn and dangerous pride.

"So Dayton was the promised land to you?"

"I thought that," Raymond says. "But I was brought back to reality. There was a little place over by the shop, a little restaurant with a bar named Mattie's, and I went in there with the white guys I worked with and we all ordered. They brought their orders out and brought mine in a paper bag. The waitress said I couldn't eat inside. I thought, 'No, I'm in Ohio now. I'm not in Texas.'" The men with Raymond threatened to leave if he was booted and after a summit with the manager it was decided Raymond could stay. "But I was so upset by then, I couldn't eat. So I knew I hadn't gone to heaven. I was humiliated, really."

"Isn't it odd," I say, thinking of the shirtless man cutting and gutting his whiting fish in Darien, Georgia, as he asked me what was wrong with him that whites despised him so. "You were humiliated by *their* ignorance, as if it were *your* fault."

"That's the way it worked. So I've known since then I'm not too far away from Texas. That's why they named this 'Up South.'"

"What's that mean?"

"The conditions down South were up here also."

In 1953, Raymond Shackleford got the break that would forever change his life and those of his children. After a battery of tests, he was picked to be the only black in a General Motors skilled trades training program organized through the Dayton Urban League, a kind of early affirmative action deal. Raymond was trained as an electrician, and he has been working at a General Motors brake and bearing factory ever since. Today, he earns $19.33 an hour. It wasn't until the sixties that most black men began doing equal work for equal pay, and many whites deeply resented Raymond's status—not only because of racial prejudice, but because of the pragmatic implications of his promotion.

"They said I'd be taking their sons' or their brothers' jobs," Raymond says. "They said I was going to open the door for more blacks." Like union membership, jobs in the great industrial factories of the North were a kind of birthright to the sons of the white men who already toiled there, an unequal privilege they wanted to keep. Yet most guys were decent to Raymond. Some even became his friends, although in thirty-eight years the Shacklefords have never been invited to one of their homes.

"You know," Raymond says, "coming from a Southern town, if I'd known I was going to be the only black I wouldn't have taken the job. I used to be very much afraid of whites. Eventually, I discovered they were just like me. They had families. They didn't know everything. I had thought, 'They know everything. I don't know anything.' They drank on the weekend, sometimes too much. Some went to church and believed; some of 'em went to church and didn't believe, just like blacks. I didn't know that before."

"You thought they were all . . . what?"

"Superior, just superior, better. It was something I had to get over. Since I got over that fear, I'm not afraid of anybody." But to this day, if Raymond is visiting relatives in Texas and he walks into a store or a restaurant where blacks were once excluded, he will sometimes momentarily feel the old fear in his stomach. "I'll have flashbacks," he says. Then he looks at Roberta, who is listening quietly. "Why don't you fix dinner?"

"I just put the bread in the oven," she says, again without apology, and then she waits for us to continue.

"How'd you two meet?"

"He loves to tell the story," Roberta says softly, "that he met me at the YMCA. And he doesn't say I worked there."

"Oh, she was the cutest thing I'd ever seen," Raymond says. "She looked like a little bunny in a red wagon, just so pretty. Oh, I chased her, and she'd go with everybody but me." Raymond smiles and I sense that this is an old and fond story.

"This is another story he likes to tell."

"It's the truth, Roberta!"

"He was so polite, it scared me."

"Women!" I say. "Points off for decency."

"Right!" Raymond says. "I don't understand 'em either."

"I had just started dating and was going off to college," says Roberta, whose father owned a prosperous ice cream parlor in Dayton. She graduated from Kentucky State College in 1959.

"So you dated off and on for years?"

"Uhm-hmm," Roberta says.

"More off than on," says Raymond, still persisting.

"He dated other people too."

"But I didn't *want* to, Roberta!"

Anyway, they eventually got married, bought their own home,

and lived through the industrial boom times of the sixties and seventies. And like the white men before him, Raymond came to believe that a high-paying job in the factory was the birthright of his sons. He told them to go to college, but he figured the factory jobs were always there for them to fall back on. His oldest son did go to college but couldn't find a job in Dayton. So in a move that reversed the migration of his grandfather, he ended up moving to Texas to get a good job. The Shacklefords' daughter was an excellent student who attended summer sessions at the elite Phillips Academy in Andover, Massachusetts, during high school and won a scholarship to the most prestigious, mostly white, private high school near Dayton. She graduated from Oberlin College and is now an estate planner for a bank in Chicago. The Shacklefords' youngest son also went to the elite private school, but he struggled as a student, just barely graduating. He later dropped out of junior college and, like the generation before him, began looking for a good factory job in Dayton. But by 1986, it was no go.

"I guess when Steven couldn't get a job in '86," Raymond says, "then I knew. And then they started closing factories." Today Raymond's plant is like a gathering of aging men each day, with nearly everybody over forty. The ride is over—for both blacks and whites. Steven now lives in Cincinnati and works two jobs to earn what his father makes at one. Without a college degree, the leg up that Raymond's good working job gave his son is lost. The Shackleford children, after literally centuries of iron-clad black exclusion from good jobs, had just one generation to make the break to the educated middle class.

Finally, we get up to eat—spaghetti and sauce topped with melted American cheese; a crisp salad soaked with Roberta's special blend of Italian, Thousand Island, and sweet and sour dressings; and homemade rolls, which I mistakenly call biscuits. "You sound like the kids!" Roberta scolds. "Calling my rolls *biscuits!* Those aren't *biscuits*, those are *rolls*." It's a good meal, and Raymond complains only once that he wanted liver smothered in onions.

After we eat, as I'm about to leave, Roberta takes my arm and guides me to the fireplace and the pictures of her children and grandchild.

"That's my daughter and son-in-law."

I lean over to look. "Hey, he's a *white* guy!"

Raymond and Roberta crack up. "When you said you had a black wife," Roberta says, "I thought, 'Won't he be surprised.'"

"I saw you two looking at each other, but didn't have a clue. What were the first words out of your mouth when she called?"

Raymond: "'I'll let you speak to your mother.'"

Again, they crack up.

"It's not worth losing a daughter over," Roberta says. Only their daughter's favorite relative—the one who as a child had been whipped by Raymond's mother rather than "Yessum" to whites— seemed angry about the marriage. "'If you can just get over him being white, you'll like him,'" Roberta told the relative. "'He's so much like Raymond. He's got that same old dumb sense of humor.'" She touches Raymond's arm. "'He just takes life as it comes. He's tall. He even resembles him.'" In the end, their daughter's favorite relative traveled by bus from the far South to attend the wedding. They've been married more than two years now, and their daughter is pregnant.

"Do you have any pictures of your family," Roberta asks, and I dig the photos out of my wallet, ones of my kids and one of my wife and me ten years ago. They oooh and aaah politely, until Raymond, smiling and waving the old photo of my wife and me, says, "This picture was taken when you still had hair." They both laugh again.

I say, "It sounds like you've had a pretty good life."

Raymond: "We've had a great life."

Roberta: "It's been a wonderful life."

1 3

RAYMOND'S YOUNGEST SON

CINCINNATI, OHIO

I can't always say exactly what I've learned from the people I'm meeting. A lot of times, I just feel something—sadness and guilt with the poor boys in Detroit; joy and exhilaration with the novelist

Dori Sanders in South Carolina; hopefulness with Jim Green, my old
college acquaintance; inspiration with teacher Nellie Cooke in Washington. With the Shacklefords, I just felt good. Being in the presence
of plain decency will do that to a person.

My itinerary didn't include Cincinnati, but I'm detouring through
the city to visit the Shacklefords' son Steven—the son who dropped
out of college, couldn't land one of Dayton's disappearing factory jobs,
and who now works two jobs for the price of one. He's the one Shackleford child who didn't make the leap to the college-educated middle
class, and I wonder about him, probably because I too was the son of
one of those stable, card-carrying union members. My father was a
Teamster, a milkman.

No castle overlooks Steven Shackleford's street, McMicken
Avenue, which flows low to high on his block and ends at a pinnacle
bluff. On one side of the narrow lane are flat-topped brick buildings
of two and three stories, which were probably family homes once, a
long time ago. On the other side are bigger, more elegant but equally
dilapidated brick buildings that tower above the street behind a tall,
cinder-block retaining wall, over which long, scorched grass has
grown. It's the only grass in sight.

In the day's ninety-seven-degree heat, the houses' screenless windows are thrown open and bed-sheet draperies are blowing freely. As
I walk up the hill in the late afternoon, someone is playing a saxo-
phone in one of the buildings and the sky has just turned dark. A
wind is gusting, and paper, plastic, leaves, and grit are sweeping violently down the tunnel that is McMicken Avenue. The wind's moist,
cool scent is quickly replacing the day's stagnant, muggy air, and a
klatch of young, skinny, stringy-haired white men with no shirts is
enjoying this in front of the Play Pen tavern. I ask for directions to
Steven's building and one of the men asks where I'm from. Then, in
an accent that gives away his secret, he says, "I'm from *waaay* down
South." He, too, has come to find work.

Steven is waiting for me on the porch of one of the bigger, more
elegant, dilapidated buildings. He doesn't invite me into his apartment—no air-conditioning—and we head off to an Arby's for chicken
club sandwiches. At twenty-four, with his tall, slender build, Steven
only vaguely resembles his dad. He has a long neck and slight shoulders, short and tightly curling hair, heavy eyebrows, a struggling
mustache, and a retiring chin. His voice is gentle and slow, and he

often looks away as he talks, as if he is uncomfortable. He says McMicken Avenue is populated with struggling whites, blacks, and Asians and that outside the Play Pen at night white guys will sometimes holler "nigger" as blacks pass in their cars. But during the day, sober, they're as friendly as can be. He seems amazed at this.

"Me and my cousin talk all the time about how the good factory jobs have dried up," Steven says, after we settle in at Arby's. "I started working when I was fifteen. I wanted new gym shoes." He chuckles. "I liked having my own money."

When Steven "bombed out" of junior college and couldn't find a factory job in Dayton, he began working as a courier. His father helped him buy a truck and in no time Steven was knocking down $125 a day, although from noon to midnight. When he learned he could make $750 a week in Cincinnati, Steven jumped at the chance. Pretty soon, he had $10,000 in the bank and decided to go into the courier business on his own. The first month, he made $70. In four months, his savings were gone—and he was $20,000 in debt for his new Pontiac Grand Am, stereo and TV, jewelry, health club membership, and the money he'd borrowed on his credit cards to pay his monthly bills after he quit his job. By the time he gave up and got another courier job, his truck was old and constantly breaking down, and he no longer had the credit to buy another. Steven was a hair's breadth from declaring bankruptcy, except that his father had cosigned his car loan at the GM credit union and Steven didn't want to embarrass his dad. So he worked during the day as a radio dispatcher in a photo lab and at night as a computer operator in a bank. This month, he should finally pay off his bills.

"My car got repossessed and my father bought it at the auction and sold it himself," Steven says. "He didn't want me to take such a big loss on it."

"A decent guy, your father."

"Hell of a guy. Hell of a guy."

"You just decided to have it all at age twenty?"

"I'll get a penny, work like the dickens to get it, and the first person who comes along with somethin' I want, I'll give it to 'im. That's something I've been trying to change. I may not have learned all my lessons, but I've gotten a lot wiser."

"How'd you fall into the mess?"

"I don't know," Steven says, but then he tells this story: Like his sister, Steven left public elementary school and attended an elite private high school. His sister thrived at the private school. She seemed to know exactly what she wanted—a good education, a leg up, and a good job someday. She seemed oblivious to the world of wealth and privilege that surrounded her. Steven, the only black in his class, was different, and he deeply resented his classmates' wealth, yearned to have it himself. But most of all, he was confused by the crosscurrents of race, class, and status. He always worked part-time so he could have nice things and money to spend, so he could fit in with the rich kids. But Steven never felt a part of them, although he was even president of his class. "We lived in an all-black neighborhood. They never came to my house."

"Did you invite them?"

"No."

"How come?"

"I didn't want my black friends to know I had white friends." Besides that, Steven's house wouldn't have been a castle to his private-school friends. He rode three buses to get to school. They got cars at sixteen. "My dad might have been makin' $45,000, $50,000 a year," he says. "Their dads were makin' $500,000, $600,000 a year." When Steven's grades crashed, his father threatened to send him back to public school, which, by then, frightened Steven. "After being with this very elite class of people who had their Mercedeses and played tennis and went to Aspen, I couldn't imagine being back in public school. I don't know, it just scared me."

"At school, you were like the Po' Little Black Kid?"

"I *was* the Po' Little Black Kid!"

"Were you a materialistic guy before?"

"No."

"The school shaped your craving?"

"Definitely."

"Didn't you understand that in America the route to *things,* even for rich kids, is college and professional school?"

"No, no," Steven says, and he looks away.

Steven was accepted at Bluffton College in Ohio, a predominantly white school, but he changed his mind after visiting, even after his father had put down a deposit. "I couldn't go through it again," he says of Bluffton. "I wasn't white and I couldn't 'act white' anymore to fit in. I felt uncomfortable around whites. In order to be accepted, I thought I had to play up to them. I don't know, I didn't have a PC or a video game at home."

"That's not white, that's rich."

"I didn't see it that way. I didn't know any rich black people. I don't. I felt that at Bluffton I would have to sell out. I would have to act like I liked white music, rock and pop. I would have to act like I didn't care about the racial jokes: 'Oh, yeah, that was funny.' Or that the room would get quiet when I walked in. Or in the showers: 'All black guys got big dicks.' You know, that kind of goings on. It really made me feel uncomfortable."

"It's like being 'on' all the time?"

"Definitely, eighteen hours a day."

"How do you feel around blacks?"

He thinks for a moment, and then says, "I'm relaxed."

Today the older, wiser Steven Shackleford has decided that more than race was at work in his high school experiences, and he's planning to go back to college. Looking back, he figures he'll never again be in a situation like high school, when he was surrounded by the children of lawyers and doctors, by all that money and easy confidence. Of his painful high school years, Steven now says, "I don't think being black had anything to do with it."

Like whites, blacks too can mistake race for deeper explanations. Steven works with mostly white people in his jobs now, and he gets along with most of them, even likes them. "We're pretty much from the same class—middle class and lower-middle class," he says. "That's how we were raised, and I think that has a lot to do with us getting along."

Yet he is not completely free. When his sister began dating her future husband, a white man whose father was the president of a prominent bookstore chain in the Midwest, race and class again intertwined in Steven's reaction. "I was, like, 'Why in the world would he marry a black girl like you? So you're educated, so what?' We yelled and yelled. I yelled that she was stupid. There was no way he was gonna marry her. There was no benefit in him marrying her. Why even think about it?"

"You thought he was slumming?" I ask.

"Maybe. I didn't want her marrying a white guy. But it turns out he treats her better than any other guy she ever had." Steven looks away. "I think we're all prejudiced."

"What is your prejudice, Steven?"

He turns back and looks me straight in the eyes: "I'm prejudiced against rich people, against a lot of white people."

And I think again of how often the two get confused.

1 4

NO MORE UNCLE TOMS

WALNUT HILLS, CINCINNATI, OHIO

Since I'm already in Cincinnati, I decide to take the morning before I leave and visit the home of the woman who embedded the words "Uncle Tom" in the American consciousness. Nearly 150 years after Harriet Beecher Stowe's *Uncle Tom's Cabin* was published, the name of her hero is still used to describe blacks who sell out their own people in return for power, money, or even respect from whites. Detroit Mayor Coleman Young cried "Uncle Tom" during the controversy over Rick Robinson's ninth-bass chair, and I've probably heard it said fifty times in my travels. Blacks use the name "Uncle Tom" the way the Norwegians use the name "Quisling." Nobody is more disgusting or pitiful than an Uncle Tom.

The Stowe House is in the Walnut Hills neighborhood of South Cincinnati, out Gilbert Avenue, past gentrified Victorians, past many more decaying homes, past Will's Jewelry & Loans and the Salvation Army Thrift Store. Sitting at the corner of King Drive, the house looks strangely aristocratic and out of place atop a hill behind a stone embankment on a huge wooded lot. It's a large white-pillared and brick house dating from the early nineteenth century. Its roof is gabled and it wears a chimney at either end. Viewing it from Gilbert Avenue, it's magnificent. But up close I see that its paint is badly cracked and peeling.

Inside, it's clear that the Stowe House, which is owned by the Ohio Historical Society, isn't a model of historical re-creation. There's a set of slave chains, a few period sketches of Uncle Tom's sale and beating and, eventually, his death at the hands of Simon Legree. That's about it.

But what catches my attention is a single handwritten page from Mrs. Stowe's original manuscript, the first page of chapter 4, "An Evening in Uncle Tom's Cabin": "The cabin of Uncle Tom was a small log building, close adjoining to 'the house,' as the negro *par excellence* designates his master's dwelling. . . ." Reading these lines, I realize that although I've often described this or that person as "an Uncle Tom," I've never actually read the book. I suddenly wonder if Mayor Coleman Young has ever read the book. Or if any of the millions of people who've called somebody "an Uncle Tom" has ever actually read the book. In 1851, it sold 300,000 copies in its first year. In Europe, an estimated 1.5 million pirated copies were sold. But that was then and this is now. Today, no doubt, *Uncle Tom's Cabin*, like Shakespeare and the Bible, is referenced far more often than it is read. So I plop down $2.95 and read the book. . . .

Never again will I derogatorily call anyone "an Uncle Tom." The man was about as decent as they come. On the surface he was docile and willing to be sold away from his family, willing to let the evil Simon Legree take all his belongings without a whimper, willing to rely on his Christian belief in the next life to give him strength. But in the end, ordered to beat another slave, he quietly and resolutely refused, unwilling to partake of evil himself—thus proving the slave's moral superiority over his master. Tom's defiant decency so frightened the evil Simon Legree that even Legree's deadened conscience was awakened. Tom's defiance so enraged Legree that Legree eventually caused Tom's death—a death that inspired the slaves whose spirit Legree had broken. Even Legree's black henchmen, Sambo and Quimbo, who are far more like the sellouts Uncle Tom has unjustly come to symbolize, were transformed by his strength. No wonder *Uncle Tom's Cabin* enjoyed a renaissance during the nonviolent civil rights era: the man was Jesus, Gandhi, and Martin Luther King rolled into one.

"How can this all too perfect servant of the Lord be confused with the type of sycophant wheedling before the white oppressor that we now dismiss as an 'Uncle Tom'?" asks literary critic Alfred Kazin in the introduction to the Bantam Books edition of *Uncle Tom's Cabin*. Mrs. Stowe's deep Christian faith, Kazin explains, may be quaint or passé to us today, but it was at the heart of her book. Its theme is that Christianity and slavery—good and evil—cannot coexist. "Against the backdrop of slavery's ultimately unfathomable cruelty," Kazin writes, "the symbolic crucifixion of Uncle Tom is a replication of the passion of Christ."

It makes sense that African Americans, tired of their freedom being dependent on guilt-inducing appeals to white consciences, would eventually come to see Uncle Tom as a fool for believing that freedom in heaven and decency on earth were more important than power on earth. But it remains that the qualities Harriet Beecher Stowe gave Uncle Tom, in her nineteenth-century view, were meant to be seen as the highest and finest in mankind. I suspect a lot of people today—black and white—would still agree with her.

1 5

"THIS IS WHAT I KNOW"

EAST ST. LOUIS, ILLINOIS

They call it the Soweto of America. Its poverty and unemployment are endemic. Nearly everybody knows somebody who's been murdered. Its school teachers earn $10,000 a year. Prostitution and drugs are cottage industries. East St. Louis, with its 40,944 people—98 percent of whom are black—is a hole down which human beings are flushed, and as I drive through its side streets, many of which are missing their street signs, I can't imagine anybody living here by choice.

The man I'm going to visit has lived in East St. Louis all his life—except for the many years he spent in prison for murder. In his middle thirties, Tyron, which is not his real name, has been in prison most of his adult life; he did his first burglary as a young teenager. Out for nearly a year now, he's got a rental house, a car, and a dishwasher's job. He's feeling proud.

This afternoon, I find Tyron in his driveway bent over the right front wheel of his old Chrysler New Yorker, which is in pretty nice shape. But the tire is flat, the wheel bent at a sickly angle, the axle locked up tight. Just last night, Tyron's parked car got hit in front of a convenience store. Some guy drove up, got out of his car to buy a soda, and left his car running. That quick, a kid hopped in and started to peel away. The guy with the soda turned, dove through an open window in the car, and struggled with the thief. It was cool until the rampaging car smashed into Tyron's New Yorker. He still owes a year's payments.

Tyron didn't have car insurance, but because his car was parked off the road, the cop, being real decent, didn't ticket him. It cost Tyron $25 to have the New Yorker towed, and his mechanic buddy says it will cost $172.60 to fix it. The car that hit him wasn't owned by the guy driving it but by his girlfriend, who told Tyron she didn't want to report the accident to her insurance company. She offered to give him half the $172.60 to forget about it. But Tyron doesn't have the other half of $172.60, and he can't see why he should have to pay for half the damage anyway. Her car hit his! He can't just jump down the woman's throat, because he's afraid he'll get in a fight with her or her insurance company and won't see *any* cash for weeks. In any event, Tyron has to get his car fixed fast, because he drives to work.

As I listen to Tyron tell me about all this, I examine the man. He's tall, handsome, well built, with longish hair brushed back from his face and forehead in a kind of African American version of the Bela Lugosi look. He wears a mustache and a little goatee, blue jeans, and a St. Louis Cardinals T-shirt. He's relaxed and soft-spoken, immediately likable. I say, "Busy night, eh?"

He laughs a good laugh.

"Can you drive it?" I ask.

"No, it can't be drived." He shakes his head, looks down at the damned wheel, and shrugs. "But I gotta get the estimate over to that woman's house today." She's waiting for him.

"You want a ride?"

"Yeah, let me get my wallet."

Behind the full-length bars that guard the door to his home, Tyron's house is really two rooms. Its walls and old wooden kitchen cabinets are freshly painted. Clean dishes are draining on the sink. Against the ninety-five-degree heat, an old window air conditioner groans away, doing the job. The rent's just under $200 a month.

"Is East St. Louis as rough as it looks?" I ask.

"Rougher, rougher! People rip you off like it's goin' outta style. But this is home."

"Which way?" I ask, as we drive off.

"OK, turn right." We drive past a fast-food joint and Tyron says, "My buddy, 'bout last night, 'bout 7:30 got jumped and stabbed in the back two times. They found 'im behind there."

"What was he doin'?"

"I don't know, man. It's some'in' else."

"Why stay?"

"Why I stay? Shit, I don't know. I can't say, man. All my family and friends here. Most a my friends in the penitentiary, though. Yep, most a mines are in the penitentiary. That's where they at, man, my old friends."

"Anybody make it outta here?"

"I got one friend. He's in California now. He's a mail carrier, some little old shit like that. He's the only one. Everyone else is here. I got an old buddy, he's a drug addict, ya dig? We just like brothers, man, I can't dis 'im. I can't just say, 'Well, go on about your business 'cause I ain't inta that no mo'.' 'Cause we grew up together. We ran these streets together."

"Which way here?"

"Keep straight."

"How'd you end up in the can?"

"OK, at a young age I started shootin' dope, when I was 'bout nineteen years old. When I got twenty, twenty-two, I caught this murder. I caught a murder makin' a burglary. Me and a couple more other guys went breakin' in a house and a girl got killed."

"Were you high?"

"Yeah, I was."

"She get raped too?"

"Yeah, she got raped and murdered."

"You did both?"

"I was involved in the murder, because when it was all over with she threw a bottle and hit me in the head—make a left right here— and that brought the murder. I had eighteen to forty-five, did 'bout fifteen." Tyron says that if he hadn't been high on drugs, he never would have killed her. "Face facts, you breakin' in my house, I'm gonna hit you with a bottle too."

"Left or right?"

"Straight. I did Menard, Stateville, Centralia, Lincoln."

"Which was worst?"

"Menard was worst, man, because at Stateville, inmates, they got a law that they catch ya stealin' from any inmate, your hand got broken. But at Menard, they didn't care. So what? Long as you ain't stole nothin' from them." That lawlessness among the lawless made Menard the worst. But Tyron asked to leave Stateville, because too many drugs were easily available. There he was—hundreds of miles from East St. Louis, locked up with nothing to do—and more drugs than back home! Women visitors smuggled in drugs hidden in balloons packed inside their vaginas.

"Turn here," Tyron says. "We *definitely* in East St. Louis!" Tyron looks around and spreads his arms, gesturing toward the old brick houses that are in various stages of falling down. It's the neighborhood of the woman whose car hit his. "Park right here." We go to the woman's front door, but no one answers. "I knew this chick wouldn't be home. It's one little thing after the other." We drive away.

"What do you make washing dishes?"

"About $325 every two weeks."

"Take-home?"

"No, that's my whole pay. Take home 'bout $220, $230. Now I got this $172.60 bill. What make it so bad is I'm payin' $126 a month for the car. It was $1,350. When you get up here to the sign, turn right. But I don't like sittin' waitin' on no General Assistance check no way. I got more pride."

"Straight?"

"Yeah. Ya know, it's all 'bout survival here. Try to get along as best you can. People get lazy. I can't deal with that. I gotta get up and go to work every morning so I got a paycheck comin'."

We drive through a grim neighborhood of boarded-up houses, and Tyron points to a vacant lot of tall grass. "They found a stud dead here three weeks ago. A dog found him, had a bone in his mouth."

As we pass just outside the East St. Louis limits, Tyron points out a nondescript building with no identifying signs. It's a strip joint and at night its parking lot is filled with buses. "This place is filled with nothin' but white guys."

"You ever been in there?" I ask.

"No, they don't let blacks in. Got security guards."

"No!"

"Yeah! It's som'in' else."

Tyron says that as a boy he bounced all around East St. Louis with his mother and his father, who had a good factory job back in the days before all the factories left East St. Louis, as did the better-off whites and blacks who lived there then. Tyron has a lot of brothers and sisters, and the sisters are all doing well, married to mailmen, bus drivers, computer operators, and such. But his brothers have had problems. One is in prison. One is on welfare. One has been shot several times. One died in a fight over a girl.

"Why are your sisters doing so well?"

"My sisters scared a goin' ta jail."

"The guys aren't?"

"Nope." With nostalgia, Tyron says, "We was poor. I knew we was poor, but we always had a roof over our head, food in the icebox. We had gas and water and electricity, ya dig? Dad was a gambler—Georgia Skin, Coon Can, Tonk."

"Tonk?"

"You don't know Tonk?" he asks, like I'm from Mars.

"It's new to me."

"OK, it's like playing Gin Rummy, but you can't spread with no ace, queen, king. Gotta be queen, king, and jack. OK?"

"Uh, sure."

"You deal five or ten cards. I seen guys play one hand a Tonk for a hundred dollars. You play Coon Can just about the same way, but you take the tens, nines, and eights outta the deck."

"Why?"

"'Cause it's just the game, come from Mississippi, ya dig? My daddy taught me how ta play cards when I was real young and I done played just about every card game they is."

"Are you sorry you killed that woman?"

"Yeah, I'm sorry I took somebody's life. I'm sorry I lost my freedom. And I'm sorry I had to go through the bullshit of bein' in the penitentiary, man. Don't ever go. You know how many wars I been through? If you won't fight, they got someplace for ya—right up under somebody's knees. And then when he got through with ya, he'd take ya and sell ya ta somebody else. I have seen mans—human beings—sold for eight caps of reefer, man, *tablespoons!*"

"Did being black matter?"

"Black ain't got nothin' to do with it. You got whites in prison. They life is fucked up too."

Soon after he got out of prison, Tyron met a woman at a party. "First thing that come outta her mouth: 'You got any money?' I said, 'You gotta find another man for that.' She said, 'I don't want no money from you. I just wanta see if you got any in your pocket.' I said, 'Why, you gonna put some in there?' She tell me, 'Could be.' She had a car, real nice, real nice. She go in the armrest and she give me $50 out of it."

"What'd she do for a living?"

"She sells drugs."

"Is it smart for a guy on parole to be with her?"

"As long as I ain't usin' 'em, I'm cool."

"What if she's stopped and you're with her?"

"See, like I always have told her. 'If anything like that happens, you take your weight.' Ya dig?"

"What if she doesn't?"

"I don't know. I ain't gonna say 'cause you never know what a person's gonna do. OK, so I seen money. Every time I needed some money, I called over to her and she'd bring me some money. Next thing I knew, she called me and said, 'Why don't you move in with me?' And she got a real nice apartment—three bedrooms, bathroom, living room, kitchen, everything you need." Let's face it, Tyron says, he's a ladies' man who could make a decent living as a gigolo if he wanted.

"Why would a woman do that?" I ask.

"Let me tell ya som'in'. Now, I told you I ain't prejudiced, but that's one thing about whites. You think you can't get no money outta a woman. You *can* get money outta a woman. Let 'em hear what they wanta hear. That's all it takes. Ain't no way I'm gonna walk the street with no money in my pocket with all these women walkin' around. These womens workin'! They got money to spare. Who better than me to spend it on? Put me some clothes on, take a bath, comb my hair, and that's all it takes. What better way to spend a day than having sex with a woman and getting paid for it?"

"How else are blacks and whites different?"

"Sometimes to me they dumb. They just act stupid. You give 'em some authority and they really take it away. They just go for it." The previous manager of the place where Tyron works used to pay him the night before payday, because payday is Tyron's day off. But the new manager won't do that—against policy. "But who's it hurtin'?"

he asks. To whites, rules are always rules, no matter how dumb.

"How'd you come out of prison without seeing every straight person as a chump to be taken as a mark?"

"I don't know if I did, ya dig? If I see a straight chump to be taken as a mark, I probl'y would, if it concerns money. I learned that on the streets. Say you get a college student, he's been to school, he got degrees. I mean like you. You got degrees. You got a good job, all this. You got a car, home, wife, kids, money in the bank, ya dig? You're set. But you don't know nothin' 'bout the streets. I think it's good for somebody ta know somethin' 'bout the streets, 'cause sooner or later you gonna be out there, even if you're goin' to the grocery store. That's the reason I say every motherfucker should know somethin' 'bout the streets. Man, I wish ta hell I did have all the education, college. I wish ta hell I did have a job, a job paying good money, the family, the home, the bank accounts, the loans, the spas. Whenever I felt like I wanta get on an airplane, I can jump on an airplane, ya dig? Like now, if I had the money, I wouldn't be sittin' here debatin' this bitch 'bout my car. If I had ta take her to court. If I had the money. But I haven't got the money. So now I gotta scheme and get my car fixed through her. I gotta use my head. What's the sense in me havin' money and I ain't got no sense 'bout how to walk out in the street and not get taken?"

I say, "Most people go their whole lives and never set foot in a neighborhood like this. That's how they do it. They avoid it, live in the suburbs, make it disappear."

"They ain't runnin' me outta my own neighborhood."

"Is it better to get stabbed?"

"No, it ain't better. It's just if you're gonna leave, make it for a good reason. It's home, ya dig? I came through it. I lived! It sounds stupid, but that's the way it is."

"It's what you know?"

"Yeah." He pauses, raises his arms, and gestures to the devastation around him. "This is what I know."

"You wouldn't rather be a straight who goes out to his house in the suburbs every night and who's got money in the bank?"

"No, no, no. That's what I was tryin' to tell ya."

"You're proud you survived here when guys like me couldn't?"

Tyron smiles and says, "You got it right."

1 6

BACK TO THE FUTURE

CARLINVILLE, ILLINOIS

Only a few minutes from Tyron's place, going north on the highway into southern Illinois, the destitution and decay that created
his strange and terrible vision of life are quickly replaced by vast fields
of corn made dry and scrawny by the heat. They are as familiar to me
as Tyron's outlook is foreign, and I feel comfortable again, back in control. This is territory I know, the countryside where I spent four years
at Blackburn College. I'm headed there to talk to black students.

Visiting Tyron in East St. Louis reminded me of a line in a song by
rap star Ice-T, whom I plan to visit later in California: Does this "look
like America to you?" Hell, no! So much drivel comes down about
how poor, city blacks have lost touch with the American values of
hard work, honesty, fairness, fair play. But like the fields of corn that
engulf me now, values begin as seeds and grow from the conditions
of the soil, the conditions of our lives. This simple truth has somehow
come to sound smarmy. But Eskimos didn't invent air-conditioning.
People like Tyron must face the world as it is, not as we who reside in
virtually another country would dream it to be. As Michael Cross
said about the third-grade boys I met in Detroit—the Tyrons of the
future—"What do you expect?"

Blackburn College, with five hundred students, is located on a pretty
little campus on the outskirts of Carlinville, Illinois, a cornfield town
of 5,416 that sits an hour north of St. Louis. It is a hub for farms, footloose factories, and even smaller and quieter burgs. It has an old two-
story town square, a movie house named the Marvel Theatre, and a
county courthouse with a giant, silver dome. It wasn't the most exciting place to spend four years, but I was a scholarship kid who went
for nearly nothing, and nearly nothing was something I couldn't
refuse.

It's always nice to go home, and I feel a rush of nostalgia cruising
over the same old speed bumps and seeing kids tossing a Frisbee on
the quadrangle, women playing tennis, a guy adjusting two kegs of

beer on the back of a pickup truck. In the middle of nowhere, tiny Blackburn was always a world unto itself. The school integrated in 1952, accepting six black students. That was a big deal in southern Illinois, where racism ran deep, where resentment of black strike-breakers brought into the coal mines in the early twentieth century still seemed fresh. Blackburn usually had about fifteen black students a year, but in 1968, the year I arrived, the number jumped to about forty, where it has hovered ever since. It was the time of Martin Luther King and Malcolm X, race riots and school busing, Black Panthers and Black Power. Even insular Blackburn crackled with black anger and white resentment.

I wonder what has changed in nearly twenty-five years. Heading back out the main gates of the campus onto tree-lined College Avenue, I find the sprawling house of Cynthia and Ed LaMar. Cynthia is a black woman who came to the campus as a freshman the year after I arrived. Ed is a white man who was a Blackburn biology professor at the time. Despite the campus gossip, Cynthia and Ed dated. Then they married. Ed always jokes that people said it would last six minutes, then six days, then six months. They've been married twenty years now. Cynthia and Ed never moved out of Carlinville, and today they run a multimillion-dollar business selling microscopes out of a warehouse just off Carlinville's square. More than a hundred people came to Cynthia's recent fortieth birthday party, including some of the town's richest and most influential citizens. That alone is quite a change.

As a favor to me, Cynthia has invited a group of black students over to talk about how they see life at Blackburn today, and she has arranged for me to meet with a dozen or so other black students over the next few days. What emerges in our discussions will leave me dumbfounded.

Blackburn continues to have its share of racial tensions between blacks and whites, slurs spoken and understood, but the racism is rarely overt and rarely do black students see an individual white's prejudice as a reflection of all white attitudes. Black student anger toward whites is clearly diminished. Cynthia has made phone calls to her old college friends during Blackburn's fund-raising drives, and she says the black students from 1968 to about 1973 are still angry about their college years. But black kids today say they've made lasting friendships with white students. When they're asked if they feel welcome on campus, the question seems to come as a surprise. *Well, yeah, sure.* When asked if they believe teachers discriminate against them—something black students in my day complained about—the question again seems to surprise. *No, no problems.* Almost all the black kids I meet say they went to elementary or high school with white kids and that Blackburn was no culture shock. Compare that with the stories I heard from my former black classmate Jim Green in South Carolina.

Today, a far bigger issue than white racism for Blackburn's black students is a festering animosity between black men and black women on campus, and this hostility reflects a dramatic change: black men and women agree that Blackburn's black men date white women almost exclusively, but that Blackburn's white men almost never date black women. "I came here and I couldn't believe it," a twenty-one-year-old freshman woman had told me earlier today. "They're just so fascinated to have a white girl in love with them. They've never done it. They call us black bitches." And her voice goes deep as she imitates a black man: "'You black women got an attitude. With a black woman you gotta tell her where you been, where you goin', what time you gonna get there. With a white girl, you can do what you wanta do.' If a white man would talk to me, I would date him, but Blackburn's white guys won't ask out black girls. They're scared."

After dinner, I sit in Cynthia and Ed's living room with a twenty-one-year-old black man who is a senior and three black women—a freshman, a junior, and a senior. The main topic of conversation is black men and black women at Blackburn. The only male student, a man who is friends with the women in attendance, is certainly on the spot. "I can see it from both sides because I dated black and white," he says hesitantly. He says black girls always think black guys date white women because they're easier sexually and more willing and able to help pay their own way. But, he says, it's also true that white women aren't so demanding of their men and that they don't keep nearly so tight a leash on them.

"To me, they don't care," says one black woman student.

The wife of Blackburn's black assistant to the president, a forty-one-year-old woman named Beverly Wallace, has joined the conversation, and she says, "They don't need the security that we as black women need. We don't trust anyone! You have to prove yourself to me, buddy, because I worked hard for what I got."

"Is this a pattern?" I ask. "You have to tie up your black man or he's out sniffin' round the pumpkin patch?"

The women nod in agreement.

"So you're saying the stereotype of the irresponsible, spoiled black male isn't a myth?"

"Oh, it's a reality," says Beverly.

The young man ventures forth carefully, saying that most black guys wouldn't look twice at a white woman if they were in, say, Chicago, "because they'd have some decent girls to pick from."

"Wait a minute!" a black woman student shouts, as the others join in with a chorus of moans, groans, and angry harumphs.

Well, the young man admits, black guys do get some "ego thrill" dating white girls. "When I came here as a freshman, I wanted to know what it was like being with a white woman sexually." He'd always heard that white women were, well, looser. I find that funny, because I know that white men often believe black women are more freewheeling sexually than white women.

"Whose stereotype is this anyway?" I ask.

Of himself and his black friends, the man says, "We sit up and talk: 'Do you think there's a difference?' I don't see it too much."

"'Too much'?" I ask.

"Let's put it this way, if I was blindfolded, I would know if it was a white woman or a black woman."

The women will not settle for his vagueness.

Bluntly, the man says that the first thing a black woman will tell a guy she's going to be intimate with is that she'll never perform oral sex. "You ask any black girl on campus," he says. Through their disgusted moans, the black women confirm the man's observation. But likewise, the women say, black men also have an aversion to oral sex. One woman says black men are always saying, "I ain't eatin' no pussy!" Says another, "Any black guy that would do it, would never admit it."

That's true, the black man says, because if he did, he'd be ridiculed by his black male friends. "I think it's a power thing," he says.

"It's *unmacho*," says a woman.

All this is a news flash to me.

As the conversation moves along, it becomes clear that besides this battle between the black sexes on campus, black kids at Blackburn are also struggling with the same raging issue blacks face everywhere: *How do I know when I can trust these white people?* The young man tells of the time he took a white student he knew home to his parents' house one holiday vacation and showed him around Chicago. The guy ate his mother's dinner, joked with his sister. On the drive back it felt like he'd made a new friend. But the next day, in the dining hall, the kid walked past, didn't say a word, and hasn't spoken to him since. A woman tells of the time she heard a white guy say blacks should "go back to where they came from," and then later saw him talking to a black guy as if he were his best buddy.

Fear of being duped. Again and again I've heard it. Too often whites seem to lure blacks into believing they're friends, only for the blacks to later discover their so-called friends were calling them "niggers" behind their back. A person feels stupid when that happens, so naive, like a dupe.

"Sometimes, with white friends," says one woman, "I don't want to walk out the door for fear they'll talk about me."

"Has this ever happened to you?" I ask.

"No, I just think about it."

"Do you think about it with black friends?"

"No."

The next evening, I go to "the ghetto"—the third floor of Butler Hall dormitory, where a lot of black men, many of them the school's best athletes, live. I've told them I'd like to talk about black men and black women on campus, and a curious crowd of black men from far beyond Butler Third is awaiting me. Over the next few hours, guys come and go, and I can't keep track of exactly who's doing the talking, but here's what they say.

"Have you seen 'em?" one guy asks, referring to the black women on campus. "It's not that the white guys don't want black girls, it's just that they're not interested in the black girls that are available. To me, that's it."

"They would not like their attitudes."

"Too forceful."

"Too manly."

"Too loud."

"White guys hate it. I hate it."

"Bad morals. They don't comb their hair when they come out to the lunch room. They don't wear dresses."

"They have no feminine ways."

"They got more masculinity than all us sittin' in this room," a man says, adding that he's heard white guys joking about how some of the black girls on campus could beat their asses. "I mean, you don't want that quality in a girl, white or black."

"If you go with 'em, they watch ya like a hawk."

"They wanta know what you're doin' every second of the day." They never trust a man. "Go to the bathroom and it's, 'Where you been? It takes you twenty minutes to go to the bathroom?'"

"Don't tell 'em you love 'em, man, they'll hold you to it."

"They put on a big hard front, but you get 'em behind closed doors and they immediately break down like a piece of fuzz." Another man says he's always heard his mother and her black women friends complaining about black men, putting them down. He's just tired of it.

After quite a while of this, I ask the men if they've ever thought about the history of black male and female relationships in America, about how black men were dehumanized, made into breeders during slavery, stripped of their dignity, and then denied a fair chance to compete with white men for another hundred years, beaten down; about how black women became the strong, resilient force that held black families together, as in the black folk saying, "Mama's baby, Daddy's maybe." I suggest that there are reasons for black women's mutual strength and frailty, bad racist reasons. "Anything to it?" I ask.

"Totally materialistic!" a man hollers, veering quickly off my question. The first time you meet a black woman, he says, she wants to know how much money you've got and what you'll buy her.

"That's the honest-to-goodness truth."

The men say that all black women aren't as they've described them, but a lot of them are. And all white women aren't otherwise, but a lot of them seem to be. Then, amid what has included a lot of laughter and goofing, one young man gets serious, saying that he just doesn't see these offensive qualities in white women nearly as much. White women seem sensitive, wanting to know how he feels, how he really feels inside. "Black girls don't want that," he says. "They want to hear, 'Oh, honey, I'm takin' out the garbage now, I'll be right back.'"

"They're very uptight that we gonna cheat."

I hear several righteously indignant declarations like this. Then I hear the story of a black guy who had a white girl in his room and hustled her out just before another white girl arrived. Afterward, he sat around telling the story: "Ya see what I did? I had sex with two girls in one night! With a black girl, there'd be no way! She'd be like, 'Where you goin' after this?'"

Quite a night. I wish I could say that I'm shocked at all this sexual bravado, that it sounds awful, just awful to me, that I was never so immature, but I can't. I mean, I'm a guy who once talked his roommate into putting a tape recorder under his bed one night before his date arrived. A lot of levels of social-sexual manipulation are going on with these young black men, and they'd also be going on if they were white. But remembering the man at Cynthia and Ed's who spoke of the "ego thrill" black men get sleeping with white women, I suspect, too, a deeper, older motive than sexual aggrandizement, and I ask, "Do you guys savor taking away the white boys' women?" After a silence, one man says, "Yeah," and the others nod and smile in agreement. One man says he sometimes even thinks about the white guys and marvels to himself, "I'm fuckin' more white girls than *you* are, and I'm black."

A dubious achievement.

Over breakfast I tell Jim Wallace, who came to Blackburn as a student the year after I did and who is today the college's director of minority affairs, about my conversations. Unlike many black kids today, Jim had gone to segregated schools until his senior year in high school. He'd grown up in the South and knew what it was to buy lunch at the back door of a restaurant. The kids I met in the last couple of days all said they had experienced no instances of overt racism until they were in their teens, maybe when a white policeman was rude to them for no reason, or a store clerk wouldn't touch their hands, or someone in town was shot in a racial incident. The students professed that these were shocking, eye-opening events that finally confirmed their parents' tales of bygone racism—stories several kids said they simply hadn't believed.

Unlike these kids, Jim Wallace came to Blackburn expecting bad racism and he found it—among students, teachers, and town folk. But Jim was never swept up in the black rage of the sixties. As a youth, Jim was living in Watts during the riots of August 1965, and he saw the National Guard come in and turn the neighborhood into a virtual prison. "I'd seen violence and the way the system thwarted violence," he says. But down deep Jim also believed that if he could make good white friends, it would somehow prove his own worth. He knew some black students would deride him for befriending whites, but he believed their criticism was really envy.

"It got that weird?" I ask.

"Oh, yeah, yeah."

Since those days, Jim has worked at all-black colleges, and, he says, they are definitely different. "There are smells and perfumes, fashionable women," he says fondly. "If you can afford it, you dress all the time." Students congregate more in groups on black campuses. They're more social. And although he knows blacks are sensitive to the supposed white stereotype that they're too loud, he says that they *are* loud: the volume on a black campus is way up the decibel scale—music and TVs blaring, kids hollering and joking. This isn't a stereotype, but a simple cultural difference, something like Italians talking with their hands.

Between our day and today, Jim says, much has changed and much has stayed the same at Blackburn. Black kids must still adjust to white ways, quiet down and explain their slang, and all the while they're looking over their shoulders for racism. But what's different is that blacks aren't nearly the novelty to white students that they once were. And, Jim believes, white kids today are just less prejudiced. It also helps, he says, that the college has four African Americans on its professional staff today, compared with none in our day.

"What about the dating?" I ask.

Jim chuckles and says it's true, and that's quite a change from his youth. "The messages I got growing up were: 'Don't date white women!'" To this day, Jim doesn't like white women to close the door to his office behind them when they enter. "If somebody yells rape, I know I'm goin' to jail whether I have an erection or not." Blackburn's black guys today don't believe that. And I think about the old, bent man I met on the street in Greensboro, North Carolina, how at age seventy-four he still felt an overpowering rage that his sexuality had not been his own, that he could have been beaten or hanged for the "reckless eyeballin'" of a white woman on the street. The man seemed haunted by this indignity.

I know that a lot of blacks will insist that this outbreak of black–white dating at my alma mater is trivial and a sellout of black values, that black men chasing white women is a psychological remnant of racism. And I know a lot of whites will insist that the dating is confirmation of their worst racist fears—that all along black men really wanted to take their white women. No matter. I believe it's progress, halting and confused, but progress still.

1 7

AN ACCIDENT OF HISTORY

EL PASO, ILLINOIS

El Paso is only about thirty-five miles out of my way on the road to Chicago, so I pull off the highway onto the straight-arrow two-lane that's dressed up with purple chicory and the sickly white Queen Anne's lace, and I whiz past agricultural America's version of the ugly billboard—tiny fencepost signs, as many as a dozen in a row, plugging a supermarket's choice of farm seeds: FS, Ffels, DeKalb, Pioneer, Frey, AgriPro, Moews, Crow. . . .

El Paso, a little farm town with 2,499 residents, had been wisely built in 1854 at the crossroads of the Illinois Central and the Toledo, Peoria & Western railroads. I'm going there because, 121 years ago, this little town was where David A. Strother became famous as the first black man in America to vote after Congress passed the Fifteenth Amendment to the Constitution, which gave black men the right to vote. By fluke, El Paso happened to have a city election on a Monday, the day before regular elections across America. In 1870 the Associated Press made David Strother a national celebrity. (At least one black man in New Jersey actually voted before Mr. Strother, but it was a century before folks in El Paso realized this.)

One of El Paso's long-time residents, a fifty-eight-year-old white woman named Marilyn Swanson, has offered to give me the David A. Strother tour, and just inside El Paso's town limits I find her house, a beautiful old brick farmhouse set way back off the road and obscured by a barrier of hickory, yellow pine, cedar, and red bud trees. Marilyn Swanson is a talkative, gray-haired woman. She has collected accounts of Mr. Strother's life and found an old photo of his house, which was a small two-story clapboard building that had no windows on the second floor and a roof that seems to have sagged a bit in the center.

I'd like to see the Strother grave, so in the high-noon sun we hop in her pickup and head east out of town to the Evergreen Cemetery, which is named after its towering trees and which sits in the middle of corn fields north, south, east, and west. Thanks to El Paso's American Legion Post 59, the Strother grave is well marked:

> David A. Strother
> August 18, 1843
> March 12, 1905.

This is Illinois, not the South, and the graves of Strother, his wife, his mother, and probably his brother are laid among the graves of El Paso's deceased white citizens. Deceased white Protestant citizens, that is, because Evergreen Cemetery is segregated not by race, but by religion. The Catholics have the northwest corner.

Judging from the accounts Mrs. Swanson has gathered, David Strother was a respected, upstanding, self-made man. His parents had been slaves who bought their freedom before the Civil War. His mother did this by paying her master $50 and then for several years contributing money for the education of her master's daughter. David was born in Missouri and had no formal education. He worked as a cook on a Mississippi steamboat. When the Civil War broke out, his cooking skills landed him a job with Company G of the Seventeenth Illinois Infantry, some of whose men hailed from El Paso. The white friends David Strother made during the war convinced him to settle in El Paso, where he borrowed $50 from the justice of the peace and set up a barber's chair. David's mother and his brother soon followed him to town, and in the next forty years David Strother became famous not only for his historic vote on Monday, April 4, 1870, but also for his Scalp-Food tonic and Genuine Rainwater Baths.

This uneducated son of slaves also came to be known for his vast book collection at a time when few whites in farm country boasted a library. "His books were not of the light, trashy sort," wrote the *El*

Paso Journal after David Strother's death in 1905, "but his shelves contained much of the highest class literature, both ancient and modern." Among them was a set of Charles Dickens's works. The *Journal* eulogized him in words that today sound patronizing but were no doubt meant then as high praise: "He always had an especial fondness for children, and they for him. Hundreds of men were dandled as happy children on 'Nigger Dave's' knee. . . . Many residents of considerable pretensions have passed away in the city but very few of them with the general regret on the part of the entire public as in the case of this honest, courteous, unassuming, gentlemanly colored man. . . . Though dark of skin his heart was white as was ever made."

Only a handful of blacks apparently lived in El Paso in the days of David Strother, and I wonder about what life is like for those blacks who live here a century later. The U.S. Census says seven blacks live in El Paso, but Mrs. Swanson knows of no blacks in town. The woman who collects the town water bills has told her that at least one black family lives in El Paso—over Schramm's Shoes on Front Street, which is El Paso's downtown drag.

I thank Mrs. Swanson, collect my car, and go downtown, which is a several-block strip of what look to have been quaint Victorian buildings before most were vandalized in the name of modernization. At Schramm's, two elderly women tell me, no, the black family doesn't live atop their store. One says she thinks they live over what used to be the old shoe store, in the last building before Rebbec's used-car lot. The other woman shakes her head. No, she believes they live over Benedict's Plumbing and Heating, which is on the way to the old shoe store before Rebbec's used-car lot.

At Benedict's, a man behind the counter says, yes, the black family did live upstairs, but they moved out two weeks ago. I ask their name and he reads it to me from an account book. I thank him and go up the street to see if the family left a forwarding address at the post office. A man there says, yes, the black family left town, but they didn't leave a change of address. He knows that for sure, because he just got mail for them today and doesn't know where to send it.

I give up. El Paso's black family must be the best-known unknown family in town, but enough is enough. It's late afternoon and my stop, after all, was only a curiosity—just as race itself, more than a century after David A. Strother, is still only a curiosity in El Paso.

1 8

"NOBODY COULD BE THIS BAD!"

CHICAGO, ILLINOIS

I grew up not far from Chicago, and the Dan Ryan Expressway, with twelve lanes of frantic drivers who rank with the freeway crazies of Los Angeles, is old turf to me. In our far-south-suburban neighborhoods, my friends and I would skip high school and zip the thirty miles into the Chicago Loop to wander the streets. Once, a rich friend and I went to the private Illinois Athletic Club, where his father was a member. We had a massage. One Friday night we all bopped into the city in a caravan of cars to a strip joint that would serve kids, no questions asked. Sometimes I took a date into the city, to the art museum or a restaurant. As it was for most folks in suburbia, the Dan Ryan was for me a railroad that made no stops between home and destination. I rode the highway as if it were a human conveyor belt built to take me where I was going without fear of experiencing the journey in between: the black neighborhoods on Chicago's South Side. I knew never to get off that conveyor belt, not for gas nor because of overheated engines, never to wander by accident or design into the surrounding jungle.

As I pull off the Dan Ryan at 87th Street, I'm lost in these memories when I'm stopped suddenly in thick traffic at the streets' intersection, where a mass of early-morning commuters is pouring across toward the train stop. They're wearing nice suits and dresses and carrying expensive briefcases. They are clearly headed for office jobs in the city, and they are all black. In the middle of the street, a man hawks daily newspapers. Another sells plastic bags filled with an apple, banana, plum, peach, orange, and a box of raisins. Another, in a bow tie and a fifties-style suit, sells the black Muslim newspaper.

In the fresh morning sunlight, the whole scene has an air of determined commerce. Yet this shouldn't surprise anybody, because 87th Street on Chicago's South Side leads into the heart of the city's middle and upper-middle class black neighborhoods, places I didn't even know existed when I was always flying past on my way to somewhere else.

Up 87th a few miles is the office of Dempsey J. Travis, a seventy-one-year-old real estate man, mortgage banker, civil rights leader, jazz musician, and author whose remarkable life has mirrored Chicago's painful race history. Born poor to parents who had migrated North at the turn of the century, Dempsey Travis went on to become rich and influential. He was one of the NAACP's original lifetime members. He was college friends with future congressman Gus Savage and the future mayor of Chicago, Harold Washington. He played piano in Chicago's famous jazz clubs and, like Ralph Cooper at Harlem's Apollo Theatre, saw white bandleader Benny Goodman come to hear the music of Louis Armstrong, before Goodman swept white America with his "new" swing sound.

Dempsey Travis was shot and nearly paralyzed in a race riot at Camp Shenango in Pennsylvania during World War II and then was forced to await surgery because of a shortage of "Negro" blood. He was denied a truck driver's job at the Quality Wet Wash Laundry because it was a good "white man's job." He was kept out of the Mortgage Bankers of America until President Lyndon Johnson intervened on his behalf. As a boy, he heard his folks tell how his cousin's family escaped a white mob during the 1919 Chicago race riot only by climbing out a bathroom window. He lived through the burning of Jesse Howell's South Side house by whites in 1949 and the 1951 Cicero riot that occurred after Harvey Clark, Jr., tried to move into that Polish neighborhood. He remembers the prostitution and gambling that white cops and pols condoned in Chicago's black neighborhoods and how integral those vices became to the black economy, with Chicago's quasi-legal whorehouses once employing two thousand black women as maids. And at an age when most men are retired, Dempsey is overseeing his most ambitious project yet: fifty-two luxury town houses in the South Side's Chatham, one of the finest black neighborhoods in America.

In the foyer of Dempsey Travis's real estate office, an old black-and-white photograph catches my eye: a young Travis, maybe thirty years old, with his wife and future mayor Harold Washington and his date. The men are in black tuxedos, the women in evening gowns. They're sitting at a small, round cocktail table cluttered with drinks and napkins and shot glasses. In the center, dominating the photograph, is a smiling Duke Ellington. Looking at the photo, I can almost hear "Mood Indigo" playing over the sound of laughter and the tinkling of ice in a hundred glasses.

"That's *some* picture," I say.

"Yeah, it is, isn't it?" Dempsey says, talking quickly and giving his head a nod of exclamation. He's a tall, slight man, bald, with glasses, wearing a pale-blue suit, pink shirt, darker pink tie, and suspenders. "It was taken at the Blue Note in 1953." He motions around the room to the other photos: Dempsey Travis with Dizzy Gillespie, Earl "Fatha" Hines, Cab Calloway, Billy Eckstine, Benny Goodman, Walter Mondale, Nelson Rockefeller, Jimmy Carter, Martin Luther King, Jr. Clearly, Dempsey Travis is not a man who hides his light under a bushel. We hop in his Lincoln Continental Mark VI, vintage 1980, and tool out past Kahn & Nate Women's Clothes, which is having an "Everything Must Go" sidewalk sale and past the only two white faces I've seen all morning—two shirtless men sweating over a steaming, stinking blacktop mixer as they repair an Amoco station parking lot.

"You know what English 99 is?" Dempsey asks.

"For the slowest college kids?"

"That's right! Remedial every damned thing!"

That's how Dempsey Travis began college. He'd been an officer in the army, scored 125 on the IQ test, graduated from one of Chicago's best black high schools in 1939—Jean Baptiste Pointe du Sable, named for the first settler, a black man, in the rugged country that's now Chicago—yet he could barely read. That first day of college, his remedial English teacher announced that 85 percent of them wouldn't last a year. "I made up my mind," Dempsey says. "I said, 'This son of a bitch is lyin'. I'm gonna get outta here.'" And he did. He even passed an American Literature 117 class that he'd accidentally signed up for. After reading Dempsey's first paper, the professor called him in and said, "Nobody can be this bad!" Dempsey pleaded to stay in the class. "Look, I'm willing to do it fifty, a hundred, two hundred times." The professor reluctantly agreed. Dempsey slept so little that semester, always staying up half the night studying, that his mother feared for his health. But one night, as he struggled with a Theodore Dreiser novel, he suddenly realized he was reading. "Great God A'mighty, Mama, I can read!" he screamed. Dempsey graduated from college and eventually earned an M.B.A. After college, he opened his own real estate business.

It's a mythical tale. Dempsey didn't sell a house for nine months. His office had a wooden fruit crate for a desk and a upside-down scrub pail for a chair. In the forties, black housing was overpriced because blacks were corralled in a few neighborhoods. White banks rarely gave blacks mortgages, and many black real estate agents worked as bird dogs for whites who would finance black homes under contract deals stipulating that the buyers lose their homes and their equity if they missed a single payment. Dempsey wouldn't play that game. Instead, he organized pools of money from two small financial institutions that would finance black mortgages and, later, from labor union retirement funds. Slowly his business grew and then flourished.

"Chatham used to be Irish," Dempsey says when we arrive in the neighborhood, which is made up of elegant old brick homes and newer brick ranch houses on landscaped lots. "Irish policemen and bus drivers." Today, Chatham is home to the black Illinois attorney general; black judges, lawyers, doctors, and businessmen; as well as double-income families of, for example, schoolteachers. Many other nice black neighborhoods are nearby—West Chesterfield, Pill Hill, Park Manor, Avalon. "But Chatham," Dempsey says, "is the diamond."

Chatham Park Place. That's the name of the diamond in Dempsey Travis's career. The development is an entire square block in the heart of Chatham that's surrounded by nice old homes that sell for about $200,000. Chatham Park Place's town houses go for between $196,000 and $350,000. Even in the midst of the nation's worst housing recession in years, a third of the homes are sold—and 95 percent of the buyers are blacks earning $75,000 to $200,000 a year. People told Dempsey he was crazy to build here, but he's confident it'll pay off. He believes that well-to-do blacks abandon the city for the white, wealthy suburbs only reluctantly because the city doesn't offer them affordable luxury housing. Walking me through his model homes, he makes no effort to hide his pride. We stop at the door to pull blue paper slippers over our shoes.

"This is thirty-six hundred square feet," he says as we enter the model's twenty-by-twenty-foot living room made to seem even bigger by a wall of mirrors, pale wall-to-wall carpeting, and high ceilings. "A guy has to have a real big ego for this one," Dempsey says.

Pointing to a window in the forty-foot-high entry foyer, I say, "I wouldn't want to have to keep that clean."

"You live out here," Dempsey says, "your 'person' will keep it clean."

Through three floors, I get the dollar tour: gourmet kitchen, breakfast nook, dining room, three bedrooms, three baths, monster rec room, laundry and sewing room, two-car garage, quarry tile, cathedral ceilings, fireplace, walk-in whirlpool tubs, intercom, and electronic security inside and out. We enter the master bedroom's walk-in closet, and Dempsey becomes uncharacteristically quiet. "I can remember when I was a teenager," he says. "My bedroom was as large as this walk-in closet." It surely is a lot of house for the money. Dempsey says it would cost a third more if it were on Chicago's elite North Side, where a lot of well-to-do blacks live tucked in among whites.

"So people get more for their money by moving into. . . "

". . . their own neighborhood," Dempsey interjects.

"I wasn't going to say that, but I guess it's true."

"I hate to see successful blacks move to the suburbs."

And that is Dempsey Travis's mission. He has spent a lifetime pursuing great accomplishments in spite of white efforts to stop him. It's not that some whites haven't been decent and fair to Dempsey over the years, it's just that they've been rare enough that it's wiser to assume they're all sons of bitches until they prove otherwise. Dempsey's *Autobiography of Black Chicago* is packed with examples of white abuses against all blacks, but also against him—and his mother, father, uncles, friends. The obscure people who decades ago died at the hands of Chicago's white rioters, the people whose homes were burned down, the people forced to crawl through bathroom windows to save their lives, are real to Dempsey Travis—he knows their names!

"I sit on many boards with whites," he says, "and I know what their damned attitude is."

"What is their damned attitude?"

"Not a damned thing has changed! Any black man who thinks he's a part of it is a damned fool. They consciously cut you out."

"What's in it for them?"

"What was in it for them to keep slaves from reading?"

I say nothing.

"Answer me!" he demands.

"They were afraid it would lead to rebellion."

He nods. Then he tells a story about how he and his wife recently went on a trip to the Soviet Union with about forty white executives and their wives. "I told my wife, 'Those bastards are so damned racist they can't stand the idea that we are here at the same level spending money just like they are, no dole.'" Sure enough, he says, when he got back, a white friend told him the only other real estate operator on the trip had been talking and talking about it but hadn't mentioned that Dempsey was along. To him, this is proof enough. Everything blacks have won, he says, since the days when they couldn't get a mortgage or a business loan, or into the Mortgage Bankers of America or into a decent neighborhood to live, they have won by fighting. Whites gave up nothing out of decency. "So don't tell me there's not a goddamned plan."

"I didn't tell you that."

"Don't tell me about these bastards!"

I ask, "But is it *better?*"

"Is it *better?*" Dempsey asks, scornfully. "White boy, I don't know what's wrong with you. What the hell are you sayin'?"

"Is it better or worse for blacks today?"

Suddenly the contentious Dempsey Travis gets calm, even solicitous, like he is taking me to school. He says whites are always asking if life isn't better for blacks today. He refuses to answer that question because it carries an implicit question whites won't ask: If it's better, why are you still complaining? Well, if somebody is beating you three times a day and they switch to twice a day, is life better? If you discover that your wife hasn't been killed but only paralyzed in a car crash, is life better? Is life in South Africa better for blacks today than it was ten years ago? The question is dumb. "The point," Dempsey says, still solicitous, "is that racism is pervasive."

To Dempsey Travis, running to the suburbs or Chicago's swank North Side to live among rich whites just because he's now as rich or richer than they are repels him. "I didn't want anybody to think," he says, "that I thought them bastards had accepted me."

And now I see. I think of the Paul Robeson quote that begins Dempsey's autobiography: "There can be no greater tragedy than to forget one's origin and finish despised and hated by the people among whom one grew up." Chatham Park Place, affordable luxury in the black city, is Dempsey Travis's way of seeing that such self-repudiation isn't the price of black success.

"It's my opinion," he says, "that you cannot bring back to the city the people I want to bring back without giving them what they can find in the suburbs—twenty minutes from the Loop! Right off the Dan Ryan!"

1 9

A RICH MAN GOES TO PRISON

CHICAGO, ILLINOIS

Ed Gardner is even richer than Dempsey Travis, and just a few blocks up 87th Street I find him at the corporate headquarters of Soft Sheen Products, a $100-million-a-year hair-care business that Gardner launched out of his kitchen sink in 1960.

Today Soft Sheen is the fifth largest black-owned business in America, selling Care Free Curl, Miss Cool, Sportin' Waves, High Five Spray, and Optimum Care, which is hawked by black pop singer Anita Baker. African Americans spend about three times more per head on hair care than do whites. Ed Gardner's company has helped create as well as satisfy that demand. In the last decade the megacorporations such as Revlon have muscled in on the black hair-care market, hurting dozens of small black-owned businesses. But Soft Sheen muscled back, introducing a bevy of new products and expanding its sales to Europe and Africa. I've come to visit Ed Gardner because Soft Sheen is a living example of black competence and achievement. Ninety-nine percent of its 550 workers—janitors, factory workers, managers, chemists, computer whizzes, and corporate honchos—are black.

I find Ed Gardner in his office meeting with a female manager seated before him and a male manager who is speaking through the telephone squawk box. While they talk, I nose around. The room has the usual wall of plaques and awards that inevitably come to rich and powerful men. But it also has these items: pictures of Martin Luther King, Jr., and Smokey Robinson; African fertility statues; the music albums of Paul Robeson, Billie Holiday, and Lena Horne. On the wall is a letter hand-written in pencil from a young black girl whose leg was shot off by a drug dealer. She is thanking Ed Gardner, who moved her and her family out of the slums into a house he bought for them after reading about the atrocity. As I explore his office, Ed Gardner listens to his managers bicker for five minutes. Then he says, "I want the disunity to stop. I'm not concerned with details. When I come back here tomorrow, I don't want to hear this mess is still going on. Is that clear?"

"Yes, sir," says the man.

"I agree," says the woman.

After they finish, Ed Gardner is all smiles and gentleness as he grabs his suit coat and leads me out the door. "I don't do that very often," he says of the dressing-down he just administered, "but sometimes you have to cut through the small agendas to remind people that the company has a common goal." At age sixty-six, Ed Gardner is a tall, trim, distinguished-looking man with thinning, wavy gray hair slicked back. He wears an expensive tan suit, a white shirt with a delicate tan pattern, a tan tie, tan shoes, and tan socks. Even his chauffeur-driven Jaguar is tan.

"Mr. G," as he's called on the factory floor, walks me through his sprawling Soft Sheen plant, which has the overpowering scent of floral perfume. We run into one of Soft Sheen's plant managers, who waxes poetic about the beauty of Soft Sheen's new MRM rotary-piston bottle filler, a state-of-the-art gadget with perfect weight measuring, no air bubbles, no messy overflow. He's a forty-three-year-old black man who previously worked at several white-owned companies. He sought a job at Soft Sheen.

"Were you being overlooked?" I ask.

"Me?" he asks, laughing. "No, not me."

"So why'd you come here?"

"Let's put it this way, politically you don't have to worry about if a person is looking at you from the standpoint of trying to make himself look good by helping a black or if you didn't get that promotion because you were black. OK? You look at how well you do a job. You have to remember that wherever I've been, I've always been the first black this, the first black that. I don't need that. Here I don't have to worry about it."

As we leave the plant, Ed says, "I used to *do* all this."

"You still enjoy poking your nose in?"

"Oh, yes! I know just enough to ask painful questions."

"So they know they're being watched?"

"Oh, yes, definitely."

This morning, Ed Gardner is going to Joliet Correctional Center, one of the state's maximum security prisons, to talk with inmates, something he does often. I'm going along so we can talk. From the back seat of the Jaguar, he points out a billboard with Anita Baker promoting Optimum Care. He points out a city bus carrying an ad for Care Free Curl, which was the product that made Ed Gardner the corporate mogul he is today. In 1979, when the Jheri curl was popular, Soft Sheen's new Care Free Curl dramatically improved the hair's curl, sheen, and natural look.

"That was the revolutionary breakthrough," Ed says.

The story of Ed Gardner's life is different, less angry, than that of Dempsey Travis. Ed's father was a laborer who studied nights and eventually became an electrician. In 1931, he managed to get a mortgage and buy a small Sears & Roebuck house in a black neighborhood on Chicago's South Side, not far from Chatham. In fact, Indiana Avenue, which borders Dempsey Travis's Chatham Park Place, was a black–white dividing line when Ed was a boy. All he knew of racism then was that he could never go east of Indiana. In school, which was integrated, he had lots of white friends. He remembers a time in high school when the white football jocks began harassing black kids, and the principal asked black parents to keep their kids home until it calmed down. Ed's father marched to the school and told the principal that there was no way his kids would stay home and miss school. Let the white troublemakers stay home.

It wasn't until Ed was in the military at Indiantown Gap, Pennsylvania, in 1943 that he saw real racism. Movie theaters in Chicago hadn't been segregated, but when he went to a movie on base and sat down front, an MP threatened to break his head if he didn't get in the balcony. "I didn't know what he was talking about," Ed says. All during the war, during his time in New Guinea, the Philippines, Japan, he and the other black soldiers were separated from whites. Once, when they were at sea, a U.S. ship appeared in the distance and its men were waving and hollering, so Ed and the black soldiers waved and hollered back. But up close, they discovered the whites were yelling, "Niggers! Niggers!" and flicking them the bird. "That really started me thinking about prejudice in America."

After the war, Ed Gardner returned to Chicago and graduated from college. Always a good student, he was accepted into the University of Chicago at a time when few blacks were admitted, and he earned a master's degree. For two decades, he was a schoolteacher and a principal at an elementary school serving the Robert Taylor Apartments, one of the roughest public housing projects in America. He earned only $10,000 a year, and so he started selling hair products door-to-door on the weekends. Eventually, he decided he could make his own products and cut out the supplier. Through trial and error, stinking up the house with concoctions of coloring, petroleum, and wax, he finally hit on a formula that beauticians liked. He quit his school job, which his relatives thought was insane, and for the next fifteen years his company grew slowly to a $500,000-a-year business. Then came Care Free Curl.

"Any time black women do something to their hair," Ed says gleefully, "it makes more money for us."

"Tell me about it," I say. "My wife goes to Bill the hairdresser every other Saturday morning."

Ed Gardner smiles. "Yeah! Yeah! A touch-up and a conditioner and a relaxer." Probably $20 a pop for the touch-ups, plus $80 every six weeks for the full treatment, which means there's a good chance I regularly drop a few coins into Ed Gardner's pot.

Getting serious, I ask, "Why have you, the son of a laborer, done so well and so many other African Americans have not?"

"I grew up with a lot of love and attention. I had a mother and a father in the house. Academically, I was prepared. And I've just always been at ease with people from all walks of life—line workers to the chairmen of major corporations. We need more opportunities to use our minds. We're spending $30,000 a year per prisoner in Joliet on those who did not have an opportunity or a father or mother who worked consistently. These prisoners are a product—like putting petroleum, wax, and coloring together."

Ed Gardner's gentle voice is getting louder now. "Black Americans have been here since 1619. No part of American society has contributed as much as black Americans and got so little out of it. For two hundred years, my foreparents gave their paychecks back to America and said, 'Use this to help build your country.' No, the English didn't do that. The French didn't do that. Nobody but black

Americans did that. And we're still at the bottom! So it can be a frustrating dilemma, if you allow it to be."

"Do you get angry?"

"No," he says, his voice going gentle again. "I just work harder."

Of poor urban blacks, particularly men, he says, "A lot of their work habits have gone down the drain. Too many poor black men haven't got the discipline anymore to stay on the job."

"You've seen this yourself?"

"Oh, yeah. We've got at Soft Sheen in our production department about 65, if not 70 percent, black women. Women will stay on the job. They are more dedicated to coming to work every day, being on time. Many of our poor black men gotta develop self-discipline. They gotta get their butts up on time and come to work in the morning. Hispanics and Asians are taking over because they got the discipline, and we've gotten to the point where too many poor black men say, 'The hell with it. I don't want a job.' It's not their skills. We lose too many black men because they drop the responsibility. But the guys in the drug life are so used to the money, it's hard for them to change." This is, for sure, harsh talk. "We do as much as we can, but then you reach a stage where they don't wanta come to work, bad attitude. Many times that's the big problem, unable to take orders. And discipline."

"This is with blacks giving them orders?"

"Yes, yes."

"What part does racism play today?"

"It's at a different level. It's economic racism. It goes back farther than education because you've got to have some dollars to support that education." Poor blacks can't learn to work, he says, if they don't have the jobs. They can't learn to aspire and to dream if they don't have real opportunities. "You talk about the imbalance of trade between the United States and Japan, but we are saying to white corporate America, 'Give us more of your business. We're buying $350 billion worth of your products every year.'"

Poor city blacks spend a fortune on Nike shoes, for instance, and so Nike should put something back. "We should be able to set up a factory in Chicago to make shoe strings," he says, adding that Kraft, Pepsi-Cola, Frito-Lay are real leaders, doing what needs to be done to make America a better country. A black-owned company next door to Soft Sheen packages chips for Frito-Lay. "They really helped him work out his problems," Ed says. "Frito-Lay is just committed." But that commitment, he says, must come from the top down, from the white corporate bosses of America, because in the bowels of their companies are "buddy-buddy" networks of suppliers and buyers who feather each other's nests. They ignore not only the financial needs of the companies for which they work but also the social needs of America. But any enlightened CEO knows that America can't have hordes of unemployed, angry, and desperate people populating its cities, not forever. It's like the old joke: If you owe a man $10,000 it's your problem; if you owe him $10 million, it's his problem. So if America's cities are filled with hopeless blacks, it's not only their problem, is it?

"Is it a conscious plot by white companies?" I ask.

"They're just not willing to share, like the Japanese."

"Is it white versus black?"

"Those who have it keep it."

"So it's not much different from white electricians wanting to pass their union cards on to their sons?"

"That's right."

"What do you think," I ask, "when you see Michael Jordan and Spike Lee hawking Nike shoes?"

"I guess to them it's a job." But then he asks, "Is Spike Lee making so much money off those commercials that it's worth it?"

I tell Ed Gardner what I learned during my visit with Spike Lee, that his Nike ads keep his name before a wide American public and contribute to the celebrityhood that brings bigger audiences to his movies. The Nike commercials aren't only ads for Nike, but ads for Spike. Ed shakes his head, not with disgust but sadness. "Something's wrong in our society," he says, "when one segment always seems to be penalized more so than others."

Joliet Correctional Center in Joliet, Illinois, is an aged stone fortress built to resemble a fortified castle. A razor-wire-topped fence replaces the moat. We are led through the security gate, frisked, and sent through a wall of black bars from which the paint has been worn and chipped and which are quickly closed behind us. Then we are sent through another wall of bars, which are closed behind us, and met by the prison chaplain, an elderly black woman. We are walked through the secure portion of the huge prison yard, where hundreds of prisoners—all black, all wearing blue prison issue—are milling about, playing catch, shooting hoops.

"They are so *young*," I say.

"They look like the few kids I had in every classroom who were way behind," Ed says. "They all say they want a job on the outside, but getting up on time and to work on time is another story, controlling their tempers." Our prisoner guide mentions that drugs are a problem in the prison and a naive Ed Gardner is astonished. How can they get drugs in prison? he asks. The guide explains, as Tyron explained to me in East St. Louis, that wives and girlfriends smuggle drugs inside balloons packed in their vaginas and that some guards are drug dealers. Ed cringes at this. "It's sad that so many black men. . . ," and his voice trails off.

We're led to the chapel, where about fifty hand-picked inmates, all but a few of them black, are waiting in wooden pews before a small stage. The door is locked behind us, and Ed Gardner and his group, which includes two young women, go onstage. I sit in the pews with the prisoners. I've never seen so many buffed and edged muscles in my life. In odd juxtaposition to the excess of beefy masculinity, the young man next to me has "I Love Mom" handwritten on his shoes.

The chaplain plays the piano and an inmate choir sings "What a Friend We Have in Jesus." Mostly, the prisoners stand quietly or whisper and moan over the women, whose legs are nicely revealed here at ground level. "Man, I don't wanna hear 'em sing!" one prisoner complains. But for the next hour, a series of speakers preach inspiration and self-help to the men, and they warm to it, begin cheering and clapping. Ed Gardner keeps absently winding his wrist watch. Finally he stands and gives his talk, telling the story of his up-by-the-bootstraps life—military, college, teaching, Soft Sheen. He says his father went to the eighth grade and had no more opportunity than any of the prisoners here. Racism is real, he says, but you must still set goals, find pride and self-respect, self-discipline and self-control. You must do your best.

"That's not asking too much," Ed says.

"No, it's not!" a prisoner hollers back.

"Yeah!" yells another in a tone of revival.

"You make the decisions—not mama, not the gang!" says Ed, preaching now. "Think about what many of you already are—fathers! Nothing—*nothing*—is more important! My father didn't accumulate any money making $19 a week. But he is *my* hero!"

Uproarious clapping.

Afterward, I ask a tall, muscular black prisoner standing beside me, a man who has served only five of his thirteen years for murder, what he thought of Ed Gardner's talk.

"It feels good," he says.

"Is it easy to make the right decisions on the outside?"

He shakes his head emphatically. "Naw, man, some things happen. You know what I'm sayin'?"

"Like what?"

"Well, dealin' with my case, I didn't know it was gonna happen. Everything just happened. It came down. I s'pposed to be in school, but I'm hangin' out with my brothers. I brought that mistake on my children."

"Does Mr. Gardner's life sound like yours?"

"Nope. In the environment I lived in, you gonna hang with certain people and there's certain schools you gonna go to. He spoke from the heart. But you gotta survive."

On the way back to Chicago, Ed Gardner is quiet.

I say, "I think if I were black I'd feel something very deep seeing a whole field of caged men, all black."

"When I first started going to prisons," Ed says, "it used to bring tears to my eyes. I've gotten a little stronger now. It's sad. And they don't even know that they're the victims as well as the ones who caused the crimes. It's their lives they're throwing away. It's their children who are being neglected." Staring out the window of his tan Jaguar, he says, "It's America's waste."

2 0

CRASHING THE COUNTRY CLUB GATES

PARK FOREST, ILLINOIS

Chicagoland has seventy-four private country clubs. Only about ten have black members. While the furor raged over the Shoal Creek Country Club when I was in Birmingham, Alabama, one of Chicago's elite clubs also was being hammered in the press— Olympia Fields Country Club, an old-line south-suburban club only a few miles from where I grew up. The black chairman of Chicago's Seaway National Bank, Jacoby Dickens, had bought a house designed by a protégé of Frank Lloyd Wright that sits just off the sixteenth green. But when he sought to join the club, he couldn't find a member who would sponsor him. Dickens, no shy guy, went public.

Dickens never got into Olympia Fields, but the embarrassing publicity spurred the club to finally think about joining the twentieth century. William Brazley, Jr., a forty-seven-year-old black architect, is expected to be one of two blacks admitted in the next year. I'm on my way to his home because in my travels I've heard black after black denigrate men like Bill Brazley, say they are sellouts trying to be white, abandoning their people for the chance to rub elbows with rich whites. I wonder what he thinks.

When I was young, Park Forest was my stomping ground. It even turns out that Brazley's street is only a few blocks from the house of the beautiful Patti Parker, an old high-school sweetheart. As a kid, I don't recall ever seeing black faces in Patti's neighborhood, unless they were delivering a Sears refrigerator. Twenty-five years later, the suburban town of 24,656 is 25 percent black, but it looks exactly the same—its middle-class homes well kept, yards trimmed, new cars parked in the driveways. I find Bill Brazley's house in a newer, more pricey section of the neighborhood. In his driveway are three Mercedes-Benzes, including a new Mercedes convertible, bright red. The house is in the woods, atop a fifteen-foot-high hill, a modern house built in two frame blocks with their natural cedar siding running at facing diagonals and leading my vision directly to the home's entryway in between. Definitely an architect's house.

Bill Brazley answers the door. He's a tall, large man with a sheepish smile and manner, a slow, deep voice. He's wearing red knee-length Adidas shorts, a red-and-white striped Izod shirt, and tennis shoes. His dark hair, flecked with gray at his ears, is cut short and natural, and he wears a mustache. This morning he was all dressed up and in Chicago bidding on an $80-million Chicago Transit Authority maintenance building, but he's relaxing this afternoon, planning to take his wife out to dinner tonight. We walk through the living room, which is a high two-story job with a brick fireplace rising to separate a great room and a TV room, where four remote clickers are neatly lined up on a leather ottoman before a huge-screen TV. Behind it is a bank of electronic devices. On the table is a lazy susan filled with compact discs—including classical, Bob Marley, the Isley Brothers. On the walls are bright African-motif prints. Bill says his wife is an amateur collector.

We settle in a rear screened-in porch, where the breeze is nice, the sparrows who live in the wall behind the floodlight are busy, and a raccoon is asleep in a tall tree.

"So why join a white country club?" I ask.

"I can't afford not to," Bill Brazley says, settling his 220 pounds comfortably into a wire-mesh deck chair. "It's not just social, but business. It's beyond being racist. It's real power. Why aren't there more successful black architects? It's because the relationships have not been developed over the years. A lot of deals that are cut are cut on the golf course and in private clubs, which we can't join. It really is a situation where people want to maintain power over people."

"And wealth?" I ask.

"That's right."

Bill Brazley then tells the story of how he came to be a guinea pig. After the public stir over Jacoby Dickens's inability to win membership, Dickens had a champagne brunch at his Olympia Fields house with several white country club members who believed it was time for a black to be admitted. Bill, a friend of Dickens, was there and he thought the whole flap was comical.

"Maybe you guys have taken the wrong approach," he said. Bill's business was in the southern suburbs, he owned property on the country club golf course, and one of his forty-two employees was the Olympia Fields building commissioner. He knew a lot of the club's members. He also was president of the American Institute of Architects local branch and one of the Institute's prestigious national fellows. "If I wanted to join," he told the men, "I certainly could." They laughed, and Bill was drafted.

"I really believed that," he says. "I was shocked to find out it was such a big deal." For the next year or so, Bill Brazley and his wife attended get-togethers and were interviewed, considered, and politely interrogated by club members. People kept asking about their kids and Bill came to believe it was in his favor that his two sons were older and gone from home. "It's a big sigh of relief," he says, laughing, "that they're not little kids who have to grow up in the club."

"They don't want your sons chasing their daughters?"

"That's right, that's right."

But that exclusion also has other consequences that Bill's sons and the children of other affluent blacks have already suffered, without even knowing it. "My white sponsor has been a member of that club since he was twelve or thirteen years old," Bill says. "His parents were original members. So some of the friends he made have maintained. They've gone to Yale together, practiced law together. They have been invaluable contacts to each other over the years, many years. He mentioned to me that one of this oldest friends was a guy who's still in the country club. That's very important."

The rippling effects of social exclusion go on and on. Bill sits on a bank board, for instance, and he's its only black member. When the board was searching for a new president a while ago, he learned that potential candidates were expected to have membership in Olympia Fields or another prestigious club. "If you want to bring in large accounts, where do you find these large accounts? I sat there on the bank board and thought, 'That automatically excludes the possibility of a black person, no matter how dynamic or creative.' Only if you were a member of a white bank board would you be able to understand the importance of being a member of a country club."

Becoming a member of Olympia Fields Country Club turned out to be painful not only for Bill but also for the white members who supported him. "I have to look deep inside myself to wonder, if I were white, would I go through the shit these guys who are my sponsors have gone through. It's a major sacrifice, when people are calling your home and saying smart-alecky things to your wife."

"Anonymous phone calls from Olympia Fields members?"

"Not to me, but to my sponsors."

"The old 'nigger-lover' stuff?"

"Or worse. And it could affect some of these guys' businesses. So when I heard this, I decided, 'The hell with this. I'll get out of this if it's gonna cause this kind of grief.' But my sponsors told me it was too late. That's another reason I have decided to stay this whole thing out. That's something that isn't said enough. Even though the country is racist, there are so many good white people who have done so many things."

Bill asks if I've seen Spike Lee's movie *Jungle Fever*, whose main character, Flipper, is a hot-shot design architect who doesn't win a partnership with his white New York firm and quits in indignation. "It's really funny," Bill says. "I had to side with the white partners." See, great design architects are easy to come by, because everybody wants to design buildings. But great designs don't pay Bill's $1-million-a-year errors and omissions insurance premium. "What are you bringing to the table?" is the question asked of new partners. So Bill could understand why Flipper's firm didn't make him a partner. That Flipper couldn't join the elite New York clubs, Bill says, certainly hurt him badly.

Bill Brazley learned these lessons only recently. He was no rich kid—his father was a waiter, his mother a beautician. They moved out of Chicago when Bill was in high school. He was a jock and got along well with white kids, felt little racism. He always wanted to be an architect, and he eventually worked his way through Purdue University. He got a job with a big firm and then left to design facilities for a new state university being built in the far south suburbs. He quit that job when a friend convinced him he could win a $6-million architectural contract with the State of Illinois under a new affirmative action effort. He quit, bought a Mercedes and new suits, set up an office—and the contract fell through. In a panic, he sent out three hundred cards to contractors and got calls to design a few decks. Soon, he was humming—and then the Illinois job came through too. Very quickly, Bill Brazley was rich enough to buy a second house on Lake Michigan, where his neighbor, the head of the Chicago Urban League, introduced him to then-congressman Harold Washington, who was planning to run for mayor of Chicago.

Bill didn't think Washington had a snowball's chance, but he agreed to throw a little fund-raiser at his house, maybe forty people.

Three hundred fifty people showed up, and Washington was so impressed he insisted Bill join his finance and steering committee. "It was an accident," Bill says. But suddenly, he was sitting around the table with Chicago's richest and most influential blacks—including Dempsey Travis and Ed Gardner. Then, amazingly, Harold Washington won. At a victory party, Washington stood up and said, "Everything Bill Brazley touches is gold." A world-wise friend said, "Bill, lightning has struck." The next morning, Bill Brazley had eighteen phone calls from big architectural firms suddenly wanting to do projects with him. "I didn't understand that when people talk about Murphy/Jahn Architects, the reason that firm grew so much is because C.F. Murphy went to school with the old Mayor Daley. In two or three years, I ended up doing the kind of work it takes firms maybe fifteen years to do." Today, Bill does business in New York, Boston, and Detroit, as well as Chicago. So he knows how important it is to be on the inside, not to be cut out.

"You know, it's funny," he says as I'm getting up to leave. "You get a couple million dollars and it just starts making money over and over again. You don't have to do anything. Sometimes, I'm embarrassed. I think people may think I'm a dope dealer."

"Does it hurt your feelings that black people say, 'That guy's sellin' out to join a white country club?'"

Bill Brazley thinks for a moment, shakes his head, and says, "It's people who don't understand corporate America."

2 1

IN SEARCH OF "PEE WEE" HAMPTON

FORD HEIGHTS, ILLINOIS

It's a little like having the same dream twice to go back to the ball field where I played when I was a kid. Today, and it may well have been even twenty-five years ago, it's in the poorest suburban town in America. The dirt infield where I played with the all-black Ford Heights team is splotched with grass now, and it's obvious nobody has played real hardball here for a long time. If it weren't for the towering backstop and the rickety team benches, nobody would even know it was once a ball field.

Walking around out at my old shortstop position, I'm surprised that I don't feel a rush of nostalgia. Instead, I have a hard time imagining how I could ever have swept a hot-hit ball out of the dirt without fearing that it would smash me between the eyes. My youthful glow of invincibility is long gone.

On my hometown baseball team from nearby Crete, I had played against Ford Heights for years, without much success. I can still remember how strange it felt to see those black guys get out of their old cars and do their slow, jivey saunter across the outfield to the dugout. They were alien creatures and the mystery that surrounded them in my mind always gave them a psychological edge. Their pitcher—the tall, dark, smiling Henry "Pee Wee" Hampton—gave them a competitive edge. He could throw the fastest pitch I'd ever seen. I don't remember getting a hit off Pee Wee, but I must have, because when I was sixteen the Ford Heights coach called and asked if I'd play shortstop for his team that summer. I don't remember why I said yes, except that it seemed like a rebellious thing to do. And I'm sure I was flattered.

Looking back, the experience changed my life. It demystified those seemingly alien creatures. I came to like some and dislike others. I learned that some were good ball players and others weren't, that some tried hard and some didn't—a version of what Ray Shackleford in Dayton had to learn about the whites he had always believed were superior to him. It seems trivial today, but at age sixteen, from my insular white world, their very ordinariness seemed novel. I liked Pee Wee the most, perhaps because he seemed to try the hardest to make me feel welcome. He was always friendly, even ingratiating, and after he once bummed a ride to an away game, I began picking him up for every game. We weren't really friends, but I've thought of Pee Wee often over the years, and I've returned to Ford Heights to find him.

The town is still dismal. It sits on the east side of the intersection of U.S. Route 30, the famous Lincoln Highway that cuts across America east to west, and Cottage Grove Avenue, which twenty miles or so to the north runs a block away from the offices of Dempsey Travis and Ed Gardner. Today 4,259 people live in Ford Heights, and 99 percent of them are black. About half are unemployed. Its per capita income is less than $5,079 a year. Its average resident got through only ninth grade. Like all the poor towns I've visited, about every third house is painted and manicured, but it's the abandoned and burned-out hulks, the ignored rental houses, and the more than three hundred public housing units that create this town's desperate visage.

Ford Heights began in the nineteenth century as a poor Italian neighborhood. Today it is really a black suburb of neighboring Chicago Heights, which forty years ago was a booming industrial center of steel mills and cement foundries. The factories supplied good-paying labor jobs to poor white men like my own father. But they also supplied jobs to the stream of black migrants recruited as cheap labor by the steel mills directly from Mississippi—including the towns of Marks and Tunica, which I have visited and which even resemble the hodgepodge, frame-house, no-curbs feel of the old Ford Heights.

Hard as it is to imagine, Ford Heights might have been worse forty years ago than it is today. People lived in garages, lean-tos, and slat-wood firetraps without running water or septic tanks. Urban renewal in the sixties paved mud streets and brought water and sewers, but it also brought the public housing projects, two of which are today sardonically nicknamed "the Bronx" and "Vietnam." Plenty of black people used Ford Heights as a way station. In its federally subsidized Sunnyfield community a stream of people from Chicago's Cabrini Green housing project bought into their first homes for $141.50 down and $87.50 a month. Some of their kids went to college and others got good jobs in the post office or the military. But with housing integration in the seventies, these successful people didn't return to Ford Heights but moved farther south to towns like Park Forest. Black flight sealed the town's fate.

With the unerring memory of a farm animal headed home at sundown, I turn off Lincoln Highway and find Pee Wee's street—Berkley Avenue. The image of black children playing catch and riding their bicycles in the summer heat flashes to mind, but today the street is empty. In place of Pee Wee's little wooden home, huge garden, and outhouse is a grassy field open to the sun. Other houses also have disappeared and two of the remaining ones are in rough shape. Up the road, a man is working under the hood of an old pickup truck and I stop to ask if he remembers a big, strong kid, an athlete nicknamed Pee Wee, who used to live—I point to the grassy field—right there, oh, maybe twenty years ago. The man looks at me with unhelpful eyes, and I'm sure he takes me for a cop. He says no. So I ask around, stop at city hall, make a few phone calls, and discover that Pee Wee's brother lives—where else?—in Park Forest, about a mile from the home of Bill Brazley.

"If you got any sense," forty-four-year-old Charles Hampton tells me when I get to his little town house, "you left Ford Heights. All these years, Ford Heights just got worse." Charles moved to Park Forest a decade ago. Most of his male Ford Heights friends who didn't move away are either dead or druggies. Pee Wee, he says, left too, moving to Minneapolis, Minnesota, nearly twenty years ago in hopes of landing a fireman's job, although that never worked out.

"How's it different living in Park Forest?" I ask.

"No abandoned cars," Charles says, adding that when he first moved to Park Forest he'd stand at his living room window night after night and stare outside into the dark. "I was lookin' to see people walkin' up and down the street makin' a lotta noise. They didn't have that. It took me a year to get used to it, where you don't hear noise at ten, eleven o'clock. It was something else. I just couldn't believe it." Charles asks where I grew up. I tell him Crete, and he scowls. Crete, he says, has a racist reputation. The scuttlebutt, he says, always has been that no blacks are allowed in Crete after dark under threat of violence. Even recently, when Charles had a part-time job delivering take-out chicken, he always hoped he wouldn't get deliveries in Crete after dark. I am amazed. "Crete?" I ask.

"That was Crete's reputation."

After getting Pee Wee's address and phone number and saying good-bye to Charles, I am still amazed. *Crete?*

Before leaving for Minneapolis to find Pee Wee, I visit a woman I learned about from people in Ford Heights. She's a thirty-seven-year-old black ethnographer who also lives in Park Forest. I was told she has studied families in Ford Heights for the last five years, and I'm curious about her findings. The woman doesn't want me to mention her name, but she's glad to share her insights. She's short, with hair tightly curled close to her scalp, big round wire glasses, a purple T-shirt, and blue jeans. She's gently unassuming, the kind of person who doesn't cut a wide swath entering a room—just the way I imagine a person must be if she is to quietly insinuate herself into other people's lives.

The ethnographer stumbled onto Ford Heights the way others do—driving through it on the Lincoln Highway on her way to the Dan Ryan Expressway headed for Chicago. "It looked like a shanty town from the Mississippi Delta," she says. Naturally, the woman knew the respectable wisdom about Ford Heights—don't ever stop, don't even break down. But ethnographers are an odd breed, and stopping is exactly what she did. Before long, she was collecting life stories, ambitions, disappointments, and resentments from about a dozen families, going to their reunions, church services, and graduations, tutoring their children. Most of the "families" she found in poor Ford Heights consisted of several generations of adult women, with men coming and going at the fringes. This was predictable stuff. But contrary to the popular idea that poor, female-headed households don't function well, the ethnographer discovered that her families worked in intricate and supportive ways through a powerfully clannish feminine family in sharp contrast and contradiction to the Middle American model.

She began poring over the studies of poor and working class families throughout the world and found resemblances to the extended families of white working-class Londoners and Irish American and Italian American families in the nineteenth and early twentieth centuries. In the turn-of-the-century writings by W. E. B. Du Bois and others she also found that extended kinship networks were common among all African Americans then, but far more powerful among the poor. These bygone kinship ways are the subject of much nostalgia today, when middle-class families are spread across the country, as children grow up and move anywhere for jobs, and the folks retire to condos in Florida. But in Ford Heights, there was also a troubling side effect of the old-fashioned extended family.

"These extended family networks people are embroiled in aren't necessarily based on these wonderful, affective feelings for kin," the ethnographer says. "People tell themselves that to help endure a leech of a brother they might have to put up with. The real flip side of the extended family is rage. There are some real tolls it takes on the individual. They're doing it for the survival of the group." Her female families coped by pooling several low-wage incomes, by sharing a single car, by shopping for sales in groups to circumvent the usual limit of three or four sale items per customer. They babysat each other's kids. Those who refused to sublimate their own desires and ambitions to the needs of the larger family were often ridiculed mercilessly. The ethnographer tells of one Ford Heights woman who lived with her mother, her sisters, and their children. This woman often put her job ambitions and her boyfriend ahead of the family— and in return was derided as selfish. "They talk about her like she's a dog," the ethnographer says. "They really lay the guilt on this woman. But if you look at her from the viewpoint of the average middle-class American family, she's doing what families raise their kids to do, which is grow up and be self-reliant, independent, and not depend on their folks."

But in these poor Ford Heights families, a daughter's success (not so much that of a son, who is expected to drift away and probably get in trouble someday) means the loss of money, help, and companionship for the family. The pressure can be enormous—especially if women decide they want to marry and leave. This woman saw one mother become despondent when her daughter announced that she and a man she'd dated for years—a man with a good career in the military—planned to marry and move to Japan. "That's just not right!" the mother said. "You don't take people from their family. She's been here all this time. Why all of a sudden now they wanta live together?" In the end, the daughter didn't marry. The ethnographer tells of another woman, very bright, who easily could have gone to college but elected to stay in Ford Heights for the sake of the family. "From her perspective she's doing what she wants," the ethnographer says. "For these women, their families are their lives. They get a message very early that the price you pay for doing well in school and work and moving away can be very high with the group. People learn not to develop aspirations that will threaten the group.

"I've been reading a lot on white working-class families and I'm amazed at the striking similarities, but the people I have studied don't think in terms of social class. They see their problems as race. When they are mistreated for non-Standard English and bad work habits, they see it as race. It's extreme class subjugation, but they see it as race. They talk a lot about how whites perceive them. People who are working often think their employer and co-workers think they're stupid. It's a big, big issue." She says that some unemployed people don't even look for jobs because they perceive potential employers looking down on them when they see their Ford Heights address.

"Is this real or imagined?" I ask.

"It doesn't matter. Such experiences are self-perpetuating."

"But it does matter in diagnosing the problem."

"For middle-class blacks," she says, "I believe racism is diminishing," but for the people in Ford Heights it's as real as ever. She says, for instance, that studies in Chicago have confirmed the suspicion that employers reject applicants with addressees in public housing projects, and she herself has experienced the kind of mistreatment her women perceive. She had repeatedly heard stories about a white doctor who took public assistance patients but who was said to treat them rudely. So when she got a cold, she went to this doctor's office.

"I go in there and there's this very young white female at the window and she's doing something and she says without looking up, 'Green card!' I say, 'What?' She says, 'Green card!' She still hasn't looked up. Finally, it clicks that she means my Medicaid card. I say, 'I don't have a green card, but I do have green money. Will that work?' For the first time, she looks up at me." When the ethnographer got to see the doctor, he asked for her medical history and she ticked it off with dates. "I saw his pencil sort of pause and he said, 'How do you know?' I said, 'I keep a record.' He said, 'You're not from around here are you?' His whole attitude about me changed. I felt what these people say they feel: whites treat them as if they're stupid. A white person becomes no longer a person who has a family and feelings, but an object of hate."

"They dehumanize whites like whites dehumanize them?"

"Exactly, exactly."

"But this mistreatment isn't unique to poor blacks?"

"That's true. But when I've often said things to people to show them that they're not the only ones mistreated, from their perspective it's irrelevant. It's not comforting to know that some low-income white kid has been shafted by the police too. It's no consolation. If nothing else, he's still white."

It's a long drive to Minneapolis, and by the time I arrive, I have realized this: Ford Heights and places like it—places like East St. Louis—are upside-down worlds. What makes sense for people living there doesn't make sense for people living in, say, Park Forest or Chevy

Chase or Bloomfield Hills, mainstream suburbia anywhere. To survive, wise people in Ford Heights live in ways that undercut their ability to ever achieve the mainstream lives they crave, because success in one world means failure in the other. It's a catch-22 that has nothing to do with character, with being hardworking or lazy. Ford Heights is a place that's judged by outside standards its people cannot sensibly share, a place that makes sense only to itself, a place where people live in unknowing and intractable repudiation of the American Dream.

2 2

STILL PLAYING AFTER ALL THESE YEARS

MINNEAPOLIS, MINNESOTA

On a Saturday morning, I find Pee Wee—where else?—playing shortstop for the River Rats fast-pitch softball team in a game against the Thumpers. It's a marathon softball tournament weekend for Pee Wee's team, which has five black and six white players. Until they lose three games, they keep playing—as many as ten games in two days. This tournament team is separate from Pee Wee's Friday night softball team, and all together Pee Wee plays about eighty games a year. I haven't played a game since college.

It's Pee Wee's girlfriend who recognizes me from my description and walks over to introduce herself as Linda Christenson. She's a white woman with a bad sunburn and short, curly, reddish-blonde hair. She points to a tan little girl wearing a pink T-shirt and black-and-white saddle shoes who's trying to balance a Thermos jug cap atop her head. She is three-year-old Natasha, Linda's daughter by Pee Wee, with whom she has lived for five years. I'd be lying if I didn't say I'm surprised to learn this about the first black man I ever really knew. Twenty-five years later, the black man has taken a white woman and the white man has taken a black woman. Linda laughs at that, saying that Pee Wee was once married to a white woman, although he did live with a black woman for years before that. Linda adds, "Hank always says that the black people with white people are the ones who want something out of life."

Linda has a red blanket spread in the shade near third base, and I sit down and watch Pee Wee. At thirty-nine, as the oldest man on his team, Henry "Pee Wee" Hampton looks remarkably like I remember him. His wide face is still unaffected and serene until it breaks out in that infectious smile. His body hasn't gone south like mine; it looks, if anything, stronger, taller, and more muscular than before. He wears a white baseball shirt with RATS emblazoned on the chest and his ball cap has an R on its face. I'm pretty sure the diamond and ruby studs he wears in his left ear have been added since I knew him.

On the field, as ever, Pee Wee leads the chatter: "Hey, batter! Hey, batter! Hey, batter!" As if to shut him up, a smoking grounder is smacked in the hole between short and third. Pee Wee instinctively takes two quick steps to his right, backhands the ball, and, without righting his now-contorted body, whips it sidearm to the out-stretched first baseman for an out. At bat later, Pee Wee still seems to drop his right elbow too low as the pitch approaches, but who am I to criticize? He pounds a ball that the right fielder, with diving luck, is just able to knock down. Pee Wee rounds the bases like a pumping machine and power slides into third base well ahead of the throw. Only then, when his hat flies off, am I reminded of the passing years: Pee Wee is bald, his head shaved and shiny brown.

As the game goes along, Linda and I talk. She met Pee Wee in her hometown of Appleton, Minnesota, population 1,552, where he had come to play a baseball game. She remembers thinking immediately, "He might steal something." She'd never known a black person, except a few foreign exchange students who'd come to Appleton and one black girl in town who'd been adopted and raised by a white family—when the girl returned from college in New York she said that the blacks she met treated her badly for her white Minnesota ways. Despite her prejudices, Linda took to Pee Wee's charm, and they eventually moved in together in Minneapolis, where she now works as a nurse's aide.

The River Rats lose this game, 12 to 7. Pee Wee jogs over to the red blanket, lights a Vantage cigarette, envelops my hand in his pow-erful shake, smiles, and says, "How are ya? Been a long time." Then he's back on the field, under the blue and cloudless sky, in the eighty-five-degree heat. He and the Rats play two more games today, both of which they win. Pee Wee gets a batch of hits, scores three times, and makes one error—on a grounder he bobbled when he started thinking about getting a double play before he'd first caught the ball. It's a Little League mistake and he'll be miffed about it all day.

On the way to Pee Wee's house, I stop and buy a case of cold Old Style, Pee Wee's choice. We break a couple and, with Pee Wee still wearing his uniform, we sit on the front steps of the small clapboard house he rents in south Minneapolis.

"So how ya been?" he asks.

"I've been good, can't complain. How 'bout you?"

"Things haven't gone terrible, but not great either. Since you called, I been thinkin' so much. We had a pretty good team! We played against Chicago Heights for the championship. We had good guys—Gregory Washington and Carl Michael. Me and Carl pitched."

"I don't remember any of that," I say. "You're the only guy I still see in my mind. I think that's because I used to pick you up and drop you off at your house. You remember when you warned me not to run over anybody on your street?"

"I was just tellin' you the honest God truth."

"What was that address?"

"Fourteen-twelve Berkley Avenue. It was a real good neighborhood. People weren't afraid to go out at night. Most people on the street owned their own houses, and most people had a mom and a dad. Everybody was family then."

Pee Wee's father, also named Henry, had come up from Louisiana and by the sixties had a job in a fertilizer plant making $150 a week, which was good money then. He built the Berkley house with his own hands. Its roof leaked and it had no running water or electricity, but even when the projects came to Ford Heights, no way was Pee Wee's dad taking charity housing. Pee Wee had two brothers and a sister, and the boys all slept in the same bed. "With arms and legs all over," Pee Wee says, laughing. He remembers often going to school exhausted even after a long night's sleep. His father's job carried no medical insurance and Pee Wee remembers that his daddy's cure for every ailment was a shot of whiskey. "Daddy never did say nothin' 'bout black and white. He said you work hard and you make it." Berkley Avenue was a good life. "Now, Sixteenth Street was *bad!*" Pee Wee says of the crossroad only a block away. "But from Fourteenth to Fifteenth, it wasn't. But we knew we was poor. We had to walk four houses every day to get water at Miss Corrine's."

"With buckets?" I ask, incredulous.

"Yeah! We didn't have no running water 'til Mom moved to the projects after Daddy died and the house burned down."

"Why didn't you have a well?"

Pee Wee grins broadly. "Why should my dad put in a well when everybody around had a well—and we didn't have ta pay?" Pee Wee says his daddy also grew a huge garden from which he sold tomatoes, greens, and peas every Saturday morning, and that in the backyard he raised chickens, rabbits, pigs, and even a cow.

"In the sixties?" I ask.

"Yeah!" he says, nostalgic now. "We was country."

"I drove in and saw a slum, but it wasn't a slum to you?"

"*Noooo!* It was a real good neighborhood."

Pee Wee learned while traveling around playing baseball that there were better neighborhoods, plenty better. He laughs to remember that he once believed nearby Sauk Village, a poor white town that also ranks as one of suburban Chicago's poorest municipalities, was luxury living. My hometown of Crete, with its big houses, new cars, and nice ball fields, was a dreamland.

"What did you think?" I ask.

Pee Wee laughs nervously. "Back then, I wished I had it."

"Were you angry about it?"

"A little, because I wasn't able to have things."

"Did you pick on the rich white kids to get back at 'em?"

Sheepishly, Pee Wee says, "Hmm-hmm."

"Did you also admire whites?"

"Yeah, to me white people wasn't that bad." He says his mother cleaned house for a white woman for thirteen years and that the white woman would do anything for his mama, that she helped the family a lot after Daddy died, that she was a good woman.

"And what about me? Why were you nice to me?"

"I was proud to have a white friend," he says bluntly. "For me back then, whites were people who knew how to make it."

"I might have taught you a few tricks?"

"Yeah, that crossed my mind."

Pee Wee was a star football and baseball player in high school, but he got kicked out of school his senior year, after a black friend punched a white kid without provocation and Pee Wee was mistakenly pegged as the attacker. He has never forgiven his friend for that. "Every time I see that man, I say, 'Ya know, you cost me somethin'.'" But back then, Pee Wee thought he had the world by the tail. He was earning $150 a week—Daddy's salary—as a roofer and $175 to $300 a month at the Ford Heights fire department. He kept playing baseball, of course, pitching for the Braves, a local semipro team. "I was proud a myself," he says. "I learnt the three-finger fastball. I learnt the split-finger. I had an overhand curve that never quit. If I had graduated from high school, I had a good chance of goin' somewhere." When Pee Wee pitched for the Braves, he was approached by pro scouts but never pursued it. "I had opportunity knockin', but after my dad died, my mom was in need of somebody bein' there," he says, reminding me of the deep commitment to family that the ethnographer found among the Ford Heights families she studied, a commitment that often kept them from moving up.

"But if you'd made it," I say, sounding very much like a middle-class kid from Crete, "she'd have been set."

"I wasn't thinking," Pee Wee says sadly. "I was a kid, I was poor, and Mom was the only thing I had."

When people began shooting at firemen as they battled fires, Pee Wee said the hell with Ford Heights. His sister had moved to Minneapolis and he moved there hoping to get a fireman's job. For years after his arrival in 1972, he applied at fire departments, but none would accept his experience in Ford Heights. No doubt his lack of a high school diploma didn't help. But the Minnesota fire departments had only a few blacks, and Pee Wee still believes his skin was his greatest liability. He found other good jobs—lifting, carrying, driving. Just two months ago, he finished training to work cleaning asbestos out of buildings. It's dangerous work, but Pee Wee says, "I can earn up to $27 an hour."

"Are you shittin' me?"

"No, man! Why you think I'm tryin' to change my life? This is somethin' I wanta do for my kids. Give them the best things I can, the stuff I haven't gave them." He sighs. "I'm livin' right now pretty bad. No job. We got a place to live, but we got in debt and they turned the lights off. It's hard times. But with this job it's gonna change. I can't afford to keep goin' back. I gotta make this move in my life, to move up."

It's a little scary talking to Pee Wee. Thousands of miles ago, black Harvard Law School graduate Bryan Stevenson in Montgomery, Alabama, told me that what separates blacks and whites is that blacks, no matter how rich and successful, cannot ever forget that only a few good breaks have meant the difference between them and the poorest black on the street. That man could be me! Knowing this forever changes the human mathematics—in the same way that my realizing that a racist cop or judge could someday shape the lives of my children. This surely changes the way I feel about racism.

It's scary talking to Pee Wee because during the time when his father was earning $150 a week and he was living in a house without electricity or water, my own working father was also earning about $150 a week. But we lived in Crete in a huge new house. I went to good schools. I imagined I would be president someday. Maybe my folks aspired higher, handled money better. But there was also the unfair advantage. On $150 a week, we could move to Crete—the town where by its reputation blacks weren't allowed after dark. At a time when Dempsey Travis was struggling in Chicago to get mortgages for even affluent blacks, my parents could get a mortgage. And my father could be a Teamster at a time when Pee Wee's father could not. This is real, only a generation past, and in my life and that of Pee Wee, these truths reach out and touch us and our children today. Except that I was white, I could have been Pee Wee. Except that he was black, he could have been me.

I tell Pee Wee these things and he listens, shrugs, and says, "It was just the life." Then he says, "I'm down on blacks. They killin' each other! It is so pitiful!" When he first came to Minneapolis, Pee Wee says, he played on all-black softball teams but then joined a white team. "I wanted to get away from it."

"Why?"

"I just wanted to play with the white boys."

"Why?"

"Why?" Pee Wee repeats, hesitating. "Because black guys fight too much. They wasn't goin' nowhere. I wanta *go* somewhere—win the division, the championship. That's the only way I got to the places I did. I been to the regional four times, the districts three times, the state thirteen times! The only place I ain't been is to the nationals, and I wanta go! Playin' with an all-black team, they get ta arguin' and fightin'. Everybody gonna get mad when you make a mistake and holler and scream and wanta fight. Then that night, you go party and they gonna wanta screw your old lady! Why do that? They don't know how to play together."

Right now, Pee Wee is putting together a team for next year that will be half-white, half-black. Even if the white guys aren't as good as black guys Pee Wee could recruit, he'd rather have them. He believes whites cool a team's emotions, make everybody play better by playing as a team.

It's a candid admission, and I suddenly realize why twenty-five years ago Pee Wee's coach probably invited me to play on his Ford Heights team. God knows I wasn't the best shortstop he could have gotten. When I was visiting Ford Heights the other day a man who'd coached there years ago mentioned that white suburban teams were often afraid to come to Ford Heights to play and were sometimes even afraid to have Ford Heights come to their towns. Sometimes the white teams would forfeit rather than play. Naturally, Pee Wee's coach knew these things, and probably figured, like Pee Wee, that having a mediocre white shortstop had other, symbolic advantages— just as Pee Wee had seen advantages in knowing me that had nothing to do with my personality and everything to do with the human dynamics of race and racism. Unwittingly, I was a character in a play I didn't even know was being performed.

"You still got your pitchin' arm?" I ask.

"Yeah, at the state fair I freak people out, throwin' the ball eighty-seven miles an hour."

"Can you still break the curve?"

"I still got it!"

"Ya got mitts?"

With excitement, Pee Wee dispatches Linda for baseball gloves and a ball, and then says in a confiding tone, "I got plans." By the time he's forty-three, Pee Wee plans to move to first base and then to pitching in slow-pitch softball. Then he's going to umpire and coach Little League. But his dream is to pitch one more year of hardball. He says, "I wanta get twenty-four more strikeouts."

"Why twenty-four?"

"Willie Mays was number twenty-four and I wear twenty-four. He was my idol." Linda returns with mitts, and Pee Wee and I spread out over a couple of front yards and toss the ball back and forth.

"Let's see what ya got," I say.

Pee Wee winds up, kicks that long leg high in the air, wheels back on his right heel, freezes motionless for an instant, and whips the ball, which flies toward me and then—*zzzzzip*—dives down and to my right, over the outside corner.

"Goddamn!" I holler.

Pee Wee answers proudly, "I can still do it!"

When we sit down, I say, "You love the game, don't you?"

"I love it," Pee Wee says reverently. "I can't do nothin' else. Ain't nothin' else to do for me. I don't wanta ever quit. If I quit, I'm scared I might. . . ." His voice falls off.

As I leave, I think to ask Pee Wee one last question. "By the way, where'd you ever get that name?"

"I was a premature baby, four pounds ten ounces," says the big, two-hundred-pound man in his RATS shirt and ball cap, a mitt in his left hand, a can of Old Style in his right. "My mama said the first thing she thought was, 'Pee Wee!' And it stuck."

An old friend of mine lives in Minneapolis and he and his wife invite me to a party at one of their friends' homes that night. An evening with friends and the friends of friends sounds relaxing after nearly three months on the road, and so I go.

My friends are white and when we arrive at the party in the Bryn Mawr section of Minneapolis, I notice we're in one of those Volvo, hardwood-floor neighborhoods that I haven't seen since leaving my own Volvo, hardwood-floor neighborhood. Inside I find maybe seventy-five laughing, friendly white people. This shouldn't surprise me, but it does. For months I've talked with white people only in stores and gas stations, motels, and libraries. The laughing, friendly people I've been with in my travels were all black, and I wander through the party, white wine in hand, feeling strangely disconnected, out of sync, as if I don't belong.

It's a quiet party, with few bursts of wild laughter. People don't holler over each other nor all talk at once. Nobody is dancing. Nobody runs to the TV at news time to check the daily lottery number. Nobody's poking merciless fun at anybody else. Strange, but after taking forever to feel comfortable in rooms full of black people, tonight I feel uncomfortable in this room full of white people. It's not because of race but because the discreet, unflamboyant, emotionless manner of these white people no longer seems necessarily natural,

God given, the way of the world. And this is a new feeling.

I'm standing at the kitchen sink, marveling, wondering if I've at last got some inkling of the tactile, intuitive gulf a black person might feel in this room, when a man touches my arm and, in a friendly way, says, "I hear you're writing a book. You gonna write about us?"

I look around at the Volvo crowd, at my own people, at this friendly man. I smile and say, "I'm reminded of what Nancy Reagan once told an adoring audience: Look at all these 'beautiful white people.'" Fortunately, the man has a wry sense of humor, and we both laugh together, although perhaps not at the same things.

2 3

THE ONLY BLACK MAN IN TOWN

OSCEOLA, WISCONSIN

Years ago, my wife's cousin Evans, then fifty-five years old, told me that the least racist place he'd ever been to was Osceola, Wisconsin. He was stationed there during the Korean War, and people had treated him so well he was plain touched. He figured folks in Osceola had never seen a black man before and just didn't know they were supposed to treat him like dirt, so they didn't.

I'd like to visit Osceola, and I see on the map that it's only a couple of hours north of Minneapolis. Being in the neighborhood, I head up on a two-laner that curves through mountain forests and around cold, glistening lakes. It must be ten degrees cooler up here. Osceola nests along the St. Croix River atop a high, perpendicular cliff of rock. As I cross the bridge into town, two canoes glide like fallen leaves beneath me on the narrow, gentle St. Croix.

A woman in Osceola's city hall had told me on the phone last week that the military base closed long ago and that the blacks living there had left with it. Although the U.S. Census claims that two black people live in Osceola, she knew of only one black among the town's 2,075 residents—a young man named Hiram Donley, who lives in the Robo Trailer Park west of town. I stop at the Robo and discover that

Hiram has just moved out, no one knows where to. But I figure the only black man in Osceola can't be too hard to find, and at the Phillips 76 station on the edge of town, the attendant says, sure, he knows Hiram. He sends me to the Cascade, a restaurant and bar on Osceola's main drag, where Hiram supposedly hangs out.

Main Street in downtown Osceola is only a few blocks long, but it's a strikingly quaint avenue of old brick storefronts. At Sunday noon, the street and its taverns, bowling alley, and antique stores are deserted, but the Cascade is open and the bartender says, yeah, he knows Hiram, saw him last night at the big softball tournament. Hiram's probably out at Oakey Park right now, where games are still being played.

Oakey Park is magnificent—with lights, a refreshment stand, dugouts, and covered bleachers. One thing's certain: Pee Wee picked a part of America that shares his baseball obsession.

But no luck on Hiram. Everybody in the refreshment booth knows him, but they say he worked the late shift in his job as an inspector at the plastics factory last night and is probably still asleep in his room in the Osceola Inn downtown. So back I go downtown, where I start knocking on apartment doors at the old, three-story, red-brick hotel. At the fourth door, a man says, sure, he knows Hiram—go up the hallway stairs and turn right to Room 207, which is where I finally find Hiram Donley.

"Anybody in Osceola who *doesn't* know you?" I ask, as we sit down in a booth at the Cascade to await our burgers.

"It's a little town," Hiram says, yawning a crooked smile. He's a young thirty-four years old, wearing blue jeans, an Oakland A's baseball cap, and a UB-40 T-shirt adorned with an abstract sketch of a black man holding his fingers in his ears, whatever that means. He neither moves nor talks quickly, and his voice—with no black accent at all—is so near a whisper that I must strain to hear him over the jukebox blare.

Hiram Donley grew up an air force brat. His father was one of only a handful of skilled black technicians in his day, and the Donleys lived in California, Colorado, Oregon, Idaho, and Spain. Hiram lived and went to school with mostly white kids. Then he went to Weber State College in Utah, about as white as a place gets. Afterward, he joined the air force and lived in Arizona and England. He got out and moved to California and later to Colorado.

For most of his life, Hiram has been a black among whites—and that's definitely the case in Osceola. Hiram was moonlighting as a ski instructor in Colorado when he met a woman originally from Rice Lake, Wisconsin, a hamlet located about seventy miles east of Osceola. The woman, white, eventually became Hiram's fiancée, but she was killed in a car crash. After that, Hiram hit the drugs pretty hard. To help him straighten up, his deceased fiancée's sister and her husband invited him to move in with them in Milltown, Wisconsin— with one black person among its 786 residents. The sister and her husband moved to Oregon soon after, but Hiram decided to stay in Wisconsin. When he called about an apartment in Osceola, he said, "I gotta tell ya, I'm a black man." The woman answered, "I don't care." She later told Hiram that thirty-five years ago she would've said "No way!" but that the years had changed her.

"So what's it been like living here?"

"It was pretty rough at first," he says. "I heard my share of Sambo jokes." He heard plenty of "big dick" jokes, a lot of "nigger" and "black nigger" remarks. Once, a drunk asked to go outside the Cascade and fight, but Hiram—a brown belt in Tae Kwon Do— calmed him down, and the man is now friendly to Hiram. The worst time was when he was standing outside the Cascade one night and two bikers said they didn't "feel like partyin' with no niggers." Hiram said, "If you see a nigger, kiss his dick," after which the bikers jumped him. Hiram beat them to the sidewalk. Word got around, and he had a lot less trouble after that. The most irksome people are the tourists from the big cities, people who seem to believe they're entering the land of the Ivory Snow people when they travel north. "You can see 'em as they drive through," he says, laughing and mimicking their dropped-jaw stare. Most people are good to Hiram here, but he still keeps a low profile. He dates a few local white women, but never in Osceola. He tells them, "Let's say we stop seein' each other, and everybody knows you were dating me. How many guys you think are gonna treat you the same as before?"

"You really believe that?" I ask.

"I *know* that! See, I know how it can get."

"Where'd you learn that?"

Hiram winces. "Colorado, Utah, Idaho, Oregon, Arizona, California—everywhere." Then he says, "But who knows, I might stay here forever. I feel a lot more comfortable now. People are more willing to accept me." Hiram says he can't even count the number of people who have earnestly confessed to him their past bigotry and said they were sorry, ashamed.

"Do people ask a lot of weird questions?"

Hiram flashes his crooked smile. "Hmm-hmm. Here's one good one: This lady at work asked me, 'Is it true that if a white woman has a baby by a black man, the baby starts out white and then turns black?' And I remember one day I was at this grocery store over here and a little kid was standin' in the middle of the aisle, and I put my hand on his shoulder and said, 'Excuse me, little man.' And he looked at his shirt. I said, 'No, it doesn't come off.' Now, every time I see that little boy, he yells hello at me. People here just aren't used to blacks being around."

It's time for Hiram to go help run the softball tournament, and we drive out to Oakey Park, where Osceola's play-by-play announcer is just saying over the loudspeaker that someone named Jim has stroked a hit past the second baseman. This afternoon, four of Hiram's friends—young white men who play on his softball team and who've spent most of their lives in Osceola—are working the chow stand, where a hot dog is a buck and a bratwurst (I mean, this is Wisconsin!) a buck fifty.

"Here's Hiram!" one of the guys says in that flat, intonationless accent of Wisconsin. "He's gonna bring a little color to the game." Hiram smiles at the joke without speaking, introduces me, and tells why I'm visiting. I play the coat-holder.

"Trouble is Hiram hasn't got anybody to date up here," I say. A roar of laughter rises up from the four men.

"He's lyin'!"

"Hey, man, those white girls like Hiram!"

The man who says this then smiles lewdly, reaches down and gives his groin a quick, firm squeeze. The men all crack up. Hiram smiles his crooked smile, looks over at me, and shrugs.

2 4

A DECENT MAN IN EXILE

IOWA CITY, IOWA

It is to be a strange and memorable evening.

James Alan McPherson has met me at the Quik Trip gas station, said, "Welcome to Iowa City," hopped back into his old bronze Datsun 510, and then led me to his house, where we have taken up position in the living room—he in an antique rocking chair and me on the edge of a couch that sags so low I slide down to the floor for more secure ground. The house isn't so much messy as it is cluttered with books, magazines, and discarded mail. It's a small, green, shake-shingled house, maybe sixty, seventy years old, in a nice neighborhood near the University of Iowa, where McPherson teaches.

In 1978, James McPherson won a Pulitzer Prize in fiction for a collection of short stories entitled *Elbow Room*. Later, he won a MacArthur Foundation Genius Award of $192,000, a no-strings-attached grant meant to free a person to pursue whatever he wishes. I love the stories in *Elbow Room*. They aren't about black people but about people who happen to be black, stories seeking truth in any color. But James McPherson, who is now forty-seven, has had no books since then, and I've always wondered why.

Certain places—Catholic churches on Christmas Eve, dimly lit piano bars, forests at sunrise—can make a person feel for a few moments that no other place on earth exits, can make a person lose one perspective so he might find another. In those places, the world seems to live within a person, not without. That's how I feel in James McPherson's house.

From my place on the floor, McPherson looks expectant in his rocking chair. He leans on its arms with his elbows, a glass of Fruit Juicy Red Hawaiian Punch in his left hand and an unlit Vantage cigarette in his right. I think to myself that he looks worn for so young a man. He wears a small straw golf cap on his head, and a few short cornrows poke out haphazardly around its rim. His plaid shirt is untucked at the side, and it doesn't match the checkered pattern of his pants. His face is dark and then darker still, worn, around his eyes. When James listens, his square jaw sets firmly. When he talks, his voice is rapid, but gentle and soft, and he often ends his sentences with the hint of a question mark, which has the effect of making me want to answer what hasn't even been asked.

We start talking at about noon and we talk until, I'm not sure, one or two or three in the morning. Into the evening, I switch from Hawaiian Punch to bourbon and he switches from Hawaiian Punch to scotch. In our conversations is a rhythm, if not a plot, that is James McPherson's story.

"That's the sinister thing about racism," James says softly. "It wants to force you to doubt your own humanity. It wants you to be a 'nigger,' to be what it says you are. It's about race, but it's also about the human soul. I shouldn't tell you this, but see that box?" James points to a coffee-table-size cedar chest on which my glass of Hawaiian Punch is resting. "I told my daughter I stole Thomas Jefferson's principles from Monticello and they're in that box. I said the white folks weren't usin' 'em." At that, James releases a tight, ironic smile and a wheezing laugh that makes me laugh too. "There is no anger in this house. Black anger fits the white expectation. They beat you and beat you and beat you, and you say, 'I'm tired, stop it!' and they say, 'Ah-hah, you're angry!' They want you to be less than human. I say no."

James grew up in the South—Savannah, Georgia—where, he says, the white motto is: I've sinned against you so much that I can never forgive you. Again, the wheezing laugh. "The black counterpart to that is, 'If the white folks are against you, you know you're doing the Lord's work.' See, they fit, don't they?"

James comes from a long line of accomplished folks. His father was once the only licensed black master electrician in Georgia, and for a time the family lived well. But James McPherson, Sr., was an alcoholic who suffered from narcolepsy. He ended up in prison for "cheating and swindling" customers, for not finishing work he'd been paid to do. James and his mother and siblings, destitute and often without heat or electricity, bounced from address to address—509 West Walburg, 2010 West Bullock, 508 East Henry, 1006 Montgomery, 316 West Hall. He remembers them all. James turned inward. He consumed comic books and then discovered the Colored Branch of the Carnegie Public Library, where he consumed Guy de Maupassant, Ernest Hemingway, John O'Hara. He talked little, and when the white boys would beat him up on the way home from school, he'd offer no defense. One year, they put him in a class with the retarded children.

When James's paternal grandmother died, they brought his father to the funeral in handcuffs, and James, in his child's world, felt humiliated. Years later, after James had become an honor student and was holding down several jobs, his father, now out of prison, sent word that he wanted to see his son. James didn't go. The last time he saw his father, the man had asked for money to buy a meal, which James had given him. A few days after his father's request for a visit, they found James, Sr., dead, frozen to death in a cheap, rented room on a dirt street in Savannah.

James climbed on. He won a scholarship to college and worked summers as a waiter on the Great Northern Railroad to get through Morris Brown College in Atlanta, a black school that drew its students from predominantly poor and working-class families. It existed as counterpoint to Atlanta's "black Harvard"—Morehouse College— where most Morris Brown students believed they could never make the cut. But James, who was a straight-A student and the editor of the Morris Brown yearbook and newspaper, signed up for a class anyway and met the kind of black prejudice he would later expose in his fiction. His black Morehouse professor asked James in front of the students if he really believed he belonged in a Morehouse classroom. When James later asked the professor what he could do to improve his mediocre grades, the professor told the future Pulitzer Prize winner, "Son, you probably can't write." Later, the same professor tried to keep James from applying to Harvard Law School, telling him he wasn't Harvard material. James applied anyway and was admitted, along with a man from Morehouse, who flunked out. James went on to win his degree.

For whatever reason of temperament or genius, James McPherson seemed to see all of our inhumanities. Naturally, he saw white racism in the South, but he also saw black prejudice against blacks and against whites. At Harvard, he saw the condescension of white liberals who ordered that he begin his first year with a tutor at his side, which James refused. He had white friends who dragged him to parties and dances so they could feel open-minded, although James hated the events and went only to make them happy. He had white professors who'd never call on black students. James also had a black

Muslim friend who railed against whites during the day and slept with only white women at night. James saw the "black hustlers" who manipulated white guilt and white fear to their own selfish advantage. And he saw the Uncle Toms (I would call them "Sambos" or "Quimbos" after reading *Uncle Tom's Cabin*) who tried so hard to be accepted by whites that they eventually became "Edwardian" in their manner, accent, and dress. James knew a black administrator at Harvard whose family had struggled to get him through the best schools. "And he's learned a few things," James says grandly. "He knows the opera. But he's completely lost his dice game! So don't overrate him!"

All of these types of people appeared in James McPherson's fiction, and as a reader I found his honesty refreshingly hopeful, thinking that if only people could stand back and see the complexities of race, class, status, and culture as they intertwined, we could move ahead.

"Yeah," James says, "those were my integrationist days."

Blinded by this hopefulness, before he had won acclaim and awards, James accepted an offer from the University of Virginia to "come home" to the South that he and generations of blacks had abandoned for the North. Come home to the New South, to Charlottesville, and teach fiction. James did, and it was a disaster.

He believed that many of his writing students at the University of Virginia were still racist. In some students, James believed he saw hatred so powerful that their eyes seemed to turn inward upon themselves. Then he won the Pulitzer and the MacArthur, and behind all the congratulations, James sensed in too many white colleagues resentment that went beyond professional jealousy: down deep they hated the very idea that a black man could be so honored. Not everybody acted this way—James made deep friendships with a handful of whites in Virginia. But he still felt constantly under assault. The message: Don't shine too bright as a black man or you'll be a target.

After his marriage to a white woman ended in a bitter divorce, James fled to Iowa, where he arrived psychologically battered and suffering from pneumonia. "They beat me half to death in Charlottesville," he says. But when James turned to an old black friend for solace, the friend ran him out of his house with a gun. James was a fool, the man said, because he'd broken the first rule they'd learned as children: Don't extend yourself to white people.

"When you're duped by a black person, you're just duped?" I ask. "But when you're duped by a white person. . . "

James finishes my sentence: "... the voice in your head is saying, 'I told you so, I told you so, I told you so, I told you so.'"

In Iowa, James began to investigate himself, to go back and reread everything he had read as boy and as a young man, to watch again the movies he remembered as his favorites. For much of his life, he'd been optimistic about race in America, believed that race was only one of many American prejudices. James could believe this no more. "Racism is out there," he says, "and it's not going to go away." With this conclusion, his optimism—the source of his writing inspiration—was sapped, stolen, gone.

James decided that he had been simply naive. When he again watched one of his favorite movies, *From the Terrace*, a 1960 film in which Paul Newman plays an executive who throws away his career rather than his honesty and dignity, James understood: coming from the bottom, this had been his lyrical view of power—honor will out, dignity and honesty are their own reward. Yeah, sure. In real life, Paul Newman would have been out of work, blackballed by his industry, and probably indicted on some trumped-up charges. He would've ended up a broken and embittered man. That was the real world. It was a place where claims of honor and honesty, appeals to morality, even charges of racism were nothing more than cynical tactics in the battle over who got what and how much of it.

"That's the system," I say.

"I see that now," James says, "but I don't like that system and so I want to avoid it for the rest of my life. I prefer to read and teach."

Rethinking his own life also made James delve into the life of his father. James discovered that his father had for years fought the white union for a chance to take the electrician's exam, and that he had suffered great racial abuse in his life. Only after his own experiences in Virginia could James understand what that can do to a man. He also began to think more about his mother, who had always been a distant, undemonstrative woman. After she died, James discovered that unbeknownst to him she had saved every scrap of memorabilia about him—elementary school awards, report cards, college diplomas, articles he'd written, and every Mother's Day card he'd ever sent. "She saved all this without saying a word," James says, adding that never in his life did his mother say congratulations—not when he graduated from Harvard Law School, not when he won the Pulitzer. "She never said a word because she was scared. She had seen so many black men beaten down if they achieved. She always kept in mind that a black man could be killed. I didn't even know my mother loved me. She never told me." Racism as his mother saw it, James came to believe, had made her withhold affection from her own son. As he says this, it seems that James is going to cry, but he doesn't. I think that he is too sad to cry.

So James rearranged his view of the world: "I see that race is a much more powerful thing than I thought before." Yet he hasn't forgotten all the other powerful things. How could he? When he was invited back to Morris Brown College to give a speech, James asked the old campus janitor, a black man he'd worked with as a student, to please attend. A university muck-a-muck, also a black man, was made so uncomfortable by the janitor's presence that in front of everybody he asked the old man to clean his ashtray. James heard blacks complaining about the power of "the Jews" on the various literary awards committees. He heard the children of the newly arrived black affluent referring to poor blacks as "those people." James heard mediocre black students threatening to charge racism if they didn't win this or that writing award.

"It's so obscene it's damn near charming," he says, laughing. "I consider them the black's revenge on the white race." He quotes Shylock from *The Merchant of Venice:* "The villainy you teach me, I will execute." Then he quotes black novelist Richard Wright: "Perhaps it would be possible for the Negro to become reconciled to his plight if he could be made to believe that his sufferings were for some remote, high sacrificial end; but sharing the culture that condemns him, and seeing that a lust for trash is what blinds the nation to his claims, is what sets storms to rolling in his soul."

"'A lust for trash'," James says. "It makes all our suffering meaningless. This is secretly the rage inside every successful black person. They thought white folks had something to offer, something great was being hidden from them, and they see there's nothing there. But I haven't given up. My idea is still that race is not the paramount standard. But that human feelings are, that you find the best people in each group, people who are human—principled, good people. I call them the 'decents.'"

Too many blacks, he says, have been reduced to amorality by success. When James was growing up the goal was not to be like whites, but to be better than whites. No more. Now the successful young blacks, those with the BMWs and the IRAs, worry only about "net-working"—using both white and black people to get ahead. He tells a story about an older black woman he knows who took a big promotion but failed to ask for a pay raise because she thought the job itself was an honor. Naive, yes. But compare her with her college-educated daughter who would not only insist on a pay raise but sue if she didn't get it. The younger woman is shrewder, but the older woman is more decent. "I accept it because these people gotta live in this country," James says. "But I feel sorry for this country, because 'What's in it for me?' is the new watchword. And when there's a crisis and they want to call on moral resources, they ain't gonna be there. 'What's in it for me?' is the question. Not, 'What constitutes a good human life?'"

I ask, "You wouldn't write *Elbow Room* today?"

"I don't know, but I'll say this much, I use my intelligence and learning in Japan, where I can talk about all the things I'm denied the right to talk about here. They want me to talk about what I know, *all* that I know—literature, technology, law, movies, music. Here, they wanta know, 'When ya gonna get to race?'" In Japan he once lectured on the connection between Herman Melville's short story *Bartleby* and *To Live*, Akira Kurosawa's classic 1952 film that every Japanese has seen. "Here, they'd say, 'Nigger, who you think you are?' In Japan, they call me a great man. I feel good when I'm there. I feel free. I feel more human. I'm not a great man, but I'm not just a race person. I've used hundreds of books in my classes and only a few are on race."

Nowadays, James searches for only the 'decents': the Japanese woman who on a crowded railway car in Japan mopped the sweat off her brow and then, noticing that James's hands were filled with bags, un-selfconsciously reached out and wiped his brow. The Jewish woman in Iowa who, when James arrived with pneumonia, came to his house and cooked his vegetarian meals, although she didn't even know him. The white man who is a Rhodes scholar but who has for years taught poor children in Chicago for next to nothing. "I look for these people," James says. "When I find the 'decents' I never let 'em go. It's not like I love blacks or whites. But you're a fool to say your own race has a monopoly on all the virtues."

"Your thinking really hasn't changed much since *Elbow Room*," I say. "In your own life, you've transcended race."

"I have but society hasn't," James says. "I'm talking about finding decent people of all races. That's all that's left."

As James talks, as I sit in his house that is like a Catholic church on Christmas Eve, I think of a passage from the title story from *Elbow Room*. It's the story of Paul, a Kansas white boy who marries a worldly black woman, Virginia, who began life in the backwoods of Tennessee. Virginia says, "'I'm black. I've accepted myself as that. But didn't I make some elbow room, though?' She tapped her temple with her forefinger. 'I mean up *here!*' Then she laughed bitterly and sipped her tea. 'When times get tough, *anybody* can pass for white. Niggers been doing *that* for *centuries,* so it ain't nothing new. But shit, wouldn't it of been something to be a nigger that could relate to white and black and everything else in the world out of a self as big as the world is?' She laughed. Then she said, 'That would have been *some* nigger!'"

That would have been. And that still is.

GOING WEST

1

WHEN DREAMS DON'T COME TRUE, PART I

NICODEMUS, KANSAS

"Go West, young man." It was America's clarion call for nearly half a century, and despite Jim Crow laws in almost every state and territory along the way—Ohio, Indiana, Kansas, Nebraska, New Mexico, Utah, Oregon, Washington, and California—blacks hit the trail. Blacks pursued the West even long before the Civil War. A black slave, Estevanico, was one of the last survivors of a European expedition into the Southwest in the early 1500s, and the stories he told led directly to the great expedition of Coronado. A black man trekked with Lewis and Clark when they charted the Louisiana Territory beginning in 1804. Blacks were fur traders and trappers, the most famous of them being James Beckwourth, who was friends with Kit Carson. Black settlements grew in Ohio and Indiana in the 1830s. A majority of the founding families of Los Angeles were black. Blacks rushed to the gold fields, rode the Chisholm Trail as cowboys, and worked as Pony Express riders. Black stagecoach driver George Monroe was so legendary that he was picked to drive President Grant through the harrowing curves into the Yosemite Valley.

Whites tried to keep blacks out of America's western bounty, and even newspaper editor Horace Greeley, who issued the call to go West, argued that the lands should be for whites only. African Ameri-

cans ignored him. But by the time millions of blacks, finally freed
from their Southern prison after the Civil War, could join the march
to acquire free land as homesteaders, much of the near Middle West
had been settled. The fertile frontier just east and west of the Mississippi River—Indiana, Illinois, Missouri, Iowa—had been conquered.
Even Kansas had been settled up to the ninety-eighth meridian at
Wichita, where the country changed from a richly watered, wooded,
and dark-loamed landscape to a forbidding place of treeless buffalo
grass and paltry rainfall—the Great American Desert. Yet after
Congress decided that the labor of former slaves, who had toiled for
as many as fifteen generations, wouldn't be recompensed with land
and after Reconstruction failed to ensure their rights and dignity,
blacks still crossed into this no-man's-land in droves.

The most famous of these migrations, the "Exoduster," began in
1879 and poured impoverished blacks into Oklahoma and Kansas. In
the following decades dozens of black towns sprang up in the Middle
West and as far away as Vado, New Mexico, and Allensworth,
California. Today, several of the Middle West's black towns still live
on, although barely, and I want to see these artifacts before they are
lost forever. So on my way to Houston to visit the man who was the
fiery black radical at my tiny Blackburn College twenty years ago (he's
a physician today), I'm swinging through Nicodemus and then down
to Boley, Oklahoma. Of all that era's black towns, Nicodemus, Kansas—
set defiantly at the one-hundredth meridian along the Solomon River
just below the Nebraska border—is among the oldest and most famous.

This morning, crossing the ninety-eighth meridian just west of
Salina, the state of Kansas isn't the psychological assault it was a hundred years ago, when whole caravans of settlers would change their
minds and turn back. At dawn, the rolling foothills are a sense-bog-
gling carpet of thick green, color so deep that as it sweeps and rolls
off into the horizon I feel as if I've driven into some computer-
enhanced land, the farmlands of Tron. When the endless fields of yel-
low-bursting sunflowers begin, it's hard to imagine how any seed
dropped on the ground in Kansas would not give birth. Because of
the wonder of irrigation and dry farming, this verdancy continues
right into what's left of the high plains town of Nicodemus. The place
isn't so much a town anymore as it is a proud, stubborn memory in
the shape of Washington Street and its few crossroads, maybe fifty
residents, twenty-five houses, a couple of churches, a squat limestone

township hall, a small senior citizens' apartment complex, and a water tower that rises like a pencil-thin landmark into a satin blue sky.

In Nicodemus I search out Ora Switzer. I find her cleaning up the old house on Washington Street where she raised her family before moving into the new retirement apartments around the corner on Fourth Street. Ora Switzer is eighty-seven years old and has lived in or near Nicodemus all her life, except for the few years she worked as a cook in Topeka to help put her youngest son through college in the fifties. Of Mrs. Switzer's six children, only Freddie, who is the mayor and deputy sheriff of Nicodemus, stayed in town. Mrs. Switzer, a large, careful-moving woman who walks with a cane, is the keeper of the Nicodemus flame. Her grandparents arrived in town in one of the first waves of migrants from Kentucky in the 1870s, and she was born—amidst the resident bugs and snakes—in a sod house dug into a hillside a half-mile northeast of town in 1903.

"I'm the oldest one left here on the town site to tell the story," Mrs. Switzer says as she uses her strong hands to wring out a soaking green rag into a silver bucket. She's wearing a blue-checkered house dress beneath a black houndstooth check raincoat. On her head is a rain cap. Nicodemus had a monster storm two nights ago, and the old house took so much water that a chunk of plaster gave way right above the front door, splattering into an awful mess. "Rain came from the northwest with high wind and whipped up the shingles," says Mrs. Switzer, who seems not at all fazed by the mishap. "Just one a those things." Since there's not a motel room for twenty miles, Mrs. Switzer is tidying up the old place so I have somewhere to stay. She didn't get it cleaned up yesterday because she was making jelly from the wild plums that grow down by the banks of the Solomon River.

"You know, I never gave it a thought that this was an all-black town," Mrs. Switzer says after we've settled in back at her apartment. "But if you're gonna get into this, you'll see where we folks been and where we're goin'."

A great deal of myth has been spun about Nicodemus, the town supposedly founded by former slaves so committed to fleeing white oppression that they were willing to lay down roots in even the most desolate environment. The truth is less prosaic but perhaps more classically American. Nicodemus was a town already under way before the Exoduster migrations from the South began in 1879. It was, according to the historical essays collected in *Promised Land on the Solomon*, a "spec town"—a town created by one of the many bands of land speculators working the frontier. The speculators' goal was not racial betterment, but profit. Indeed, the group's moving force was an experienced white town developer named W. R. Hill. The plan was to lure blacks in the upper South to Nicodemus to set up homes, shops, stores, and businesses in the "Largest Colored Colony in America." Like other speculators, Hill and his partners resorted to exaggeration and bald lies about the richness of the land, game, and timber at the barren one-hundredth meridian. One group of blacks was so elated at what they found upon arrival in the Promised Land that they tried to lynch Hill.

But after a period of desperate poverty, when many black settlers in Nicodemus existed on charity, the town began to thrive. With the arrival of more affluent black settlers and the slow but successful establishment of the poor settlers' homesteads, Nicodemus burgeoned to almost seven hundred residents. But contrary to the image of Nicodemus as a "Colored Colony," several white businessmen and the town's white banker were actually among its most influential residents. Even the newspaper editor was white, and he worked for W. R. Hill, who lived in another of his spec-town creations, Hill City, about ten miles west. The town's prosperity grew not from the grit and guts of its poor black inhabitants but from the promise of an approaching railroad, which attracted prosperous blacks and whites.

Nicodemus never got its railroad, but according to historian Kenneth Marvin Hamilton in *Promised Land on the Solomon*, Hill City did, with the help of one of its richest investors, millionaire James P. Pomeroy, the son of the president of the Atchison and Pike's Peak Railroad Company. Nobody—black or white—in Nicodemus could match that clout.

The final demise of Nicodemus came in 1888 when the Union Pacific Railroad laid its tracks six miles to the southwest, where the railroad had created its own spec town of Bogue, thereby reaping not only railroad profits but land development profits as well. Within months, every white-owned business in Nicodemus had left, most of them setting up shop in Bogue. But money knows no racial bias— dozens of black businessmen in Nicodemus also fled town, many for Bogue. What happened to Nicodemus, wrote Hamilton, happened to hundreds and hundreds of fledgling towns bypassed by the railroad.

Nicodemus was at a singular disadvantage because—romantic folk-lore aside—its black residents simply didn't have channels to the big eastern investors who backed much of the frontier's development. And the hard reality, wrote Clayton Fraser in a companion essay, was that if a town—black or white—didn't get the economic boost of a railroad, a county seat, a university, or a prison, it was doomed. So much for hard work and determination.

What made Nicodemus unique was that after winning none of these perks, it didn't fold up and die. Up until the Dust Bowl droughts of the thirties, Nicodemus hung on as the area's social center of black life. After the depression, Nicodemus, like all farm towns, suffered slow strangulation as children abandoned the farms for jobs in the cities. Today, only one teenage boy lives in Nicodemus, and there are literally no children there. But in the last decade or so a small but constant stream of former residents has returned to retire in this town, which has lived on fondly in the minds of those who once lived here. As evidence, the annual Nicodemus homecoming draws more than a thousand folks from all over America.

"You know what?" says Ora Switzer, "I just have ta say this, it's not braggin' on myself. A lotta people have had a lotta problems with the white folks, but I haven't. I just can't say I've had a hard time, went through any slavery thing, more than just workin'." Yes, there was prejudice in Kansas. Black homesteaders were harassed by whites. A white surveyor who worked for blacks was found shot dead. Mrs. Switzer can recall when blacks had to sit in the balcony at the movie theater in Hill City. In nearby Oklahoma, racism was rampant and violent. But blacks in Nicodemus Township, with a huge electoral majority, held all the key political positions, and a black man from Nicodemus, Edwin P. McCabe, was elected Kansas state auditor and vied seriously for the governorship of the Oklahoma Territory. Mrs. Switzer's schools were always integrated. And there was none of that shufflin' and jivin' for white folks. Blacks never waited in stores patiently while white customers jumped ahead. Blacks talked back, fought back. They weren't afraid. So if a person had to be poor and black, Mrs. Switzer figured, it was better to be poor and black on the high plains of Kansas than in the backwoods of Kentucky.

When I get to the house of the mayor of Nicodemus, Freddie T. Switzer, the sixty-six-year-old son of Ora Switzer is in the backyard feeding his hogs, a luxury not allowed in most towns these days.

"I thought I smelled hogs," I say, scowling.

"You smell money!" Freddie Switzer says emphatically.

"Does that make you stinking rich?" I ask.

Freddie laughs, finishes his job, and then, oblivious to the great swarm of black flies and the finger-sized grasshoppers that abound, he gives me a quick tour of his hog pens, the roofs of which are secured by the weight of old car tires in the practical way of country people everywhere. Mayor Switzer is a big man, nearly three hundred pounds, and he takes off a leather work glove and consumes my hand in his. He has the large voice of a large man. He wears Big Smith bib overalls, heavy boots, a white short-sleeved shirt, and an orange Kansas Department of Transportation cap tilted back high on his head of thick snow-white hair. He's clean shaven except for a rail of fuzz above and below his lips.

"Everybody left town but me," Freddie says proudly as we climb into his red Dodge pickup and head out for a tour of town. Freddie occasionally ventured out to visit Los Angeles or San Francisco. "But they didn't show me nothin'," he says. "Look how you can breathe out here. Nobody comin' up knockin' you in the head." He gestures to the town around him. "This is history! This old town is nothin' but history."

A tour of Nicodemus isn't a lengthy affair. We stop at the marker where the old Mason's hall went up in 1893. Nicodemus had some wild parties there. Kansas was a dry state from 1880 to 1948, but bootlegging was a cottage industry. Freddie's uncle, eighty-two-year-old Lloyd Wellington, who left Nicodemus in 1932 and returned to retire in 1982, always told great stories about the wild times—the bootlegging parties, the "sportin' women" black and white men would take out for a twirl in the corn fields, the music bands from as far away as Salina, the local ragtime guitar pickers who played W. C. Handy's "St. Louis Blues." On weekends, the streets of Nicodemus, which by the thirties was a desperately poor town of dilapidated houses on dirt streets, were filled with people.

Freddie remembers the last days when Nicodemus was still a "real town"—with a couple restaurants, a dentist, several churches, a post office, and a grocery store, which was run by the grandfather of great Chicago Bears halfback Gale Sayers. Today, Freddie can name every house and building: Ernestine's barbecue restaurant, which is boarded up; his uncle Lloyd's house; the old post office; the trailer of his brother Veryl, who visits regularly; the vacant gas station; the stucco-walled and shake-shingled AME Church built in 1885 and shrouded in trees and uncut scrub grass today; and the abandoned hip-roofed District No. 1 schoolhouse that's being renovated into a VFW hall. Then there's the old baseball diamond, which gets used only on homecoming weekend these days but once was graced with the pitching of Satchel Paige, who came to town with the Kansas City Monarchs to play the Nicodemus Blues.

"I stayed here and gathered the moss," Freddie says. "If I'd a had the opportunity my kids had, I'd a been—wooo-*eeee*—but it just wasn't my day. I could run like a deer, weighin' two-thirty, and I could hit that ball! Oh, I shoulda been goin' on, but when I come along, Jackie Robinson days wasn't quite ready. But it don't make me sad, 'cause I got it through my kids. I had one son play for the Buffalo Bills." Perhaps more significant, Freddie Switzer's six children also went to college. Today they live all across the country and work at good jobs. "Time has changed everything," Freddie Switzer says. "One a my sons said, 'Dad, if you got the qualifications today, you can do anything.'"

I ask Freddie if he ever had any trouble being a black man in rural Kansas, and he says he had trouble only once in his life, back fifteen, twenty years ago when he was a road-crew supervisor for the state. A hefty, six-foot-six good ol' white boy from Oklahoma didn't want to take orders from a black man, and he kept seething for a fight. Finally, Freddie waited until five o'clock, gave the strapping kid from Oklahoma the first lick, and then hit him so hard he knocked out two teeth. "I was sorry I hit 'em," Freddie says, smashing his right fist into his left palm and sounding not very sorry at all. "But what ya gonna do? I took enough!"

I ask, "Did you get along after that?"

"Oh, yeah," Freddie says cheerfully. "We was fine after that."

2

WHEN DREAMS DON'T COME TRUE, PART II

BOLEY, OKLAHOMA

Looking up the main street of Boley, I think for a moment that I'm a time traveler. As I stand where the old Ft. Smith & Western Railroad tracks once crossed Pecan Street at the southern edge of town, my mind flashes to a picture of Boley that I have seen—a faded black-and-white photo taken about 1910—and I think that the town should seem more alive than in the old gray photo. Today the sky is painted blue and the trees and grass are a collage of greens, yet Boley looks eerily dead. The old colorless photograph of civilization on the prairie seemed to announce triumphantly that men and women had breathed life into this harsh and desolate landscape. But today the bright colors of reality make it seem that while the landscape has lived on in Boley, the life has been sucked out of it.

In 1910, spindly power poles lined the wide street and many of the buildings that housed the town's businesses sported awnings. It's the same today, but the businesses that flourished then are long gone—seven restaurants; three pharmacies; five groceries; barber shops; a bank; five hotels; a movie theater; a jewelry store; real estate and insurance agencies; a loan company; dress shops; a lumber yard; four cotton gins; two photo studios; a newspaper; a taxi service; the offices of seven doctors and three lawyers; the three-story State Masonic Temple building; power, water, and phone companies; a brick factory; a soda factory; and two colleges. Gone as well are most of Boley's four thousand black residents. Unlike Nicodemus, Boley was a prosperous town—and it was owned and operated by blacks. But its wealth was rooted in the farm and cotton economy of the region. As that economy failed with the Depression, the towns it created and demanded failed too, black and white.

The history of race cuts deep and bloody in Oklahoma. The original Oklahoma Territory was the national hotbed for the "black town" movement of the late nineteenth and early twentieth centuries. More than two dozen black towns sprang up in Oklahoma, according to Kaye M. Teall's book *Black History in Oklahoma*. For decades, the rallying cry of westward-migrating blacks, most from the South, was that Oklahoma could become a state controlled by a voting black majority, a place where black rights and black dignity could be assured. Tens of thousands of blacks left the South for Oklahoma, and for twenty years Oklahoma existed in a state of racial siege, as blacks and whites battled for political control. The black towns of the era offered the reverse of white racism, with Boley and another black town, Wybark, reportedly posting signs outlawing whites on their streets after sundown.

As they did on the high plains of Nicodemus, blacks in Oklahoma were determined that they would never again play the compliant, shufflin' Negro. Boley town marshall John W. Owens armed his townsmen in anticipation of attack, and it was said that white lawmen were determined to kill Marshall Owens. Victory eventually went to white Oklahomans as laws were passed restricting black suffrage and segregating public schools and transportation. Oklahoma finally became a parody of the South, going so far as to require separate black and white phone booths. Oklahoma became one of the country's most violent segregation states, where politicians backed by the Ku Klux Klan often won handily. In the twenties, martial law was declared to stop thousands of reported floggings of blacks. In 1921, the Tulsa race riot—in which thousands of armed whites attacked Tulsa's black neighborhood, killing dozens of men, women, and children—became one of the saddest chapters in America's sad race history. But Tulsa's blacks hadn't played dead. They had fought back, killing many whites in return. This eye-for-an-eye justice is believed by some to have sharply diminished later attacks on blacks. Black Oklahomans never stopped battling in the courts or on the streets, and it was in Oklahoma City that some of the nation's earliest sit-ins against segregated stores and restaurants were launched in 1958.

But with each step toward racial equality, Boley stepped backward economically. What's left of the downtown is about the length of a football field. I park at the south end of Pecan Street, near the post office, and walk Pecan's length toward the north. Most of the buildings are brick and a single story high. For every one in use, two or three are shrouded in boards and abandoned. Mr. Truelove's

World's Best Hamburgers is boarded up. Squirrel & Janet's Place is burned up and hollow. The Progress Laundromat is in business, although nobody's inside. Out on the street, an old white Oldsmobile 88 has its doors open and rap music pounds out into an empty road, no listeners. At Sherman Street, sky-high to the right, rusted and retired, is Boley's original two-hundred-thousand-gallon water tank, which had gone up in 1911. It is supposed to be a monument but it looks more like a skeleton. The two-story Boley Hotel, which still says HOTEL in faded white letters across its red-brick front, stands alone, resembling the symmetrical head of some giant robot: its boarded-up front door and lower windows for a mouth and cheeks; two gaping glassless windows on the second floor for eyes; a slightly lower second-story window, closed with cinder blocks, centered neatly for a nose.

I must look for a long time before I find anyone in downtown Boley. Finally I come across William Brooks, owner of the Boley Liquor Store, which is in a building barely distinguishable from the abandoned buildings around it. Mr. Brooks is a seventy-one-year-old man with a stand of gray hair that starts high on his head. He's short and slight, his chest a little sunken, his face tired, his brow deeply furrowed. His liquor store is like none I've ever seen. The yellow plaster on the walls of the tiny room is cracked and peeling to reveal old turquoise walls beneath. There's a fan, but the room's air is hot and heavy, more so than outside in the midday sun. Four shelves run the length of two walls. Most are empty, except for a top shelf that sags under the weight of seventy-two bottles of Thunderbird wine. The other shelves hold a few scattered half-pints of whiskey, vodka, gin, brandy.

"So how has Boley changed?" I ask.

"Oh, man, it changed like night and day," Mr. Brooks says as I keep an eye on the wasp circling around my head. "When I left, there was almost five thousand people here. Didn't have an empty spot on either side a the street." William Brooks was born in Boley, where his father owned the liquor store before he did. But as a young man, Mr. Brooks left town for Detroit and good jobs in the car factories. To his amazement, he discovered that Detroit was even more racist than Oklahoma. He laughs darkly and says it had a street where blacks could walk on one side but were arrested if they walked on the other. He remembers whole restaurants that would clear out their customers and lock the doors rather than serve a black. Mississippi on Lake Erie.

"Man, that was the most segregated city in the world. That was true clean up into the fifties and sixties. It didn't change till the riots." Over the next fifty years, Mr. Brooks returned home only rarely, and so he saw his hometown's demise in a kind of time-lapse photography, watching it not dwindle away but disappear before his eyes in a few visits over the decades.

"Were you saddened?"

"Yeah, in a way, but you had to figure that this used to be cotton country and when cotton went people had to go somewhere to make a livin'."

Today Boley is kept alive by its 908 residents, a lot of whom are retired people and folks who commute to jobs in Oklahoma City and Tulsa, both about sixty miles away. As a bedroom community, the town is healthier than its main street looks, with fourteen churches, a community center, and a restaurant and gas station on the outskirts of town.

As a final question, I ask Mr. Brooks if growing up in Boley made a difference in his life. He thinks a moment and then says that when he got to Detroit he was surprised to learn that black people there didn't have the confidence he had. So many believed they couldn't amount to anything because white people would never let them.

"You didn't believe that?"

"No! I figured if I wanted ta move that building, I could move that building. I just had that kinda confidence."

A few doors away, I walk into Kees Department Store, which isn't a department store in the way of Montgomery Ward. It's one room, every inch of which seems to be piled with items a person could use—wigs, hats, sunglasses, watches, shirts, women's dresses, men's suits, bed sheets, underwear, reading glasses, socks, ties, shoes, stockings, cowboy boots, oil lanterns, Vaseline, Old Spice, flashlights, batteries, deodorant, watches, greeting cards. Under a glass counter is a laminated front page of Oklahoma's *Okemah Daily Leader* from November 23, 1932, the day after Boley's bank president was killed in a sensational daylight bank heist by members of the Pretty Boy Floyd outlaw gang. Boley's famed Marshall Owens, sixty-four years old then, arrived on the scene too late to save the president, but as a dead-eye marksmen he knelt in the street and shot one of Pretty Boy's men dead.

I'm beginning to wonder if anyone is in Kees Department Store this afternoon when an old man who turns out to be Bienville Kees, age seventy-six, walks through a door at the back of the store, where he lives. Mr. Kees talks slowly and his face seems locked in a sad expression, or maybe he's just not prone to chatting with strangers. He sees me looking at the report of the Pretty Boy Floyd gang's robbery and he nods out the window to where the bank used to be. "He was killed right there," he says, pointing.

Mr. Kees was among those who fled the South for freedom in Boley. He arrived in 1945 from Jena, Louisiana, a burg located about fifty miles west of Natchez, Mississippi—hard racist country then, Richard Wright's boyhood crucible, the place where Denise Ford's daddy was blown to bits after applying for a supervisor's job at the Armstrong Rubber plant. In 1946, Mr. Kees opened his store, which is, he's proud to say, the oldest remaining business in town. "You just never was a man," Mr. Kees says of living in Jena. "You never grew up to be grown, because you were treated as a child. It was so much better here. You was just as big as anybody else." Back in Jena, a black man always had to be on guard, looking to avoid certain white people who were trouble, looking to protect his fragile dignity. In Jena, he says, a black man had to call fifteen-year-old white boys "Mister."

During World War II, Mr. Kees served overseas and discovered that life everywhere wasn't like life in Jena, and he wanted out of that evil place. He'd only heard of Boley, but he packed up and moved. "It was a matter of freedom," he says. Sure, he found plenty of racism in Oklahoma. But it was a different kind of racism, one a man could face and fight, a straight-out battle for power, not an insidious racism that permeated a black man's every psychological fiber, even his dreams. Black children raised in Boley, he says, just grew up free. A smile finally creases Mr. Kees's face: "It wasn't like Louisiana." If you didn't want to call a white man "Mister," Mr. Kees says, still smiling, you didn't.

Ronald Shelton was a black child who grew up free a few miles outside Boley. Today I find him and his wife at the R & F Hardware and Supplies store across the street from the post office. R & F Hardware is the closest thing Boley has to a social gathering place, and the store is the town's most modern. The Sheltons remodeled the building when they bought it in 1984, and today R & F looks like any hardware store in suburbia—a concrete floor painted grass-green, a drop ceiling, fluorescent lights, new white shelves, a Coke machine. People pick up their mail across the street and drop in at R & F for a soda, or to pay their rural water bill, or to pick up brake fluid, Ajax, septic root destroyer, or a BEWARE OF DOG sign. And they drop in to gossip.

Ronald and his wife, Francis are Boley's new generation. He's forty-six and she's forty-four. They both grew up here in the forties and fifties, and Ronald's father, a farmer, got around in a horse-drawn buggy. But they aren't country people today. They're urban people, relaxed and casual, quick with a cynical joke, quick to laugh. They too live behind their store, but the old storage rooms they've turned into their home resemble a Soho loft, with fifteen-foot ceilings and exposed pipes, with modern furniture all around. After high school graduation in 1963, Ronald moved to Oklahoma City and got a job as a shipping clerk, while Francis went on to finish college. They married and raised two kids. Then, when the company where Ronald worked for twenty-two years went belly-up, they decided they'd return to Boley. Francis has kept her job as a lab technician in Oklahoma City and for five years now all their income from the hardware store has gone toward buying supplies and paying off the seven-year, $500-a-month mortgage on the store. Once that's retired, they'll make a profit.

"When I left in '63, everything was still in operation," Ronald says of Boley. There were grocery, clothing, and shoe stores, gas stations, restaurants, Saturday night entertainment. "From one end of the street to the other," Ronald says, "it was full." As a kid, he had no idea Boley was in any way special, even though the bathrooms in the stores in nearby Paden were segregated, and in Okemah blacks still had to take restaurant food by the back door. But Ronald says that living in Boley—where he saw black people rich and poor, successful and struggling—he never took the outside insults to heart. Just as a white man's self-esteem isn't shattered because he might not be welcome in, say, a tavern in a black neighborhood, Ronald's self-esteem wasn't damaged by his occasional exclusion. He never took it personally. After he moved to Oklahoma City, he learned "there's a whole lotta hate" in the world. But he figures that's a lesson better learned as an adult than as a child.

Ronald tells this story: In 1980, he and several family members arrived in Pine Bluff, Arkansas, for a family reunion. They stopped to eat a picnic lunch in a public park. Soon after they'd taken a table, a white family nearby got up and left, and a black man walked over and told them they were sitting in the white part of the park. "You walked right up like you owned the place," the black man said. "Y'all are goin' home," he added anxiously, "but I gotta live here." Then he hustled himself and his child out of the park. What a lesson for that child to learn. "See, I didn't know I wasn't free," Ronald says of growing up in Boley. "I thought I *was* free." And that feeling has always stayed with him, even through some rough times.

Then it hits me. Confidence. Of course. Confidence, I finally see, is what Boley gave William Brooks, Bienville Kees, and Ronald Shelton—at a time when the rest of America was determined to rip it away from them like flesh off their bodies. Black people weren't hiding out in towns like Boley. They were seeking what was a natural right to white Americans, the chance to be proud and dignified and accomplished, the chance to feel good about themselves.

I was wrong. I'm not the time traveler moving backward to visit Boley, and this town's life hasn't been sucked out of it. Instead, the town has been consumed in the breath and existence of those who lived here at a time when options were few. The spirit of the town has traveled with them and has been breathed into their lives and, inevitably, into the lives of their spouses and friends, children and grandchildren. That is time travel. And that, not a rusted old water tower, is Boley's monument.

3

SLAVES, INDIANS, AND AN IRISHMAN

FORT TOWSON, OKLAHOMA

Fort Towson, in Oklahoma's Choctaw County just above the Texas border, is a couple of hours out of my way to Houston, but I detour onto the Indian Nation Turnpike, get off at Hugo, cross the Kiamichi River, and enter tiny Fort Towson, which is only about an hour west of Little River County, Arkansas. Buried in a cemetery here are Uncle Wallace and Aunt Minerva, an old black slave couple who composed the legendary spiritual "Swing Low, Sweet Chariot." Somewhere I've been told that they were owned by a Choctaw princess, which would be no surprise. After reading Kaye Teall's black history of Oklahoma, I realize that Native Americans often owned a lot of slaves, and the destinies of blacks and Native Americans were constantly intertwined, not only in Oklahoma but everywhere the two peoples met.

From the beginning of slavery in America, blacks had escaped into the wilds and ended up living among Native Americans. The Seminole and Creek people had little racial prejudice and often treated runaway slaves as equals. The Chickasaws, Choctaws, and Cherokees, on the other hand, were often as bigoted as whites. But escaped slaves also fought beside Native Americans against U.S. soldiers in many battles before Native Americans were driven from the southeastern United States. The Seminole War of 1817 included as many as six hundred black warriors fighting in Florida, and Andrew Jackson even called the Seminole War "this savage and negro war."

Native Americans owned slaves, but their slavery was often quite different from Southern slavery, with intermarriage between slaves and Native Americans. In the Creek Nation, blacks eventually became so numerous that a black man became one of its chiefs. In the 1830s, when Native Americans began to travel the Trail of Tears into the new Indian Territory that included Oklahoma, thousands of slaves went with them. After the Civil War, the defeated Native American nations, which had fought with the South, were forced to give to blacks living among them full rights as citizens. The Creek and Seminole nations did this, but other nations, particularly the Chickasaw, discriminated against black "freedmen" and denied them the right to vote and their children the right to attend Chickasaw schools. How crazy is our racial history: red men discriminating against black men in white America.

I've come to Fort Towson on a whim and have no idea where Uncle Wallace and Aunt Minerva are buried. Fort Towson is a wide spot in the road, and I stop at the Corner Store, a cinder-block place, to ask advice. I figure everybody knows everything in a town of 568 people, or they know somebody who does. True to theory, a young white woman buying a tin of snuff hasn't heard of Uncle Wallace or

Aunt Minerva, but she gives me the name of a woman to call. That woman gives me the name of a man to call, and that man, Chester Merritt, knows all about Uncle Wallace and Aunt Minerva. He gives me directions to the graveyard, where he'll meet me.

From the Corner Store, I follow what the locals call the Red Road (so named because of the red clay in which it was dug) and come to the Fort Towson Cemetery, which is surrounded by a fine, three-foot-high stone fence. It's a huge cemetery and the grass has just been cut. In the cooling heat of the late afternoon, the bleeding blades give off the strongest scent, which mingles with the citrus smell of the plentiful bois d'arc fruit. At an old stone chapel with a white cross on its front, I find a marker so old its inscription is nearly worn away:

> Tryphena Wall Stewart was a remarkable,
> well-educated, and beautiful Choctaw girl,
> was called a missionary to her own people
> and became a legend in her own time.
> She died at the age of twenty-five in 1849.

Wandering among the gravestones, I find a tall, flat, dirty marker that says simply, "Tryphena's Grave"—an enigmatic epitaph confirming her local fame.

Chester Merritt arrives. He's a short, stocky, sixty-seven-year-old white man wearing work boots, blue pants, a blue flannel shirt, yellow-tinted shades, and a red fishing cap that reads "crappie fisherman." He has an interesting hybrid accent—slightly southern and slightly western. Strictly Oklahoman. Mr. Merritt is a member of the community association that runs the cemetery, which dates back to the 1840s, and he has mapped all its graves, named and unnamed. Wherever I heard that Princess Tryphena owned Uncle Wallace and Aunt Minerva, he says, the information's wrong. The slaves were owned by Britt Willis.

Mr. Merritt then refers me to the story credited to a Mrs. Jimmi Kirby in Frances Imon's local history book, *Smoke Signals from Indian Territory*, which he has brought along. Jimmi Kirby was the granddaughter of Britt Willis, who is also buried in the Fort Towson Cemetery. He owned not only Uncle Wallace and Aunt Minerva but about three hundred other slaves. Willis was an extravagantly rich Irishman from Hickory Flat, Mississippi, who had married a Native American woman. When the Native Americans made their journey on the Trail of Tears, Britt Willis, his wife, and their three hundred slaves went too, settling on a plantation south of Fort Towson.

"Mama said it was a hot August day in 1840," Mrs. Kirby told Frances Imon. "They were hoeing the long rows of Grandpa's cotton. As Uncle Wallace rested a moment on his hoe he could only see endless rows of cotton. . . . No doubt he was very tired. . . . South of the field he could see Red River shimmering in the sun." Mrs. Kirby's mother told her that at that instant Uncle Wallace simply sang out:

> *Swing low, sweet chariot,*
> *Comin' fo' to carry me home!*

Aunt Minerva chimed in with:

> *I look over Jordan an' what do I see*
> *Comin' fo' to carry me home. . .*

And then together, in a cotton field south of Fort Towson on hot August day in 1840, the old husband and wife composed and sang their now world famous spiritual.

The story sounds, well, a touch poetic, but I won't quarrel with poetry. Later the superintendent of a nearby school for Native American children was supposedly in New York on a business trip and introduced the Choctaw County spiritual to the Fisk University Jubilee Singers, who later sang "Swing Low, Sweet Chariot" before Queen Victoria. That's the story.

"So where are they buried?" I ask.

"We wish we knew," says Mr. Merritt.

We know where Britt Willis is buried. We know where the Choctaw princess Tryphena is buried. But the old man and old woman who left the world one of its most enduring spirituals are buried in markerless graves. And not here with Willis and Tryphena, but over there, in the slave section of the cemetery, which is still separated by a wire fence that's overgrown with possum grapes.

As we walk in the shadow of the cedar trees on the slave side of the cemetery—which includes forty-three known graves, only fifteen of which are marked—Mr. Merritt says he figures most of the ground beneath us contains the graves of nameless slaves who died without markers. He wants to be sure I understand that the fence separating black from white and Native American dates back to the days of segregation. A couple of years ago, a black high school student began a petition calling for it to be removed, which the cemetery association was willing to do. But when local blacks (the U.S. Census reports that only eleven blacks live in Fort Towson) were asked their opinion, Mr. Merritt says, they wanted the fence left there.

"There's a couple spots down here," he says. "If I was guessin', this is where I'd guess they put 'em." He stops at two graves, side by side, that are outlined as one by rectangular stones. "I'd say that's special."

By the standards of antebellum Oklahoma, I suppose this was a glorious send-off for slaves. The graves are even located inches from the possum-grape fence, so close to the white and Native American side that maybe an old black man and woman were supposed to feel honored. But a century and a half later, I stand in the shade of the cedars and marvel at the irony: the wealthy Irishman Britt Willis and the beautiful Choctaw princess Tryphena, so honored in their lifetimes, are forgotten, while two old slaves buried in markerless graves are immortal. I recall a line from Thomas Gray's "Elegy Written in a Country Churchyard": "Some mute inglorious Milton here may rest."

Or perhaps two. Two that we know of anyway.

4

WHAT THE DOCTOR HAS LEARNED

HOUSTON, TEXAS

On the road to Houston. . . .
After visiting Nicodemus, Boley, and Fort Towson, I keep thinking of a painting my father did after he visited drought-choked Kansas in the summer of 1936. It hangs in my living room—a picture of an abandoned farm house and barn at dusk, the grounds and buildings dark and cold and without detail, beneath a flaming sunset of reds and yellows that rises and roils violently and then disappears

into a high, black sky. "Faded Dreams," my father called it, in memory of the human wreckage behind the spoils of the Dust Bowl, which spurred the exodus of the poor white dirt farmers John Steinbeck immortalized as the Joads in *The Grapes of Wrath*.

I keep thinking about that painting and that book and how they fit the places in Kansas and Oklahoma where I've just been, places where people were exploited, harassed, and despised; assaulted by the choices of Wall Street bankers and railroad magnates; then buried without markers. And I think of these metaphoric lines in Steinbeck's book: "And over the grass at the roadside a land turtle crawled. . . . Pushing hind legs strained and slipped, boosting the shell along. . . . But higher and higher the hind legs boosted it, until at last the center of balance was reached, the front tipped down, the front legs scratched at the pavement, and it was up."

How close Steinbeck's sentiment is to that of a poem by the revered black author Langston Hughes entitled "Mother to Son":

> *I'se been a-climbin' on,*
> *And reachin' landin's,*
> *And turnin' corners,*
> *And sometimes goin' in the dark*
> *Where there ain't been no light.*
> *So boy, don't you turn back.*
> *Don't you set down on the step*
> *'Cause you finds it's kinder hard.*
> *Don't you fall now—*
> *For I'se still goin', honey,*
> *I'se still climbin'.*

Faded dreams are faded dreams—for dirt farmers and poor mothers, black or white. They are kin. But so is the spirit behind the dream, the ambition. And that's at the heart of what America honors most: resilience. Fall down, get up. Never say die. Claw with those hind legs. A black friend once told me, "Black people are the most American Americans we've got." I didn't understand what he meant then, but I do now, after more than fifteen thousand miles. It's not amazing that so many African Americans are poor. What's amazing is that so many aren't. It's not remarkable that so many African Americans feel hopeless. What's remarkable is that so many have hope at all. It's not shocking that so many African Americans have given up on America. What's shocking is that so many haven't, that so many still believe they can have their turn and are willing to prove they deserve it. I wonder how many whites would have been so strong for so long in the face of so many faded dreams?

But enough, *enough!* I've got to shake this gloom that has settled on me since Nicodemus. I fear that I'm feeling the sentiment that has always kept right-minded white people from really understanding African Americans. Oh, these poor people, we like to think as we wallow in our guilt and easy sympathy. The black people I've met aren't gloomy. They don't pity themselves. They've been mostly enjoyable, spirited, optimistic men and women, clear-eyed and realistic about the world around them, turning injustice into darkly comic lessons for life.

Here is one dark joke I've heard: A black man is standing on the top of a tall building watching a white dude jump off and then rise up to stand on the roof again. The white convinces the black to try it—and he falls a hundred stories to his death. The moral: even Superman don't like niggers. Among themselves, black people will laugh at that joke until they cry, because they carry sadness along with a life-affirming vibrancy, the spirit of the blues. The black people I've met spout few of the white liberalisms about how society is to blame for black poverty and despair. They believe it and reject it at once, because it's no use telling a boy he's a victim of his environment. He's gotta get up and do it, carry the extra weight, or sink. Compare him with young people who coast through excellent schools and by osmosis learn enough to get into college, who call Daddy's friends for jobs. Who most deserves our respect? Who is more American? Face it, blacks are the most American Americans. They're more like us than we are.

The Davill Armstrong I remember from college was a smart and angry young man. I respected him. But he also had an arrogant, dismissive laugh that galled me. I thought the guy was a know-it-all. I think most white kids and many black kids on campus agreed with me. But black rage was in the air in 1968, and Davill was really my only window to that emotion. From a distance, I thought I shared and understood his anger. But I was in the era's hands-around-the-world-in-love-and-peace mold, and my opinions were well felt but not very well thought out. Davill, as the reigning campus black radical who lived in the dorm room next to me my freshman year, played the brick to my glass house. So it is a genuine letdown when he tells me he doesn't remember me.

"I lived next door to you in Graham Hall," I say, trying to hide my disappointment. "We used to argue. You wouldn't play on the same basketball team with me, said I was a racist."

He shrugs sympathetically. "I'm sorry."

I laugh to myself, thinking that maybe it's better Davill doesn't remember me, that he probably wouldn't talk to me if he did. Davill's wife is out of town picking up their twelve-year-old daughter from a summer camp in the Catskills. His eight-year-old son is visiting the grandparents. So Davill is less pressed for time than usual. We sit at the dining room table in his modern Victorian-style home—a big but not showy house in a mostly white suburban neighborhood of such homes—and share a glass of jug wine. Davill Armstrong, M.D., age forty-two, wears an old T-shirt, black sweat pants, and black sneakers, no socks. The man is well preserved: trim and fit, with all his hair, a short black beard, a tad of gray at his chin.

"I think it was just a different time," Davill says of our college years. "Race was more polarized, because everything was so segregated. Looking back, I think a lot of my time was taken away from studies I should have been doing." But then he laughs fondly: "We were always into something, some kinda controversy." Davill remembers when he and Jim Green, whom I visited in Columbia, South Carolina, vandalized the science experiment of a professor they believed was racist, and the time they broke windows in the home of a college dean. He tells me about heated negotiations with the college administration over creating a black gathering room. After winning the room, Davill then got the administration to repaint it—solid black! He laughs at the memory. "Hey, man, that was the mau-mau days!"

But Davill also organized a black culture week and served soul food in the dining hall, where I tasted bitter collard greens for the first time. He donated black history books to the library and showed black films. I remember the award-winning David Loeb Weiss anti-war documentary *No Vietnamese Ever Called Me Nigger*. Davill doesn't recall, but I bet it was at one of these events where I first heard the black poet and novelist Ishmael Reed, whose work I've continued to follow for twenty years and whom I plan to visit in California.

"It was a good college experience," Davill says, adding wryly, "I had no illusions about white people after Blackburn." But living among whites at Blackburn and later at Rutgers University medical school, Davill also learned that all white people weren't bad, at least not as many as he had once believed. "There's a lot of white folks who will step out," he says, who will judge people without regard to race. "You gotta take people as people, because sometimes people will pop up and be nice from the strangest places." Davill's father, who attended law school but worked as a railroad laborer, had communist affiliations during the McCarthy-era witch hunts. He introduced Davill to radicalism early, and Davill came to believe that a handful of rich people, almost all white, ran America for the benefit of themselves and their social class. But when it came time to enter medical school, Davill saw that system work in his favor. Davill's father knew a New Jersey state senator who helped Davill get into Rutgers. Through the Urban League, Davill also met then-New Jersey senator Harrison Williams, Jr., who helped him get financial aid. "I was a token at Rutgers and I knew it," he says, "but they needed blacks. Hell, ain't nobody smarter than anybody else. It's politics, or at least enough of it is."

Politics or not, Davill grabbed the brass ring. Out of five blacks in his class, only two graduated. It was rough. Most of his classmates hadn't gone to backwater colleges like Blackburn, but to schools like Harvard and Princeton. These people weren't just coasting on family privilege. They were well trained, hardworking, and smart. But they knew something else too. "Those white boys knew the system," Davill says, with respect. "We blacks didn't know nothin'. They got old tests to study. I studied my notes."

After medical school, residencies, and a couple of years in a poor neighborhood clinic, Davill launched his own practice in the Acres Homes section of northwestern Houston, a neighborhood of poor and working-class blacks. Today Davill's practice is thriving and he's a rich man. But he isn't at all flamboyant, still wearing old slacks and sneakers and open-collared shirts to the office and hospital. He believes whites resent blacks who flaunt their wealth or success. Rich or not, he still votes Democratic. "Basically, I benefited a lot from Reagan," he says. "But we don't even need all that we have." Davill agonizes over the disparity, gives a bundle to charity. And, he says, "I'm a doctor in a poor community," where even most black professionals won't work. It's not glamorous. He sees a lot of poor people's diseases—syphilis, obesity, diabetes, hypertension, arthritis. When he was taking Medicaid patients, people would clog up the drains and steal the toilet paper. Somebody used a sledge hammer to break through the clinic's brick wall to get to the pharmacy. He had to install plastic windows. He understands why black professionals flee to the white suburbs.

When Davill set up his clinic, he was determined to hire only black contractors, lawyers, and accountants. "But it didn't work out," he says. In the middle of construction, his black contractor requested more money. Davill refused and found another black contractor, but that contractor hired whites. Of his black accountants Davill says, "After you start making a lot of money, they couldn't really help you," because they were used to handling "mom and pop" clients. It hurt, but Davill found new accountants, and they were white. Ditto for his black lawyers. "The bottom line," he says, "is we got better service from the white guys than we did from the black guys."

It isn't that Davill thinks less about race these days, because it's always there. "But if we want to go to Sydney, Australia, we got the money to do it," he says. "We stay in the best hotels. Life is more important than having money, but that lets you know that you can do certain things. I can go to Australia, France, send the wife to China, send her to India. Yeah, I can do it. That's what everybody wants to do, bottom line, right? It comes down to an individual thing. It's like at the hospital, the whites control it, but they let me in because I could do it. I've got patients. I go over and do my work and everything is up to snuff. Individual initiative, individual determination, individual achievement. That's what life is about. I think there's no excuse why you can't try to do something.

"Now there are people who come from a background where there's been so much negativism, it's hard to get over that. We see that every day in our practice. We have a wasteland of human beings out there, man! On every corner in Acres Homes there are groups of young black men doing nothing. I see a lot of their children, and now their children are beginning to act like them. You see the lack of self-control, the lack of any ethical boundaries. And the loitering, the giving up, no hope. You talk about people on Medicaid. They think society owes them something. Yeah! They demand more than the person who's paying. And I'm not the only one who will tell you that, everybody will. But the society created that. We're not stupid. People in the black community see welfare as a bad thing. We see it as a way to control people."

Davill is pessimistic about the future. He says America will find a way to cut young blacks and Hispanics into the system, or there will be violence in the streets, as there was in the sixties. But this time, Davill says, the new generation of well-to-do blacks will probably side with white America. "I think what it's coming down to is class," he says. "People vote for their own self-interest. If you're doing well, you wanta stay well."

I'm beginning to think that the anger I saw in Davill as a youth has dissipated in his middle age, but then I ask him what he thinks about the troubles of former Washington, D.C., mayor Marion Barry, who was convicted of cocaine possession in what became a sensational circus trial. Immediately, the old Davill flashes, waving his arms and raising his voice in anger: "Even the most rich black man knows he is vulnerable in this society!"

I push the issue: "If black people want to hold power, don't they have to take responsibility for it, too?"

"We just want a fair, equitable, equal system! That's what we want! The black man doesn't want any more than the white man. We want to be treated fairly. We know a lotta white politicians stuff their pockets. This is a serious system in America. *They* don't want anybody to challenge this thing."

"Who is 'they'?"

"What the fuck you mean, who is 'they'?" Davill asks scornfully, dismissively. "The same people who killed Kennedy. The same people who killed Malcolm and Martin. There is a group of people who control this society, and if you get out of line, whether you're Kennedy with money and the presidency, they will *kill* your ass. They know if you give everybody an opportunity, there's a lotta whites who won't have much. White folks always think you're kinda crazy if you think that. But black people all believe it at some level."

I think, Now that's the old Davill.

Truth is, I share a lot of Davill's biases. You don't grow up the son of a milkman without getting lessons in the Philosophy of Life Looking from the Bottom Up. I know something of what Davill felt when he arrived at Rutgers, at least I think I do. When I was a young reporter at the *Washington Post,* it didn't take a wizard to see that the place was wired with Ivy League graduates. My wife joked that I should be considered an affirmative action hire because I hadn't gone to private prep school. And while blacks and women at the paper were always complaining that the place discriminated against blacks and women, it seemed it was really kids of the working class who were slighted. Even many of the blacks and women hailed from solidly middle- to upper-middle-class families.

"Where I part company is when you say 'they'," I tell Davill. "I don't think it's a conspiracy." Black people have expressed Davill's view to me again and again, and I know the outlook runs deep and is sincerely held. But I've heard it one time too many, and I give a little speech about how those who spend their time worrying about people conspiring against them don't understand that powerful people are always fighting among themselves and that there are many sources of power in society and organizations. Merit may not be the only thing but it does matter. And the number of years a person stays in school is still the best indicator of the kind of job he will hold. Not only is this view of the world more accurate, I proclaim, but it also readies a person to grab opportunities as they arise.

End of dramatic speech.

Davill eyes me for a long moment. Then, with perfectly deadpan humor, he says, "Yeah, that's what a white person can do."

And we both crack up.

At 5:30 the next morning, I meet Davill for his early hospital rounds. He likes to visit his patients before the hospital has begun to bustle, while the nurses have time to talk about each patient, before the TVs are glaring and folks are eating. This morning is typical. He has a woman with a tumor in her uterus that will need surgery, a boy with pneumonia whose grandmother is sleeping in the hospital bed with him, a woman with a breast cyst that has turned out to be benign, a woman with an infection in her leg that won't heal, and an old man who came to Davill through the emergency room after a bad fall. Only the old man is white. In the silent hospital, Davill pads from room to room, dressed in old slacks and tennis shoes, and he flicks on the lights and gently awakens each patient. It's a pleasure to watch him with these people, and I know they appreciate the genuine respect he shows them. He is gentle and warm, downright kind.

The old white man is already propped up in bed, smoking a cigarette, when Davill walks in. He's seventy-five years old, very thin, bald, and with a huge, bulbous nose and a sunken mouth and lips that disappear with each puff of the cigarette. Rough-looking dude. Davill gently takes the cigarette and puts it out. In a voice that manages to be assertive and friendly but not condescending, he asks the old man if he remembers what day he came to the hospital. He does, which is a good sign that his mind is clear.

"Do you have relations in Houston?" Davill asks, after he glances at the chart, replaces it, and looks back at the man he has never met before yesterday.

"No, I don't have a goddamned one."

"You hurt anywhere?"

"Hell, no, I'm not hurtin'. The way they juggle me around in here, I oughta be hurtin' ever'where."

"How's your appetite?"

"I eat three meals a day, small ones, and a snack or two."

"You cook for yourself?"

"What little I do, with my left hand."

"What about your right hand?"

"It ain't worth a crap. Use it a little for smokin'."

"OK," Davill says cheerfully, "see you later."

In the hallway, Davill explains that his questions were meant to discover, before the old man leaves the hospital and disappears, if he's able to take care of himself, if he needs other medical care. With a shrug and a gesture toward the hallways, Davill says, "These are the people I see." I'm surprised at how relieved I am to know this, to learn that Davill didn't grow up to be, oh, I don't know, a plastic surgeon or a diet doctor. I didn't like Davill or understand him as an angry young man, but I always respected him. I'm glad to know I respect him still.

"By the way, Jim Green told me to tell you you're still ugly."

Davill laughs. "Man, that was a long time ago."

5

WHEN COWBOYS RODE THE RANGE

HOUSTON, TEXAS

Michael Solomon wears one glove, on his left hand, but he doesn't resemble Michael Jackson in the least. No, he looks like a cowboy, and in some ways he is. Out in the horse stalls of the Taylor-Stevenson Ranch on the outskirts of Houston, a ranch that has been owned by a single black family for 125 years, Michael digs into the front right pocket of his jeans, already dirty just a few hours after dawn. He pulls out his pocket knife, and in two quick motions cuts the hairy twine that crisscrosses a bale of sweet-smelling hay. He stuffs a few fistfuls of hay into a red nylon-rope feeding sack that he then hangs over the horizontal slats of the stall's cedar fence. Michael, thirty-nine years old with the taut, wiry body of a jockey and a slight limp (a horse he was once training broke his left ankle), spits up particles of hay and dust that float thick in the atmosphere of the small, sunlit cubicles. He wears tan cowboy boots into which the tight legs of his jeans disappear, a tan-and-white western shirt with plastic black-pearl snaps, and a green ball cap that reads "Newport Alive with Pleasure," his only nod to modernity. When he leans over to dig a coffee tin of sorghum and rolled oats out for feeding, his shirt pulls damp across his back, and even amid the competing scents of hay, feed, horses, sheep, ducks, chickens, turkeys, peacocks, and a long-horned baby bull, Michael emits the proud, distinct scent of hard work.

"A man that works is the backbone of the country, no matter what color," he says without interrupting his chores. "We been joinin' together to keep the country up."

"We haven't been joinin' together enough," I say, smiling.

For the first time, Michael shows some expression. He chuckles. "Not enough, no. That's the truth."

"What's different about working for a black rancher?"

"Whites tend ta pay more."

"So it's better to work for whites?"

Michael nods. "It's better," he says, because white ranches are bigger and make more money. For a half-day's work here, Michael earns about $25. Working at a more prosperous white-owned ranch, he figures, he'd earn half again as much. "I feel like I have ta make a little more money," he says. "I hate to leave her, though."

The woman Michael hates to leave is Mollie Stevenson. She's forty-four years old and one of the keepers of the Taylor-Stevenson Ranch, which is no longer the working cattle ranch it was a hundred years ago. The family leases out some of its several hundred acres these days, and Mollie, who returned to the ranch after years working as a model and a secretary in New York, Kansas City, and Houston, runs a fledgling "western entertainment" operation. She boards horses, gives hay and horseback rides, and operates a little museum that honors the tradition of America's cowboys, including the blacks, women, Native Americans, and Hispanics who were written out of history. When she returned nine years ago, the place was a mess, a sad cry from the old Taylor-Stevenson Ranch.

The ranch dates back to before the Civil War when a white rancher named E. W. Taylor paid $1,500 for a young slave woman whose job it was to nurse his son back from tuberculosis. Patient and nurse fell in love. Marriage between blacks and whites was illegal in Texas then, as it still was in sixteen states when the U.S. Supreme Court finally struck down the laws in 1967. But young E. R. Taylor moved onto land deep on the family spread and with Ann, his common-law wife, raised six children. Mollie is a descendant. All of Ann and E. R.'s children married blacks, and the Taylor-Stevenson dynasty was born. Mollie's seventy-eight-year-old mother was the glue and grit that held the ranch together in her generation, and it was her inspiration that kept five of her six children on the ranch while so many others of their generation left the land behind.

"Blacks are always amazed when they find out how many black cowboys there were," says Mollie Stevenson, who has joined Michael and me in the dusty corral. She's a tall, thin woman wearing a red bandanna around her neck, cowboy boots, a blue-jean skirt, a T-shirt, and a straw cowboy hat. "We didn't write the books. We didn't produce the movies. So we were politely deleted." Mollie recently entertained a group of black dentists who had traveled all over the world. "But they didn't know nothin' about black cowboys," Mollie says, adding that the very name "cowboy" comes from the low status of the blacks, Mexicans, and poor whites who worked the western ranges and the great nineteenth-century cattle drives. "They were 'the *boys* who worked the cows,'" Mollie says. "In the movies, they became Roy Rogers and Clint Eastwood."

They say it is the victors who write the history books. Delving into the history of black cowboys—like the repressed black history of Colonial Williamsburg and the ignored black history of the West's settlement—is more frightening evidence of that truth. As I was reading *The Negro Cowboys,* by Philip Durham and Everett L. Jones, and *The Black West,* by William Loren Katz, I imagined that I was feeling something of what a person feels when he discovers he was actually adopted. How can this be? How could this have been kept from me so long? No wonder Davill Armstrong can be so cynical and conspiratorial in his view of white America.

William Loren Katz writes that when white historian Ray Allen Billington published his definitive 933-page book *Westward Expansion* in 1967, it included not one reference to a black who helped conquer the West. Yet an estimated five thousand black cowboys worked the western ranges—as many as a third of all working cowboys—and many were among the most respected and famous of their rugged lot. Britton Johnson was said to be the best shot in Texas. Bill Pickett created the rodeo event of bulldogging and boasted Tom Mix and Will Rogers among his assistants. (Later, Rogers would use the word "nigger" on his radio show, and Tom Mix would defend lynching.) Nat Love became the self-created prototype of the dime-fiction character Deadwood Dick, after he won several events in the Deadwood City rodeo of 1876. As late as 1913, "Peerless" Jessie Stahl was ranked as the best wild-horse rider in all the West. And these are only the black cowboys who became celebrities. Any ranch in the West, write Durham and Jones, welcomed good black ranch hands, and they were everywhere: Jim Perry, who was renowned as a rider, roper, and cook; a cowboy named only "Frank," who was so skilled a roper he wasn't required to work night-herd duty; and Bose Ikard, who became the close friend of legendary Texas cattleman Charles Goodnight, who said of Ikard, "I have trusted him farther than any living man." Black cowboys even ranked among the West's most notorious outlaws: Cherokee Bill was certainly as ruthless as Billy the Kid.

"I always knew about black cowboys," Mollie says, "because black cowboys used to work all over our ranch." And even today, she says, not a weekend goes by in the summer when some little Texas town isn't hosting a black rodeo. Mollie's own twenty-six-year-old nephew, Ben "Legs" Stevenson III, is today ranked among the top ten professional rodeo bull riders in the country, black or white. Says Mollie proudly, "He learned to ride right here."

Michael Solomon and I are leaving the ranch about the same time, and so I offer him a ride to his home in Houston's poor black neighborhood of Sunnyside. Michael is a cowboy who doesn't own a horse, doesn't own a car and lives with his mother. I offer to spring for lunch, and we stop at McDonald's, where over hamburgers Michael talks about his life.

One of seven children born to a mother on welfare, Michael grew up without his father. He dropped out of school in ninth grade and has worked a series of decent warehouse jobs off and on over the years. He was heavy into drugs until about five years ago when he kicked the stuff. He has a daughter and two sons who are grown, pretty much without his help. One of the most painful moments of Michael's life was when he learned that one of his sons had denied to his friends that Michael was his father. He's been training horses since he was a teenager, just something he picked up, along with the belief that whites are superior to blacks.

"Mentally, IQ level," Michael says, "because I know for a fact by the history books that blacks did not create all the modern things, the conveniences, like cars, airplanes, boats that traveled the water. Whites were adventurers. They were conquerors. I always thought of them as good. They were always Mr. This and Mr. That. I respected that they were strong. When I would have to go in through the back door, I knew there was a reason for this and this was to gain control over a nation. The black man was as an animal in Africa, ya know what I mean? I felt gratitude that they wasn't just takin' their guns and shootin' all the black men down."

"I know for a fact by the history books. . . " That's what Michael said. He didn't learn in school that blacks helped settle the West, that they battled with fist, rifle, and law books in an effort to control the entire state of Oklahoma, that they struck out impoverished by the tens of thousands to homestead the desolate desert, that they escaped their slave masters and entered the Florida swamps where they became guerrilla fighters, that black explorer Estevanico's travels through the southwest led to the Coronado expedition. And that's just the tip of

what he—we—didn't learn. We didn't learn that the Egyptians were black, that Ptolemy studied geometry in Timbuctu, that Africans sailed with Columbus on both his voyages to the New World.

Michael was always behind in school. "I didn't have that hands-on learning at home and this is what's needed," he says. "Education is something that is inherited, ya know what I mean? My sons are intelligent, but educated, no, because I didn't sit down and help them with their homework—two plus two plus two. I feel cheated. I feel cheated to the point of not bein' able to teach my children the right way to go. But my father was cheated too. Society might look at me and say, 'Oh, that's his fault.' But it's not my fault. I was a little child. I coulda made it if my dad had been concerned that he had a son. I don't even know if he's still alive. I hated that I didn't have the things the other guys my age had—a father, a home. I feel like I was self-taught. I explain it as not *my* fault. This is not a cop-out. This is the truth.

"I've been down and I'm just now startin' ta get a spiritual lift from a young lady. With me workin' and having enough gumption to go out there and do what I can, clean up this stall or that stall, try to make a dollar, it's got where I can find me somebody that likes me for me. Without money you can't get a girlfriend." A woman wants at least $50 a week from her man, he says. She's looking for a guy with a job and a car and maybe even marriage. "I want marriage," Michael says. "Come home and dump my paycheck. Or go to the bank and deposit my whole paycheck."

"Have you ever had a checking account?"

"Never! Never in my life!" Michael would like to earn $4.50, maybe $4.75 an hour. "I could live comfortable," he says. "I could own that car I never owned, sleep in that bed that never belonged to me. These are the things I owe myself as a human being. The world don't owe me nothin'. I owe me somethin'."

Back in the car, Michael directs me to his house through another of what I've come to see as America's classically poor neighborhoods—about two out of three houses are dilapidated, but about every third one is in nice, tidy shape, the grass cut and the siding painted. But Sunnyside, like Davill's Acres Homes, is a hard place, where ten, fifteen, twenty young black guys with no shirts are milling on strategic corners, sitting on car hoods, leaning against fences. And after about a dozen lefts and rights on Sunnyside's narrow streets, I

realize I've got no idea where I am. Just then, it strikes me that I don't
know this guy Michael Solomon from Adam. I'm relieved when we
get to his mother's house, a nice little green home with clean white
shutters and clean clothes drying on the line.

"Thanks for the lift," Michael says, as he heads for the house.
Once again my fears are unfounded.

6

THE UNSUNG ENFORCERS OF EMPIRE

LAS CRUCES, NEW MEXICO

The territory patrolled by the Buffalo Soldiers—the Ninth and
Tenth Colored Cavalry regiments formed in 1866—began east of
Big Bend, the desolate southern toe of West Texas at the Rio Grande
River, and swept through thousands of miles of Indian territory in
Texas, New Mexico, Arizona, Colorado, Oklahoma, Kansas, Mon-
tana, and the Dakotas. Even after the Civil War, the Native Americans
of those lands—Apache, Cheyenne, Ute, Arapahoe, Comanche,
Lipan, Navajo, Kickapoo, Kiowa, Sioux, Pawnee—were still the
major barrier to the land's settlement and exploitation.

From the early battles in West Texas before 1870 to the final massacre of Sitting Bull's Ghost Dancers at Wounded Knee, South
Dakota, in 1890, the black soldiers, always commanded by whites,
were in the thick of conquest. Equipped with third-hand weapons,
aged horses, and rancid food, they still won numerous awards for
valor and had the lowest desertion rate in the army. But they were
ignored or even demeaned by the military establishment. They
tamed the West but, like black cowboys, were written out of American history for a hundred years.

The Buffalo Soldiers weren't the first blacks to fight for the
United States. As many as 5,000 blacks fought in the Revolutionary
War, and about 180,000 fought for the Union in the Civil War. But it
was left to their new enemy—Native Americans—to bestow upon the
black troopers their highest honor: the moniker Buffalo Soldiers,

which probably grew from the belief that their hair resembled buffalo fur. Some Native Americans, unaware that African Americans too were a subjugated people, even believed they'd been vanquished not by a distant white power but by black warriors on horseback.

I'm on my way to Las Cruces, New Mexico, to visit the first black woman born in that city, in 1909, and her son, a retired junior high school history teacher who was once named New Mexico's public school teacher of the year. But I'm also visiting because fifteen miles north of Las Cruces, a city of 62,126 people that sits an hour above Mexico and at the southern edge of the San Andres Mountains, is the ruins of Fort Seldon, one of the many army encampments that dotted Indian Territory to protect the settlers, travelers, mail riders, and miners who ventured west. Between Houston and Las Cruces was a long string of fortifications, including Forts Brown, Clark, Concho, Quitman, Sill, and Stockton. All of this is found in historian William H. Leckie's *The Buffalo Soldiers*, which also describes the men's grueling lives—one-hundred-mile-a-day horseback pursuits of marauding Indians in winter ice storms or scorching summer heat.

In our fast-food, Holiday Inn world, I figure it's easier to imagine these men's lives if I get off the super-highway and see the terrain more as it was then. So at Fort Stockton, Texas, the location of one of the key Indian war fortifications, I go south toward Big Bend, the scene of many bloody fights between bands of, say, fifty Buffalo Soldiers and equally small Native American contingents. By modern standards, these battles weren't much. But such skirmishes—in which one, two, or three soldiers and Indians might be killed or wounded and a dozen cattle or horses might change hands—defined the war for the West. As long as small bands of Indians terrorized the countryside, the land wouldn't be settled. The Indians knew this well, and their guerrilla warfare tactics had discouraged massive white settlement since the Spanish arrived in the Southwest in the sixteenth century.

The trip to the Tex-Mex border—even in a car, even 120 years later—still offers a kind of primal deep breath, with desert and cactus disappearing into the horizon in every direction. For ten, twenty, fifty, a hundred miles there are no cars or people, just a roadrunner, leaning ahead of itself like an Olympic sprinter, dashing across the road in ninety-five-degree sun with a wiggling lizard in its mouth. Dreamy black-to-red-to-mauve plateaus and mountains rise in misty terraces amid bony mesquite sculptures softened only by a sky so far away and so blue it looks unreal, like a painted dome. This terrain hasn't changed in seventy-five million years.

I stop and walk a football field's length into the desert and sit down. You are truly on your own out here—you and the owls, coyotes, six-foot rattlers as thick as your calf, wolves, and mountain lions that come out when the desert goes dark and cold. But if the West Texas badlands are sobering today, imagine what they were like for twelve men on doddering horses with canteens and hardtack—with Apaches, revolutionaries, bandits, and desperadoes lurking behind the cacti and hunching in the arroyos. It's as rough and frightening and lonely out here as the pulp writers of the nineteenth century and the moviemakers of the twentieth portrayed it. Except for one difference: John Wayne was black.

Sad news greets me in Las Cruces. During the night, the eighty-two-year-old woman I've come to visit died in her sleep. Gertrude Fielder's son, Clarence, who is sixty-three, tells me this at the front door of his mother's yellow adobe house in what is clearly a poor Hispanic neighborhood. Her house and others are nice, but gang insignia adorn the walls of water-stained adobe shacks, and Budweiser cans are cast about the streets. With only a 2 percent black population in Las Cruces, there's no isolated black neighborhood, and blacks live in poor to rich sections throughout the city and suburbs.

Clarence and I stand quietly for a moment beneath the two towering mulberry trees in his mother's front yard. He says his brothers and sisters will be coming to town for the funeral. He is very calm. I say I'm sorry and that I'll be on my way, but he says no, he'd still like to take me around, talk with me about his life. Clarence is a deeply religious man, and he says he's trying not to feel sad. His mother is in better hands.

"It's too bad you couldn't meet her," he says later, when we meet back at his house a few blocks away. "She could really have told you."

Clarence Fielder retired from his job as a public school history teacher a few years ago, but he still teaches black history at New Mexico State University in town, and for that course over the years he has collected pieces of the ignored black history of Las Cruces.

Clarence's grandfather had been a railroad cook, and he settled in Las Cruces as a chef at the fancy Don Bernardo Hotel on Main Street downtown. Later, he opened a restaurant—the Jitney Cafe—and eventually did well enough to own a house in town, a house in the country, and a dairy farm.

The early black settlers in Las Cruces included unskilled farm laborers, but also an electrician, a welder, a tailor, a mine owner, a grocery store owner, and the owner of a pool hall and rooming house. Clarence believes a majority of the early blacks in Las Cruces were prosperous. When the White Sands Missile Range opened outside town in the forties, it also attracted a small group of highly educated blacks. Today a black city councilman who works at White Sands is running for mayor. Clarence says such black prominence isn't new. One of the city's richest men until his death in the fifties was E. D. Williams, a black barber who parlayed his hair business into tremendous real estate holdings.

"His barber shop catered only to whites," Clarence says.

"He wouldn't cut black hair?"

"No, blacks couldn't even go in."

Clarence is telling the black history of Las Cruces from the notebook cards he uses in his black history class. He's sitting in a stiff-backed wooden chair in a living room that's overflowing with books and documents—*County by Race, Black History, Black Defiance.* On his wall are portraits of Martin Luther King, Jr., and Malcolm X. He keeps glancing back and forth from me to his notes, pushing up his round glasses. He's a large, gentle man with a high forehead, heavy brows, and a vague mustache and goatee. He has a lyrical voice and a good, deep laugh. Like so many blacks I've met, he gets a kick out of men like E. D. Williams, who put the lie to white stereotypes about black incompetence and laziness.

Until 1925, the schools in Las Cruces were integrated. But an influx of white Southern landowners led to demands for segregation. Clarence's mother told him that the black kids just came to school one day and were told to go home. She and the few dozen other black children didn't go to school for a long time. Then a little church school opened. Then two small tar-paper shacks were built. In 1933 a black school finally opened. "My mother used to say that when they first came, some of the Southern kids were nice, but that others called them names in the hallway and spit on them." But Las Cruces was

spared the violent racism of the South and Oklahoma and Texas. Boy
Scout troops and social clubs were never segregated, and when the
Supreme Court ended segregated schools in 1954, Las Cruces inte-
grated without trouble.

After Clarence graduated from New Mexico State, which had just
integrated, he went into the army and was sent to Georgia, where he
discovered that many of the college-educated blacks in his unit, from
segregated colleges in the South, resented that he'd gone to college
with whites. "It wasn't true, but they felt I felt superior," he says. As
Clarence got to know them, he realized that many felt deeply inferior
to whites, a feeling that he hadn't experienced while growing up in
Las Cruces. Shipped off to Korea, Clarence was put in charge of a platoon of ninety men, only one of whom was black. This was unheard
of, and he got some strange looks. His men, on the other hand, got a
crash course in racism when they began being scheduled to eat last at
chow time. "They were pissed!" Clarence says, laughing. "I said,
'Now you know what it feels like.'" But Clarence's wartime experiences were not deeply tainted by the racism of the era. When
Clarence tells his college students this, they don't believe him. He
says, "I'm here today because white guys came back and got me."

October 25, 1951, near the tiny village of Magori, South Korea,
two in the afternoon: Clarence had been ordered to lead his men on
an assault against snipers, but when he stood to bark the command, a
bullet ripped through his thighs. He couldn't walk and when one of
the two men carrying him out had his head shot off, the other man
fled. Clarence was pinned in a hole, his legs wrapped with tourni-
quets, for four hours. Four white soldiers in his platoon finally fought
their way back through pieces of head and leg and gut that lay all
around. They carried Clarence out and both his legs were saved. It
wasn't until he was recuperating in Japan that he understood why
he, as a black man, had been put in charge of whites. He was called to
the colonel's office and when he walked in, the colonel said, "Goddamn, they *did* make a mistake!"

"What's wrong?" Clarence asked.

"They got you down as Caucasian."

The colonel said he'd get the records fixed, but when Clarence got
back to New Mexico they still listed him as white. Again officials said
they'd fix it. Clarence laughs. "They never did change it. On my things
from the Veterans Administration everything is still listed as Caucasian."

* * *

Clarence has a friend who would like to go with us to Fort Seldon. We stop by his house on Paxton Street, which in the fifties was the only affluent black neighborhood in Las Cruces. We get to Dessalines C. Johnson's house soon after he has returned from his morning nine-hole round of golf. He's seventy-two years old, a mathematician retired from White Sands, and an indomitable character with the throaty voice of a cigar smoker. His nickname is D.C. In his house he's surrounded by his own sculptures and paintings, more than a few of which are nudes. "He understands his symmetry," says Clarence, winking. With his shaved head and mustache that drapes around his lips, Dessalines looks like Lou Gossett, Jr., maybe forty pounds lighter.

In World War II, D.C. was in the Ninth Cavalry—the direct descendant of the Ninth Cavalry of the Buffalo Soldiers stationed at Fort Seldon, in which D.C.'s grandfather served from 1897 to 1927. D.C. has lived in Las Cruces thirty-nine years, always meaning to get out to Fort Seldon, but he never has. So he'd like to tag along. D.C. has his old Ninth Cav yearbook out and it's all here—the Indian Wars; the Battle of San Juan Ridge in the Spanish-American war of 1898, when the Buffalo Soldiers beat Teddy Roosevelt and the Rough Riders to the top of the hill; the Buffalo Soldiers quelling rebellion in the Philippines in 1900; their Mexican border duty from 1913 to 1915; their service throughout the South Pacific in World War II.

"How'd it feel to fight for a racist country?" I ask.

"Look, that was always something you thought was ridiculous," D.C. says, dismissing the question. "But it was that way. You took it. You didn't like it, but you understood it." D.C. moved to Las Cruces after the war, because he was once stopped by a city policeman here early in the morning and he was treated respectfully. That impressed him, because D.C. was from San Antonio, Texas, where he knew a white cop who bragged that his pointed cowboy boots were for "putting up niggers' asses." D.C. doesn't remember integration coming to Las Cruces quite so smoothly as Clarence recalls it. He says whites burned one house down when blacks bought into a white neighborhood. But all in all, he says, Las Cruces was a good place for black folks.

Under a rainy-season sky of monstrous cumulus clouds, we arrive at Fort Seldon. The adobe fort hasn't held up well over the years. It's in ruins, with only stubs of walls standing like a salmon-colored Stonehenge protruding in some meaningful but obscure pattern. It's impossible to see in these remains the post's dirt-floored, dirt-roofed, single-story buildings that were laid out in a rectangle surrounding a desert parade ground. Or to imagine that the soldiers' day went from sunrise to 8:30 at night and was filled with grueling, mindless labor of upkeep and make-work. What's easier to imagine is the isolation, and how desperate a man—black or white—had to be to sign up for this $13-a-month duty. No wonder it was newly freed slaves who were recruited to go west and replace the white volunteer troops stationed here during the Civil War. War has forever been a poor man's business. Fort Seldon then was like Big Bend today, except more so. The closest railroad was 549 miles away. The closest telegraph station was 263 miles away. And the scenery: spineless prickly pear cacti, creosote bushes, yucca plants, spiny ocotillo, and staghorn cholla. Not to mention the snakes, scorpions, and tarantulas. And the stupefying heat.

Fort Seldon was occupied from 1866 to 1891, when it was finally closed with the end of the Indian Wars. But in those intervening twenty-five years, thousands of black troopers passed through these adobe walls. The remaining black-and-white photos of the Buffalo Soldiers reveal tough, cocksure men who stood straight and stared hard, with hats cocked at jaunty angles, white scarves tied cavalierly around necks, guns dangling confidently from lean hips. God knows tough men were needed. In the two years from 1865 to 1867, according to a report cited by historian Leckie, Native Americans killed 162, captured 43, and wounded 24 citizens in Texas alone, while stealing four thousand horses and thirty-one thousand head of cattle. Today we are prone to sympathize with the embattled Native Americans. "Look," says D.C. Johnson, "the Indians' cattle—buffalo—were slaughtered by sportsmen shootin' 'em for the hell of it. Well, shit! Naturally, they're gonna strike back. If it'd happened to you, you'd a done the same damned thing."

I suppose. But that's insight by hindsight. If it hadn't been for the American mentality of conquest, D.C. Johnson and Clarence Fielder wouldn't be living in Las Cruces today, nor would the barber E. D. Williams have become one of the richest men in town, nor would Gertrude Fielder have died here peacefully in her sleep. In some way, shape, or form, the demise of Native America was inevitable. What I find so poignant about the Buffalo Soldiers, about these crumbling adobe walls that house their ghosts, isn't that they helped white America conquer Native America unjustly, but that they did exactly what America believed it had the right to do—exterminate the Indians. The lowest of the low did the bloody deed, but they received none of the bloody glory. That is truly a double-bind, truly a poetic injustice.

7

FROM *SOUNDER* TO "STAR TREK"

HOLLYWOOD, CALIFORNIA

Paul Winfield, alias Dathon the Tamarian, has been here on Paramount Pictures' cavernous sound stage number 16 since 3 A.M., and he's dragging by lunchtime. It's an eight-day shoot for this weekly episode of "Star Trek: The Next Generation," and Paul must be on the set every one of those eight days. Everybody else can get here after breakfast, but the elaborate, molded mask for his sci-fi character takes three hours to fit. The mask is sealed to his skin except for perspiration drains into his clothing, and it's hot, wet, and itchy inside. Glamorous work, this Hollywood. But at least he's playing a hero—a brown, pig-nosed, bald, bony-headed hero with three seams of vertebral nubs running like a crown on his red-veined skull. He looks something like a lizard man in his green boots and space suit. It's scene 22, in which Paul ritually tosses Dathon's talismanic jewelry around a campfire before lying down to sleep amid the fake rocks and real dirt of the freezing Planet L. The campfire won't burn right, so they shoot it over and over.

"Cut!" the director finally hollers. "Print it!"

Paul Winfield, a very tall man who turns fifty-two today, has gone thick in the belly since his famous 1971 role as the poor black sharecropper in the movie *Sounder*, which earned him his only Oscar nomination. (He lost to Marlon Brando in *The Godfather*.) But otherwise, he's still powerful in the chest and shoulders, narrow at the

hips, still carrying himself in his slow, muscular manner. After scene
22 wraps, he strides over to the snack table and from among the
muffins, fudge, and rippled potato chips picks up a handful of carrot
sticks and, with a sigh, settles into the high director's chair desig-
nated for the guest star.

I've come to southern California to visit Paul Winfield and other
blacks in the film industry—Charles Burnett, a respected young filmmaker not at all in the Spike Lee mold; talent manager Dolores
Robinson; her daughter Holly Robinson, who starred in Fox-TV's "21
Jump Street"; and gangster rap star and actor Ice-T. After my time in
the old black towns of the West, at the graves of Uncle Wallace and
Aunt Minerva, at the black cowboy museum and the desert remains
of Fort Seldon, I felt as if I were lost to the twentieth century, gone,
immersed in a deep pride and dignity that only the truly dispossessed can ever achieve. Now back in the present, I hope to learn
something about what it's like to be black in Hollywood.

Paul Winfield isn't the biggest black star in America, but he has
been around a long time, doing movies as memorable as *Sounder* and
as forgettable as *Damnation Alley*, in which he's eaten by radioactive
cockroaches. He has seen public interest in black movies rise, wane,
and rise again. He has watched his white contemporaries such as
Harrison Ford and Jack Nicholson go from acting classes with him to
leading roles, while he has rarely landed a lead. Even in supporting
roles, he's almost always killed before the credits. "I die in almost
everything!" he says with a belly laugh. "I even die in this." But that's
white Hollywood. For seventy-five years, since the first full-length
movie—D. W. Griffith's *Birth of a Nation*, a blatantly racist apologia
for the Ku Klux Klan and the disenfranchisement of blacks after
Reconstruction—the movie industry has mirrored the changing and
unchanging racial realities of America.

In my travels across the country, I stopped at Indiana University's
Black Film Center Archive and watched *Birth of a Nation*, which today
is offensive almost beyond belief. Its hunched, apelike white actors in
blackface ogle, eyeball, and assault innocent Southern belles. It makes
Gone With the Wind look like a civil rights tract. Except for stereotypical roles as tough-but-loving mammies, ghost-fearing chauffeurs, or
nightclub bandleaders, blacks were rarely seen on screen until the
fifties and the arrival of Sidney Poitier.

Superb movies did slip through the cracks—Paul Robeson in *The*

Emperor Jones and *Sanders of the River*; Ethel Waters, Eddie Anderson, and Lena Horne in *Cabin in the Sky*; Sidney Poitier in *Lilies of the Field* and *A Raisin in the Sun*; James Earl Jones in *The Great White Hope*; the little-known but brilliant *Nothing but a Man*, which portrayed the demeaning choices a black man faced in the pre-civil rights South; and *The Learning Tree*, Gordon Parks, Sr.'s autobiographical tale of a black boy growing up in rural Kansas.

Then in 1971, the year before Paul Winfield's Oscar-nominated Best Actor performance in *Sounder*, everything changed with the wild success of Melvin Van Peebles's independent, shoestring flick *Sweet Sweetback's Baadasssss Song*, the story of a black sex-show entertainer who finds his racial pride when he attacks two white cops who are beating a black man. The angry, authentic film launched dozens of cheap "blaxploitation" film rip-offs such as *The Mack, Mandingo,* and *Super Fly*, until the films finally lagged at the box office in 1976.

There were decent film and TV productions over the years— "King," which starred Paul Winfield; *The Autobiography of Miss Jane Pittman*; "Roots"; *Conrack; A Soldier's Story; Mississippi Burning;* and *Glory*, to name only a few. But what such movies usually had in common were plenty of good-willed white characters for white audiences. Films made for blacks went into eclipse after the blaxploitation era, until the success of Spike Lee turned the heads of Hollywood's bottom-liners and spawned a new crop of black-directed movies for black audiences, such as *The Five Heartbeats, Boyz N the Hood, New Jack City*, and Charles Burnett's beautiful *To Sleep With Anger*.

Although too brief a history, this hits the high points. Hollywood has gone from stereotyping blacks as buffoons or monsters to portraying blacks as creatures worthy of white pity and white guilt in civil rights–era flicks to glorifying lawless black bucks fighting against a corrupt white system to finally putting black portrayals firmly in the hands of black directors.

Dathon the Tamarian has lived through it all.

"It really all started for me with the civil rights movement," Winfield says, sitting stiffly in his high chair, hands resting on his knees. In his Tamarian getup he must swivel his entire torso to look me in the eye, and he does. In his voice is the soothing, liquid archness of the stage actor. All around us the fifty or so grips, actors, and technical people are shouting orders, laughing, talking about evening cocktails, replacing props, studying scripts, adjusting lights. Winfield is

oblivious. "For the great white unwashed"—he chuckles gently—
"before the sixties it was as if we lived on the other side of the moon.
I mean, unless you had a black servant, you just didn't think about
black people. But when you started seeing them in your living room
every evening on the news, having dogs sicked on them or being
beaten just for the right to vote or sit at a lunch counter, it really got
white America curious about who these people were."

Paul Winfield grew up in Los Angeles and Portland, Oregon,
where his parents had moved to take jobs working for rich relatives
in the hotel, restaurant, and casino business. He acted in high school
and won a scholarship to the University of Portland. In those days he
planned to teach and do a little stage acting on the side, because in
the early sixties he saw few black movie actors. "There weren't any,"
he says. "There was Sidney Poitier. There were musicals. There were
comedians. And that was about it." But Paul didn't sing, dance, or
tell jokes. On stage, however, actors such as James Earl Jones, Ossie
Davis, and Ruby Dee were doing memorable dramatic work. Then
came the 1965 race riots. "I was out of college doing LeRoi Jones's
Dutchman and *The Toilet* here in Hollywood. Burgess Meredith was
directing. And the Watts riots happened and brought home this racial
tension." Hollywood woke up. "They saw this as a *real* story, and I
started being cast as angry, young black men. Right place, right time.
I was playing villains because I have acne, and I wasn't great looking.
My big breakthrough role was *Sounder*." The film was shot near
Baton Rouge, Louisiana, and it was Paul's first trip to the South.

"You'd see these beautiful plantations, these beautiful mansions,
the wonderful craftsmanship that represented a wonderful, stylish
way of life, a kind of gentility. Then you'd go in the back where the
slaves lived and see how they *got* all this. It was a real eye-opener.
After a hard day on the set, we'd jump in the motel pool with everybody else. And in about five minutes, we'd look around and nobody
else is in the pool. Gee, that's strange. But we didn't think about it.
We'd go back to our room to a get a little bite, come back out, and the
pool is full again. So, ah-hah, I get it!" He shakes with laughter. "So
we'd torture those poor people. We'd get in, they'd get out. We'd get
out, they'd get in. Back and forth, back and forth." And he laughs
again.

"You know, there was an actor named James Edwards, who made
a big impression on me as a boy. He did a picture called *Home of the*

Brave that Stanley Kramer directed in '49. It changed my whole outlook. I was living in Portland, Oregon. I remember all of my neighbors in my parents' kitchen talking about this movie and that they
weren't gonna sit in the balcony to see it, because the lead character
was a black man who wasn't a Stepin Fetchit or a servant, but a *real*
man. And I had thought we always sat in the balcony because that's
where we wanted to sit! But they had Jim Crow laws even in Portland. Well, everybody came down en masse from the balcony. It was
simply, 'We're not gonna take this shit anymore. This is *our* movie
and *our* theater and *our* city, maybe even *our* country!' It was a major
social change resulting from a movie." Years later Paul told Stanley
Kramer what had happened, and Kramer said the same thing had
happened throughout the North. "To me, that was the best thing
about being an artist, that you could really change society. It seems
presumptuous but it worked, and not by standing on a soapbox and
preaching and organizing, which wasn't my style."

But the great parts came only rarely. "This didn't piss you off?" I
ask.

"It seemed to me you had to be realistic."

Then he returns to his story about the actor James Edwards. "He
didn't have the career that he thought he deserved. He became an
extremely bitter, angry man. It just consumed him. He would blow
up. 'Look what *they've* done to me!'" Like so many blacks I've met,
Paul learned that no matter how legitimate his anger, it could still
destroy him. "No matter how great you are," he says, "if you can't
get a job, what the fuck difference does it make? That's the way it
was. I mean I just liked living too much to make myself sick worrying
about things I cannot personally change. Oh, I wanted to do costume
dramas. The *Three Musketeers* was written by a black man! I would
like to have done, God, I still want to do *King Lear*. I still want to do a
remake of *Cabin in the Sky*. I really thought *The Great Santini* should
have been done by a black. I think the black army brats have never
been done—being black and brought up in Germany and then coming back here! I'd like to do *Death of a Salesman*. But after thirty years
of this, I just feel lucky to be alive, still working and not at the Betty
Ford Clinic."

"You don't feel slighted as a black actor?"

"Hell, no, I've had wonderful roles. And I am an *actor!*" Besides
being in *Sounder* and playing Martin Luther King, Paul played the

bitter stepfather in the PBS version of James Baldwin's *Go Tell It on the Mountain.* He did *Richard III.* He played the elder generation to Denzel Washington's young Buppie character in *Checkmates,* a play that had a nine-month run on Broadway. Sure, he did *Damnation Alley* and *Serpent and the Rainbow,* in which he had his head ripped off in the grand finale. He did *The Charmings* on TV. He does voice-overs for radio commercials ten times a week, if he can. He'd like to do more stage acting, but that just doesn't pay the mortgage. Right now, with a recession in the film business, he's just glad to be working at all.

"So you figure this black man is who you are, and this is the reality of the world and the roles that come from it?"

"Yes."

"Just like a woman isn't going to play the Terminator?"

"And neither am I."

"There has to be a relationship between the world you're creating as an actor and the world as the audience knows it?"

"Yes, right!"

"It would be like you playing a Southern cop in 1932?"

"I'm getting to that," he says, laughing. "I was once cast in a federally funded theater program under President Johnson. We did plays for high school kids around the country. André Gregory was the Los Angeles director. In the first play, *Tartuffe,* he cast Louis Gossett, Jr., as Tartuffe and set it in Spanish California with Indians and cowboys. The school teachers just screamed: 'This is not the Molière in the book!' Well, Gregory was on probation after that. The next show he cast was Tennessee Williams's *The Glass Menagerie.* Bonnie Bedelia played Laura—and *I* played Jim O'Connor, the gentleman caller! Well, they went totally off: 'Oh, you can't do this! For brother Tom to bring home a black man for his crippled sister, for his mother who is a former Southern belle, would be an act of cruelty. That's not what the play is about.' André Gregory was summarily fired. The board met and the man who came to my rescue was Gregory Peck." He took the money out of his pocket and sent Paul to the Twentieth Century Fox makeup studio, where they came up with a nose, wig, opaque makeup, and blue contact lenses. "I looked like this Greek-Irish guy. I didn't tell my parents about it, and they came to see the play and said, 'Where's Paul?'"

"Did you enjoy playing a white man?"

"Oh, yeah! I know what those white guys are like," he says,

showing for the first time a hint of bitterness. "I've seen 'em all my life. You know that sort of guy who believes if you just say the right things—the Dale Carnegie secrets of success—who is so enthusiastic but to me rings so shallow. I mean, you'll sell your soul to succeed! And to be in a white world where everything is geared for *your* success! All you need to be is smart enough to take the bull by the horns and ride a ladder of success. It's all there waiting for you. I did it with a vengeance!"

We have been talking off and on all day, and Paul has been up and down, going back to the set, shooting a scene, speaking in Tamarian—as in, "Jalad of the Kituay. Kadir beneath Mo Moteh." The campfire never does cooperate, and it takes twelve hours to shoot three pages of script. Exhausted, Paul says his lines again and again and again without complaint.

"Does it do you any good to play a role where nobody can recognize you?" I ask, just before the day's close.

"It's a release!" he says, melodramatically spreading his arms and turning his Tamarian face upward. "Who will ever know?"

And it does pay the mortgage.

8

EVERYBODY HAS A CHOICE

LOS ANGELES, CALIFORNIA

A black friend turned me on to Charles Burnett's movies. He said, "They're like reading a James Alan McPherson short story." What he meant was that Burnett's films have no high-speed car chases, no pimps, drug dealers, or hookers, no nudity, no vulgarity. They are about people—in this case black people—struggling to sort right from wrong while maintaining humanity and dignity in lives that are, from the world's perspective, insignificant. They're films about morality in its most intimate clothing.

Charles Burnett's first movie, *Killer of Sheep*, follows the daily struggles and responsibilities of a man who works in a slaughter-house. It is a black-and-white film shot on a shoestring budget. But along with *The Godfather* and *Citizen Kane,* it has been honored as one of fifty treasured American films listed on the National Film Registry by the Library of Congress. But Burnett is considered an artsy film-maker, and if it weren't for his house-painting income, National Endowment and Guggenheim grants, and a $275,000 Genius Grant from the MacArthur Foundation, there'd be no movies. To make his second film, *My Brother's Wedding,* Burnett used the money he and his wife had been saving to buy a house. He lost it all.

Charles Burnett's so-called commercial debut came with *To Sleep With Anger,* which stars *Lethal Weapon*'s Danny Glover. It's the story of Harry, a malevolent trickster from African American folklore in the Gullah tradition. He drops in on a family of old friends who migrated a generation ago from the rural South and are now living the good, middle-class life in California. Harry's demonic powers soon begin to magnify the buried anger within the seemingly happy family, even-tually forcing its members to face their own simmering resentments. This beautiful film is about as commercial as a book of Portuguese poetry. So far, it has earned Burnett $30,000, which is lunch money in Hollywood.

I've come to visit Charles Burnett because his films are so unlike those of today's popular young black movie directors—Spike Lee's raucous, obscene, and iconoclastic films; John Singleton's ghetto drama, *Boyz N the Hood;* Keenen Ivory Wayans's *I'm Gonna Git You Sucka,* a parody of the blaxploitation flicks, and his smash TV series, "In Living Color"; and Warrington and Reginald Hudlin's *House Party* movies. With the exception of poignant Spike Lee characters such as the Reverend and Mrs. Purity (played by Ossie Davis and Ruby Dee) in *Jungle Fever,* I don't see in these movies many of the black people I've met in either my wife's Kentucky family or in my travels. The characters are too often young, urban hipsters—who per-fectly conform to movie-going audience demographics. I've met plenty of urban hipsters, but I've met far more people like the charac-ter in *Killer of Sheep*—a man teaching his sons when fighting is right and when it isn't, searching for a cheap engine for his old car, and looking for time to lay a new floor in his kitchen.

So on a quiet Sunday afternoon, I find the Burnett home in the pricey View Park neighborhood of Los Angeles, which surprises me.

It's not way up the hill in what the locals call the "Cosby" neighborhood, where Keenen Ivory Wayans lives, but I doubt many starving
artistes live in these nice houses, many of which are obscured by
mature trees and red and pink blooming camellias. When I arrive at
the Burnetts' pale yellow rancher, Mrs. Burnett is at the door straightening the ties of her two young sons. She too is dressed up, and
everybody except Charles—in chinos, a frayed gray sweatshirt, and
green Reeboks—is ready to walk out the door for services at the
nearby Jehovah's Witness Kingdom Hall. The house, a mess after two
months of renovation, is a new acquisition bought with the
MacArthur grant money. The Burnetts were bankrupt when that
money fell from heaven.

"It's going to be pretty," I say.

Without expression, Charles says, "Hmm-mmm," and I wonder if
he's indifferent to the fruits of affluence or if perhaps he's even
embarrassed by them, at age forty-seven still feeling guilty about
having finally achieved the kind of material status any moderately
successful lawyer or laundry owner would expect. His wife seems
not to have any such ambivalence, and she immediately delays her
departure to give me a tour of the house, leading me on a walk
through narrow pathways that wind like animal trails through a forest of packed and stacked cardboard boxes: the formally furnished
living room with the grandfather clock and the oriental rug, the new
kitchen with the tile countertop, the well-stocked wine rack, the vintage gas stove bought at Antique Stove Heaven, the new Mexican tile
floor in the sun room, the new wall of French doors, the new patio,
the new cedar-lined walk-in closets—a large one for her, a small one
for him. She is very proud.

"You don't go to church?" I ask Charles after his family has left
and we've settled into what used to be his study before everything
got ripped up and his papers, books, and computer printouts got
heaped in random, uneven piles.

"Well, I'm Baptist, but I don't go too often."

"You want your kids to grow up Jehovah's Witnesses?"

"It's either that or go myself."

Charles Burnett is a small, compact man whose feet don't reach
the floor when he sits down on a tall stool in the middle of his office.
He's got a little mustache and short, tight, balding hair that's laced
with gray. His left eye is just slightly wider than his right eye. He has

the vague hint of a boyhood stutter and, as he talks, he often looks away shyly until it is my turn to speak. His voice and his manner, like his movies, are gentle. I tell him about my travels and about the people I've met and how they are not like the people I see in the new crop of black movies. For the first of many times, I ask what he thinks of these films.

"I don't make those kind of movies," he says, and for the first of many times he fails to answer my question. "I have to be careful to remember that mine is not the only vision. But you look for films that try to communicate some values and what do you have? None, basically, very few. I get American Movie Classics on cable and you see some really great movies. The writing is better, the photography is better. I don't care what anyone says. When you grew up on those kind of films you got a sense of right and wrong."

"What do you think of Spike Lee's movies?"

"A lot of Americans are asleep," Charles says, "so Spike waking them up, fostering dialogue, is good."

"But does he create the kind of black images you want to see?"

Again Charles slips the question. "He has his sensibilities and I have my sensibilities."

"What do you think of 'In Living Color'?"

"I've only seen it a couple of times."

"But what do you *think* of it?"

He sighs. "I think it can be damaging in many ways," he says, finally getting out the criticism that his films, by juxtaposition, clearly imply. "Their thing is that there is a message behind it. I don't know if that can justify it, because I don't think people see that. They just see what they see."

"The Homeboy Shopping Network of stolen goods?"

"Yeah, and for a lot of people it confirms perhaps a lot of their stereotypes." And then there's "The Cosby Show."

"It deals with race," I say.

"But it's superficial," Charles says softly, reluctantly. "There's no distinction between the characters in his show and, let's say, 'Cheers.' People are very lazy. People don't want to turn the TV off and think about what they've seen." Too many black films, he says, present "an image of black people that is similar to what you get on the six o'clock news. It's not challenging. The films are not made to deal with people's humanity." Black people face the reality of racism every day, he says, but they also have childhoods, families, careers, love and loss, menopause and old age to face.

As I've seen again and again in my travels, black people live complete lives beyond the matters of race and racism. "But you don't see a 'thirtysomething' with blacks," Charles says, "shows trying to deal with, say, the real growing pains of adults." Charles first saw this bias as a young film student at UCLA, where most black film students were making angry, political films with characters struggling against injustice and exploitation. "The people I knew didn't live like that," he says.

"You had a problem with plot?" I ask.

"I had a serious problem with plot. Life isn't such where things are resolved. People keep struggling."

Conversation with Charles Burnett doesn't flow smoothly from point A to point B. He talks slowly, and the remnant of his stutter occasionally intervenes. He's not the kind of thinker whose thoughts flow in even, articulate waves. His words wander off in long asides and tangents, and his sentences are peppered with "sort of," "you know," and "I mean." He's always rethinking what he's thinking even as he's thinking it, layers of nuance atop layers of nuance.

Charles was raised by his grandparents in what is today South Central Los Angeles, very tough territory but which in the forties and early fifties was more rural than urban. The neighborhood was populated with families like the one in *To Sleep With Anger*—tight-knit families still holding to their rural southern values as well as their chickens, country gardens, swamp-root medicines, blues music, and bad-luck superstitions. Charles and his brother raced their bikes up and down the roller coaster hills of Devil's Dip and spent whole days shooting their bows and arrows and BB guns in the nearby swamp. He remembers this as an idyllic time, before the relativistic morality of today, a time when right and wrong were clearly taught. The challenge was always the same: How do you do the right thing even if everybody else is doing the wrong thing? The films of the blaxploitation era, he says, did great harm within the black community because they argued that it was impossible to tell the good guys from the bad guys. Pimps and drug dealers were transformed into antiheroes, their corruption and immorality justified and rationalized by the rampant corruption and racism of the white world.

"No!" Charles insists. "You don't join them!" He says that people who make films should think about what impact their films might have on the people who see them. He then tells a story. A youthful acquaintance of his once robbed a store at gunpoint. The storekeeper ran into the street with his own gun in hand, and Charles's acquaintance shot and killed the storekeeper. Charles went with the family to the trial, and during a break the family sat talking about how their relative was sure to get off because he had shot the storekeeper in self-defense. "I was like, 'Huh?'" Charles says. "I was the only one who had a different opinion. My whole thing was that he was"—and he pauses—"*guilty*. The guy did this robbery and as a consequence this man was killed." But the family couldn't comprehend this view. They were so out of touch with this clear and simple moral reasoning they couldn't imagine how anybody could see it as anything other than self-defense.

"Is this the inmates running the asylum?" I ask.

Charles nods sadly. "Yeah." He says that even as a young man he knew he could never be a spokesman for that segment of black America. Such flawed moral thinking, he believes, now permeates American culture, black and white. But because blacks are under constant assault by racism and poverty, it has damaged them even more. Likewise, the invasive commercialism of American culture has damaged everyone by ceaselessly claiming that the road to happiness is a new Volvo or tennis shoes or an eight-ball jacket. But again, this societal drift has damaged African Americans the most by eroding what was their greatest strength—their moral fiber.

Charles is always amazed when he talks to elderly blacks, those who suffered the worst of American racism but who proudly and stubbornly clung to the idea that they could still be decent human beings, that they could be morally superior to their oppressors if only they didn't sink to the oppressors' level. In Iowa City, James Alan McPherson had made exactly the same point. Today, Charles says, far more young blacks—without the benefit of moral bearings—are crippled by a racism that, ironically, isn't nearly as severe as it used to be. I'm struck by the similarity between Charles Burnett's moral thinking and what is today considered the quaint Christian morality that Harriet Beecher Stowe gave to Uncle Tom. In the end, both Stowe and the filmmaker believe a person's goodness isn't measured against the worst in others but against what should be the best in all of us. For Charles Burnett, morality boils down to the choices each of us makes about the only thing we can really control: our own behavior.

These universal themes, filtered through the lens of African American experience, are the meat of his movies. "It's hard to make a serious film, period," Charles says. "But there is resistance toward black subject matter on every level—marketing, production, you name it. It's a 'black film.' The niche is very difficult and if it's a family drama, a serious piece, well, then it's even more difficult. But if you want to do a film about the negative, pathetic side of black life you can always get funding." Right now Charles is working on a film project about the Black Panthers of the sixties and a feature movie about the Harlem Boys' Choir for MGM. Neither is a done deal, money in the bank, but it's far more lucrative work than he was doing a few years ago.

I ask Charles if he ever worries that the new public interest in black movies is only a temporary blip, that they will again go into eclipse and that he and other black filmmakers will go with them. His answer is uncharacteristically blunt. "I don't care one way or the other." He says he'll be making movies whether or not the public is interested, whether or not black films are making money, whether or not he is making money. "I can only do what I can do," he says. "I'd rather try to say *something* to a few people than say *nothing* to a mass audience. You make movies for yourself."

After a few hours, as I leave Charles Burnett's new home, running through my head are the words of William Faulkner who once said that he worked "in the agony and sweat of the human spirit, not for glory and least of all for profit, but to create out of the materials of the human spirit something which did not exist before," as he struggled to understand the nature of human compassion, sacrifice, and endurance. "The poet's, the writer's, duty is to write about these things. . . . The poet's voice need not merely be the record of man, it can be one of the props, the pillars to help him endure and prevail."

Charles Burnett, writer and filmmaker, is doing his duty. It's a shame more people—black and white—aren't listening.

9

"I'VE BEEN BLACK LONGER THAN YOU"

BEVERLY HILLS, CALIFORNIA

Edward Scissorhands would be in heaven in Beverly Hills, because the place must be the topiary capital of the world. It may even have more ornamental bushes, hedges, and trees than it does Mercedes-Benzes, but I wouldn't bet on it. Sitting at the stoplight at Robertson Boulevard and Burton Way, beneath a California canopy of sunshine and palm trees, I count two Mercedes-Benzes on my right, four on my left, and two in front of me. Beside me is a gold Rolls-Royce convertible wheeling a tanned, blond, fiftysomething Troy Donahue type who's puckering his lips and bobbing his head to music. For all I know he may be Troy Donahue. But more amazing than any of this are the street signs. All the streets have street signs! The streets are even announced by extra street signs a block ahead, making Beverly Hills a perfect reverse-image of, say, East St. Louis, where finding a street sign in some neighborhoods is about as common as finding a $100 bill at the bus stop.

This town is America at two extremes: rich and white.

Among the city's handful of blacks are Dolores Robinson, one of the hottest personal talent managers in the movie and TV business today, and her daughter Holly, who plays a young cop on TV's "21 Jump Street," the show that catapulted actor Johnny Depp to fame and, come to think of it, landed him the role of Edward Scissorhands. Over the years, Dolores has represented veteran actors Martin Sheen, Randy Quaid, Harry Hamlin, and LeVar Burton, who played Kunta Kinte in "Roots." But her white-hot status grows from two young clients—black actor Wesley Snipes, who starred in Spike Lee's *Jungle Fever* and in Mario Van Peebles's *New Jack City,* and white actor Jason Patric, who played a punch-drunk boxer in *After Dark, My Sweet* and a cop in *Rush,* but who's best known for having taken Julia *Pretty Woman* Roberts away from Kiefer *Flatliners* Sutherland only days before their scheduled Hollywood wedding.

I know this sounds like "Entertainment Tonight," but there are things a person must know before entering Dolores Robinson's Beverly Hills office, which is done up with deep-green carpeting that matches the waiting room's modern-art painting, which looks as if it has had a run-in with a plasterer's brush. Dolores is prone to modern art—clouds floating in a blue sky, a garish Hollywood couple at a coffee shop, black-and-white photos tinted in pastels. As far as I can detect, none of her office artwork is African American, which is unusual compared with the homes and offices of the other successful blacks I've visited.

From her desk, telephone to her ear, Dolores motions me to a chair with a quick, jerky flick of the wrist. She's a fifty-five-year-old woman who still looks almost girlish. Thin and supple-skinned, she wears her black hair pulled back in wavy rivulets and tied in a knot at the nape of her neck, gold-wire glasses hiked atop her head, a tan-striped jacket over a black turtleneck, two silver rings, and an amber and silver necklace. On her desk is a liter of Evian water with lipstick around its lip. Most striking is the wall of movie scripts—scripts stuffed in bins and stacked on shelves, scores of scripts, maybe hundreds: *Color of Valor, Love Abuse, Nervous Ticks, Zero Tolerance, City of Joy.*

Into the phone, Dolores says, "Everybody's got a Black Panther project, I swear." She says this in a way that manages to be gracious and curt at once, in a voice that reveals little tolerance for fools, in the voice of a deal maker. "I went to dinner last week with Joel Silver and Wesley—Black Panther project! Suzanne DePasse has a Black Panther project!"

I interject, "And Charles Burnett."

"Charles Burnett has a Black Panther project! And there's Meryl Streep's 'Fay Stender' project! So when Wesley was in your director's face, he didn't have the career he has now. Here's what you do. Send the script to me. 90210." Now, in a sweet voice, "Have you talked to my ex-husband lately?"

When Dolores is off the phone, there are no introductions between us. She's off and talking. "When a career's on the way up, you have to be careful. You gotta know when to say no. The toughest thing you've got to do. . . " She hesitates, leans across her desk conspiratorially, and says that the toughest thing for Wesley Snipes is saying no to his old black friends, because he doesn't want to be seen as a "brother" who forgot his roots. And his "brothers" play that card for all it's worth. "That's why he's gotta have a big old can of Raid called me! It was a thrill last month to walk into Warner Brothers and have them ask us, 'What movie do you want?' I mean for a black actor, it's unheard of! Wesley can carry a movie!" She gets conspiratorial again: even Denzel Washington is threatened by Wesley's rise. "Hollywood isn't set up for black actors," Dolores says. "There's only room for one lead black actor. If one is up, the other is down."

Naturally, much of this is hype. I know it. She knows I know it. I know she knows I know it. That's the rapacious charm of Hollywood, a town that lives by one commandment—making money, behind which race and racism, or motherhood, or patriotism, or faith, or family will forever be distant runners-up. Live by the commandment and you may prosper. Forget it and you're emotional fishbait for the sharks. Dolores puts it this way, "If you're looking for love, go home." That, too, is hype.

But how Dolores Robinson, whose mother cleaned the homes of Philadelphia's old rich, got to be a Hollywood queen bee isn't hype at all. She grew up in the tiny town of Penllyn, Pennsylvania, in a shack that was nothing more than old servants' quarters for the Mayflower types who lived on the estates nearby. Dolores knew these people well, because when her mother cleaned their homes Dolores often helped. Dolores, whose father had abandoned the family, wore the hand-me-down clothes of little Penny from the big house. "My mother loved and respected white people, the people she used to work for," Dolores says. "She talked nicer about those kids—little Penny and Andy—than I ever heard her say about me."

"Did she have any idea she was hurting you?"

"Not a clue."

"I bet you never wanted to clean another house."

"No, but I learned a lot. I always thought I had it over middle-class and lower-class white people, even rich people who have no taste. They were never exposed. I was lucky to be exposed to these things." The homes were remarkably elegant, filled with artwork and antiques. Not to mention the style and comfortable confidence she saw in the people for whom her mother worked.

"What did you think of those people?"

"I wanted what they had. I wanted to live in their houses. They had these wonderful clothes. They lived in houses with running water! I had no running water. I was the only person in the town.

There was a pump in the back yard and an outhouse. When I'd go home from college, I'd go back to that."

"Did you ever have white school friends over?"

"One time. I remember Phyllis and Robert coming to my house and me saying, 'Step over,' because there were holes in our floor and you could just step and go right through."

"Were you humiliated?"

"Absolutely, totally humiliated. I remember that clearly."

But Dolores had an edge. "Everybody loved me. That's how I got over. I was never really angry. I just wanted what they had. Luckily, I just got a double dose of positivity. It wasn't confidence, it was positivity." Dolores says she never felt confident, even though she always got better grades than her white classmates. "It was clear to me I was smarter," she says, "but I wasn't better." In an awful, nagging way, Dolores always believed in her gut—even after she graduated from college, taught school in Philadelphia, won her own local TV talk show—that whites were better than blacks, better than she. Only great success in Hollywood has finally put most of those fears to bed. But sometimes, even today, if she walks into a room of white strangers, the old fear will flash, like the occasional ache of an old wound. For just an instant, Dolores will recognize it in the pit of her stomach. She will ignore it and tell herself, "This is what you are. You were born to it. You have to fight it all the time."

In 1974 Dolores and her husband, who was the original Gordon on Sesame Street, separated. Against the advice of everybody, she sold her furniture at a yard sale, took the $500 she earned, packed the two kids in the car, and moved to Malibu, California, where she crashed at the home of black actor Cleavon Little, whom she knew from his stint as an actor on Sesame Street. "Everybody kept saying, 'You're totally California, you're a total show-biz type.' I didn't know they meant I could bullshit." From her Malibu perch, Dolores saw a lot of people getting very rich, going off to Spain or Italy to movie shoots, then returning to the beach for a couple of months, before going off again. And they didn't seem that bright. "My whole thought was, 'Why can't I do that?'"

"Did you ever think that there were no black managers?"

"No, never."

At age thirty-eight, Dolores got a job working as a secretary for

Cleavon Little's agent. Through the contacts she made answering the phone, she had nearly parlayed her way into a job as an agent but for one tiny detail. She had failed to tell her future employer she was black, and when she walked up to him at their first lunch together, he said, "Holy shit, why didn't you tell me?"

"What was I supposed to tell you?" Dolores asked. "'Hi, I'm Dolores Robinson, I'm black.' What's that have to do with what I do?'" He liked that, thought it was gutsy. She was hired, although she soon left the agency business to become LeVar Burton's personal manager—the liaison between an actor's agent, lawyer, publicist, and business manager. After more than a year working only with Burton, she signed Powers Boothe, Martin Sheen, and Emilio Estevez, and the industry took notice. "What I had done was cross a barrier in Hollywood. I had become a black manager who managed white clients. Until I signed those white actors, everybody who sent me clients sent me black clients"—usually faded actors from the blaxploitation era. But knowing the racial biases of Hollywood, Dolores wouldn't take them. That would have put the same ceiling on her own success that Hollywood imposed on black actors. Dolores was determined to be not a manager of black actors but a manager who happened to be black, and she succeeded. Today, she represents eleven actors, nine of whom are white.

A few years ago, Dolores noticed Wesley Snipes playing bit roles, saw something special, and made her pitch just before he hit it big in *Mo' Better Blues*. "Why'd he pick you?" I ask.

She flashes a smile. "He liked that I have a Mercedes."

No conversation with Dolores Robinson goes uninterrupted. In and out the whole time is her secretary. And her associate Scott Lambert. And Brian Medavoy, a young talent manager from down the hall who used to work for Dolores. He's the son of Mike Medavoy, the president of Tri-Star Pictures and one of the most powerful men in Hollywood. Then comes Dolores's daughter Holly, who takes a call from Los Angeles Raiders star Marcus Allen, who pretends to be Denzel Washington. It's like clowns in a phone booth. Then somebody phones Dolores to say Jason Patric and Julia Roberts have made Suzy's gossip column in today's *New York Post*. They were sighted kissing in his black Porsche outside Mortons restaurant. Amid this madness, Dolores watches Joan Rivers on TV.

Dolores is also on and off the phone: "Which movie has Denzel

Washington starred in on his own that's made as much money as Wesley Snipes starring on his own? Tell 'im, 'Dedicate some a that Nike money to me, Spike. Dedicate some a your two million or your three million, whatever you get.'" And, "I said, 'Nancy, you've been a casting director a long time and you know they pay black actors less than white. He's a guy who is box office! You wouldn't pull that on a white actor.'" And, "I really think they think I'm a dumb black bitch." And, "Guess how Harrison Ford's gonna feel when Dennis Haysbert walks in and looks down on him? Harrison Ford's ego is not gonna have this big old guy, bigger than him. Physically, it's Wesley. So try and get some money. Go for it!"

Currently Dolores is angling to win Wesley Snipes a costarring role with Harrison Ford in a planned movie tentatively titled *Night Ride Down,* and she's simultaneously miffed at Spike Lee. "There's a problem because Spike wants Wesley to do a part in *Malcolm X.*"

"You don't want him to?"

"Well, not with Spike making his three million and Denzel making his three million, and they offer Wesley scale, plus ten."

Money, babes, money. The first and only commandment.

While Dolores runs off to a lunch, her daughter and I talk. Holly is twenty-six years old and beautiful. Not so-so beautiful, but truly beautiful, spin-your-head-on-the-street beautiful—with smooth, dark skin, perfect teeth, a great smile, and long hair that she nonchalantly runs her open hand through as she flicks back her head in that timeless, confident manner of pretty rich girls all over the Milky Way galaxy. I'm not surprised to hear she graduated from high school in Malibu and then Sarah Lawrence College. She has no black accent. She wears jeans and a loose black blouse decorated with white stars. No makeup, no fingernail polish. On her left hand is a giant engagement diamond. She's relaxed, friendly, and remarkably candid.

"There's a sense of establishment that I've had," she says in a slow, deep, sensuous voice, in a languid California drawl. "I feel prepared." But she says she also knows a lot of people in Hollywood have a problem that she's marrying a white man. This is news to me. "Spike Lee had to go do a movie and give a catch-phrase name to interracial relationships. Now you could be with someone ten years and have twenty kids and be happy as a lark, but now you've got *Jungle Fever.* We get ostracized a lot."

"In Hollywood?" I ask, amazed. "By blacks or whites?"

"More by blacks. Blacks are more obvious about it. Whites will talk behind your back, pretend. Blacks are more vocal." She slips into mocking dialect: "'Oh, you too fine, baby, why you with that white boy?' That's just plain ignorant. I have no time for that." Her mother didn't object when she announced her engagement, but her father did. "He has a problem with it." He told Holly that racism is on the rise, and he asked about her career: "You gonna get labeled a black woman who likes white men."

I ask, "Who would care?"

"A famous, well-known director has a *big* problem with white men dating black women."

"Spike?"

"Yeah, everybody knows it."

"But he wouldn't hold that against you?"

"I think he would," Holly says. "I have no doubt that he would. He's in a position of power, and he's a short guy who's not that good-looking who gets women because of his power. Yeah, he does exercise his political beliefs in casting sessions. I like his films so much. I just don't like him." Holly says she has auditioned for Spike. "He'll ask, 'You still with that white boy?'"

"My God, that's obnoxious!"

"Well, yeah, that's obnoxious. Whoever said he wasn't? The bottom line, he's in a position of power."

I tell Holly that when I visited Spike he argued that it's impossible for black people in America to be racist, because to be racist requires societal power to shape other people's lives. Blacks, he said, don't have that power, so blacks can't be racist, just prejudiced. By his own definition, Spike Lee has the ability to be more than prejudiced.

"I don't wanta be jerked around," Holly says. "And I have girl-friends who have white husbands or boyfriends who feel the same way. There aren't that many middle-to-upper-middle-class black men who are willing to be a little more flexible with their women. There's a whole 'that's-ma-woman' syndrome. But I know a lotta white guys who are like that, too. There's just not that many men, period."

No, Holly says, she doesn't feel out of touch with what it means to be black in America. She's close to her mother's working-class family back in Philadelphia. And sometimes, when she's with her fiancé's Jewish family, she senses how they must make an effort not to mention race in her presence. "They think of blacks as thugs. I once heard his mother say, 'When *those* people do this.' She referred to black people as *those* people. 'You know how *those* people are.' And I was, like, *those* people?"

Even living in Beverly Hills, even being rich and famous, Holly's not totally insulated. Last year, for instance, she was driving into Beverly Center, the ultimate in decadent shopping malls, in her Saab convertible with the top down, and a white guy on the sidewalk yelled out, "Fuckin' nigger!" She freaked, jumped out of her Saab, ran up to him, started pummeling him. He pushed her away and said, "You're even an ugly nigger, too. I'm not even gonna hit an ugly nigger." Nobody had ever, *ever*, talked to her like that. "It was really, really weird. I was dumbfounded for a week. This is Beverly Hills—three blocks from my mom's house! There is a snobbishness that goes on with rich Beverly Hills people anyway, but they don't come out and say, 'Fuckin' nigger!' I felt there's some scary, angry things goin' on right now."

But more important to her is the way race will inevitably shape her career. She admits that she got her role on "21 Jump Street" because she's black. But when the show got rolling, it was America's white teenyboppers who fell in love with Johnny Depp and who put the show over the top. "Jump Street" has a black male cop, a black female cop, a Vietnamese cop, and a WASPy cop as lead characters. "Who did all the story lines go to?" Holly asks. "The WASPy cop, Johnny Depp. He became a star. The whole first year, every show was written for him."

"Is that racism or reality?"

"I see it as racism when after the show has gotten off to its start, you're still sitting here with these characters and you end up not using them." Many times the producers told Holly, "Well, look, we really would rather cater to a young white audience than a young black audience." You don't have to be a rocket scientist to understand why. White kids are the people whom advertisers want to reach—they're richer and greater in number.

I ask a final question: "Is it more limiting to be female or to be black in Hollywood today?"

"Black, no doubt," Holly says, but then she hesitates. "I don't know, that's hard. It might be neck and neck. There's some white women who are trying to get jobs and they have to always be bangin' the lead guy in the movie, not to get the job, but that's the role—the girl on the arm, the big boobs. So, no, I think it's about neck and neck."

Dolores returns from lunch and asks, "You wanta travel?"
"I'd love to. Where we goin'?"
"To show the flag."
And we're off—to the warehouse district of Los Angeles, where, after a ride up a freight elevator, we enter a huge, whitewashed room with a blue-gray floor and metal-mullion industrial windows. It's the set of Midnight Heat, which features Daphne Ashbrook, a white actress Dolores represents. The place is stone silent, and in the corner under glaring lights is Little Richard, wearing a hot-pink shirt untucked like a short skirt over black pants over suede boots with silver-tipped toes. In his makeup, he looks like a Kabuki dancer. Dolores and Daphne chat for a while, long enough for Dolores to prove her attentiveness.

In the car on the way back to Beverly Hills, Dolores says of white people, "They're always shocked when you speak their language. I can say, 'Oh, say can you see by the dawn's early light,' and they would say, 'Oh, she's brilliant!' Nobody heard a word I said. White people are so easy. If you talk like them, they think you're like them." She laughs. "They're so easy! If I was into doin' my Black English thing, they wouldn't think I was so smart. I really am smart, but they don't know it. They feel comfortable with me because I'm like them."

However, she is not like them entirely. She notices that in her sixteen years in Hollywood she and Suzanne DePasse, the producer of the TV mini-series "Lonesome Dove," are still the only blacks at most business gatherings. She notices there's only one black creative executive in the business, a woman at Columbia Pictures. She notices there's not a single major black talent agent in Los Angeles or New York. And she notices that despite the success of Wesley Snipes, Denzel Washington, and Whoopi Goldberg, the NAACP Image Awards committee had to drop its Best Female Leading Actress award category this year, because there were none. Of being black and female, Dolores says, "The double whammy."

But Hollywood's first and only commandment—making money— is as much to blame as racism. Dolores says all actors outside the mainstream are mistreated. Any character played by her client A Martinez, a soap opera star, will first be given a Hispanic name. "I'd really rather him be a character named David Winston," Dolores will say. And the studio execs will look shocked, nervous. It's a constant battle to keep actors from being cast into the stereotypes they fit, and it's especially true for black actors. Dolores is now in a battle with studio executives who want to put a black director on one of Wesley Snipes's next movies. "I say no. I want him for career's sake to move into the white world, because you gotta cross over before you start reaching those upper echelons. And if you keep doing black projects, this town will slot you: 'Oh, yeah, that's Wesley Snipes, he does great black movies.' I don't want the perception of it being a black film. I want the perception of it being a white film, because I want a full, long career." That's why she so badly wants Wesley to costar in *Night Ride Down*, the movie with Harrison Ford, even if it's a flop. "It moves you into what I call 'white world.'" Of course, this is the reverse of the tack used by Spike Lee, who made movies for black audiences first and who reshaped the film industry in the process.

"If anybody is instrumental in changing the business—as much as I don't get along with him—it's Spike." He kept control of the whole creative process more than any white director. And he used race to his advantage. "He beat 'em over the head with, 'You don't understand!' And it's true." White studio executives really don't understand blacks. Dolores recently had lunch with a Hollywood executive who was telling her about a planned movie about the life of Martin Luther King, Jr., and he mentioned that as a boy King was taken by his father and immersed in water as part of a Baptism ceremony. He said, "It must've scared the kid to death." Dolores was incredulous and explained that any child growing up in the black church has seen that ritual dunking every other week for years. "They don't know! They have not a clue!" And more than once, she has given white studio executives her patented line, "I've been black longer than you have."

But Dolores's job isn't to change the world. Her job is to make her clients rich and successful for as long as possible. To do that in America, she believes, black actors must "cross over"—appeal to white as well as black audiences. Just look at Bill Cosby—and Paula Abdul, Michael and Janet Jackson, Whitney Houston. It's no secret that the big bucks and the career longevity are in the crossover. Remember Sammy Davis, Jr.?

"Do black actors resent this?" I ask.

"You have to explain to them that to get the power to do what you want, you gotta have box office strength." The historic break, the profound change, Dolores says, will come when blacks are able to play roles that portray universal themes independent of race. Dolores mentions a new movie, *Strictly Business*, in which a black yuppie character and a black mail-room worker help each other succeed. Their race is incidental in this little-man-wins-out tale. "It's a wonderful story," Dolores says. And then she explains why she is hopeful that *Strictly Business* will help change the way black actors are typecast: "This film can make money."

1 0

CROSSING OVER WITH ICE-T

IRVINE, CALIFORNIA

I must be lost. I'm supposed to meet the meanest, bad-ass, straight-up, def (hipster for "cool") nigga' king of gangster rap, the I-had-enough-shit-up-to-the-eyeballs costar of *New Jack City*, the Fuck-you!, kill-a-cop, bang-a-bitch-with-a-flashlight, hip-hop man of South Central L.A. himself: Ice-T. Or, as he says, "Ice *Mutherfuckin'* T."

But what I find at the Lollapalooza (Spanish for "huge and great") Festival at the Irvine Meadows Amphitheatre, where Ice-T will crime-rhyme this afternoon, are fifteen thousand white kids. There's a guy in a black-lace shirt and tights and purple lipstick, a girl in a Raggedy Ann doll wig, two blond-haired twin sisters in matching orange jumpsuits. Everybody wears something black. And tattoos—rattlesnakes, roses, peace symbols. And hair colors—red, orange, green, white, and the always popular purple. For sale are T-shirts that read: "I used to be a white American, but I gave it up in the interests of humanity." Baffled, I ask a young woman in the parking lot, "Excuse me, but why are all you white kids going to a rap concert?"

The woman is wearing black shorts, a black halter top, black shoes, a silver peace sign medallion, and what looks to be an African tomb-bead necklace, circa A.D. 500. Only when she looks me up and down hesitantly through her black sunglasses do I realize how strange I must look in my $7.99 Payless tennis shoes, my baggy Banana Republic shorts, my no-brand Izod knock-off T-shirt, my $3 fake-aviator sunglasses, and my yellow Clarksdale, Mississippi, Delta Blues Museum baseball cap. I mean, like her father, man! I suppose she decides she's safe with all these people around, and she says, "Just one act is rap. Mosta the acts are Modern Rock, music called New Wave or Alternative, Punk. The stuff nobody wants ta play on the radio. But Ice-T is cool! He's not just a rap artist. I admire him. Everything he has ta say is intelligent, *extremely* intelligent. Are ya stayin' for Jane's Addiction?"

"Ahh, Jane's Addiction?"

"The hottest cult band in England!"

"What time they on?"

"Last act, prob'ly ten or eleven."

"I might have ta miss 'em."

It turns out Lollapalooza is a white-child middle finger flicked in the air at the status quo. These affluent-looking kids and the event's once-over-lightly antiestablishment tenor remind me of rock festivals in the sixties—except that Lollapalooza is clearly more slick: security guards everywhere, plenty of bathrooms, earplugs for a buck, dozens of food vendors hawking vegetable pie, falafel, Jamaican chicken, and deep-fried plantains. The pleasant scents of barbecued chicken and Coppertone mingle in the air. Under a huge white tent cooled with nine gigantic fans are a bevy of "radical" groups making their pitch—Greenpeace, the National Abortion Rights Action League, Handgun Control, Inc., even the League of Women Voters. On the electric sign-board atop the stage flow these messages: "75 percent of all bombs dropped on Kuwait and Iraq missed their targets" and "Save the Whales." Onstage will be in-your-face bands that are the obscene Country Joe & the Fish and the bad-boy Rolling Stones of today: Jane's Addiction, Siouxsi & the Banshees, the Butthole Surfers, and the Rollins Band, which is just now playing so loudly that my breath and my heart seem to catch for a instant on each thunderous beat. And Ice-T!

I scan the huge outdoor arena and see maybe a dozen black kids. The black woman I sit next to turns out to be the wife of Ernie C, the guitar player in Ice-T's new hard-rock band, Body Count. Ice-T was heralded in the white rock music press when his last album, "O.G. Original Gangster," which included the theme song for the movie *New Jack City,* blended hip-hop, rock, and rhythm and blues. Years before, he'd been simultaneously praised as a poet of the urban dispossessed and excoriated as an obscene, violence-worshiping woman basher. It will be another year before Vice President Dan Quayle will attack Ice-T for his still obscure song "Cop Killer." But even before this notoriety, Ice-T had already begun to temper his screw-the-Skeezers lyrics and preach against violence and drugs, and he was being hailed for having matured, which is one way to look at it. After having visited Dolores Robinson, I know there's another way: the crossover. As the wife of Ernie C says, it's hard to find venues for straight-up rap shows, because too often the hard-core rap fans cause trouble. Ice-T, one of the country's biggest rap stars, isn't alone in seeking a path to that lucrative white audience. Next week, Public Enemy—the rap band that sang "Fight the Power" in Spike Lee's *Do the Right Thing,* the rap band with the strongest Black Power overthrow-the-system message—is performing here with Anthrax, a popular heavy-metal, screw-the-system band that will draw a young, rebellious—but rarely violent—white crowd.

Whatever Ice-T's motives, I've come to meet him because the girl in the black halter top is right: his rap is intelligent. His tales of "the killing fields" of South Central Los Angeles are beyond chilling. I have listened to his song "Midnight" alone in my house at midnight and gotten up to check that the doors were locked. As Charles Burnett's movies seem to be about life itself, so do Ice-T's songs, although about a very different life. They are, as he says, "a walk through hell."

> Place my crosshairs on my vics eye,
> squeeze the trigger, watch the brains fly.
> Violent? Yea you could call me that . . .
> You think I'm crazy? You ain't seen shit yet.

The white kids love him. In two minutes, Ice—every move of his body angry, muscular, and wild—and his Rhyme Syndicate hip-hop band have them to their feet, something none of the other bands has achieved today. "I don't know how many y'all ever been to a rap show before," Ice snarls, "but I'm gonna teach you how it goes. *This ain't Bob Hope!* Git your motherfuckin' ass up outta the chair!. . . *I'm your mother, I'm your daddy, I'm that nigger in the alley!*. . . Now all you sucka motherfuckers who wanta stay sittin' like you lookin' at some damned Lawrence Welk Show, *fuck you!*. . . The Syndicate has a motto. It goes like this: 'What good is a beautiful woman . . . IF THE BITCH WON'T FUCK!'"

That does it. For nearly an hour, Ice-T takes this crowd on a journey into a dark, forgotten corner of America. Around me are rebellious kids, angry at injustice, at the raping of the planet, at the excesses of capitalism, at the abuses of politicians, at the brutality of cops, at the scourge of crack, at the excuses and failings of their parents, of people like me. Between his harsh lines, Ice-T preaches peace, love, and togetherness among blacks and whites. The kids are up, screaming, cheering, rhyming along.

Ice, mean and low-down: "America was stole from the Indians, . . . A straight-up nigga move. . . . Yet they complain when a nigga snatch their gold chains. What is nigga suppose to do? Wait around for a handout from a nigga like you?"

Ice, taunting: "I'm the one your parents hate!"

Ice, slow and melodic: "Sometimes I sit at home and I watch TV and wonder what it would be like to live someplace like the 'Cosby Show' . . . where cops come and get your cat outta the tree, all your friends die a old age. But, you see, I live in South Central Los Angeles and, unfortunately, . . . SHIT AIN'T LIKE THAT!"

Ice takes these kids into the streets to meet his homeboy friend Evil E. Ice cradles a Tec 9 weapon in his lap. Ice's imaginary crew has blow, cash, and a stultifying, mesmerizing rage at the injustice of it all: "You'd know what to do if a bullet hit your kid on the way to school, or a cop shot your kid in the backyard. Shit would hit the fan and hit hard! . . . ON WITH THE BODY COUNT! . . . Does South Central look like America to you?" The white kids are soon screaming, dancing, shaking fists.

As a grand finale, Ice chants: "Fuck the police! Fuck the police! Fuck the police! Fuck the police! Fuck the police! *I can't hear ya!*" The kids join in—louder, louder, louder.

Kids: "Fuck the police!"

Ice: "Louder!"

"FUCK the police!"

"Louder!"

"FUCK THE police!"

"Louder!"

"FUCK THE POLICE!"

Ice: "COP KILLER! Everybody!"

Kids: "Cop Killer!"

"Louder!"

"COP KILLER!"

Ice: "What you wanta be when you grow up?"

Kids: "COP KILLER!"

Ice, with humor: "That's a good choice!"

Kids: "COP KILLER!"

Ice, with a blaring rock 'n' roll riff to end it all: "I'm a mother-fuckin' . . . COP *KILLLLERRRRRRRRRRRRRRR!*"

Backstage, while the Nine-Inch Nails manage to bring the entire crowd back to their seats, a guy in an Original Gangster T-shirt and cranberry tennis shoes carries two huge ice tubs filled with Corona beer and Andre champagne into Ice's dressing room. Ice is off in a corner striking cop-killer poses and flexing biceps for a photographer from *Rolling Stone,* and I look him over. He's old for a rap singer, somewhere in his early thirties, although he won't say exactly. He's short and stocky, strong but not edged and buffed like the guys stretching time in Joliet Correctional. He's dressed in black. He wears his cap backwards. One of his pale brown eyes has a dark shadow on its lower right side, and a little mole dots his right cheek. His palms are smooth and soft, almost feminine, but his fingernails look as if he were changing the oil in his Porsche last night. He's light-skinned, and when he takes off the shirt over his black sleeveless T-shirt, his arms are rimmed in a truck-driver's tan. Both hands flash gold-and-diamond rings, and on his left wrist is a diamond-studded, gold-and-silver Rolex.

"You really wear a Rolex?" I ask, probably signaling in my tone that I think this isn't cool.

"Pavé," he says in a hard voice, referring to the name of the extravagant multidiamond setting on the watch's face.

"How much?"

"Ninety thousand."

"My God!" I say with disgust.

"Suck my dick! Can't fit no mo' diamonds on it."

We both smile and I ask, "What's goin' on? There's more blacks onstage than in the audience."

"This is an alternative music concert, and I'm just as much alternative as any a them," Ice says, with the same pounding, musical, rap lilt that hovers in his stage voice. "In rap, I'm alternative. I'm not the rap that gets on the radio. I'm a little hard for even black people sometimes. I still got the hard-core black audience, but these white kids wanted to see Ice-T. But they haven't had a chance to really see me in a black arena, because they might've been scared, ya know?" Besides all these high-minded reasons, 80 percent of Ice-T's records are sold to white kids.

"How's this tie into South Central L.A.?"

"See, I'm growin', dude. I come from a background where, ya know, white people were victims to be victimized. And why the fuck should I trust 'em? But I ain't a hateful person. I don't believe that a white kid is born racist. I might hate your parents, but I think the kids have a chance. White people gotta learn that maybe not them but their ancestors were savages. White people have to be willing ta look at people as equals. They gotta be willin' *not* ta be the shit! Black people, which is gonna be harder, gonna have ta learn to trust white people. I got kids growin' up in this world and that hatred ain't gonna help nothin'."

"Did you feel that way ten years ago?"

"Naw, ten years ago I was just a ignorant kid. The kid that I rap to now, that's who I was. Now I'm tellin' 'em that fast lane ain't the way. You're gonna end up in prison." He says blacks must do what the Japanese did. They were bombed and conquered but came back to compete intellectually. "We ain't gonna win with no hostile takeover. We'll definitely lose that war. They say, 'Judge the devil by his deeds.' Judge people not by their skin color but how they treat you. I just learned that all that hate gets you nowhere. When I got in the movie *Breakin'*, for the first time, I was meetin' white people who was treatin' me like a person. Before, all I knew was cops, teachers, and vics."

"Vics?"

"Victims. I don't look at it as a race issue. I think the white people were the first people to have money so they decided, 'Well, we're runnin' this country so let's make sure we always stay in power.'

Money *is* another race. A broke white kid could walk into a hotel and he'll get thrown the fuck out. A black guy with a suit and money, he'll get treated different. So if I wear my hat like this"—backwards— "as long as I can talk point ratios and overseas sales, they're gonna take me ta meet with the boss. That's what I'm tryin' to get my brothers and sisters to understand."

"As a kid, did you think you were as smart as whites?"

"No, I thought white people were smarter. I don't know how I learned, man. I just started thinkin' more. I mean when you're down and you're stuck and you're broke, you're emotionally charged, not mentally charged. You're not thinkin'. Now you get a little cash flow, you're able to sit back and analyze, think, size it up. I got a lotta brothers who are still down with me who got that anger and I'm tryin' ta say, 'Hey, look, that ain't the way. You gotta work within this, if you wanta survive."

"Is there hope for kids in places like South Central?"

"The black kids need to go to school and escape. Get out! Move into the suburbs. Move right next door to the white family. Leave it an urban wasteland!" He quotes one of his songs: "Hit the gate, bro! Get the fuck out!"

Ice-T must leave the dressing room for another press photo shoot, and I tag along. I agree with most of what he has said. But then, I would. I'm a white guy. He's telling black street kids to cool it, give up the life, go to school, get a job, join the system. Soothing stuff to white ears. Words of wisdom from a convert? Maybe. Or maybe Ice *Crossover* T is just telling white people what they want to hear, as he goes for the gold. Or maybe Ice-T is telling the truth, maybe he has grown, maybe he has seen that the view from South Central isn't always 20/20. I suspect it's a bit of both. It's a strange moment, for instance, when at the photo shoot eight security guards walk past Ice-T as they forcibly eject a black man from the concert. (Only eleven left, I think to myself.) As the black man passes, he nods angrily at Ice, who has brought along a pistol in order to vamp bad-ass gangster-style for the photographer. To the black man, Ice instinctively flashes a salute with his gun. Perhaps less instinctively, he then flicks the peace sign. Neither gesture does the man any good—in another instant, he's gone, tossed out the gate on his black ass.

11

O.G., ORIGINAL GANGSTER, WITHOUT POETRY

SOUTH CENTRAL LOS ANGELES

There is no chalk for the pool cues and the tips have gone hard and dark and glassy, but the half-dozen boys, thirteen and fourteen years old, who are circling the table or leaning against the walls watching aren't bothered by the edge this takes off their game. Outside, a burglar alarm is *whiiir-whiiir-whiiiring* somewhere on this graffiti-decorated street of single-story warehouses and rundown apartment buildings. In this neighborhood of Watts, where the riots of 1965 left thirty-four people dead, nobody pays much attention. (It will be another eight months before South Central Los Angeles again explodes in violence after the infamous Rodney King jury verdict.)

This morning I've come to the neighborhood's youth center to meet a bona fide Original Gangster. That's the respectful street title given to men who were among the original Los Angeles "gangbangers"—argot for gang members—in what are now scores of youth gangs that the songs of Ice-T and the movies *Colors, New Jack City,* and *Boyz N the Hood* have immortalized. While I wait for O.G. Fred Hill, as he was once called, I challenge one of the kids to a game.

"Straight pool?" I ask.

"Eight ball," he mumbles.

"No chalk?"

"Nope."

"You wanta break?" The kid points to me, and so I break, dropping no balls. He then sinks the 11-ball on a long table shot. "Where'd you learn to play?" I ask, trying to get the conversation past dead silence.

"Watchin' other kids," he says flatly. So far, none of the other boys have spoken. They just keep staring at the table and stealing furtive glances at me. They're all young-looking, thin, well-scrubbed black kids. One wears braces on his teeth. None is wearing expensive designer clothes or tennis shoes.

"My father taught me to play when I was your age," I say, as I line up a long shot at the 6-ball. I blow the shot. "I'm so *baaad!*" I say, and then, noticing the boys glancing at each other, I add, "I don't mean *baaad*, like good. I mean *baaad*, like bad."

"You live in Los Angeles?" a wall-leaner finally asks.

"Nope, near Washington, D.C."

"You a cop?"

"No."

"You ever meet the president?"

"Well, yeah, a couple a times. I'm here to visit Fred Hill. You guys gangbangers?" Everybody looks at one kid.

"He be in a gang," a boy says tauntingly as he points at a boy who is smiling shyly along the wall.

"So you're an O.G.?" I ask, and all the boys have a laugh at their friend's expense. "What'd you think of *New Jack City?*"

"That's neat!" the gangbanger says, coming to life. He mimics cradling a shotgun in his hands: "BOOM!" he hollers, firing.

"What'd you learn from *Boyz N the Hood?*"

"If Ricky hadn't messed with 'em, he'd a never got shot," the gangbanger says, referring to a promising black kid in the movie who's blown away after he accidentally bumps shoulders with a punk who believes in determining his manhood with a shotgun.

"That was the message: 'Shut up and you won't get shot'?"

"Yeah!" says the gangbanger, as the other kids moan in disgust and laugh derisively at their buddy.

"Why don't you guys join a gang?" I ask.

"Nothin' in it for me."

"You get killed."

"Ain't worth it."

"Whatta you kids wanta be when you grow up?"

"Football player."

"Computer operator."

"Teacher."

"*He* wanta be a gangbanger," one boy says of the gangbanger kid, and they all laugh at him again.

"How you guys do in school?"

"B's."

"A's."

"*He* don't go ta school. He a fighter." More laughter.

"*He* got kicked outta every last school he went to."

"Did not!" the gangbanger says defensively. "I didn't get kicked outta Walter Reed."

"Why'd you join a gang?" I ask.

"What you call that? Hmmm . . . peer pressure."

"You seem like such a nice kid, but you wouldn't hesitate to shoot somebody for steppin' on your shoes?"

"I wouldn't shoot nobody for nothin', but if they messed with me real bad? Like said, 'Fuck you!'" The boy says this in a changed, cold voice, not the voice of thirteen-year-old.

"They deserve to be dead for that?"

"I shoot 'em in the foot. They keep talkin', I shoot 'em in the leg. Keep talkin' and I'll kill 'em."

"That's worth going to prison?"

"Police won't catch me."

A chorus of moans rises up from the other boys.

"Police dumb!" the gangbanger says.

I turn to the other boys. "You know a lotta guys who think like that?" They all roll their eyes and shake their heads yes. On the eight ball, I scratch, lose the game, and go out to the street to wait for Fred Hill.

Gang experts estimate that no more than a quarter of the kids in neighborhoods such as this are gang members, but they are a powerful minority. This weekend alone, Los Angeles saw eighteen violent deaths, many gang related. Last week, a kid was killed in a gang incident just across the street from where I'm standing. In school, the kids have drive-by shooting drills where they practice hitting the floor as quickly as possible. The ongoing transformation of South Central Los Angeles from a black to a Hispanic area (by 2010, Los Angeles is expected to be 40 percent Hispanic and South Central is expected to be overwhelmingly Hispanic) has done little to slow the gangs. The much-publicized battles between the Crips and the Bloods over drug turf and the protection-extortion rackets continue even though the membership of some traditionally black gangs is now one-fifth Hispanic. City gangs of poor kids aren't new, with the Irish and Puerto Ricans, among others, in New York doing a deadly job of it too.

The street I'm on is in Crips territory. The tall building I can see a few blocks away is in Bloods territory. The L.A. gangs today have become so Balkanized that every few blocks is the territory of a different gang, usually factions of the Crips or the Bloods. The scribbling on walls everywhere in South Central is the equivalent of animals urinating on bushes to mark their turf and warn off competitors foraging the same landscape.

Within this arcane world is still another subgroup—taggers, who are free-lance graffiti writers not connected with any gang. By coincidence, sitting on the sidewalk in the hot sun amid the strong smell of motor oil from the nearby car repair garage are four kids, all in their early teens, who are taggers. They're looking across the street admiring their last night's work. They climbed on the building across the street and tore off about half the plastic letters that announce the name of a local business—the R, S, T, A, L, and S. With other expropriated items, the kids plan to spell out their tagger nicknames and then take snapshots for posterity.

"Exactly what is a tagger?" I ask.

"Somebody who doesn't get shot," one kid says, explaining that tradition allows taggers to go into any gang territory and spray-paint names, artwork, and characters without bringing the gangbangers down on them. Taggers, whose real identities are kept secret to the nontagger world, challenge each other to graffiti duels: whoever tags the most and the best in the next two weeks is judged the winner. The loser must abandon his tagger name for another. None of this tagger graffiti, the boys explain, should be mistaken for gang markings. "We have a different style than gangbangers," one boy says, bragging. "We write fresher than they do." He points across the street to a wall of black spray-painted scribblings, none of which I can read.

"What's it say?" I ask.

"In Memory of Miner," a boy says. "Look at that M. Now see how ours are?" He points to more scribblings. "See how theirs are? We make our letters better than theys. This is a gangbanger L." He points again. "A tagger, this is how he writes an L, with loop."

"And why does it matter?" I ask.

"Because we got more style. They got a cheap style."

"And you get a reputation, get known, get some pride?"

"Yeah," says one boy.

"That's right," says another.

* * *

Fred Hill is a short man who looks like he might have been a mid-dleweight boxer in his day. He's thirty-three now, young for most men but old in the world of boxing or gangbanging. He wears a white T-shirt, tan shorts, white socks pulled up over his calves, and white sneakers. He wears a black, red, and green necklace—the colors of the *bendera*, the African American flag created generations ago by black nationalist Marcus Garvey. His face and his nose are thick, his eyes narrow, his laugh shy. He doesn't look in the least bit scary, but he is buffed in the way Ice-T is not, real muscles. He got that way in San Quentin, where he spent five years for shooting and paralyz-ing a man who had refused to give him his cut in a drug deal. That was in 1979. In those days Fred was called O.G. Snoop Dog, and as the founder of the Rolling 60s Crips gang in South Central's Cren-shaw neighborhood, he was feared and respected in the streets, where his gang sold marijuana and angel dust and fought interlopers with knives, clubs, and pistols.

While Fred was in prison crack cocaine arrived—and the money, violence, and fire-power multiplied. The Rolling 60s, born on the block where Fred Hill grew up, went national with chapters in thirty-three states and became one of the most violent gangs in the country. Two Rolling 60s gangbangers got death sentences for killing the mother, sister, and two nephews of former National Football League player Kermit Alexander, after the Alexander home was mistaken for an enemy drug house and the family was gunned down with a .30-caliber M-1 carbine.

In prison Fred learned a new philosophy and came out believing white America wants black America to kill itself off, stay divided, stay conquered. Blacks killing blacks, he came to believe, were only playing into white hands. He got a girlfriend, had a son, went straight. Today he's a paid street gang counselor. Too often he's called out to the scene of still another gang killing, sometimes of kids he knows.

"You started one of the worst gangs in America," I say as we drive over to Rolling 60s territory. "How the hell you feel now?"

"I regret it a lot," says Fred, who has a deep, raspy voice like that of radio's Wolfman Jack. "But it woulda started anyway. I didn't know it was gonna be this worse. I didn't think there'd be nine guys on death row from my street gang. It just escalated."

"How 'bout the guy you paralyzed?"

"Now I regret that I shot him. Now! After years have went by, over eleven, twelve years ago." But in the old days—following the convoluted values that so appalled filmmaker Charles Burnett as a young man—Fred figured the guy shot himself. The guy owed him money, welched on a deal, wouldn't pay.

"The guy fucked up?" I ask. "It was *his* fault?"

"Right, exactly! That's how I looked at it."

"Where are we now?"

"We're on 82nd and Avalon. This is a Blood area. These are the Swans. See on the wall over there? See where it say, 'Mainstreet Bloods, CK'? CK means Crip killer. Farther down on 70th and Avalon, it might say 'East Coast Crips, BK.'"

"Were you a bad actor as a kid?"

Fred laughs softly, gruffly. "Yeah, I was a bad actor. We was into takin' over Centinela Park in Inglewood by force." All the Crips hung out there in the early seventies. But then they all started fighting each other. "The East Side Crips stayed on the east side, and the West Side Crips stayed on the west side, and then the West Side Crips broke off into street-number gangs, into like Rolling 60s, 8-Trey, Playboy Gangsters, or School-Yard Crips. Now the Bloods defend Centinela Park and don't no Crips really go up there, not unless, say, Crips go over like with cars deep, seventy-five strong. If they go over there with guns and strong numbers, they can beat up some guys and rape some a their girls, take over their liquor stores. It's like a street riot."

Fred motions to the neighborhood around us. "This is the front 'hood of the Rolling 60s. We're just comin' out of 8-Trey Gangster neighborhood. We're on Western and Florence, the dividing line. Like ya see on the wall 'ETG.' That's 8-Trey Gangster. That's their moniker. And you might see '60K.' That's '60 Killers.' Just like in the 60s 'hood, you'll see '8-Trey Killers.'"

We arrive at Horace Mann High, where Fred went to school. To my amazement, it is a beautiful neighborhood—palm trees and blossoming shrubs, even some Beverly Hills topiary trims, clean yards, nice little Spanish-style homes, a well-kept working-class neighborhood. Fred says his mother's house is worth $135,000 today. "See this kid over here?" he asks suddenly. "He could get shot down just from wearin' khaki pants in this area. He's wearin' the wrong Crip moniker."

"Maybe he doesn't know."

"He know what area he's in! It's part of growin' up."

"Not where I'm from."

Fred nods thoughtfully. Then he shows me his arm, where "RSCG"—Rolling 60s Crip Gang—was tattooed while he was in prison. "That's their moniker," he says, adding, "This is a strong dope block right here. I done found a buddy a mine layin' dead up under there." He points between two nice little houses. Two blocks later, he says, "My little brother got shot on this block." He points out bullet holes in the walls of the nice little Spanish-style houses. "It's like a ghost town," he says, after we park the car and get out to walk the quiet, quaint, sunny street. "It's summertime, but the kids are not outside playin'." In these neighborhoods, Fred says, a person must know exactly where he is all the time, street by street.

"From the outside it looks so crazy," I say. "But from the inside it doesn't seem crazy at all, does it?"

"It's simple, simple."

"This sounds awful," I say, "but it's as if you got so little to fight over, everything becomes important."

"That's it! Everything is! That's it! A fuckin' street!" Fred pauses and his voice gets reflective. But think of all the guys in the Rolling 60s who died or went to prison in the name of defending that street, Fred says. It's like soldiers fighting an unjust war. No matter how bankrupt their cause, they will still honor each other's bravery and their dead friends will become justification and cause enough. Fred says the 8-Trey Gangsters and the Rolling 60s have had a running feud, with retaliation after retaliation, since 1979, when an 8-Trey shot a Rolling 60. But the young gangbangers today, he says, like young Hatfields and McCoys, don't even know that's why they're still fighting.

Up Central Avenue we stop at Greta's Place, a little street-side soul food restaurant with formica tables and green vinyl chairs and pictures of palm trees on the walls. We meet a teenager who's a member of a Crips gang. I'll call him James. Fred wants me to meet James because he's a kid who could go either way—go straight if he gets a couple of breaks or go deep into the gang life if he doesn't. He's not a big-time gangbanger, neither a wild gunman nor a heavy dope dealer, although he has dabbled in both. He's your average street gang member about to reach maturity, thinking about getting married, looking for a decent job—and knowing that gangbangers can have a short half-life. He's awaiting word on a job that would earn him about $1,500 a month. For that kind of money, he'd kiss gang-banging good-bye. So would a lot of other guys, he says.

Before James got booted off his school sports teams for skipping school, he was a star athlete. Everybody in the 'hood knew him and respected him. After he lost that reputation, he felt naked. A guy doesn't have to be in gang, he says, but he does need a rep. As an athlete, he could "walk alone." As just a guy, he couldn't.

"I was just drawn in hangin' round with the fellas," James says. The gang was like a social club—friends, drinks, girls. Last week, his gang went over to a friendly Crips territory and had a barbecue. The girlfriends cooked. On the Fourth of July, they always have a big picnic with a disc jockey. Somebody videotapes it so everybody can get a copy for their scrapbooks. "It's a lot more to it than just being in the gang. It's about bein' *down* with your neighborhood." It's about respect. Gangbangers don't respect "busters"—wimps, guys who let somebody bump their chair or push 'em outta the way. It's not just status. If a guy gets a buster rep, he's gonna be a mark, get beat up for fun, have his money and his coat stolen.

But just hanging around on street corners, James says, will make trouble find you. "You're a target," he says. "It's like Vietnam. Nine outta ten kids hangin' out are packed, strapped. The kids' mentality is, 'Well, if they bust on us and miss, we gonna try to shoot them back in their car. Or we try to get them before they get us.'" James, not even a particularly violent gangbanger, has at times packed .22-, .25-, and .38-caliber pistols.

Truth is, the gangbanger life is exhilarating as hell. Nobody in a gang has to go on an Outward Bound expedition or leave Yale for a foreign war to prove his manhood or to experience the exhilaration of danger. After a gang has driven past shooting, and James and his homeboys have reached for their guns, dived for the dirt, and fired back, it is an unimaginable high. "'Fuck the niggers!'" James says they holler afterward. "'You see how he fell? You see how he dropped when the bullets riddled through his body? Let's get another brew.' It makes you feel like you're somebody. Sometimes you don't have that, a lotta people showin' you a lotta respect. I ain't no straight-up ass-hole. I don't like to hurt people, but I had to sometimes. I'm tryin' to get my mind straight." For years, he just felt like "Fuck it!" He just didn't care—get shot, shoot back, go to jail, who cares? "Fuck it!"

He still feels that way sometimes, but Fred has shown him there's another way—a man can still be proud of his neighborhood, down for his buddies, and hold a job, have a girlfriend, a son. Fred, who taught him that black people are being pitted against each other to keep them down, inspired him. James remembers how inexplicably proud he felt when Fred told him that scientists believe the first humans evolved in Africa and then spread across Europe, Asia, the New World. "It just made me feel better about myself and my people." Through all the bravado, James confides, he had always believed blacks weren't as good as whites.

"Why?" I ask.

"Just look around you."

"What about selling drugs?" I ask.

"Well," he says, "that comes along with the territory." James sold crack, making about $300 a week, but he never flaunted it, never let his mother know, always kept a part-time job so he could cover up his cash purchases of nice clothes and jewelry. "Us black guys is not the ones droppin' the drugs down from the planes, ya know? We don't own any yachts, ya know? Somebody else is bringin' it over here. We're just the pass-on so they can make their money." (The conversation hushes abruptly when Greta brings lunch—baked short ribs and a choice of collard or mustard greens, candied yams, corn, okra, lima beans, rice, and black-eyed peas—for $6.65.)

I ask James, "Is a rich white person profiting from getting people addicted and fucked up any worse than a poor black person profiting from getting people addicted and fucked up?"

"He's worse."

"How are you any different?"

In a whisper, he says, "I'm not, not at all. I'm just makin' less money. But believe me, if I could get it, I would."

"If you could be a drug kingpin, you would?"

"Yeah!" James sees sixteen-year-old kids tooling around in new BMWs. "Like, it looks good!"

"You ever think of the lives they ruined for a BMW?"

"I don't look at it like that. If I see someone in a fancy car, lots a money, I'm like, 'Hey, whoopty-doopty-do!' If I don't sell it to him, somebody else will. So why can't I go ahead and do it and make me a little money? Like why not? It's America!"

"You really believe that?"

James nods yes and then gives me a lesson in the drug economy. Everybody who sells drugs doesn't end up dead or in prison, like everybody who cheats on their taxes doesn't get caught. A lot of guys sell dope until they get a stash and then go into a legit business. He says everybody knows that a lot of rap singers supported themselves and paid for their demos with drug money before they hit it big. Everybody knows men who own, say, a beeper or phone service, a liquor store, a tow truck business—all of whom got their stake selling dope. I think of something my wife's uncle Bobby told me of his bootleg liquor days in Glasgow, Kentucky: "You won't find a black in Glasgow who's got anything that somewhere along the line bootlegging didn't touch their lives. Because the people workin' weren't paid anything. It was work and be dirt poor, or be a bootlegger." True in Glasgow in 1938, true in South Central today—people without a chance will take a chance.

"So why not go big in the drug business?"

James laughs at the question. "It ain't that easy. If I could get the connections to where I could make it like that, I'm gonna jump on it. But you gotta have money to get money, ya know?" In the straight world, the impression is that anybody can be a drug dealer if he wants to be a drug dealer, but that's not true. Like the lucrative medical profession, the lucrative drug-dealing profession is highly competitive. "And the way the laws is now and with everybody tellin' on everybody," James says, "it's hard bein' a drug dealer. Ain't too many more big drug dealers." Most dealers are like James used to be—a guy with a job who deals a little on the side. "But I don't wanta go that route right now."

I ask, "Not because it's wrong but because it's risky?"

"Yeah."

"If you don't get a job will you sell drugs?"

"If I have to."

After James is gone, Fred says the kid's conflicting feelings about the thrill of the gangbanger life versus the reliable predictability of the respectable life will be with James forever, as will the upside-down values of his world. Sometimes, Fred says, even he still feels the tug of the gang life's exhilaration and profit, especially when he's pounding his head against the wall at work for $18,000 a year. After all these years! Individual conversion of one sort or another, he says, is the only way out of this place. Either find God or find a racial pride that won't let you exploit your own people. Only these roads to Damascus are powerful enough to fight what has been bred into these boys, these urban soldiers. Because once you've known the life of gangbanging for profit, it's always a temptation.

"Like Ice-T," Fred says scornfully. "When they make those damned videos and the fifteen- and sixteen-year-old kids see that shit," they don't see any antigang message. They hear the hip-hop beat, see the flashy cars, and gold chains, the women and the easy money. That's the message.

Of Ice-T's carefully cultivated stage image as a bad-ass gangbanger, Fred Hill laughs bitterly, and growls, "Ice-T was *not* no fucking gangbanger. Me and Ice-T went to Crenshaw High in the same years. I knew Ice-T! Ice-T was a pop-lock dancer. Any O.G. gangbangers you'll meet, you just mention Ice-T, they'll start laughin'. He was not a gangbanger! Him and a kid by the name a Hot Dog was in a dance group. Ice-T wasn't never no banger, never."

"Well," I say, "he was right about one thing."

"What's that?" asks the real O.G., Original Gangster.

"South Central doesn't look like America to me."

1 2

HOT COMBS, CURLING IRONS, AND DISHWATER

BAKERSFIELD, CALIFORNIA

Geri Spencer's beauty salon isn't the hippest place in Bakersfield for a black woman to get her hair done. It's tucked between the Bangkok Noy Thai Grocery Store and Pablo's Mexican restaurant on Chester Avenue, a four-lane strip that separates mostly black neighborhoods from mostly white neighborhoods about a dozen blocks south of downtown. Bakersfield is a city of 174,820 people plopped down between unforgiving mountains and desert to the east and the fertile San Joaquin Valley to the northwest. For more than a hundred years, the croplands near this south-central California city have drawn poor blacks and far more poor Hispanics looking for subsistence work, which is how Geri's family got here a half-century ago. Today, a tenth of Bakersfield is black.

Geri's salon is about the size of Floyd's barber shop on the old "Andy Griffith Show," with two hydraulic chairs on a faux-tile, wax-free vinyl floor surrounded by new rose carpeting, four space-helmet dryers posted against a white wall, a garden of plastic bottles and sprays and gels, a black counter full of curling irons and combs, a miniature silver oven in which to heat them, and two small round mirrors for when Geri swivels her women around for the final look-see. Oprah's on TV with fathers who always try to seduce their son's girlfriends, but who's watching?

"Did you think you were goin' into a big fancy place?" Geri asks pleasantly, as she deftly divides a woman's hair into small geometric patterns with a rat-tail comb and then squeezes a bead of Soft Sheen's creamy-white Optimum hair relaxer along the pathways of scalp. Geri is giving this woman a root touch-up so that her new hair will be as straight and soft as her old hair. Meanwhile, two women sit quietly under the dryers. One thumbs through the pages of *Black Passion International Hair Magazine,* filled with jazzy hair-styles that few of the middle-aged women who come to Geri these days would risk wearing. The other woman, elderly, seems to be either asleep or praying, with eyes closed, shoulders set straight, and hands folded demurely on her lap.

"No, they just said you run the best beauty shop in California," I say with mock seriousness. Geri is a short, girlish, fifty-three-year-old woman who's wearing casual red slacks and a white T-shirt emblazoned with a huge American flag. Her hair is cut in a clipper trim along the sides and back. On top, it's only a few inches long, straight and swept over from left to right, where it ends abruptly in a stark ledge. It's a dignified punk-rock look she improvised when she accidentally clipped too much off one side. Her hair is various shades of man-made reddish-blond—lighter at the ends and darker at the roots, which nicely matches her reddish Irish American/Native American/African American complexion. At my quip, Geri tosses back her head and, without missing a twist of her rat-tail comb, laughs convincingly. Clearly, she's a woman experienced at laughing at other people's jokes, funny or not.

I'm visiting Geri Spencer because my wife insisted on it. "You gotta know hair to know black people," she told me. I had no idea what she was talking about. With exasperation, my wife said, "Just go to a beauty shop." And so here I am. Along the way, somebody told me about Geri, a talkative philosopher of hair who has been fashioning heads in Bakersfield for thirty-five years. She's done stints in fine salons, as well as eight years as the convention-show stylist for Willie Morrow, the inventor of the Jheri curl, which revolutionized black hair-styles in the late seventies. Geri's husband is a Bakersfield land-use planner. With their three kids grown and through college, she can take it easy these days, working only on regular customers.

"If you were black when I was a little girl," Geri says wistfully, "you wanted to look like Shirley Temple."

"Weren't there little black girls you emulated?"

"Where'd you see 'em? They all looked like us—all raggedy, hair stickin' all over your head. Everybody wanted Shirley Temple curls." Geri was maybe five or six, but she can still remember flicking her head back and flipping those long curls with her hand. "You know how a little girl do when she get her first curl?"

"My Mama got it so straight," says a woman in the chair, "it looked like silk when she got through with it."

Geri turns serious. "Up until ten years ago, you could never sit here and talk to any a these ladies about their hair the way you are. They would not have even came to the shop if they knew you were gonna be here! They would not have answered *no questions,* and may not have came back! It was a thing we didn't want white people to know—the texture of hair we had—because we felt like we were judged on our hair texture. Even though whites were judging us by our skin, we still felt"—and she laughs sardonically—"it was our hair. People would have been very angry for telling anything about our hair to somebody white."

"Why?" I ask. "It's just hair."

"It was *kanky,*" says the woman in the chair.

"It's still *kanky!*" I say. "What changed?"

"It used to be—what do you say?—an embarrassing situation," says the woman. "Now, we don't care. Amongst you guys"—meaning whites—"we used to use the word *kanky,* but with each other we said, 'You know, ma hair sho is nappy!' And we'll still say, 'It's just like sheep's hair!'" Until about a decade ago, Geri says, black beauty parlors were even divided into individual booths so other black women in the shop couldn't see each other's hair. "You definitely didn't want white people seein' your hair, but sometimes you didn't even want black people to know what kinda hair you had: 'Oh, girl, you got *baaad* hair on your head!'"

"Why, if you all had kanky hair?"

"I don't know why," Geri says. "Just coming up as kids, you learned to hide it. Black people, like whites, came to judge each other's worthiness on the texture of their hair. We were ashamed of our hair. I'm not ashamed anymore."

"Geri!" the woman in the chair squeals in high-pitched, playful exclamation, "if I had a grade a hair like you got. . . "

"Your hair is better than mine!" Geri howls.

"No it's not!"

"Is too!"

I say, "It looks about the same to me," but I'm ignored.

"Your hair do *not* bead up on you in back! Mine's like wire."

"So use the clippers."

"I don't like shavin' it."

Geri looks at me. "Just because they don't see beads on my neck—they call 'em BBs 'cause they ball up—they say I've got good hair. *I* put chemicals on my hair."

"Girl, you don't put *no* chemicals on that neck!"

"I don't have to!"

"I know you don't! That's what I'm sayin'!"

Perhaps noticing my confusion, the sleeping or praying woman under the dryer stirs, touches the nape of her neck, and says, "We call it the 'kitchen.'"

"Why?"

"I don't know," she says, pausing with perfect comedic hesitation, "maybe because it always needs to be cleaned up."

And the women laugh wildly.

This new, casual, confident attitude about hair first burst on the scene in the sixties when the Afro and the political philosophy of Black Power purged much of the embarrassment that these women say they felt about having hair that wasn't like white folks'. "The Afro was the best thing that ever happened to us," says Geri. "It gave

us pride." The technical breakthroughs of the chemists at Soft Sheen
and other black hair-care product companies accelerated the change,
because they allowed blacks to straighten and soften their hair and
easily keep it that way, freeing them to wear their hair any way they
wanted. Today black hair-style has become mostly devoid of political
symbolism.

But before effective, safe, and quick chemical straighteners, a
black woman who wanted to wear her hair straight had to oil it with,
say, Vaseline, lanolin, lard, or even greasy dishwater and then laboriously comb it from the roots up with a straightening hot comb, which
had itself been a technical breakthrough in black hair care in 1905.
The meeting of oil and hot comb often resulted in a putrid smell, plus
too much hot combing could damage the hair. Even then, if a woman
wanted to keep the look, she couldn't take a shower, go swimming,
get caught in a rainstorm, perspire, or live in a humid climate or it
would mat up: "Goin' back home," they called it. So men often wore
their hair greased flat like Nat King Cole. Women wore their hair
similarly or in short, tightly crimped curls put in after hot-comb
straightening, which would last two weeks, max.

"Wasn't your hair awfully greasy?" I ask.

"Really!" Geri screams, laughing. "When they said, 'Fried, dyed,
and laid ta the side,' that's what it was—*fried!*"

"Wasn't this all a pain in the ass?" I ask.

"Yeah," Geri says, "I don't know why God did that to us."

I say, "As punishment for looking so young so long?"

Says the woman in the chair: "I'd a rather had straight hair,"
which evokes another round of cackling laughter from the women.

Naturally it was more than hair. One of Geri's brothers and her
sister had light skin and straight hair, taking more strongly after the
Native American and Irish blood in the family. When the kids were
young, the family lived outside Bakersfield in rural Edison. Few
blacks lived in the area, and the children went to school with mostly
white kids. Geri remembers that it was usually the light-skinned
blacks that the white teachers and children seemed to like best. Later
she realized that light-skinned blacks usually married only light-
skinned blacks and that they always seemed to get ahead faster, that
whites always seemed to favor them. Light-skinned blacks often
seemed to accept, even glory in, the white premise that they were better than dark-skinned blacks.

But it wasn't only straight hair or light skin that blacks resented, Geri says, but the practical advantages these qualities symbolized. For instance, my own wife's family in Burkesville, Kentucky, and Mollie Stevenson's family in Houston, Texas, both got a leg up in the world when the black side of their family married into white affluence. The bonds no doubt lightened the families' skin, but they also heavied up their equity. Black resentment of blacks with light skin ran deep, and when Geri's family moved to the segregated Mayflower neighborhood in southeast Bakersfield, her light-skinned brother and sister took the grief. Black kids even held down her brother at knife-point and cut off his curly hair.

"Why do you wear your hair straight?" I ask one of Geri's customers, a manager in a large Bakersfield business.

"It's just easier," she says.

Geri knows better and she elaborates. "On a lot of jobs straight hair still makes whites accept you more."

Customer: "Well, you do have to fit in your executive environment. It's just conforming to the business look."

Me: "The business look couldn't be a nice tight curl?"

Customer: "No, they'd think I was a rebel."

Me: "That's dumb."

Customer: "That's life."

Geri: "You always have to explain yourself when you're black."

Customer: "They'd say, 'Why'd you wear your hair like that?'"

Geri: "White people watch everything you do when you work with 'em. They say, 'Oh, you got *another* new dress?'"

Customer: "Or they say, 'Oh, those colors look so good on *you,* but I couldn't wear that.' They're strange!" Of her straightened hair, she says, "This is just one less problem." As she rises to leave, she whispers, almost to herself, "Strange people."

"You know why I wear my hair short?" Geri asks. "I think I'm being rebellious." She chuckles. "Every black woman is still concerned about wanting long hair. I was just as bad. But our little girls feel the thing that makes them beautiful is havin' long hair. And I think we are beautiful without it."

"It's gone too far?"

"I think so. It's almost like your hair is a designer label. Bakersfield is probably like a lot of other places where black people have moved up and moved out, and they are becoming just as prejudiced toward blacks as any white person. They think being a role model is standing up and saying, 'Well, I made it. You can make it.' They get in their Mercedeses and go back across town."

"You've seen this?"

"I observe it all the time. People are getting so caught up in materialism, getting ahead, and being recognized that they judge you by where you live, what you drive, and what you wear. It's not the color of your skin. It's money, education, jobs."

I ask, "Just like white people?"

The philosopher of hair nods and sadly says, "Yes."

Before I leave town I'd like to see the old Mayflower neighborhood, Bakersfield's historic black neighborhood where Geri and just about every other black in the city grew up until a few decades ago. Blacks first came to Bakersfield to work the cotton fields, and by the 1920s they were segregated outside town on Cottonwood Road. Although people lived in boxcars and lean-tos and shanties, the Mayflower neighborhood had grown to 6,200 people by 1950, when the community became part of the city, and bus, sewer, and water lines were finally extended. As with other black communities once made whole by segregation, the advent of open housing led affluent blacks to spread out across the city, and today Mayflower is a poor neighborhood, nearly half Hispanic. Geri's brother Larry Floyd, who has quietly sat listening in her shop during my visit or gone about sweeping the floor, offers to show me Mayflower.

Larry's a small, frail, forty-four-year-old man in an ill-fitting suit and tie. His shirt is too big at the collar and his neck seems to disappear into it. He says he's living in abandoned houses, storing his few belongings in the trunks of junked cars, mooching change from strangers on the street, saving enough to rent a room and a bath every few days. He rolls his own cigarettes from Buglar tobacco, buys a pack of Camels when he can afford it. There's no spirit left in his voice. "I'm homeless," he says. "I'm a bum." Larry figures he's spent ten years of his adulthood in prison for drugs, burglaries, rubber checks, petty crimes—San Quentin, Soledad, Tracy. He's been out three years now. "I'm retired. That's the reason I'm on the streets now. Before I would do somethin' to make some money illegally. I also used to make money sellin' drugs, but I don't wanta do it. I'm tired of it. I don't have too many years left, and I don't wanta spend those locked up." He says Geri and the family have helped him again and again, but now he's on his own. "I just got too many problems. I don't blame 'em."

Larry's most striking feature, the one that has shaped his life, is that he is a black man who looks white. Not just light-skinned, but absolutely European—his nose, cheekbones, lips, and hair, which is combed back straight and curling over his collar. All his life, he has been mistaken for white by both blacks and whites. It was rough coming up, he says, but not out in rural white Edison, where Geri felt out of place. No, Larry loved it out there. "I had a little white girl-friend. Her name was Susan."

"Did she know you were black?"

"I don't know."

It's remarkable how much alike poor neighborhoods look every-where in America: the concrete main drag with gas stations, liquor stores, black wire-mesh windows, gaudily painted little churches identified with hand-scratched signs, the de rigueur half-built brick church of glorious ambitions that's been under construction for ten years. Mayflower has all these generic landmarks, plus Louie's Bail-bonds and the Cotton Club. On its side streets, the American pattern continues, with nice, well-kept little homes demarcated by dumps and boarded-up hulks. Mayflower does have one of the cleanest-looking public housing projects I've seen anywhere, and a beautiful park. But the whole neighborhood is marred with gang markings. The Los Angeles Crips have come strong into Bakersfield—and, nat-urally, Mayflower, with so many poor blacks, is its main breeding ground. The neighborhood is divided among the East Side, West Side, Spoonie G, and Country Boy Crips, whose graffiti abound. Even a big-time Rolling 60s crack distributor was arrested in Bakersfield a few years ago, although he didn't live in Mayflower but in a well-to-do apartment complex.

"They sell heroin right over there," Larry says, pointing to an alley where Hispanic men are hanging out. "The Mexicans sell heroin, the blacks sell rocks, crack. You want speed or weed or LSD, you go to the whites." We weave around through Mayflower's side streets until Larry stops me in front of a nice house. "My father built this house," he says. His father picked cotton, worked on nearby ranches, washed city trucks—anything for an honest buck. As the payoff, he owned what was then one of the nicest homes in

Mayflower. A huge evergreen tree today consumes the front yard, and Larry says, "We planted that tree as a baby tree."

"The one with the sign: 'Warning: Security Dog'?"

"Yeah."

As a boy, Larry was called "white paddy" by Mayflower's black kids. Once, when he ran into his beautiful new home from a fight, his father made him go outside and face it. He won that fight, but lost many others. His life has gone on like this—back and forth, trapped between the worst in the American psyche long after the myth of the tragic mulatto is supposed to have become a historical footnote. As one of Bakersfield's "original hippies" in the sixties, Larry had a lot of white, hippie, love-one-another-right-now friends. Eventually he discovered they called him "nigger Larry" behind his back. In prison, where violent racism is an inmate's code of life, Larry aligned himself with Hispanic prison gangs because neither white nor black really accepted him.

"See, my sister and all them, they don't understand how I feel," he says without emotion. "They don't understand what I been through. They been knowin' me all my life, right? And I'm one a them. And they think everybody else looks at me the same way as they look at me. But everybody else don't. If I'm around whites and they don't know me, they'll be talkin' 'bout 'nigger this, nigger that.' I have walked past cops and heard 'em say, 'Yeah, I guess I'll go kill me some niggers tonight.' 'Cause they think I'm one a them, white. I hear things blacks wouldn't hear. I know that certain whites who they think is their friends is not. They say things in front of me they won't say in front of them. And they think other blacks look at me as black. But it's not the case. If they don't know me, I'll be white to them. Blacks and whites both think the same in a way. They both prejudiced. They both bigots.

"And blacks are prejudiced against themselves. They don't like blacks of different colors"—high-yeller, light-skinned-with-good-hair, yellow, tan, brown-skinned, black, black-black. "I just got tired of explaining what I am all the time. I used to fight a lot about it with black and white. I just got tired a fightin'. I used to say something when I heard derogatory remarks about whites. I don't say nothin' no more. And if a black thinks I'm white, I don't say I'm black. I'm what-ever you want me to be."

We are done with my tour and for his time I slip Larry a $10 bill and buy us both hamburgers at Andre's drive-in, where we eat out-side at a picnic table under a large shade tree. I say, "You see the worst, lowest, meanest, racist side of everybody, don't you?"

"Yeah, I do. It has affected me. I get depressed."

1 3

TWO MEN'S DREAM IN THE DESERT

ALLENSWORTH, CALIFORNIA

The women in Geri's Beauty Parlor knew my next destination. They had visited Allensworth during its twice-a-year festivals, when thousands of black people from all across California pour into the little Lower Sonoran Desert town to celebrate the memory of one of America's most ambitious all-black towns. They had talked of their visits with emotion, about how beautiful the town is, how good they felt walking its streets.

Allensworth was the dream of Colonel Allen Allensworth— escaped slave, Union Army soldier, restaurateur, Baptist preacher, chaplain to a regiment of Buffalo Soldiers for twenty years, the highest-ranking black in the U.S. military at his retirement in 1906. He was an accomplished man whose final dream, like that of other blacks of his era, was to create a thriving all-black town, where the skill, brains, ambition, and respectability of blacks could be paraded, while they lived in dignity outside the indignities of the white world. Allensworth, which sits midway between L.A. and San Francisco, was virtually gone in 1969 when Cornelius Ed Pope stopped by to see what had become of the town where he had lived as a boy. From his visit grew Allensworth State Historic Park, the only park of its kind in America.

From the road map, I can't tell how to get to Allensworth off the highway, so I stop at a little roadside restaurant, the kind for truckers and farmers. At the coffee counter sit two old white men with vein-laced faces—one wears a Ford cap and the other a dressier hat made of straw. When I ask them the quickest way to Allensworth, malevolent smiles suddenly stain their faces.

"You got a load a watermelons?" Ford-cap asks.

They chuckle.

"You a reverend?" straw-hat asks.

"Everybody goes through here's a reverend," says Ford-cap. "You know, they're all preachers when they need to be."

They chuckle again.

"Better be outta there by dark," says straw-hat.

"You a federal agent?" asks Ford-hat with widening eyes.

"Just passing through."

"He's a federal agent," says Ford-hat.

Straw-hat agrees: "You're a federal agent."

"So how do I get there?"

Through grape orchards and forests of pecan trees planted in fields of black-eyed peas, through seas of purple-flowering cotton and oceans of desert scrub, past mountains of hay stacked as tall as a barn, and the purple, pink, and green shacks of poor Hispanic families, the two-laner finally arrives at Allensworth, which is just to the west of the railroad tracks that were once the town's lifeblood. The place is like the Twilight Zone. On forty-two acres of flat sand and clay grassland sit a dozen new clapboard buildings painted gray, green, tan, brown, white—the schoolhouse, the library, Singleton's General Store & Post Office, Grosse's Drugstore, Dodson's Restaurant, Colonel Allensworth's house. The streets are named after the famous African Americans Sojourner Truth, Frederick Douglass, and Paul Laurence Dunbar and after the author of *Uncle Tom's Cabin*, Harriet Beecher Stowe.

The Visitor's Center is open and the artifacts of Allensworth are on display—photographs, hand tools, a bent fork, a corroded spoon, an eighth of an ounce of Deux Vies perfume. I wander around the ghost town for an hour but find no people. Near the schoolhouse, two lawn sprinklers have exercised themselves into a small lake, a blunt-nosed leopard lizard runs for cover, and four black-shouldered kites flush and flutter from sagebrush as I walk past.

But no people.

That night, I track down Cornelius Ed Pope, and the next morning we meet at Allensworth, where one lonely carload of campers is packing up after having stayed the night. Ed is a tall, sturdy, intense man, sixty-one years old, with short dark hair and a gray-flecked mustache and goatee. He smokes Pall Malls.

Without Pope, Allensworth would not be. He was a draftsman for the state twenty-two years ago when he realized that in all of California's state park historical system there was only one reference to blacks: three miners who in frontier days turned to cannibalism rather than starve to death. The neglect was an insult. To help settle California, blacks had fought every inch of the way, because "free state" California was like the rest of America: blacks were denied the vote and the right to testify in court. Real estate covenants restricted black property ownership. Schools, hotels, restaurants, and swimming pools were often segregated, and white labor unions excluded blacks from membership.

Allensworth became Ed Pope's mission. Black politicians pulled together, pushed through the plan, and by 1976 the land was bought and the park launched. At the time, four hundred thousand people a year were expected to pass through Allensworth. But over the years, state support flagged. Today, only an estimated twelve thousand people visit Allensworth each year, about half of them during its two annual festivals. The park has no full-time ranger assigned to it. The maintenance equipment has been reassigned to other parks. The campground has no electricity. Although personal items in the home of Colonel Allensworth are irreplaceable, the park has no security. Vandal graffiti has been appearing recently. This morning, "Allens Boyz" and "Joe Freak" are spray-painted on the wall of the schoolhouse. But Ed Pope continues his mission. A few months ago, he retired from his job in Sacramento and moved near Allensworth.

"It's good work and it needs to be done," he says in a slow, deep voice as we head out into the ninety-five-degree heat, among the warbling meadowlarks and cavorting monarch butterflies, to walk the deserted streets of Allensworth. "There's too much here to let it go to waste like this," says Ed. "But we're on the verge. I see it popping wide open, living history like at Colonial Williamsburg. Once we get the hotel open in October—it's a humdinger—there's no reason it shouldn't take off. I'm lookin' for thousands and thousands of people comin' in over those railroad tracks, and they'll all leave out feelin' a little better."

Ed Pope would know about that. He was an eight-year-old boy when his parents, migrant crop workers, found their way to Allensworth during the Depression. By then, the great dream of Colonel Allensworth was dead. From its founding in 1908 until 1914 skilled craftsmen, farmers, businessmen, and laborers from across America had heeded the colonel's call, pulled up roots, and moved to Allensworth. For those years, it thrived. The first black justice of the peace and constable in the state of California were elected in Allensworth. The colonel had picked the spot because it had plentiful water and was a grain transfer point on the Atchison, Topeka and Santa Fe Railroad. The population jumped to a thousand overnight.

Black masons and carpenters won building contracts in nearby towns, and black farmers grew grain, cotton, and sugar beets and raised dairy cattle. Stores and businesses, a bakery, a barber shop, and a newspaper appeared. A state-of-the art school opened and a public library filled with books so quickly that there were calls for investigations about what all those black folks were reading out there. The town had debating societies, classical concerts, and stage plays. Colonel Allensworth, like Booker T. Washington, saw black equality coming through education and independent black achievement. He immediately drew up plans for a Tuskegee Institute of the West and went to the California legislature for funding. But powerful blacks in Los Angeles opposed the colonel's school because it smacked of segregated education, which they had fought bitterly.

During one week in 1914, Colonel Allensworth was killed in a motorcycle accident and the legislature killed his school. Within a decade a new railroad transfer depot was built in nearby Alpaugh, and the deep artesian wells that had watered Allensworth began to go dry. Then came the Depression. By the time Ed Pope's family arrived in 1938, Allensworth was doomed. But Ed Pope didn't know that.

This morning we enter a hip-roofed, bell-towered Allensworth schoolhouse that's almost exactly as it was when Ed Pope first entered it as a boy. "This is the first school I ever went to regularly," he says. As the child of migrant workers who harvested cotton, peaches, tomatoes, onions, and oranges, Ed had fought his way in and out of white schools all over the San Joaquin Valley. "We were poor. We were defenseless. It was kind of a bummer." But in Allensworth his family lived in a house instead of a tent, and he saw a black teacher for the first time in his life. Instead of pencils, the school used inkwells and fountain pens. And he didn't have to fight. The kids welcomed him. "I just loved it," he says, gesturing around the huge one-room school, his voice cracking hard against the wooden floors, walls, and ceiling. The old desks are lined in sentry rows, copies of the *Farm Life Reader* atop each, the teacher's Bible is open to the "Song of Solomon," and fountain pens and inkwells sit on every desk.

"This is where I started learnin'," Ed says. "I said, 'Hey, a fella can actually learn somethin' in one a these bad boys.' I felt protected." Ed stayed in Allensworth only three years, but those three years were enough. He left out "feelin' better." Later, in high school when a white teacher told him, "You're wastin' your time kid 'cause there's no black draftsmen," Ed Pope ignored him.

He picks up an inkwell off a desk and turns it slowly in his hands. "I've tried to see that the room is set up just the way it was." At the door, Ed stops, tugs the school's bell rope, and three strong gongs cry out: **RIIING. RIIING. RIIING.** "It's hard to pull," he says. "You gotta get it swingin' and catch the swing comin' back." On the third try, I catch the swing comin' back: **RIIING.** "You got it!" he hollers. "You got it!"

We walk the pale cracked ground for a couple more hours— through the drugstore, library, post office—and Ed shares his dream for Allensworth. The seven-room hotel and restaurant and the Amtrak station are done deals. But he wants to see people living in the stores and running them as tourist concessions, a small field of cotton, and an annual cotton-picking contest so kids can know what it was like, the newspaper publishing, twenty houses with people living in them and working in the town, lines with clothes drying and chimneys with smoke rising, the livery stable housing seven or eight horses, an air-conditioned tour bus, the cemetery a few miles away cleaned up and on the tour, a full-service campground, a Holiday Inn, golf course, and clubhouse just outside the town like at other state parks, the library filled with books, and a church up and running. "The preacher will preach and the choir will sing," Ed says, "and give 'em a good blast of gospel!"

At the house of Colonel Allensworth, Ed unlocks the door and stands back for me to enter the meticulously reconstructed home. "My God, it's beautiful!" I say.

"Isn't it a dream?" he says. As a boy, Ed Pope and his family actually lived in Colonel Allensworth's real house, which was a shambles by then. Ed loves this part of the tour. "This little chair sitting back here in the corner, that was Colonel Allensworth's chair," he says.

"All the pictures are authentic to the house. Mrs. Allensworth was an accomplished pianist and she had pictures of Beethoven and Mozart. That was her dish. That's a picture of Colonel Allensworth's daughter. That's Colonel Allensworth in the cavalry. That's the little speller his slave master's son taught him to read out of. These are letters from him to President Grover Cleveland." He stops and reaches into a shadowed corner and pulls out a gold-plated walking cane and hands it to me. "I always tell everybody, 'This was Colonel Allensworth's cane. It was his actual cane.'" Ed carefully takes it back. "Let me just set it back down there." Then he says something he probably understands better than even he knows: "Colonel Allensworth could take a man who did not read or write and had very little self-esteem and lift him right up and get him off and on his way."

And that, I now realize, is what Allensworth—and Nicodemus, Kansas, and Boley, Oklahoma, and all the dozens of turn-of-the-century black towns—did for Ed Pope and thousands of other Ed Popes long forgotten. This is not *black* history. It is human history—a testimony of perseverance, pride, dignity, strength, resilience. Allensworth should be completed. And the two old white men with vein-laced faces in the roadside restaurant? Tie them up, gag them, and make them take Ed Pope's tour.

"It looks like it's dead," Ed tells me through the open window of my car as I'm driving away. "But I don't see it as being dead." He is hollering now. "I see it as being *alive!* THIS BAD BOY'S JUST ABOUT READY TO POP!" And in my rear-view mirror, I can see Ed Pope in the bright sun smoking his Pall Mall, the only person in Allensworth, a town he understands in a way few others can.

1 4

THE FIRST BLACK LADY OF BASEBALL

OAKLAND, CALIFORNIA

I know I'm getting close to Oakland, because I can finally get something other than top pop 40 on the radio. And at the end of the FM
dial I find Johnnie Johnson, the former piano player for Chuck
Berry—the black great-granddaddy of rock 'n' roll—playing his new
album, "Johnnie B. Bad." Oakland is what you might call the
Allensworth of today: a modern black town. Like Washington, D.C.,
or Detroit, it's got all the woes that poor people bring to a city—
poverty, drugs, and crime—but it also has Aissatoui Ayola Vernita's
one-of-a-kind soul food art collection; African American poet, novelist, and playwright Ishmael Reed; and a cadre of well-to-do blacks,
including the Oakland A's Sharon Richardson Jones, the first black
female front office executive in professional baseball.

It's a perfect day to watch the world champion Oakland A's play
ball—sunny, but not too hot at seventy-nine degrees. And I've got a
seat along the third-base line, in the shade of the upper deck, where I
plan to watch the A's play the Seattle Mariners, eat a couple of hot
dogs, and drink a beer while forty-seven-year-old Sharon Jones talks
about being the first black lady of baseball. The buzz in the stands is
that Oakland rookie Scott Brosius, in his first major league game, is
playing right field for José Canseco, the five-million-dollar man
who's out with a stiff back. Sharon—a large, pretty woman with short
softened hair and a funky purple and turquoise jacket—and I are
barely in our seats when Brosius wallops a hanging curve down the
left-field line for a double in his first-ever big league at bat, knocking
lead-off hitter Willie Wilson from first to third.

"It's nice to see *real* grass on a ball field," I say.

Sharon laughs. "It's a spiritual experience to watch how they
groom it." When Sharon Jones began working for the A's eleven
years ago, everything from grooming the grass to signal calling to
batting averages was new to her. The only time she'd ever been in a
baseball park was decades ago when she and a girlfriend came to the
Oakland/Alameda County Coliseum on "hot-pants" day. Any

woman in short-shorts accompanied by a paying male got in free, which Sharon did. She was mortified to learn that she and all the free-loaders had to strut their stuff around the field during the seventh-inning stretch. Her only other baseball story comes from her childhood, when she was growing up in nearby Berkeley. One day, everybody on Sharon's street was outside waiting for somebody named Jackie Robinson to visit one of their neighbors. Little Sharon, never a shrinking violet, walked up and knocked on the door and asked Jackie Robinson who in the world he was that everybody was so excited. Robinson invited her in, treated her to ice cream, and explained that he was the first black man ever to play in the white major leagues, that's who.

"I just remember his hands were big like my father's," Sharon says, as the crowd roars its approval when Dave Henderson grounds out to second and Willie Wilson scores from third. "Before the A's, those were my only two baseball stories." Sharon graduated from Mills College and worked as an assistant to a dean at the Wharton School of Business while her husband, a sociologist, taught at the University of Pennsylvania. They returned home to the Bay Area and Sharon worked as an assistant to the Oakland Symphony's Calvin Simmons, the first black maestro of a major American orchestra. Sharon also volunteered her time to a half-dozen civic causes, and over the years she came to know everybody in Oakland's black power structure. So when the owners of San Francisco's Levi Strauss fortune bought the A's, Sharon Jones knocked on another door and convinced them that as white outsiders they needed her to be their eyes and ears in Oakland.

"I had no idea I was the only black female executive, the only black anything," she says. That was not how Sharon thought about herself. She grew up in mostly white Berkeley, went to school with whites, and had a lot of white friends. Because the University of California is in Berkeley, the city has always been ragingly liberal-to- radical, and even in the fifties it was common to see black and white couples on the streets. Sharon's mother was a secretary at the university and she was accorded considerable status in the black community as a result. Sharon's father was a union longshoreman at a time when few blacks held such jobs, and the family owned its own house and bought a new car every year. Four of Sharon's seven brothers were able to inherit their father's union "book" and snare good-paying jobs themselves. As ever, power and opportunity bred power and opportunity.

"I always wanted to be where decisions are made," Sharon says. "I wanted to see *how* they're made. I think I have learned some things black people were not allowed to learn, because they were not allowed to be that close to power. When Billy Martin got fired, I was there, a fly on the wall. It's very exciting to be an African American woman. There are lots of challenges that other people don't face at all. I think that African American people should stop comparing themselves to whites and just say, 'This is me, this is my culture, this is what I bring to the table. I accept myself. I embrace myself.' It's very freeing. I think a lot of us are being bogged down by how we perceive white people perceiving us. To me, that's not important."

"How do blacks perceive whites perceiving them?"

"They feel they're not gonna get a fair break. I think they feel they're being judged all the time in a negative way."

"*Are* they being judged that way?"

"Sure, but I'm not gonna let that paralyze me with any kind of fear. I'm gonna continue to set goals and achieve those goals and not give a damn what anybody thinks, white or black." Of course, racism and sexism are real. Whenever Sharon travels, people always assume she's an entertainer, a teacher, or a stewardess. And in her affluent, predominantly white neighborhood recently, her teenage son was running to catch a bus and the police stopped him. When Sharon recently asked a woman if she could please make an emergency call on the pay phone the woman was guarding, the woman said, "Look, nigger, I'm using this phone."

"I just don't think we have to focus our entire lives around racism," Sharon says. "Otherwise, why bother to get up in the morning? We've got to see ourselves making major contributions to the world and be the best person we can be. I think some black people— and people in general—are often limited by themselves. They're not really setting goals for themselves because they think there's no need, somebody's gonna be there to stick their foot out or white people are not gonna allow them a chance. Blacks have a lot of preconceived notions about whites—that they're not gonna get a fair break at anything. That they don't want to live next door to them or marry their daughters. And there's a million others. This limits their power to make creative choices and to think big. I mean, I'm black and I have a whole black family and a black network, and I see what they're doing and I see what they're *not* doing. I don't think people are living up to their full potential. I see people who are satisfied on jobs they've been on for twenty years, and they're still not close to the power and they're very comfortable with doing nothing.

"They feel racism and say, 'Why try?' I think this is just as real today as it was on the plantation. I think it's all in the manner of how we chose to see it. Racism hasn't gone away. But I just don't think that everything we do should be centered around what we *think* we'll be allowed to do."

"But the A's wouldn't have hired you in 1930."

"But with my personality, I would have tried. Sojourner Truth met with the president when women couldn't vote. Some people just see themselves as losers. I mean, they've had losing experiences. Every white person they see is an authority figure—policemen, social workers, even teachers. They have to put all those bogeymen in the closet and release their creativity."

Sharon, a great success in black Oakland, believes that growing up among whites helped her a great deal because she was never afraid of them, nor did she wonder if she was really as smart or as good as they were. Whites never seemed mysterious or superhuman to her. Sharon found her confidence living among whites, whereas Spike Lee found his confidence living among blacks. Obviously, there's no one route.

I ask, "Do you ever get angry at blacks and think, 'Get it together and don't be so sorry?'"

"Hmmmm." There is a long pause. "I probably do. I don't feel it's all black people's fault. But on the other hand, I think maybe they should get rid of this excuse-itis. I'm tired a hearin' this stuff about 'why I didn't succeed.' The rod of our deliverance is in our own hand. We've got to grab the mike, make some plans."

Sharon must go back to work, but I stick around for the rest of the game. It's a 6–1 rout for Oakland, but the joy of the afternoon is that rookie Scott Brosius comes up a second time and smacks a line-drive homer into the right-field bleachers—only the third rookie in Oakland history to hit a homer in his first major league game. The kid nearly flies around the bases, pumping his fist in the air as he rounds second.

It's a day of rare achievement for Scott Brosius. And it has been a lifetime of rare achievement for Sharon Richardson Jones. I've learned enough by now to know that plenty of blacks would think she has lost touch with hardship, that her criticism of black America is, well, white. But I've also learned enough to know that plenty of blacks would agree with her. Sharon Jones is saying candidly what blacks have told me again and again, often in secretive whispers: racism still rages, but it is for too many blacks also an excuse. Blacks don't shout this from the housetops for fear it will fuel white racism. But quietly, among themselves, many believe it.

As a white man I'm not supposed to know that.

1 5

HONORING THE BONES OF SHAME

O A K L A N D ' S   I N N E R   H A R B O R

Aissatoui Ayola Vernita taught me this: When we say somebody is living "high on the hog," we are paying homage to the eating traditions of African Americans, who during slavery believed it was a great treat to get their hands on a piece of pork cut from anywhere on the pig's body above its feet. Vernita, the name by which she prefers to be called, is a "soul food" artist—probably the only one in America—and it's hard to imagine how her artwork can be anywhere near as beautiful as I've been told it is. I mean, art made from chicken and catfish bones, collard greens and watermelon rinds, sweet potatoes, pig ears, and sassafras roots? Out of curiosity, I look for her Ebony Museum of Art along Oakland's waterfront.

Vernita is a short forty-nine-year-old woman with a slow, deliberate way of speaking and the hint of, perhaps, a West Indian accent. She wears a green sack shirt decorated with black and rose flowers, which was designed by a friend. An African rope belt in black, gold, and green is tied around her waist. She wears a necklace of malachite and silver and brass-and-ivory earrings, all of which she made herself. On her wrists jangle twelve bracelets from all over the African continent. Vernita is a collector, and some of her five thousand

African pieces date back three thousand years—everything from a bathing bowl for the child of a Senufo chief to handwoven Kuba fabric to animistic sculptures by the Makonde to a Bambara chieftain's mask. Her modern pieces include seven hundred black dolls and thousands of "degradation" memorabilia—ashtrays, ads, product wrappers, and statues that portray American blacks as happy and fat-lipped. But it's her soul food art that is unique.

"I wanted to bring the old eating habits of African Americans out of the closet," Vernita says, as she walks me from her gallery's African room over to her soul food room. "For so long, we were ashamed of the foods we ate. We must remember them with pride." To my amazement, the tiny soul food room is filled with designs of stunning beauty. From the remains of remains, Vernita has crafted necklaces, bracelets, earrings, a rocking chair, a mourner's bench, a bone quilt, statues, and dioramas. All of them made from dried bones, vegetables, herbs, and roots that African Americans ate in the time of slavery. They've been dried, cured, sprayed with acrylic, and painted black, green, red, turquoise, every imaginable color. They are no longer garbage, but whatever it was that Vernita saw in her mind's eye: a fatback wall-hanging reminiscent of a Picasso painting (reminding us that Picasso was profoundly influenced by African art), a necklace of chicken feet that recalls a voodoo priest's adornments, a cabin and front porch of pork ribs and collard leaves that are dead ringers for the wooden shacks of the rural South.

"You know what this is?" Vernita asks in her singsong voice, as she gently touches a structure the size of a Lincoln-log house.

"Hmmm," I say, buying time as I peer into the hut, which is painted inside with tiny fish and flowers. "An outhouse?"

"Right!" Vernita sings, elated at my lucky guess. "It's made of chitlins and collard greens."

I straighten up and ask, "Where are you from anyway?"

"My parents were West Indian, but I was born in Arkansas, Foreman, next to Texarkana."

"Foreman, Arkansas? Little River County? I was there!"

"In Foreman?"

"To talk to an old man about a lynching in 1899."

Vernita is silent for a moment. "I remember when I was a kid and the river would overflow and we'd say, 'Look at that red mud!'"

"Red River, it had just flooded—red mud everywhere!"

She cocks her head and raises a brow: "This is eerie."

It turns out that Vernita was a brilliant little girl and by the time she was twelve her mother wanted her out of racist Foreman, where the family owned twenty acres of tobacco land and lived pretty well. But the atmosphere was oppressive and the black schools were awful. Vernita, like so many others separated from their families to get away from the South, was shipped to an aunt in Kansas City. She married a military man and they lived overseas for many years. They settled in Oakland in 1967 and Vernita finished college, collected art-work, and made jewelry. She has no idea where she got the idea for soul food art. "I think it might have been something from the beyond, from a spiritual power," she says, quite seriously. Vernita thus became fascinated with the history of African American foods.

White food critics were just beginning to discover "soul food" in the late sixties, she says, but many blacks, particularly successful blacks, were ashamed of it, embarrassed to eat catfish, chitterlings, or watermelon. But Vernita came to see the history of African American foods as symbolic of the black struggle to find not only sustenance, but dignity. Slaves had little time to grow gardens so they became experts at foraging the wilds for dandelion, watercress, pepper grass, and poke salads. Whites fancied turnip roots, so blacks turned the discarded leaves—the greens—into a mainstay. Slave masters boiled the small intestines of hogs to make soap and passed the cooked guts on to their slaves. Chitlins became a delicacy. Blacks weren't allowed to hunt with guns, so black children learned to run down rabbits on foot, men trapped raccoons and possum, and everybody kept an eye out for turtles when the creeks ran low. What justice it was, Vernita came to believe, that slave masters and their families often suffered from scurvy and the joint-aching pain caused by trichinosis, while slaves—filled with turnip greens high in vitamins C and A and eating low on the hog away from deadly larvae—rarely suffered from these diseases.

Joyfully, Vernita says, "People are always saying, 'I didn't realize the food I eat could be so beautiful.'"

I think of the joke I heard in Epes, Alabama, about the blacks who died, went to hell, and then beat the devil by air conditioning the place. I think of the words of John Oliver, a working black man quoted in the book *Drylongso* by black anthropologist John Langston Gwaltney, a man I'll be visiting in a few days. The day Gwaltney interviewed John Oliver, he served rabbit in sassafras gravy, turnips, and salt pork for dinner. With glee, he said of white folks, "They keep thinning this soup and we keep coming up with chicken fricassee!" If the defeatism Sharon Richardson Jones talks about runs deep in African America, so does the resilience of the John Olivers. This, Vernita knows.

"You made something out of nothing," I say, and the laughing woman turns serious, relieved that I have gotten the point.

"That's the whole thing," she says. "The whole thing."

1 6

THE GUMBO THAT IS AMERICA

NORTH OAKLAND, CALIFORNIA

For months, I've been excited about visiting Ishmael Reed. It's the kind of excitement that I'd guess other people feel about meeting, oh, maybe an old baseball idol. Twenty-some years ago, I heard Ishmael Reed recite his poetry at little Blackburn College. Why he was there, I have no idea. At that time, he'd published only his first two novels, *The Free-Lance Pall Bearers* and *Yellow Back Radio Broke-Down*. But a few years later his weird, satiric, pseudohistorical novel *Mumbo Jumbo* would be nominated for the National Book Award, and Ishmael Reed would be compared with Richard Wright, Gabriel García Márquez, and Mark Twain. I don't remember a word he said two decades ago, but I've never lost the image of the goateed, Afro-coifed, iconoclastic poet and author whose message of Black Power was quite a shock to kids in the Illinois sticks. When I later read his poem, "Visit to a Small College," I knew he could have been talking about Blackburn:

> *you invited me here but*
> *don't have my books on your*
> *list, or in your*
> *bookstore.*

Indelibly touched with curiosity about the man, I haphazardly followed the burgeoning body of his work over the years—eight novels, several collections of poetry, two collections of essays. In *Mumbo Jumbo,* one of Reed's characters says, "Why must you mix poetry with concrete events?" That's exactly what Ishmael Reed does, blending the jazz age of the 1920s with voodoo and plots by the great men of American civilization—guys in the Masons—to stomp out the dangerously nonrational, emotional, mystical, African influences emerging in the guise of jazz. Or blending the Civil War, Abraham Lincoln, and an oversexed Harriet Beecher Stowe into the novel of Southern debauchery and self-delusion, *Flight to Canada.* A person has to suspend a lot of disbelief to be taken for a ride in one of Reed's novels, but the payoff is always in his point that the world was not necessarily constructed the way European Americans have reconstructed it.

Ishmael Reed forever reminds us of the two-way street that is culture. Igor Stravinsky composing Ragtime. George Gershwin and Aaron Copeland copping jazz. Beethoven borrowing Turkish marches for his Ninth Symphony. French Impressionist painters influenced by Japanese art. The Cubists cribbing African art. The French declaring the nineteenth century African American Cakewalk dance "poetry in motion." Suppressed claims that President Warren G. Harding's father was black. Psychologist Carl Jung decrying the impact jazz might have on Christianity. Black San Francisco madam Mammy Pleasant servicing the white titans of California industry. Poet Walt Whitman influenced by the poetry of Native Americans.

Always, Reed's novels and essays remind that African Americans derive from a different culture, an African culture that is more intuitive—magical, if you will—than Western culture, more deeply rooted in the feeling, the *soul* inherent in African American blues music, a culture in which mind and body aren't distinctly separated into intellect and sensation but are intertwined, creating "the manic in the artist who would rather do glossolalia than be 'neat, clean or lucid.'" That, in a nutshell, is Ishmael Reed.

His street in North Oakland, a street of large-to-small older clapboard homes, is neither rich nor poor. Cars with different-colored fenders and a two-ton work truck are parked on the street, but so is a new Volvo. I see nobody outside in the bright morning sunshine except a class of elementary school children walking in a tidy straight line with a woman in the lead and a woman at the rear. Everybody is black. Reed has written about this neighborhood, ironically describing it as "a predominantly black neighborhood," as the newspapers (and I) would put it. He called it the kind of neighborhood where he grew up and from which his mother and stepfather had spent much of their lives trying to escape.

Reed, too, had escaped to live in well-to-do white neighborhoods. But when he moved to North Oakland, he realized that this neighborhood was different, at least for him. People were friendlier, more watchful of each other's homes. A vendor actually came around selling fish and yelling "Fish man!" In the old Southern tradition, people got together for New Year's Day Hoppin' John meals: black-eyed peas, collard greens, ham, corn bread—foods that ensure good luck for the coming year. I know, because my wife throws a Hoppin' John party every New Year's Day. North Oakland was like the neighborhood in Charles Burnett's *To Sleep With Anger*, and Ishmael Reed felt as if he'd come home.

His huge cream-colored Victorian, eighty-six years old, seems to lord over the street. It's got to be his house, because parked in front is a Toyota with a bumper sticker that reads "My Kid Is A Poet." Can't be many people in North Oakland who'd think to publicize that achievement. At the door, Reed, at age fifty-two and although grayer than in Blackburn days, is a lot like I remember him: tall, round-headed, wide-faced, thick-haired, bearded, and incessantly frenetic. He leads me to the dining room with quick, assertive motions. Around us, the house is decorated in grown-up collegiate modern. Nothing fancy, no matching sets of Ethan Allen furniture. Just a worn purple couch, old cabinets for the stereo, simple metal bookshelves, a piano, plants and woven baskets, some genuine Eskimo art, a reproduction of Hiëronymus Bosch's "Adoration of the Magi," and two David Levine caricatures of Reed himself.

But the reigning theme of Reed's home is, as it should be, paper—stacks of it: newspapers, magazines, file folders overflowing with sheets of paper, cardboard boxes overflowing with stacks of file folders, and, naturally, books, mountains of books: *Notes of a Hanging Judge. Capitol Hill in Black and White. Satchmo. Chicago Politics. American Irish Culture. Indians of the United States. The World of Thought in Ancient China. Romans and Blacks.* A glutton for paper, Ishmael Reed consumes five newspapers a day and five books a week. We sit down at the dining room table and he begins to talk rapidly in bursts, changing subjects, returning, telling a joke, laughing from the belly, but then laying his head on his hand and listening intently, his eyes locked to mine. I liked Ishmael Reed two decades ago, and I like him now.

He says, "If there's an isolated America, it's white America."

"What is 'White America' these days anyway?" I ask.

"It's more of an attitude and a style than anything else, because people considered 'white' here are not considered 'white' in Europe today. You're Italian or you're French or you're Icelandic or Nordic. But there's no 'white'—the white thing is here. I once said that Irish Americans were the first runaway African American fathers, because they didn't leave any assets to all those black ladies they had babies by. A lot of us have Irish blood. I do. Alice Walker does, Alex Haley. It's very common, because Irish Americans were in the South. You had Scarlett O'Hara. They were the overseers and there was a lot of cohabitation. The Irish themselves were brought to the West Indies as slaves, actual *slaves.* Irish Americans don't want to recognize the mixed Irish American ancestry of many African Americans. Blacks have people like Clarence Thomas who think they're Anglo, but Irish Americans have Pat Buchanan, who sees himself as an Anglo. And these are people who have been oppressed in Ireland for eight hundred years! I mean if Patrick Buchanan were in England, he'd be sweeping the streets!" Reed loves this notion and bellows at his joke. "They hate the Irish in England. He'd be after *me* for help!"

"You've come to see the African American experience as only one of many minority experiences everywhere?" I ask.

Reed nods. America's obsession with black versus white, he says, is nothing more than a myth created centuries ago, when African Americans had to be seen as different from everyone else to justify their enslavement. But the intricacies of race, class, ethnic and nationalistic enmity go far beyond black and white, not only in America but worldwide.

Reed's list is a long one, and his examples pour forth in a torrent. While Koreans in the United States are considered a model minority, the Japanese bias is that they're lazy. And the Japanese don't despise only blacks, but also anyone with a hairy body. As whites used to say of blacks in America, the Japanese often say all foreigners stink. In Switzerland the Italians are looked down upon. In Iceland the Swedes are looked down upon. In the nineteenth century there was a joke that said the solution to the race problem was to have an Irish-man kill a black and get hanged for it. Today Blanche Knott's *Truly Tasteless Jokes* includes this funny one: "What's the American dream? A million blacks swimming back to Africa with a Jew under each arm."

A professor at Berkeley teaches that blacks and women have small brains—the same thing once said about the Irish. It was even argued that the missing link between apes and Africans was the Irish! The Germans used to say the same thing not only about the Jews, but the Hungarians! And the Nazis also exterminated Gypsies and gays. During the great Italian migrations to the United States, a common slur against Italian men was that they all wanted a white woman—the same slur heard against black men today. And how often have you heard it said that as soon as a Jewish man gets rich he gets him-self a Christian woman? And while it's blacks who are constantly dis-paraged for welfare dependence, two-thirds of the people on welfare are white, as are two-thirds of America's teenage mothers. And don't forget that it wasn't only African Americans who lightened their skin and straightened their hair to blend in, but Jewish women had nose jobs, Irish and Scots dropped their brogues, and generations of immi-grants dropped the "vitch" or "ski" from their last names. "The U.S. is gumbo," Ishmael says. "It's better that we know this."

One of Reed's friends, an Irish-Italian-American named Jack Foley, tells this story: His son came home from school complaining that blacks were allowed to wear T-shirts that read "Black By Popular Demand" but that white kids weren't allowed to wear shirts that said "White By Popular Demand." Foley told his son, "That's true, but you *could* wear a shirt saying 'Irish is Beautiful' or 'Italian is Beauti-ful' or 'Jewish is Beautiful.'" Writing in *Konch*, a literary journal Reed edits, Foley said, "The point is that *white is not an ethnic group*. It has no traditions, no culture. . . . To speak of multiculturalism, therefore, is to speak of a way of seeing the world *without whiteness*."

In a nation polarized by black versus white for centuries, this is a radical notion. Many black leaders have decried multiculturalism as a slippery slope down which the distinctly searing quality of discrim-ination against blacks (along with special resources aimed at redress-ing that discrimination, such as minority scholarships and business set-asides) will be lost in a muddle of claims by minorities who have suffered far less. In some ways, this has already happened as discriminatory claims are increasingly made by women, gays, and white males charging reverse discrimination. Reed knows these things. He says such claims water down the meaning of discrimination and oppression, making just about anybody able to lay claim to the title of "victim." Trouble is, the multicultural model is just plain closer to the truth.

"The word *oppression* should be reserved for the most unfortunate," Ishmael says, "whether they be white, black, men, or women." Today Ishmael Reed would rather see scholarship money go to a poor white kid than to the child of a well-to-do black family just because he or she is black. Yes, racism against blacks is still rampant. Reed sees it every day, when he is eyed suspiciously by police or searched for drugs at the Burbank airport. Or when he sees George Bush race-bait America for a few lousy votes. Or when the bank offers him the loan over the phone but then turns him down in person. But there is more to heaven and earth.

"The error among some African American intellectuals is that they suffer from agoraphobia," Reed says. "They specialize in the so-called African American experience and if they started studying these other cultures—Chicanos, Irish, Italians, Indians, white ethnics, Japanese—they'd learn something about themselves too. They would find that the problems they think are acutely African American are shared by any number of other groups. They would find a shared experience instead of being dismissed as paranoid. African Americans feel alone, and they're not alone. Not in their individual experiences, which are part of their group's history, which are part of other low-status groups' histories."

"Is poverty still the key?"

"Absolutely," Reed says. "I believe that."

1 7

WHEN THE PAST IS THE FUTURE

SACRAMENTO, CALIFORNIA

Ikeep thinking of something Dempsey Travis, the wealthy real estate developer in Chicago, told me months ago. He complained that white people are always pointing out that life for black people in America is better than it used to be. He angrily called that crap, because better is still bad. I respect Dempsey Travis, but I believe that better is also better. It took violence, it took threats, it took bold political power, but for a lot of black Americans I've met, life is pretty good these days. The worst indignities are gone. Ishmael Reed told me that in the old days middle-class blacks were terrified of being humiliated day-in and day-out—when they walked into a restaurant or a hotel, when they tried to use a public bathroom. Today blacks with the scratch are usually treated respectfully. Everyone from Ishmael Reed to Ice-T to Pee Wee Hampton to Dr. Davill Armstrong said this.

That's the new black America.

On Broadway Avenue in Sacramento I'm reentering the old black America, the one many people never left. It's the same one I saw in Tunica and Marks, Mississippi; Landover Hills, Maryland; Detroit, Michigan; East St. Louis and Ford Heights, Illinois; Watts, Los Angeles; and the Mayflower neighborhood of Bakersfield, California. I'm stopping on Broadway in Sacramento so that my head isn't ringing only with recent memories of Sharon Richardson Jones, Aissatoui Ayola Vernita, Ishmael Reed, Dolores and Holly Robinson, Paul Winfield, and Ice-T, black people doing quite well, thank you.

In Sacramento, Brenda isn't doing well. She's thirty years old and the mother of two young children. Her husband is in prison, again. She lives on $694 a month (soon to be reduced to $663 because of welfare program cuts) from Aid to Families with Dependent Children and $134 a month in food stamps. She has a high school diploma and six hours of college, but she doesn't have a job. Her one-bedroom apartment costs $290 a month. It is so infested with cockroaches that Brenda can sometimes feel them crawling on her legs in bed at night. Brenda's neighborhood is rough, a neighborhood of auto parts shops, a check-cashing outlet, a used-appliance store, a bailbond office. On the corner, a man is jumping up and down, flailing his arms, cursing at an old, primer-gray Oldsmobile, its tire having just blown out with a ka-**boom!** At night the hookers are everywhere. Brenda is proud she has never sunk to prostitution.

Brenda doesn't want me to come to her apartment, so I meet her at a free day-care center where she drops off her three-year-old daughter. I suggest we go to breakfast, and with her one-year-old son we head to a pancake house Brenda knows, although she's so nervous about seeing me she keeps giving wrong directions. Once in the restaurant she eyes the menu nervously.

"Get what you want," I say. "My treat."

Brenda, who has a big, shy smile, wide eyes, a high forehead, and unruly hair brushed high on her head, laughs. "It's been a long time since a man say I can get whatever I want. OK, let me have a ham and cheese omelet. Omelets, they all four seventy-five?"

"Don't look at the price. Get what you want."

"Pork chops and eggs, *boy,* that sounds good!"

"Well, get it."

"Yeah! Pork chops and eggs!"

Just then, the waitress, an older white woman with one of those patented blue-collar hairdos, arrives. "What ya gonna have?"

"Pork chops and eggs," says Brenda cheerfully.

"How ya want your eggs?"

"Over easy, with the yellow comin' out."

The waitress scowls. "With the what?" she asks disdainfully.

"With the yellow bursting out," Brenda says weakly, as if she's suddenly confused. "How would you describe that?"

"Over easy," the waitress says flatly.

An edge comes into Brenda's voice. "So I was right."

"Well, I didn't hear ya. Pancakes or hash browns?"

Again Brenda seems confused. "Ah, pancakes and hash browns."

"White, rye, wheat, sourdough?"

Brenda looks at me blankly for an instant. "Ah, white."

The waitress leaves and Brenda sits expressionless. I ask, "Did you think that woman was being rude to you?"

"No, not really," she says, almost inaudibly.

"Did you feel uncomfortable when she talked to you like that?"

"A little." Brenda hesitates. "You picked it up? I thought I was right when I said 'over easy.'"

I look around the crowded pancake house and see that it's filled with mostly white working-class Joes. I ask, "Was she acting like you don't belong in this restaurant?"

Brenda shrugs and looks away. "Somewhat, yeah." Her voice is a whisper. "I always get it like that. And her seein' me with you. They don't like that, a black woman with a white man. But I try not to 'go off.' Some blacks, they'd say, 'You heard me, b—!'" Brenda, who dislikes cursing, is too polite to use the word bitch. "But you don't give 'em what they want, so they can bounce you right out. Don't give 'em what they expect. My mother taught me that." Proudly, she says, "I haven't been on welfare all my life."

The surly waitress arrives again and while she's delivering our mountain of food, she also sets a pot of hot coffee inches in front of Brenda's one-year-old son, who has been reaching out and grabbing anything in range. I say sharply, "Move that coffee before the boy grabs it." Without expression, the waitress takes the pot and walks away. I look at Brenda: "A sweetie, huh?"

"Hmm-hmm," Brenda says absently. And while we eat, I hear the story of her life. Brenda grew up in Los Angeles. Her mom was poor and out of work for a while, but she went back to school, graduated from junior college, and got a decent job in a day-care center. "I call her my champion," Brenda says. They lived in a rented duplex, not public housing, and Brenda and her sister always had nice clothes. "We had four TVs!" Brenda says. "We never saw a hungry day." Her father was long gone, and it wasn't until she was sixteen that she finally met him, discovering that he didn't even know the date of her birth. She called her step-father "Daddy." Although his was an on-again, off-again marriage to her mom, he was always good to Brenda and her sister.

It was from her mother and grandmother that Brenda learned about white people. "My mother and grandmother used to sit down and tell stories about you guys—how you guys mistreated us." Brenda's grandparents had lived near Houston, Texas, and she heard the story about the time Brenda's aunt had beaten up a white girl and the police came and said they were going to kill her aunt right then and there. "My grandmother was begging them not to kill her, please don't, please, they'd give up their house, anything, just let my auntie live." The cops relented. And she heard the story of her uncle who had been castrated by whites in the army decades ago. And the stories about black women who were murdered by their white lovers so the women could never reveal the affair, about the time her old and frail grandfather was slugged by a young white man for not stepping off the sidewalk fast enough, about the white kids hollering "'igger, 'igger" before they were old enough to holler "nigger."

"Whites were not to be trusted," Brenda says, adding that when she went into the hospital to have her babies, she was terrified the whole time, afraid the white nurses and doctors might poison her. (I remember Dempsey Travis saying that his own father had been terrified to go into the hospital for the same reason—but that was fifty years ago!) "I was scared to death," Brenda says. "I'd be cryin' and prayin' because doctors get away with death and I'm just a black person." Brenda says she sometimes wonders if even heaven will be run by white people. I laugh, thinking she's joking.

"I *was* thinkin' that," she says.

As we talk, I notice that Brenda is beginning to eat her pancakes with only butter and I ask if she'd like some syrup. "A little," she says, taking it from me. After a moment, she adds, "I don't even know how ta eat in a restaurant, really." She says she doesn't even know which silverware to use. At the risk of seeming to act like a big shot, I laugh and tell Brenda not to worry, that when I worked as a newspaper reporter I was once invited to a lunch at the house of George Bush, who was then vice president. "When the waiter brought around the salad bowl, I forked it out onto the wrong plate." I tell her that I didn't realize I'd screwed up until I saw Bush—apparently worried about embarrassing me—glance at my empty salad plate and then hesitate before dropping his salad onto the correct dish in front of him.

"Now that's worse than picking up the wrong fork, isn't it?" I ask. For the first time, Brenda seems to feel momentarily at ease and she lets out a loud laugh. She tells me that in high school she was bused out of her black neighborhood to "this sweet white school" in San Fernando.

"How'd you get along with the rich white kids?"

"I got along and I didn't," she says. "I was just waiting for 'em to say the word 'nigger.'"

"Did they?"

"Yeah!"

"What'd you do?"

"Fight!"

But Brenda says that her best friend from those days was a white girl who withstood the taunts of "nigger lover" from other white kids. Brenda says she knows that her mother and grandmother weren't completely right, that some white people are decent. But as a rule it's just safer to steer clear. "Deep down inside they hate us and they think that they better," she says. "I felt like when I went to junior college—all my teachers were just about white—they didn't want black people to pass. They got the power in their hands. Whether blacks do the best or not, they still fail 'em. 'Cause I went to one class, and God know I did the best I can, and she still gave me a terrible grade."

"Did you deserve a terrible grade?"

"I would say like this: it needed some correction, but I don't think I deserved to fail, cause I was goin' there on the bus and I was tryin' and even willin' to do make-up and she didn't even want me to do that, like I wasn't teaching material."

"You felt. . . "

". . . less than."

"Did you feel deep down inside that maybe you really weren't as good as the white kids in college?"

"Somewhat. Just goin' to school and walkin' among 'em. They would come inside the bathroom and say, 'Oh, my hair.' They would give ya certain looks, like shit is on you. Strokin' their pretty hair. They language is much better than ours, educated, where we have to struggle and be classified as dumb. They would say, 'Brenda, what are you gonna do for this summer?' and I would lie, 'Oh, we're goin' to Hawaii,' when I know we ain't goin' nowhere. Let's just face it: white people are nice-lookin' people. Straight hair, blue eyes. We don't have none a that. Our hair is not straight. We have to press out our hair. You guys have natural oil. We gotta put grease in ours." Brenda then tells me that a man she was once involved with had an affair with a white woman and when Brenda found out, it broke her heart. After that, whenever a TV commercial with a pretty white woman came on, she'd holler, "You want her? You lookin' at her? I know her hair's straighter than mine!" Brenda asks me, "Would you say my nose is too fat?"

Her speech has nearly brought me to tears. It's almost the year 2000, and blacks like Brenda still must live with this garbage polluting their heads, terrorizing them, tearing them down, making them unable to withstand fools as insignificant as a waitress in a pancake house. For all the progress, this continuing tragedy we must never forget. I say, "I think you have a pretty nose, a beautiful face, high cheekbones, elegant skin."

"But the Mormons believe we are cursed by Canaan!"

"Even the Mormons don't teach that anymore."

"But they don't like us!"

"Brenda, let me tell you a secret. My wife is black and we have two kids." At this she is dumbfounded. Immediately she must see pictures, and I pull them out of my wallet. I'm not surprised at Brenda's reaction: "Oh, she's a light-skinned black," she says of my wife. "Oh, he's cute," she says of my son, "but he look all the way white." Of my daughter, she says, "She's darling! They look practically white, though." For Brenda, that's the bottom line.

We're about ready to leave and I see that Brenda has been able to eat only about a third of the food she ordered. I gird for the last confrontation and tell the waitress we'd like a doggy bag, which she brings and drops rudely on the table among the remaining food. I say to the waitress, "You can take it all and put it in the box for us," which she does without enthusiasm. I ask Brenda, "Would you ever think to order that woman around like that?" She shakes her head an emphatic no.

"This is *your* world," she says, "We just live in it."

Out in the car, I tell Brenda I'd like to buy her some groceries in return for the time she has given me. She jumps at the offer and we go to a bulk-food store, where she reveals herself to be a very practical shopper. She fills the cart with twelve bars of Ivory, a bottle of dishwashing soap (she has run out and has been cooking Ivory hand soap in water on the stove to make dishwashing liquid), eighteen rolls of toilet paper, forty-four paper diapers, a pack of ice cream sundaes, a straw broom, a huge pack of turkey lunch meat, butter, bacon, milk, Froot Loops, two jars of Vaseline, deodorant, Binaca breath spray, a super-size box of Tide, batteries, and a carton of no-brand cigarettes.

"I guess we can go ta my house," she says, "if you don't mind the roaches."

"I don't mind."

Brenda's apartment is indeed nothing fancy—a tiny living room, small bedroom, and an alcove kitchen. No phone. Very ragged furniture. Mattresses on the floor for beds. Even in the bright light, the cockroaches camped around the washed and stacked dishes on the sink don't bother to hide. "I'm really embarrassed for people to come over, because they be crawlin' on the rug, the ceiling," Brenda says. "That's why I didn't want you to come to my house. I'm sure you used to bein' in finer homes than this."

"I've been in finer homes, but I've been in worse."

"You have?" Brenda asks, seeming happy to hear this.

Thinking of Sims Street in Marks, Mississippi, I say, "A lot worse."

Brenda has her apartment decorated with plants and baskets, and on the wall is a collage of pictures and drawings of her children, mother, and imprisoned husband, who is a handsome man. "This is me and him right here after he got outta the pen," Brenda says, touching one of the photographs gently. I ask her why, if he's been in and out of prison, she doesn't just dump him. "I love him. My mom says I deserve better. I do *not* see any better."

"Do you know any black man who has a job, picks up his kids after work, goes home and helps fix dinner, watches some TV, goes to bed, and gets up for work the next morning?"

"No."

"Not one?"

"No."

As I'm about to leave, I ask, "What are you most proud of in your life, Brenda?"

"That I survived. I could have been dead a long time ago."

1 8

THE EXTRAORDINARY IN THE ORDINARY

LACOMB, OREGON

As they say, there's no there there.

The town of Lacomb is really the Lacomb Grocery, a one-room job where you can buy the necessities, plus worms and Lotto tickets.

A person could count the abandoned Lacomb Cafe, with its peeling white paint and rusted 7-Up sign that's squeaking in the wind, or the Baptist church up the road, or the nearby and noisy breeding farm for what the locals say are fighting cocks, but that would definitely be it for downtown Lacomb, which sits unbothered by its simplicity just west of the lavish Willamette National Forest, a couple of hours south of Portland, about fifty miles inland from the Pacific. This is the lush and sprawling territory where in 1844, by state constitutional provision, all blacks were formally expelled.

Even deeper into the dense forest of towering Douglas firs that disappear like Jack's beanstalk into low, troubled clouds, backed up to Crabtree Creek beyond which the Cascades begin to rise, below the town of Jordan, and above the town of Sweet Home, I am to find black anthropologist John Langston Gwaltney, whose book *Drylongso* is the most disturbing racial document I've ever read—more disturbing than Richard Wright's *Native Son* and Malcolm X's autobiography. More disturbing even than the screeds of the Klan.

Drylongso is the old Gullah word for 'ordinary' or 'adequate', and Gwaltney's 1981 book is a compilation of ordinary African Americans talking about their lives and their attitudes toward whites. Gwaltney, a blind man who spent years interviewing 307 people for *Drylongso*, was convinced that American social scientists had never captured the essence of what it means to be black in America, and so through his oral histories he identified what he calls the values of America's "core black culture."

Gwaltney's black Americans are people working at working jobs, neither poor nor affluent. They are down-to-earth and practical people who value actions, not words. They are suspicious of written "paper" knowledge and respectful of oral knowledge passed between generations. For them, neither great people nor great books are trusted guides in life. Their philosophy is rooted in daily, concrete experiences, which are considered life's only trustworthy data. They're a people who walk through life with a cool, wry, suspicious, distrustful, even cynical eye. These traits, Gwaltney argues, grow from a blending of the practical, clear-eyed ways of ancient West African tradition and nearly four hundred years of oppression.

Yet it's the picture Gwaltney's people paint of whites that is so stunning. White people are dogs—selfish, cruel, and spoiled. They are dirty, picking their noses in public. They teach their children cruelty so they, too, can grow up to brutalize black people. No white person is ever to be trusted. *Never!* Whites care nothing of right and wrong, but ask themselves only, "Can I get away with it?" Example after example of horrendous personal experiences are these people's teachers. To Gwaltney's blacks, white folks live in a fantasy world of "liberty and justice for all," while blacks live beyond such childlike imaginings. For example, Rosa Wakefield told Gwaltney, "They asked a little white girl in this family I used to work for who made her cake at one of her little tea parties. She said . . . the good fairies made it. Well, you are looking at that good fairy. Black folks don't have no time to be thinking like that. If I thought like that, I'd burn cakes and scorch skirts."

After more miles of mountains and forests, gnarled live oaks crying tears of moist green moss, an acrobatic flock of black-hooded and pink-flanked Oregon juncos, and endless fields of what should be named America's national weed, Queen Anne's lace, I find the silver mailbox of John Gwaltney and a long, narrow driveway that tunnels though pines rising seventy-five feet and darkening the way. The drive opens to a sunny clearing and a little tan house, newly built. Seeming to peek out of the big woodpile is a carved head resembling the Greek god Poseidon. Red clover surrounds the bird bath and in the air is the scent of mint, which is growing in the nearby herb garden. In the distance, vaguely seen, down a sloping field two hundred feet away, is, *holy shit*, a brown bear! On a much closer second look, I see that the bear, like Poseidon, is a sculpture. Off in the opposite direction are three very live mule deer nibbling casually at a field of clover. At the front door sits a squat pre-Columbian stone head. Interesting place, this house in the middle of there's-no-there-there.

"So these pines are what Christmas trees grow up to be?" I ask John Gwaltney, as he leads me into a large, sunny room where he has been carving a wooden mask at his work bench. Since age seven, John has been a wood carver in the Gullah tradition, as were his great-uncle and uncle before him.

"Now there speaks an Easterner!" John says in a deep, resonant, almost Shakespearean voice, a James Earl Jones voice. As he takes a seat near his bench, he punctuates his remark with a raucous, hearty laugh. John says that his wife, Judy, who is a white woman, gets credit for the grounds and the gardening. With clear pride, he says, "My wife has always displayed a great genius for making something from very little." The words echo in my head, knowing that Judy's ability is a quality that black Americans traditionally prize.

As John talks I look at him closely, feeling oddly embarrassed that I can examine him but he, as a blind man, cannot examine me. At sixty-two John Gwaltney is neither thin nor portly, but hovering in between. Although the hair that rims the sides of his head is still dark, his beard is nearly gray. He's a small man, with compact hands and feet. An anthropologist to the bone, he wears a brown-and-white pullover shirt that's decorated in some kind of smiling primitive-god motif. His dark glasses dominate his face in repose, but when John throws back his head and laughs—his gold-rimmed front tooth glistening, his arms waving in exclamation—the man's energy and wit are ingratiating.

I ask, "Didn't the people in your book know any *decent* white people?"

At that question, John, who I know cannot eye me, seems to eye me anyway, although perhaps he is simply evaluating my voice in the way my eyes have evaluated him. He takes a deep breath. "Look, the people in that book were talking about life as they had experienced it." His words are slow, rich, and well formed. "Look, let's be realistic. If, when you came in that door, I had taken a dollah hanging on the wall"—he motions to the many hand-carved Gullah canes he has crafted over the decades—"and hit you with it, you would develop a quite natural prejudice against me." He laughs mightily. "I mean, we live in a world where for most of our history it has been very fatal to assume civilization on the part of white people. Look, when I was a youngster I remember a trial at which white people had been speedily acquitted after having wounded several black youngsters who were swimming in the river. They did that simply because it was *OK* to shoot black people! If a black person went into a strange town and treated everybody as if they were sane, civilized, and reasonable, it would land him in jail! You can't afford to take chances. That isn't prejudice."

"What would you call it?"

"Good sense!" And John Gwaltney shakes with laughter and then takes a deep breath, as if he is weary of stating the obvious. "Look, most white people have inherited a horrendous backlog of privilege, which they take for granted and which shows up in thousands of ways. Can I go there? Of course I can go there!" Great laughter. "I'm free, white, and twenty-one!" More great laughter. "I can do what I want. I was born deserving. Well, I still don't have that feeling. I mean, for most of my life I have been obliged to ride on Jim Crow trains. I have been obliged to look for protracted periods of time to relieve myself, get a drink, or get a sandwich. You don't do that for three hundred years and have people feel that all the natural entitlements of humanity are theirs! But three hundred years of living that way does not make you feel that the people who do have automatic entitlement are any more deserving than you."

"But is this 'black culture' or powerlessness speaking?"

"It is both. Black culture developed *against* something. It had to overcome. And what it had to overcome, in plain words, is white caste. Now, I have met civilized whites. But it took a lot of pain and anguish for me to be able to see white skin as anything but an imminent sign of disorder and early sorrow."

"But Judy, your wife?"

"She is a civilized person. I have known white people, a very small minority, who have been able to get themselves free of the formidable impediment of the caste which they bear. Each time a white person is born they have a decision to make: am I going to stand on my own merits and do what is good and just, or am I going to relax in the sea of privilege I've inherited?"

"But isn't that the issue people born to privilege face in any culture anywhere?"

"Of course it is!"

"Are whites different than blacks born rich in Africa?"

"I don't think they are different. We're talking about the weight of caste, psychological and otherwise. I didn't say whites are in a unique position, but they are in that position, along with upper classes everywhere."

"What about whites *not* born to privilege?"

"To one extent or another, in America, they all are. Since the country started, we've had a racial ethic which says that the passport of a white skin entitles me to more of the good things in life. If I don't have them, there was always Andrew Carnegie and other role models, who were all white." I tell John about the actor Paul Winfield talking about the time he was made up to play the white male suitor in Tennessee Williams's *The Glass Menagerie*, and the way Winfield felt in the role, as if for the first time he could sense what it meant to

assume that if he were only personable and hardworking—a practi-
tioner of the Dale Carnegie techniques—that good things would
come to him. As a black man, Winfield had never had that feeling,
had never been able to draw upon the motivation that such optimism
breeds. John Gwaltney loves the Winfield story and he laughs
uproariously.

There's a joke reported in *Drylongso*: Three astronauts—one
black, one Italian, one Jewish—are in an overloaded spaceship and
one must be sacrificed. So the command devises a fair test to pick the
doomed man. The Italian is asked who discovered America. "Columbus." The Jew is asked the name of a ship that sank after hitting an
iceberg. "The Titanic." The black is asked to give the first and last
names of all the people who drowned when the Titanic sank. With
John, I laugh until my eyes water, but it's not the first time I've heard
the joke. My wife's uncle Bobby, a great teller of stories, told it to me
years ago. Its sardonic and suspicious humor reminds me of the joke
about the blacks who air-conditioned hell (again, making something
out of nothing) and the joke about the disguised Superman fatally
luring a black man over the edge of a high-rise (again, never trust a
white man). The jokes turn hardship into humor at the same time
being harsh object lessons for life—like the fables of Aesop (who was
once a slave) or the collected fairy tales of the brothers Grimm.

"Black culture is not romantic," John says. "It is faced with what it
is faced with, and it has to deal with that. Every black person has to live
in a very hostile world. It isn't his imagination that it's hostile. It *is* hostile! Prudent black people think this way. Sometimes they think so only
unconsciously, but most think this way. We are not romantics." John
laughs and recalls that as a boy he had a white New England school-
marm scold him for agreeing with British philosopher Thomas Hobbes
that most people's lives were "nasty, brutish, and short." He says, "She
felt that was a very wicked thing to say. Well, I would say the same
thing today! Now that is the way most black people see the world."

"But do you wear a set of lenses that assumes these awful things
will be in front of you when they aren't?"

"You're pleasantly surprised if they aren't."

"But wouldn't you have to assume the worst for a long time
before the best would ever seep into your thinking?"

"I don't know, because we've never been faced with that. It has
been constantly pretty bad for most of us."

For six hours, through lunch and a snack of chocolate chip cookies, John Langston Gwaltney regales me with the stories of his life
and the breadth of his knowledge. The ancient Gullah folktales that
his grandmother would tell him before bed. Stories of long ago when
animals talked like humans and the turtle was slow and wise and the
monkey was not. ("The monkey is curious but not wise," John says.
"One reason he is not wise is because he is too curious"—once a cru-
cial lesson for black children to learn.) Stories, like the jokes of today,
with lessons of caution, stories meant to warn children that the *buckra*
could not be trusted and that this secret must forever pass from black
generation to generation. Stories of the white musicologist in graduate school who insisted there were no African pan pipes in North
America and who refused to relent even when presented with an
actual musical instrument of the kind he said did not exist. How the
famed anthropologist Bronislaw Malinowski had referred to his
Melanesian field subjects as "niggers." Patrick Henry's black son.
Thomas Jefferson's black mistress. A third of the "white" Southerners
estimated to carry black genes. On and on and on John goes, with
cynical, life-affirming glee. Stories of the arrogance and self-delusion
of the imperial white mind.

Naturally, African Americans aren't the only victims and white
Americans aren't the only conquerors. The Romans subjugated much
of the world. The English subjugated the Irish, who as the queen's
military enforcers later helped subjugate India, much like the Buffalo
Soldiers later helped subjugate Native Americans for the white
nation that had subjugated blacks. The Jews have been set upon by
most everyone. And nobody expects the Ukrainians to trust the Rus-
sians, who subjugated them. Any conquered people, John says, will
come to see their world with the same cold, clear, unromantic eye
African Americans use to see their place in America and the white
people around them. It is the reverse image of the imperial eye of the
British poet Lord Byron, who in 1811 said, "The rest of the world—
niggers and whatnot."

"In 1811!" John says.

"A man ahead of his time!" I say.

"Amazing forethought!" roars John.

"What is it white people need to learn?" I ask.

"If you had asked my great-aunt this question," John says wryly,
beginning to chuckle even before the punch line, "she would have

said, 'What white people need to learn is that their shit *does* stink.'"
With that, he howls and slaps his thighs.

Finally, I tell John Gwaltney that what disturbed me most after reading *Drylongso* was realizing how I, as a white man, am so thoroughly dehumanized by most black people, how my individual traits count for so little in their minds, how I am judged on experiences I've had nothing to do with. John smiles at that, because it's exactly the way African Americans have always been judged by whites. I say, "I don't like being reduced to a bundle of prejudices and stereotypes."

"That is the ruler's price of empire," John says.

"Or black people's price of domination?" I ask.

John, smiles, spreads his arms, and, for perhaps the first time, laughs gently: "Ah, they are the same thing."

I've been told that the most magnificent sunset I will ever see is to be found not far from John Gwaltney's house on a long stretch of Baptist Church Road, just outside Lacomb. Since I must pass that way, I make the right turn and drive ahead a hundred yards, pulling onto the grass and the wild garden of Queen Anne's lace that inevitably lines the narrow road. To my right is a regiment of Christmas trees, all the same height, about six feet, all looking as if they were planted on the same day, at the same hour. To my left is a wide pasture of unharvested hay, which is tossed by a sweet, piney breeze from the southwest. Ahead a half-mile or so is a forest line running the width of the horizon, where the sun is falling.

In rainy Oregon, clear bright days are rare, and John's wife had said that today was one of the prettiest days of the year. But I wouldn't know it from this uninspiring sunset. It's only 8:06 and sunset isn't until 8:19, but already the sun is obscured by the soaring trees and the sky is so clear that its light is without refracted color, faded to a pale yellow haze that lays atop the trees like thin fog on a valley. Disappointed, I sit on the fender of my car and absently watch as yellow goes to colorless gray.

It has been a long trip. I am tired, and wondering if I have learned anything, when at my feet, rising up to my knees, I again notice that Queen Anne's lace. It has seemed to follow me everywhere—from my home back East to Pulaski, Tennessee; to El Paso, Illinois; to Lacomb, Oregon. Tough stuff, this distant relative of the carrot. Woodsmen once grated the root of Queen Anne's lace and salved burns with it. The juice from its stems was once eaten as a cure for parasites. But today Queen Anne's lace is a weed, with a long green stem no thicker than a phone cord and a dirty-white bonnet a few inches in diameter. Whole fields of it seem to have no scent at all.

For all the times I've seen Queen Anne's lace, I've never really looked at it. So I snap one off, turn on my headlamps in the early darkness, and study the lace under the light. The weed's flat, round bonnet isn't actually dirty-white, but rather several shades of white— stark white around the edge and then, in narrowing circles, its shade turns deeper until, at its center, it is light gray. But most startling is that Queen Anne's lace is not a single flower at all, or even buds on a single flower. Queen Anne's lace is hundreds of tiny, delicate, five-petaled umbels floating in a single umbrella bouquet. Each umbel, the size of a contact lens, is its own constellation of microscopic buds that, when seen together, resemble nothing so much as snow crystals laid in their illusory white blanket on the ground. And it does have a scent, though not perfumey. Queen Anne's lace smells to me like collard greens have always tasted—strong and pungent, hard for me to appreciate. But I realize that in scent and appearance it is distinctive and beautiful nonetheless. As I think that thought, with one of those fighting cocks crowing violently at the dusk, I realize that I have learned something after all.

I have one last destination.

EPILOGUE: HIGH SCHOOL, REVISITED

CRETE, ILLINOIS

THE MUSIC IS THE MESSAGE

All around the dance floor, as the disc jockey segues artfully from "I Wanna Sex You Up" by Color Me Badd to "Bizarre Love Triangle" by New Order, the black kids stop dancing and the white kids begin. Then, as "Electric Boogie" by Marcia Griffiths folds in, a line of black kids appears doing the electric slide, and the white kids wander back to their tables, except for one raucous guy doing his Vanilla Ice imitation amid a circle of bellowing white buddies.

On and on this goes late into the night, with such predictability that the disc jockey can accurately whisper "black," "white," or "black and white" to me before each song. I promise it wasn't like this when I was at Crete-Monee High School's dances in 1968. We had bands at our dances, often REO Speedwagon, a Chicago hard-rock group that hadn't yet made it big. Everybody loved the Speed-wagon. Today Crete-Monee can't have a live band because no single band could satisfy its new rainbow audience, especially not a hard-rock band. Today the reigning consensus of style and taste that once governed my white suburban Chicago high school is dead.

I try hard not to reveal—or for that matter even feel—shock or nostalgia at Crete-Monee's racial transformation, but it's not easy. Out on the dance floor, I notice a young black man with a snow-white fur wrap draped over his tuxedo. He wears a top hat and carries a cane. Neither I nor my friends would've gotten out of the house alive wearing that kind of getup.

I think of the scene in *Dr. Zhivago* where the young physician returns to his family after the Russian Revolution and discovers thirteen strange families living in his house. "But it *is* more fair," says Dr. Zhivago. "Why does it sound so funny?"

My sentiments exactly.

There was at least one black girl out of about eight hundred kids when I went to Crete-Monee High. Her name was Naomi, but I didn't know her. In those days, my friends and I, our school and our town, were out of central casting for a fifties bobby-socks movie: popularity contests, student council elections, cars, sports, and dates were our worries. The racial tension and violence of the nation's cities in the sixties might as well have been happening on Jupiter.

The changes began in the early seventies, a few years after I left Crete for college. Affluent blacks began moving into University Park, a new community west of town. Their children entered the high school with little trouble. They were middle-class kids, and as students they were often superior to Crete's native white stock. As ever, it was the children of the area's poor whites who were at the bottom of the school's status ladder—the guys who wore oily ducktails and a pack of cigarettes rolled up in their white T-shirts, the girls who wore teased hair and pale pancake makeup. I had moved to Crete, which is located about thirty miles south of Chicago, from one of those poor enclaves at age twelve, when my own working-class parents moved up to a nicer home. In town, my new friends called my old neighborhood "Skunk Hollow"—a slur that drove my normally placid mother to angry exasperation.

It wasn't until the late seventies that the high school saw real racial change. As a nice suburban community that wasn't hostile to blacks, nearby University Park attracted more and more black families, and an old, ugly cycle unfolded. As its black population neared half, whites were increasingly hesitant to move in—and affluent blacks and whites increasingly moved out to nicer neighborhoods. Real estate steering no doubt played some part in University Park's segregation, and it is common today to hear whites tell of agents who openly discouraged them from moving to the town ten and even fifteen years ago. University Park is today a town of 6,204 people that isn't a slum by any stretch of the imagination. It includes abandoned houses but also beautiful homes that would be worth far more than their $100,000 value if they weren't in University Park, which is now 79 percent black.

The rest of the area around my hometown has also changed. The township that includes Crete, with its 6,773 people, has several predominantly white affluent neighborhoods that are now well integrated. The village of Crete itself is still nearly all white, but the changes around it have added up to this: Crete's high school is today 36 percent black. After traveling twenty-five thousand miles around America, I've returned home to discover that my old high school is a laboratory specimen of the complexities of race, class, and culture that are so baffling to America today.

"Everybody knows there's a problem," says Jane Castle, a white woman who has taught French at Crete-Monee since 1969, the year after I left. "But nobody knows what to *do* about it. So we don't do anything."

"Sometimes," says Shirley James, a black woman who has taught math for seventeen years, "all I can do is shake my head."

After a week of walking the hallways, listening to students, black and white, I know the feeling. It's as if I've been talking to these kids everywhere in America.

A BULL SESSION WITH BLACK KIDS ALONE

"Nothin's changed," says Scott Williams. "It's still geared toward the white society."

"Last year," says Tasha Johnson, "we studied *Black Boy* by Richard Wright and two white girls were offended and went to the principal and didn't have to participate in class discussion."

"We once read a book of short stories," says another girl, "and some had the word 'nigger' in them, and my mother complained."

I ask, "How is that any different from the two white girls complaining about having to read *Black Boy*?"

No one answers.

"Everybody gets along fine in class," says Stacy Sublett. "We talk and laugh, really do. But in the hallway, you see those same people, they don't make eye contact, they don't say hello."

Scott says he was friendly with a white girl in class. But when he said hello to her in the lunchroom, she gave him a dirty look. "Don't come over here when I'm with *them*," she told him later. "You don't understand! A guy at the table had just said, 'Man, I *hate* niggers,' and then you come over."

I ask, "Does this hurt your feelings?"

"Yes."

"It's like it makes you wanta kill 'em," says Emael Graham. "It makes you so mad I just wanta fight 'em."

And everybody nods in silent agreement.

A BULL SESSION WITH WHITE KIDS ALONE

"I live in University Park and I see how they're brought up," says Bryan Tsikouris. "They're less open to friendship. With me and even with each other. I have black friends, but not really close, close friends because I can't really get close to 'em. It's hard to explain, but they're less open to being themselves, less open to telling you how they feel. They're just a lot more guarded."

I ask, "More cautious?"

"Yeah," Bryan says.

"More cynical?"

"Yeah."

"More distrustful?"

"Yeah."

"They have to uphold a black image," says Sharyn Tylk. "If you're friends with a white person, then you're a sellout, an outcast. You're going to be discriminated against just as much as they discriminate against white people."

I say, "But I've been told that if whites are friendly with blacks then they'll be outcast by whites."

"Yes," Sharyn says. "The rednecks, yes."

"I understand that black kids might get harassed," says Angie Kochel. "But when I walk down the hallway when I do attendance second hour, I get practically molested. They say, 'Hey, baby, why don't you come over to my house?' But if I say anything, they say, 'Oh, you're just prejudiced because I'm a black person. You don't want black people touching you.'"

"I've learned now since I moved here," says one boy, "that there really is, there's black people and there are niggers."

EPILOGUE: HIGH SCHOOL, REVISITED

There is a chorus of "mmm-hms" around the room.

"A black person," he continues, "tends to be well educated,
comes from a better community. A lot of black ministers are more like
white people. A nigger is basically the kind a people you see outside
our school with their hats tipped to one side, who don't give a flying
hoot about school."

A BULL SESSION WITH THE SAME BLACK AND WHITE KIDS TOGETHER

The black kids chuckle.

"I don't think it's a racial thing," says Stacy, a black girl. "It's a
guy thing."

I say, "But she says only black guys do it."

"They probably want to kiss her," says Emael, a black guy. "They
think she's cute."

"Hormones, you know," says Scott, also black.

I ask a black girl, Tasha, "How would you handle it?"

She smiles widely. "I'd say, 'Look but don't touch!' If she walks
down the hall like she's scared, they're gonna bother her."

"I remember," says a white guy, "when Ron once said to me in
the library that there's black people and there's niggers."

"What I meant," says Ron Tinsley, who is black, "was that blacks,
whites, Hispanics—any kinda race—can be a 'nigger.' It means a very
ignorant, stubborn person. So when somebody says I'm a nigger, I
say, 'No, I'm not.'"

"Who are *you* to judge?" asks Scott, a black guy whose ire is rising. "You live where? In University Park, right? Your parents may
have a couple extra dollars and so you don't have to act in an
uncouth way, unfit. But other kids don't have that. You're not in a
position to judge these people and say, 'You're a nigger.'"

"I have relatives on the West Side of Chicago!" insists Ron. "I
know what rough means!"

"Hey, I *was* on the West Side of Chicago!" insists Scott. "I probably know even a little bit better!"

"You're talking about the West Side of Chicago!" hollers Sharyn, a white girl. "This isn't the West Side of Chicago. You're talking about people who call you 'nigger.' I didn't call you 'nigger' and nobody in this room called you 'nigger.' You're bringin' the problem from someplace else."

"I don't think that in this school there's any integration program," says a white kid. "We're tryin' to change people who used to be slaves into people who are the same as regular white people."

"See!" hollers Scott. "That's the type of ignorance that needs to be stopped right here! No, we're tryin' to change *ourselves* into something else! *You* changed us into slaves!"

"I didn't do it!" yells Sharyn.

I think to myself, *Will this never end?*

"WHITE NIGGERS"

I haven't heard it said in twenty-five years. But back in Crete, visiting old friends, someone says it of their neighbors. You know, folks with junk cars and dead washing machines in their yards, who whitewash the bottom few feet of their trees, folks always screaming at each other, folks quick to slap their kids, throw a punch. They are a type. And being a native of Skunk Hollow, I once knew them well.

Earlier, I had talked to Neale Miller, a history teacher who has not only taught in Crete all his career but also graduated from Crete-Monee in 1958. I had mentioned to him that good black students often say they are under pressure from lousy black students not to get good grades, that they're called "white" if they do. Neale—a strong, robust, soft-spoken man who said he has never had any special trouble with black students—laughed at that. "Ah, come on," he said, "that's nothing new. That happened when I was kid. Only it was the poor whites. You don't break out, don't try to be better and leave the folks behind. It's as old as the hills."

Unexpectedly, Neale Miller had touched some deep memories in me, and with his words in mind I make an unscheduled detour and drive out to Skunk Hollow. It's still there, on a country road crowded with small frame houses. All the people I see are white, but the place makes University Park look like Beverly Hills. My old cinder-block house, now painted brown instead of white, is still there, too, set way off the road, looking pretty nice. Farther up the street, where it was always the worst, it's still the worst.

Dandelions envelop an old junk car, and there's the rusted hulk of a dump truck in a field. On this stretch of road is the house where an old man and his teenage son, or maybe it was his grandson, once scared the hell out of me. I had gone to their door selling garden seeds one winter night after dark. Maybe I was eight years old. They invited me in and closed the door. Never had I seen or smelled such a place. At a small table sat the old man, slicing something, maybe fruit, with a paring knife. I can still see the knife. He asked me to sit and he asked me my religion, which was Catholic. Then, for what seemed an eternity, the old man railed. He sliced and railed against the Catholics. I hadn't known that anybody hated Catholics, and I've always believed that the old man was my first encounter with plain, old-as-the-hills prejudice. I watched the knife. I was terrified.

When I drive past that house today, I'm stunned to see the old man's son, or maybe his grandson, outside. All grown up. His back is to me. He wears a hat. I know that I should stop and talk with him. Perhaps we'd laugh at my memory. But, to be honest, I am afraid. After thirty years. How deep and lasting are the experiences of such indignities, for blacks or whites, for anybody.

As a boy, my family left Skunk Hollow for town. We did what Crete-Monee's new black immigrants are now doing. We moved up, leaving the old, failing neighborhood behind. My new friends were the children of teachers, bankers, businessmen, lawyers, stockbrokers, and real estate and insurance agents. As an adult, I've wondered if those parents ever worried about their children being friends with me, the son of a milk-man from that awful place in the country. But I fit in—took ballroom dancing, learned to play golf. My friends from Crete have done well. They are teachers, contractors, bankers, dentists, lawyers, businessmen. My old friends from Skunk Hollow? One went to prison, one is an auto body repairman, one a cosmetologist, one a cop, one a janitor.

"It's as old as the hills," Neale Miller had said, and I am in those hills now. I am of those hills. The American playing field isn't level for anyone born in Skunk Hollow or worse, whether black or white. It also isn't level for anyone born female, whether black or white. Catholic. Jewish. The list is endless. But as much as I'd like to believe, as some do, that being black is today no more important in determining a child's future than is sex or religion, I don't. In hundreds of conversations with African Americans across the country, I've heard too many terrible stories to believe that.

I think of Crete, which Pee Wee Hampton's brother said has had a racist reputation for decades. While in town, I ask around and discover that Pee Wee's brother was right. One of my old teachers, Tommy Thompson, recalls being at the annual Crete carnival in the fifties and seeing a group of white men tell a group of blacks they would have to leave because dark was approaching. An old friend tells me that a retired Crete policeman once told him he would follow any car with black occupants just to make sure they left town without stopping. Another old friend says he recently asked men working on a new park facility in town why they weren't putting in basketball courts and the worker told him candidly that basketball courts attract blacks.

Ah, my hometown.

After all the miles and the people, places, and conversations, I'm left with one not-so-grand thought: When it comes to race today, I must learn to keep more than one idea in my head at once. Only a generation ago, discrimination—legal and social—was all that a person needed to understand most of what was happening between black and white Americans. It will no longer do. Discrimination alone can't explain what's happening to the poor women and their daughters in Ford Heights, or the Fleming family in Tunica, or Brenda in Sacramento and what's happening to black millionaire Bill Brazley in Park Forest, or brilliant Karama Neal in Little Rock, or Holly Robinson in Beverly Hills.

Today, the advantages of privileged birth and excellent education are as real for blacks as they are for whites, and it's simple dishonesty or disingenuousness to deny it. But so also is it true that white prejudice and discrimination are real and are not going away soon. In short, race *still* matters, but it is no longer *all* that matters. It is time for whites to admit that despite all the changes of the last several decades, racism is still a plague on America. It is time for blacks to admit that as bad as racism is today, great strides have been made.

I think of blues music: Good *and* bad, true at once.

After my travels, I wonder if it is not our continued failings, but rather our progress—the end of the most grievous forms of discrimination, the integration of our schools and work places—that haunts us most today, as we are left to struggle with social and psychological intricacies that most of us, black and white, never had to face in the old, awful world of straight-out legal discrimination. Look at Crete-Monee's kids: Progress has complicated their lives with the daily anxieties of race and added to the mix our "old as the hills" biases about class, status, and respectability—all of which are often mistaken by blacks and whites for matters of race.

Yet amid this new complexity, our ways of seeing race remain compartmentalized, with people squabbling over what is supposed to *best* explain the conflicts of black and white in America: white racism and discrimination, *or* deep inequities rooted in social class, *or* differences in black and white "cultures," *or* the inability of blacks to seize new opportunities open to them. But what I found at Crete-Monee, what I found all across America, is *all of the above*, and more.

I found white prejudice, black prejudice, white ignorance, black ignorance, affluent whites *and* affluent blacks naive about the profound impact of growing up poor, whites cowering defenseless at the charge of racism, underachieving blacks trying to pull down those breaking from the pack, blacks reluctant to confront this racial mau-mauing, and whites *and* blacks ignorant about their deep cultural differences. With befuddlement all around.

I think of Ishmael Reed, who told me that African Americans need to learn that they aren't alone, that people all over the globe, forever, have been conquered and subjugated, oppressed. Reed believes that African Americans would be liberated from a kind of psychological jail if they could only see themselves in the experiences of the Irish, Asians, Native Americans, and even poor whites in this country. I believe it is even more true that white Americans would be liberated from their own psychological jail if they could learn to see themselves in the experiences of African Americans. If they could only rediscover the Skunk Hollows of their own pasts. The words of my black friend keep ringing in my head: "Black people are the most American Americans we've got." They are us! They are the most up-by-the-bootstraps Americans ever. They were the poorest, least educated, most despised, most disenfranchised, least capitalized of immigrants. But look how many have made it!

As Americans, it is our common ground.

After my journey, frankly, I'm less frightened of black people, and I downright admire their humor, their worldly-wise skepticism, and their amazing ability to make something out of nothing. I know now that black people are like me and *un*like me at the same time. The white liberal piety—"those people are just like us"—is wrong. Good-hearted whites who buy that line are shocked, baffled, and even angered when they discover that black people *aren't* just like them. In the way that men and women are the same *and* different, in the way that the people of France and Germany and Japan are the same *and* different, blacks and whites in America are the same *and* different. How could we not be? We have literally lived in a different land and country for four hundred years.

I keep reading in the papers that race relations in America are getting worse and worse. After my wanderings, I simply don't believe it, not as a long-term weather report anyway. I believe there's an abiding *fear* that race relations are getting worse. But if anything is clear to me after my travels, it is that two black Americas have emerged—one whose children have been cut in and one whose children are still cut out and living in places like Marks, Tunica, East Detroit, Ford Heights, East St. Louis, and Watts.

One hundred and fifty years from now people will look back at these abandoned enclaves of destitution and human waste and see them as the great moral crime of our era. And they will wonder at how we could have closed our eyes to these people in the same way we today wonder at how gallant men of the South could have seen slavery as noble. They will wonder at how we could ever have argued that the poverty of the people in Ford Heights is their own fault. In 150 years, people will ask of us the question Michael Cross asked me in Detroit: "What do you expect?"

This hopeless, entrenched poverty is bad and getting worse. But I wonder if the pessimism of relatively affluent blacks I met around the country isn't a different animal altogether—less a child of racism than of the daily requirement that people must now wrestle with the trivial human conflicts of race, class, and culture that our progress has exposed. Spike Lee, usually seen as some kind of black nationalist, is really the voice for the new black affluent who are often struggling to reconcile their modest roots with their new lives at the top, while their families and old friends often still live at the bottom. It is a painful door through which all travelers going up have always had to pass.

As Neale Miller said, "It's as old as the hills."

I began this trek for deeply personal reasons: I wanted to leave for my children a document that captured the breadth of black America.

I wanted to be the blind man who touches the whole elephant. For my children, I rest easier. I know now that there's no one way to be black in America and that, despite racism, black people have been getting along, living full lives quite nicely, without white people for hundreds of years. I wasn't a neanderthal on race when I took to the road; a mossback wouldn't have married a black woman in the first place. But I've been awed by how much I didn't know, by how much there *is* to know about black America. I have learned this: We white people would be better off if we opened our hearts and our heads, listened more and talked less.

But what I discovered while sitting in the dentist's chair more than a year ago, what I learned from the dentist who stopped by and casually told a racist joke about a black man who was stupid, still remains the greatest insight I have to share:

The idiot was talking about my kids!

I remember a time when my son was a baby. It was late at night and only the light in the hallway was alive, pouring a shower across my knees as I sat in the dark of my son's room, rocking him through some unknown annoyance. Rocking to the hum of the air-conditioner, the flutter of the cat scurrying on the stairs, the hollow groan of the water turning on and off in the apartment upstairs. I watched his face grimace and flex in the shadows. And then, in time so short it passed only in the mind, my son was gone and I was the boy annoyed, and my father was me. I could feel the mannerisms, the voice, the phrases that would be mine someday. And just as suddenly, I was gone again and the light was falling across the knees of my son, who was grown, who was a father, who was me. All in time so short it passed only in the mind.

This kind of understanding changes everything. Only when I *became* black by proxy—through my son, through my daughter— could I see the racism I had been willing to tolerate. Becoming black, even for a fraction of an instant, created an urgency for justice that I couldn't feel as only a white man, no matter how good-hearted It is absolute proof of our continued racism that no white person in his or her right mind would yet volunteer to trade places, *become* black, in America today.

If you are white, be honest: Would *you*?

So when does a journey end? Is it when you finally arrive back at home, kiss your wife and kids hello, unpack your bags, and slide into your favorite chair? Or is it when you realize that what had baffled you before baffles you no more, what had frightened you before frightens you no more? That's the way it is for me anyway. I'm going home. I'm done. Black America cannot be truly understood or explained, not by me or anybody else, black or white. Like every nation of people, it's too great and too petty, too beautiful and too ugly, too generous and too selfish for that. But it can be experienced. It can be demystified. It can be made whole.

I think of something an old black man named Porter Millingham told anthropologist John Langston Gwaltney: "We know white folks, but they do not know us, and that's just how the Lord planned that thing. . . . Now, I have thought about that thing all my life, but nobody ever came over here and asked to hear what I think."

Well, I have asked. . . and *asked*. . . and *asked*. Looking back, I don't know if it was the answers or the asking that has made me feel better. Looking back, I don't believe it matters.

AUTHOR'S NOTE

The people portrayed in *Crossings* are real. None are fictional and none are composites of several people. A few names and details have been changed at the request of major subjects and as a condition of their agreement to talk with me. When pseudonyms are used, they are noted in the text. Characters who appear briefly are often left anonymous. Sometimes even I did not know their names. Except for people I met in passing encounters, all other subjects were told I was a journalist working on a book about race in America.

Crossings is based on numerous handwritten notes taken on the scene and more than 250 hours of taped interviews with subjects and my own taped observations during my travels. More than fifteen hundred photographs were taken in the course of travel and served as a documentary record of numerous details. Quotations attributed to subjects are usually their own words exactly, although for readability I have eliminated the use of ellipses to indicate deletions and breaks in conversation and sometimes altered the sequence in which remarks were made. I also have taken the liberty of, for instance, changing pronouns to nouns when necessary or adjusting tenses for consistency. Whenever I have felt the need to substantially alter quotations for accuracy, clarity, or brevity, I have read them to the subjects for approval. Still, readers should know that the interpretation of all events and conversations in *Crossings* is strictly my own.

In order to eliminate intrusive footnotes, I have cited published source books and articles in the text. But numerous other sources were used for background, context, and detail—everything from the 1990 U.S. Census of Population, to travel brochures, to U.S. Soil Conservation Service topographical maps, to local newspaper articles, to local and state history books such as *Clarksdale and Coahoma County: A History*, by Linton Weeks; *Little River County*, by Bill Beasley; and *Afro-Americans in California*, by Rudolph M. Lapp. Books about America's race history also were important as sources of historical background and context, including *A Documentary History of the Negro People in the United States*, edited by Herbert Aptheker; *Eyes on the Prize*, by Juan Williams; *Bearing the Cross*, by David J. Garrow; *Parting the Waters*, by Taylor Branch; and *The Promised Land*, by Nicholas Lemann. Also important were reference books such as *The Negro Almanac: A Reference Work on the African American*, the *Encyclopedia of Black America*, and the *Encyclopedia of Southern Culture*.

The help and advice of numerous people whose names do not necessarily appear in *Crossings* also were invaluable. With that in mind, I want to thank Ken Kipps, Jesse Jackson, Lynda Edwards, Richard Harrington, Thanh Vo, Hal Sieber, Willie Mae Harris, Welton Reynolds, Kelly McGillis, Jewell Thomas, John Zippert, Sid F. Graves, James Figgs, Oscar Hamilton, Donna Matteson, Linton Weeks, Calvin Norwood, Gloria Gibson-Hudson, Tierney Hamilton, Lorry Hester, Vernon Jarrett, Sharon Hicks-Bartlett, Charles Gordon, Diana and Len Witt, Nancy Callahan, Frank Whelan, Maurice Mondell, William Lee, Rudolph M. Lapp, Tommy Thompson, Joe Collins, Lin and Dave Waterhouse, Tina and Pete Pearce, Jan and Randy Martin, Karen Olson, Margaret T. Burroughs, and James Bottrell.

I also want to thank the reference librarians at the West Street Branch of the Anne Arundel County Public Library in Annapolis, Maryland, and librarian Rosalie Sherbrooke for their help. I am indebted to Leonard Downie, Bob Thompson, and John Cotter at the *Washington Post*, which published portions of *Crossings* in the form of magazine articles before the book appeared. Without this financial support, *Crossings* could not have been undertaken. One of those articles was the recipient of Northwestern University's John Bartlow Martin Award for magazine reporting, the money from which also helped support my research. Thanks also to Jay Lovinger and Steve Petranek, editors at *Life* magazine, which also published an article based on material that later appeared in the book. Both men have been a source of inspiration and practical advice for many years and strongly encouraged me to pursue this project.

Several people read all or part of *Crossings* in draft and made suggestions that improved the book immensely. I want to thank for performing this task Pete Earley, Mike Sager, Steve Weinberg, Deborah Fleming, John Cotter, Leon Dash, Carol Melamed, Steve Petranek, and Jay Lovinger. Thanks also to my agent Amanda Urban, who believed in the project from the beginning; my editor Terry Karten; her editorial assistant, Charlotte Abbott; copy editor Sally Jaskold; and attorney Chris Goff. Ms. Karten literally bought an idea that many other editors considered either too vague or too grand. She later made hundreds of editorial suggestions, and her important contributions run silently throughout the text.

I want to give a special thanks to my wife Keran Elliott Harrington, who encouraged me to undertake the book, and to our children, Matthew and Kyle. Although my long absences from home interfered with their own lives, they did not complain.

Finally, thanks to the people who let me write about them.

INDEX

ABOUT THE AUTHOR

Molly Roberts

An award-winning journalist and former staff writer for the *Washington Post Magazine*, Walt Harrington is currently Professor of Journalism at the University of Illinois at Urbana-Champaign. He is the author of *At the Heart of It: Ordinary People, Extraordinary Lives* and *American Profiles: Somebodies and Nobodies Who Matter*, available from the University of Missouri Press.